AF710383

WITHDRAWN

W. Schertler, B. Schmid, A M. Tjoa,
and H. Werthner (eds.)

Information and Communication Technologies in Tourism

Proceedings of the International Conference
in Innsbruck, Austria, 1995

Springer-Verlag Wien New York

G
154.9
.I457
1995

Univ.-Prof. Dr. Walter Schertler
Strategisches Tourismusmanagement
Universität Trier, Trier, Federal Republic of Germany

Univ.-Prof. Dr. Beat Schmid
Institut für Wirtschaftsinformatik
Hochschule St. Gallen, St. Gallen, Switzerland

Univ.-Prof. Dipl.-Ing. Dr. A Min Tjoa
Institut für Softwaretechnik
Technische Universität Wien, Vienna, Austria

Univ.-Ass. Dipl.-Ing. Dr. Hannes Werthner
Institut für Statistik, Operations Research und Computerverfahren
Universität Wien, Vienna, Austria

This work is subject to copyright.
All rights are reserved, whether the whole or part of the material is concerned, specifically those of translation, reprinting, re-use of illustrations, broadcasting, reproduction by photocopying machines or similar means, and storage in data banks.
© 1995 Springer-Verlag/Wien
Printed in Austria

Printed by Novographic, Ing. Wolfgang Schmid, A-1230 Wien
Printed on acid-free and chlorine-free bleached paper

With 85 Figures

ISBN 3-211-82669-6 Springer-Verlag Wien New York

PREFACE

Due to the great success of the First International Conference on Information and Communication Technologies in Tourism which took place in January 1994 there was common agreement among the participants as well as among the Programme Committee to organize the second Conference, contrary to the original intention, as soon as 1995 instead of 1996. A two year break in an area of rapid technological development might otherwise result in a completely different landscape of telecommunication with hardly any connection to the first Conference.

The recent development as well as the publicity with regard to the so-called information highway has justified this decision far beyond our expectations. The Programme Committee has decided to choose "Electronic Marketing" as the central topic of this Conference.

The international network is opening up entirely new information and booking channels. Printed information is not disappearing from the scene, but is acquiring competition in the form of electronic media. That means new dimensions in the presentation of the selection, new ideas as to informative contents, new, direct paths from suppliers to potential clients - making their choice at home in front of their screen and able to book immediately - and, finally, a new form of democracy. The small economic units which shape tourism thus acquire more interesting opportunities. Information that can be published fast and easily updated, effective alliance and networking make it possible for the small to participate with the great and to safeguard their own interests. It is our task to facilitate access to the great information highways in order to avoid landing in an economic cul-de-sac. New technologies demand new understandings in the working world: the market advantage lies in conveying the latest information fast and in sensitive dealings with the various new media, geared as far as possible to the individual target groups and to the type of information. It means a fresh understanding for cooperation within the tourism industry.

Finally, we want to thank the organizers of ENTER: the Tirol Werbung (Tyrolean Tourist Board), especially its managing director Andreas Braun for his continuous support. Mayor credit for the success goes to all of our colleagues who submitted papers. Many persons contributed numerous hours to organize this conference. The names of most of them will appear on the following pages. In particular we wish to mention Arno Ebner, Thomas Schierer, Kathrin Schöpf, Michael Spechtenhauser and Almut Wolfsgruber. We also want to mention the reviewers, who refereed the papers and improved them by providing helpful comments. Silvia Schilgerius, at Springer-Verlag, moved the editing process along with patience and steady persistence. To all of them our special thanks.

Walter Schertler	Trier
Beat Schmid	St. Gallen
A Min Tjoa	Wien
Hannes Werthner	Wien

CONTENTS

Programme Committee xii
Index of Authors xiii

Multimedia and Virtual Reality I:

The Holiday Supermarket
S. Musil, G. Pigel, M. Tscheligi 1

A Virtual Reality Based System Environment for Intuitive Walk-Throughs and Exploration of Large-Scale Tourist Information
K. Szabó, P. Stucki, P. Aschwanden, T. Ohler, R. Pajarola, P. Widmayer 10

Virtual Travel: Promoting Tourism to Unfamiliar Sites Through Pre-Trip Experience
C. Bauer, R. Jacobson 16

Tourism and New Technologies I:

A European Electronic Market Place for Tourism
P.F. Byerley, J. Ewers, G. Lella, G. Lo Reto, U. Zobel 22

ISDN in the Travel Industry - A Catalyst for Change?
W.J.M. Teunissen 33

Mobile Computing in a Reservation Application
O. Wolfson 43

Economic and Business Issues:

The End-User Acceptance of New Information and Communication Technologies in Tourism
W. Schertler, M. Maier, S. Rothe 46

Regional Integrated Computer Information Reservation Management Systems and Tourism Distribution Channels
D. Buhalis 53

Marketing and Information Technology in the Hospitality Industry. A Strategic Approach
P. Desinano, C. Vigo 65

Simulation of the Logistic and Information Infrastructure, Applied in the Value Chain of Tourist Enterprises
D. De Reus, C. Meijs 76

Airline Hotel Reservation System Improvement: the Contribution of Value Chain Analysis
G.E. Haramis, G.J. Siomkos 85

New Requirements and Architectures:

Changes in the Leisure Travel Market Result in New Requirements for Tour Operator Systems
M. Weber 95

Information System Architectures and Benchmarks for Local Tourist Offices
C. Meijs, G. Dijks 103

Electronic Networks: New Challenges for Tourist Organizations?
R. Maier, W. Röckelein 112

Designing an Interactive Telematic System for Small Businesses and Private Households
C. Kuhn 124

Multimedia and Virtual Reality II:

Virtual Tourism - a Realistic Assessment of Virtual Reality for the Tourist Industry
I. Benjamin, M. Cooper 135

Explorative Analysis for Development of a GIS-based Tourisminformationssystem
G. Trichtl 144

An Information CD on India
A. Rao, S. Sethi, K. Sharma 151

Managing WWW Documents in Distributed Editorial Environments
F. Burger, S. Reich 160

Social and Legal Implication:

Legal Aspects and Security in Electronic Markets for Tourism
B. Wildhaber 171

An Anonymity Service for Targeted Advertising
N. D. Griffeth, J. Katz 180

Multiperspective Hypermedia Representation of Customs and Rituals: Implications for Tourism
H. Lukas, J. Stockinger 192

Information Systems and Databases:

Beyond ISO 9000: Trends in the Standardization and Certification of the Quality of Information Systems Development
G.J. van der Pijl, J.G. Verrijdt, G.J.P. Swinkels 202

Database Support for PC Software Configuration and Version Management in the START Network
S. Auerbach, A. Buchmann, I. Buchmann, T. Kudraß, K. Lange, C. Lier, K. Weidmann 212

Electronic Market Support for the Tourism Industry: Requirements and Architectures
M. Merz, K. Müller, W. Lamersdorf 220

Adaptable Object-oriented Distributed System Integrating Multimedia Resources
V. Wietrzyk, V. Ramaswamy, A. Ginige 230

From Structure to Process: a Vision of a Process-based Organization
K. A. Simon 239

Multimedia and Virtual Reality III:

Evaluation of Hypermedia Tourism Applications
F. Garzotto, L. Mainetti, P. Paolini 249

Tourism Promotion Needs Multimedia Information System
J. Berce, A. Oblak, I. Tran 260

Multimedia Information Systems for Hotel Guests
C. Weiser 268

Expert Systems and Decision Systems:

OuR TOWN: a Distributed, Multi-media System for Travel and Tourism
S. W. Clyde, T. Landfried 278

Business Travellers' Expert Advisor
F. Y.Y. Ng 288

A Decision Support System for Tourism Destination Choice
R. Mulye, J. Rickard 299

Tourism and New Technologies II:

International Marketing via Broadband Networks - Building the Local Network in a Norwegian Region
K. Aanonsen, Y. Lindsjorn, G. Kamfjord 308

Macrodata-integration Support for Electronic Tourism Marketing
K. A. Froeschl 318

Industrial Papers:

The System Architecture of CitySoft/GermanSoft
R. Fleck 328

Tourism and Technology
P. Kruger 333

OOSEM - a Complete Oo-development Process for Developing Touristic Framework
J. Withalm 336

PROGRAMME COMMITTEE

International Conference on Information and Communication Technologies in Tourism
Innsbruck, Tirol, Austria - 18 - 20 January, 1995

Chairmen:

TJOA A Min	Technical University of Vienna, Austria
WERTHNER Hannes	University of Vienna, Austria

Co-Chairmen:

SCHMID Beat	Hochschule St. Gallen, Switzerland
SCHERTLER Walter	University of Trier, Germany

Members:

AIVALIS Constantin	University of Crete, Greece
BAUKNECHT Kurt	University of Zürich, Switzerland
BRANDES Wolfram P.	Arthur D. Little Int., Germany
EBNER Arno	TIS GmbH, Austria
HITZ Martin	University of Vienna, Austria
JAFAR Jafari	University of Wisconsin, USA
KASPAR Claude	Hochschule St. Gallen, Switzerland
KUBICEK Herbert	University of Bremen, Germany
MAARTMANN-MOE Erling	Norwegian Computing Center, Norway
MATA-MONTERO Erick	Instituto Tecnólogico de Costa Rica, Costa Rica
MAZANEC Josef A.	University of Economics, Austria
MEIJS Chris	Wageningen Agricultural University, The Netherlands
OSTROVSKI Doreen	Travel Trust International, Canada
PAOLINI Paolo	Politecnico di Milano, Italy
PERONI Giovanni	CST Perugia, Italy
REVELL Norman	Middlesex University, Great Britain
RIBBERS Pieter	Tilburg University, The Netherlands
ROITHMAYR Franz	University of Innsbruck, Austria
SHELDON Pauline	University of Hawaii, USA
STOCK Oliviero	Istituto per la Ricerca Sientifica e Technologica, Italy
WAGNER Roland	University of Linz, Austria
WEIERMAIR Klaus	University of Innsbruck, Austria
WIETRZYK Vlad	University of Technology Sydney, Australia

INDEX OF AUTHORS

Aanonsen K. 308
Aschwanden P. 10
Auerbach S. 212
Bauer C. 16
Benjamin I. 135
Berce J. 260
Buchmann A. 212
Buchmann L. 212
Buhalis D. 53
Burger F. 160
Byerley P.F. 22
Clyde S.W. 278
Cooper M. 135
De Reus D. 76
Desinano P. 65
Dijks G. 103
Ewers J. 22
Fleck R. 328
Froeschl K.A. 318
Garzotto F. 249
Ginige A. 230
Griffeth N.D. 180
Haramis G.E. 85
Jacobson R. 16
Kamfjord G. 308
Katz J. 180
Kruger P. 333
Kudraß T. 212
Kuhn C. 124
Lamersdorf W. 220
Landfried T. 278
Lange K. 212
Lella G. 22
Lier C. 212
Lindsjorn Y. 308
Lo Reto G. 22
Lukas H. 192
Maier M. 46
Maier R. 112
Mainetti L. 249
Meijs C. 76, 103
Merz M. 220
Müller K. 220
Mulye R. 299
Musil S. 1
Ng F.Y.Y. 288
Oblak A. 260
Ohler T. 10
Pajarola R. 10
Paolini P. 249
Pigel G. 1
Ramaswamy V. 230
Rao A. 151
Reich S. 160
Rickard J. 299
Röckelein W. 112

Rothe S. 46
Schertler W. 46
Sethi S. 151
Sharma K. 151
Simon K.A. 239
Siomkos G.J. 85
Stockinger J. 192
Stucki P. 10
Swinkels G.J.P. 202
Szabó K. 10
Teunissen W.J.M. 33
Trichtl G. 144
Tršan I. 260
Tscheligi M. 1
Van der Pijl G.J. 202
Verrijdt J.G. 202
Vigo C. 65
Weber M. 95
Weidmann K. 212
Weiser C. 268
Widmayer P. 10
Wietrzyk V. 230
Wildhaber B. 171
Withalm J. 336
Wolfson O. 33
Zobel U. 22

THE HOLIDAY SUPERMARKET

Sabine Musil, Georg Pigel, Manfred Tscheligi

Vienna User Interface Group
Lenaugasse 2/8, A-1080 Vienna, Austria
{musil, gp, mt}@ani.univie.ac.at

ABSTRACT To reduce staff costs in travel agencies a TACRS (Travel Agency Clerk Replacement System) was prototyped. As these systems have to be used and accepted by occasional users a non standard metaphor based non standard interaction system was developed. Due to the non standard nature of problem and solution novel development methods such as "vision presentations" (roughly spoken verbal prototypes) had to be explored. Low quality video prototyping has shown to be a valuable designer's tool to transport non standard design ideas to the users.

1 Introduction

Costs of labour are increasing in the Western European states with densely webbed systems of social security. Therefore also enterprises offering services to the costumer feel the pressure to make use of their staff more efficiently than before. A good examples for this (at least in Austria) are banks: The customers are served more and more by machines instead of human clerks behind the counter. This trend also spreads to other traditionally very staff intensive service industries, e.g. travel agencies. In Austria, it was even considered to have the customer pay for the advice in travel agencies if it does not come to a booking. Of course this would lead to strong resistance from the customers' side. Therefore travel agencies are looking for a possibility to automate the advice before the booking. Existing TIS (Tourism Information Systems) [15] offer basically only interactive information on a certain topic, i.e. you point to a certain sight on the screen and get a digitalized videoclip on this topic, but are not able to explore the likes and dislikes of the customer in order to suggest an appropriate holiday as is done (or should be done) by the personal interview with the customer. Therefore traditional TIS have to be enhanced to replace the personal interview between clerk and customer by an automatic advice system, which will be called Travel Agency Clerk Replacement System (TACRS) in the following.

This paper presents the functionality of a TACRS and the design process of such a non standard metaphor based non standard interaction system. It is demonstrated how the vague vision of a metaphor can be shaped during the process of designing a series of prototypes. From the verbal presentation of a metaphor to the users in a vision presentation, the sequence of static pictures supplemented by oral explanations of paper and pencil prototyping, cheap, quick and very detailed but non interactive low quality videoprototyping, up to an interactive softwareprototype the metaphor based interaction system is designed in more and more detail. This paper presents and discusses each of these steps of the design process for non standard metaphor based non standard interaction systems.

2 System Requirements

A TACRS shall provide users with the possibility to interactively figure out their wishes and demands for a holiday. Certain criteria that determine the quality of a holiday like means of transport, duration, destination, accomodation, sporting facilities, entertainment facilities etc. shall be offered with many options for the user to choose from. For example, the criterion accomodation would come with the options hostel, private bed&breakfast, guesthouse, hotel and luxury hotel. Users can choose options as they like, exchange options and also abandon them if they change their minds. At the end, when the users are happy with their choice, the system automatically will generate some offers, according to the criteria options chosen.

Underlying this automatic offer generation must be a database, that includes all offers of as much travel organizers as possible. It also would be helpful to have a kind of intelligent agent, that looks for senseless combinations (like South Sea and -10 degrees Celsius) and recommends certain combinations.

3 User Requirements

TACRS can only be of any value if the customers (users in the rest of this paper) accept them. The success of the automatisation of banking services was due to the special conditions in this ecconomic sector: Cash machines for example have a horrible user interface, but they are the only way to get some cash when the banks are closed, and opening hours are extremely limited! So the users have no choice and have the advantage that they can get cash now at any time. That's why they use cash machines despite the frustrating experiences they often have. Travel agencies cannot rely on similar conditions. If users are to prefer using TACRS instead of talking to a human clerk it must be fun and very impressive. To guarantee this, the following requirements have to be assured when designing a TACRS:

- The way the TACRS works has to be comprehended by users without thinking twice. Even people who never before had anything to do with computers have to understand how to get information out of the TACRS. The interaction with the TACRS should be based on knowledge everybody can be assumed to possess. Reusing knowledge from one domain in another domain generally is called a metaphor [3] based style of interaction. The TACRS should be based on a metaphor taken from a domain everybody can be assumed to have experiences in.

- The TACRS must be easily usable. Usability must be checked and evaluated during the whole development process of the TACRS. Not only the metaphor forming the basis of interaction but also its implementation have to be evaluated over and over again. It's essential during these evaluations that actual users take part. As every evaluation can lead to considerable changes in the design, iterative prototyping is the fitting paradigm for this style of development.

- The TACRS must attract potential users. Common styles of human computer interaction like clicking with the mouse on cute little pictures or pointing with the finger on a touchscreen won't do. These interaction techniques are too commonplace and remind too much of work. But TACRS are to sell holidays and hence reminding the users of their dull, daily routine can have a very negative impact. Holiday, travelling and everything connected with it should be attractive, extraordinary and sensational. If you believe newspapers and and other mass media [1,13,16], the most exciting recent development in computer science is Virtual Reality (VR) [11]. Taking into account that the average user of a TACRS knows about computer science only from these sources, it's evident that one should sell extraordinary travels with an extraordinary, en vogue system which includes a touch of VR technology. If VR techniques are considered a means to design human computer interaction one easily sees that they might allow a more convincing design of real world metaphors [19] which is another strong argument for the incorporation of VR techniques in a TACRS.

A TACRS designed according to these requirements has good chances that interacting with it will not be considered operating a complicated automaton, but a futuristic experience, an exciting game. Only then users will be willing to exchange a conversation between humans against an interactive experience with a machine. Under any other circumstances the TACRS will have little chance of being accepted and frequented by customers.

4 Meeting the Requirements

We developed a software prototype of a TACRS. The stress of the development was on the design of the human computer interaction according to the requirements mentioned above. Iterative prototyping was chosen as development paradigm. In each iteration a more detailed prototype was developed with higher effort but considering the experiences and points of critic the evaluation of the predecessing prototype had provided. This prototyping can be divided into the following steps:

- Searching for an appropriate metaphor as basis for the interaction with the TACRS. The metaphor based system at this early stage of the design process not being much more than a vague vision is presented to the user as a verbal prototype in an evaluation session called "vision presentation".

- Design of paper and pencil prototypes to enhance the vision of the system with static visional elements. In a succeeding evaluation these prototypes were demonstrated to the users in a Wizard of Oz technique manner [18] and the metaphors incorporated in these prototypes could be tested on their comprehendability and interpretability [9].

- Making a low cost video prototype to provide a more detailed impression of the interaction style to the users during the evaluation session. The transition between the static visional elements which were faked by the presentator in the last step can be seen actually in the video, thus making it a appropriate tool for designers to present their ideas to the users despite non professional technical quality.

- Development of a software prototype with a PC-based VR tool.

Each of these steps was iterated if necessary, i.e. if the evaluation session proved unsatisfying and if because of the defects and shortcomings of the existing prototype it seemed too early to produce a more detailed one. For example there were several versions of paper and pencil prototypes.

4.1. Finding an Appropriate Metaphor

The basis of the TACRS is a metaphor, which had to be generally understandable. A real world metaphor (which is built on a system existing in reality) was considered more appropriate than an abstract metaphor. Real world metaphors are easier to comprehend and the a priori knowledge can be used in a more concrete way. Two metaphors looked promising:

- The metaphor of a supermarket in which the users can select their wishes concerning climate, culture, sports etc. off the shelves in the according department (see Figure 1) and collect in the trolley. On the cash desk the users receive a list of suggestions for the destination of their holiday trip.

Fig.1: A typical aisle of the TARCS

- The metaphor of a wide open space containing objects incorporating aspects of the holiday trip like means of transport, climate etc. These objects can be opened and allow the selection of the desired option out of a three dimensional map stand (these three dimensional map stands are similar to cone trees [1]).

Both metaphors were evaluated in a vision presentation with two different groups of users: The presenter explained the metaphor and the system based on this metaphor verbally. Comments and reactions of the users were taperecorded for later evaluation. An evaluator kept a protocol of the evaluation session.

In the vision presentations users' reactions encouraged to enter the next design step with two alternative metaphors.

4.2 Paper and Pencil Prototypes

Now paper and pencil prototypes of the system based on these metaphors were created. Typical user tasks (according to task centered design guidelines [8]) in interacting with the TACRS were drawn as a sequence of sheets of paper. During the evaluation session the presenter played the part of the computer. This way the users got a visual impression of the metaphor. It was possible to detect unclear details and shortcomings of the metaphors during the evaluation sessions. For example, it was totally unclear what to do with the selected items in the card stand metaphor. Nevertheless it must be kept in mind that only static pictures were presented to the users and the transitions between those static visual impressions had to be faked by the presenter.

In the paper and pencil prototyping sessions the supermarket metaphor proved to be much more intuitive. First of all no explanation how to understand the metaphor was needed. It also matched well into the context: as users buy nearly everything in a supermarket, they will very likely accept the fact that holidays can be got there, too. And as shopping is fun, relaxing and very much contrary to working, this metaphor seems to fit for a TACRS perfectly. The card stand metaphor was abandoned.

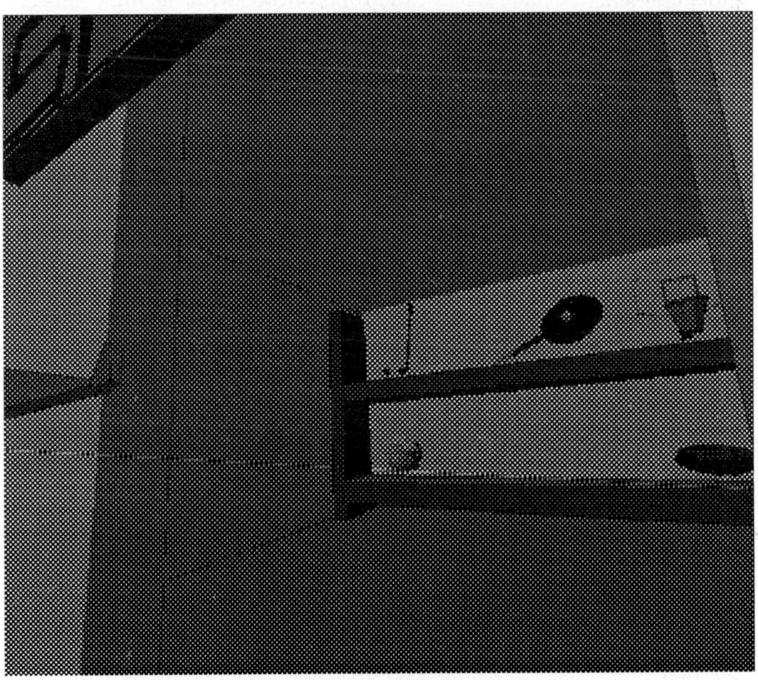

Fig.2: In the sports department

The behind the holiday supermarket is that of users putting together their dream holiday by selecting the desired features in the form of objective symbols off the shelves and collect them in their trolleys: For example, the users go into the sports department of the holiday supermarket and put a tennisracket and golf equipment into the trolley to indicate that they want to play tennis and golf (see Figure 2). Or the users head for the climate department and take a thermometer showing 25 degrees celsius as a symbol for the desired temperature. There is no need to stroll through the departments of the holiday supermarket in a certain sequence. It is also possible to put items back into the shelves or to exchange symbols. At the cash desk the users finally get a list with suggestions for holiday trips fulfilling their desires. The booking itself is still intended to take place outside the system.

4.3 Video for Prototyping

On the one hand paper and pencil prototypes only give a very rough impression of the interaction style of a system. On the other hand a software prototype demands very high effort especially when dealing with non-standard metaphors and VR techniques. This calls for another, cheaper way of creating a prototype for early design stages which nevertheless gives a better impression than a paper and pencil prototype. We found a solution in video mockups.

We intend to use video prototyping as a cheap and simple means to create a prototype to ensure usablility of a system with non standard interaction techniques, as a designer's tool [5], not a marketing division's tool. Therefore we require only low-tech equipment and a simple cutting facility. Tognazzini points out in [17], that video mockups only make sense when produced with a high budget using professional video clip quality. But he considers video prototyping solely as a marketing tool for convincing managers and the broad public that their company's money is well spent for research work which will show its fruits only in years to come. His video prototypes are movies "to communicate a vision to the audience", whereas we see it as a usability testing device. Therefore the experiences of Tognazzini cannot be mapped one to one onto our video mockup.

The video prototype was an intermediate step between the rough paper and pencil prototype and a "real" working software prototype. It gave us the possibility to demonstrate the details of interacting with the TACRS. Of course, a video prototype lacks interaction. So our mockup showed a typical human-TACRS interaction which gave our test users the possibility to comment on the system just as if they were peeping over someone's shoulder, who was interacting with the real system. The typical task selected demonstrated the arrangement of a sporting holiday in the southern seas.

The video mockup allowed us to discuss a complete interaction including all details which had to be neglected due to the fact that paper and pencil prototypes only consisted of a sequence of static pictures. Despite the low technical quality of the video prototype (it was filmed with a normal video camera and cut on two video recorders without specialized equipment) the evaluation session with the users lead to valuable results and hints on how to improve the interaction: for example, we found out, that it was very annoying that all items existed only once in the shelves. This not only proved to be annoying to our users, it also violated the metaphor, as supermarkets shelves are never empty but always promptly refilled by the staff of the supermarket. Therefore the interaction was changed. Now each item taken out of the shelves is automatically replaced by a new one.

4.4 Softwareprototype

The TACRS includes VR techniques. VR systems are divided into such forcing the user to wear special equipment as helmets, HMDs, DataGloves etc. [10,12,20] and systems which avoid such encumbering equipment [2,6,7]. For the TACRS the latter class of VR systems was preferred. A screen for a pseudo 3D display of the virtual holiday supermarket combined with a 6DOF input device provides all the equipment needed for interaction. The reasons for that were manyfold:

- What users would voluntarily use a TACRS if they had to put on a helmet, adjust the HMD and slip on the DataGlove? Most likely the holidays would be over before users had started interacting with the TACRS.
- It is not very comfortable to wear such an equipment. Besides that, the question of health hazards caused by this equipment is not definitely answered yet [4].
- TACRS should lead to a decrease of staff costs. But if users had to wear special equipment to interact with the TACRS they would need someone to assist them in taking it on and off. Developing TACRS would then no longer be reasonable from an economic point of view.

To implement the software prototype a PC based tool, VIRTUS Walkthrough, was used. As usual with human computer interaction prototypes not the whole functionality of the TACRS was implemented (the data base functionality which would be of extreme importance in a TACRS is of no interest when developing the interaction techniques), but only the parts of interest for evaluating the usability of the chosen interaction style. Of crucial interest in this context were for example the way users find their way in the virtual supermarket (Fig.1) or how to select items and put them into the trolley (Fig. 2).

5 Conclusions

The pressure towards rationalization on the service industries increases the demand for systems which can be operated by users without experience or training on the system. Additionally users must prefer using such systems compared to human assistance. Therefore special requirements must be met:

- the way the system works must be easily comprehended,
- general usability must be guaranteed,
- and the system must be highly attractive to users.

The methods to achieve these goals consist of a non standard, real world metaphor forming the basis of the human computer interaction, iterative prototyping as development paradigm and of including latest trends and ''en vogue'' features.

As a design example the development of a TACRS to reduce staff costs in travel agencies was outlined.

The resulting prototype shows all salient features of the applied interaction techniques which have been developed as a result of the evaluation of preceeding prototypes. Future work will include the implementation of a prototype with superior performance. Also the efficiency of the interaction with the system will be improved as a result of extensive testing. The idea of an intelligent agent could be included in future versions. The add on of the actual booking process into the TACRS is also under consideration.

The crucial goal of this work was to search for alternative interaction techniques and metaphors for a non standard problem domain. Alternative interaction techniques and metaphors can only be implemented to a certain limit with conventional tools. Especially in the early design stages the designer has to look for ideas how to demonstrate non standard solutions. A simple, but effective means to evaluate metaphors in the very early design phase has been developed with vision presentations. Low cost, low quality video prototyping as used in this work has shown to be very well suited to transport ideas and design philosophies to the users.

6 Acknowledgements

We would like to thank C. Biedermann, M. Kirmair, T. Kreuzhuber, M. Posch and M. Schwarz for assisting us in getting this work done.

7 References

1. Bauer, C.: Psychotrip im Cyberspace. OUTPUT + micro, No. 10, 20-23 (1992).

2. Cruz-Neira, C., Sandin, D.J., DeFanti, Th.A., Kenyon, R.V., Hart, J.C.: The Cave - Audio Visual Experience Automatic Virtual Environment. Communications of the ACM, Vol. 35, No.6 (1992).

3. Indurkhya, B.: Metaphor and Cognition. Kluwer Academic Publishers (1992).

4. Kalawsky, R.S.: The Science of Virtual Reality and Virtual Environments: A Technical, Scientific and Engineering Reference on Virtual Environments. Addison-Wesley (1993).

5. Kolli, R:. Concept Prototyping: A Designer Based Approach to Envisioning User Interfaces. In: Proceedings of Computergraphics'92. 355-367, (1992).

6. Krueger, M.W.: VIDEOPLACE-An Artificial Reality. In: CHI'85 Conference Proceedings, ACM, 35-40 (1985).

7. Krueger, M.W: Artificial Reality II. Addison-Wesley (1991).

8. Lewis, C., Rieman, J.: Task-Centered User Interface Design - A Practical Introduction. Shareware, P.O. Box 1543, Boulder, CO 80306 (1993). Original files for the book are available via anonymous ftp from ftp.cs.colorado.edu.

9. Musil, S., Tscheligi, M.: Breaking the Chains: How to Design Non-Standard Interaction Environments. Tutorial Notes CHI'94, Boston (1994).

10. Pausch, R.: Virtual Reality on Five Dollars a Day. In: S. P. Robertson, G. M. Olson, and J. S. Olson (eds.): CHI'91 Conference Proceedings. ACM, 265-270 (1991).

11. Pimentel, K., Teixeira, K:. Virtual Reality: Through the New Looking Glass. Intel/Windcrest/McGraw-Hill, Inc. (1993).

12. Rabb, F., Blood, E., Steiner, R., Jones, H.: Magnetic Position and Orientation Tracking System. IEEE Transaction on Aerospace and Electronic Systems, Vol. 15, No. 5, 709-718 (1979).

13. Rheingold, H.: Virtual Reality. Summit Books (1992).

14. Robertson, G.G., Card, S.K., Machinlay, J.D.: Information Visualization using 3D Interactive Animation. Communications of the ACM, Vol. 36, No. 4, 57-71 (1993).

15. Schertler, W., Schmid, B., Tjoa, A.M., Werthner, H. (eds.): Information and Communications Technologies in Tourism. Springer Verlag Wien New York (1994).

16. Hot Stuff!, From the Land of High-Tech Gizmos, More Techno Toys. Time International Magazine, December, 51 (1992).

17. Tognazzini, B.: The "Starfire" Video Prototype Project: A Case History. In: Adelson, B., Dumais S., Olson, J. (eds.): Proceedings of CHI'94. ACM, 99-105 (1994).

18. Tullis, T.S.: Screen Design. In: M. Helander (ed.): Handbook of Human-Computer Interaction. Elsevier Science Publishers B.V. (North Holland), 377-411 (1988).

19. Väänänen, K., Schmidt, J.: User Interfaces for Hypermedia: How to Find Good Metaphors? In: Proceedings of CHI'94, Conference Companion, ACM, 263-264 (1994).

20. VPL-Research: DataGlove Model 2 Users Manual. (1987).

A Virtual Reality based System Environment for Intuitive Walk-Throughs and Exploration of Large-Scale Tourist Information

Kornél Szabó[1], Peter Stucki[1]
Patrick Aschwanden[2], Thomas Ohler[2],
Renato Pajarola[2], Peter Widmayer[2]

[1] University of Zurich
Department of Computer Science
MultiMedia Laboratory
Winterthurerstrasse 190, CH-8057 Zurich
ph: +41 1 257 4346; fax: +41 1 363 0035
email: szabo@ifi.unizh.ch
http: //www.unizh.ch/kornel.html

[2] Swiss Federal Institute of Technology
Institute of Theoretical Computer Science
Haldeneggsteig 4, CH-8092 Zurich
ph: +41 1 632 7402
email: pajarola@inf.ethz.ch
ttp: //www.inf.ethz.ch/
hdepartment/TI/pw/staff/pajarola.html

Abstract

This paper describes the concept and a prototype architecture for Virtual Reality (VR) based generic (X) Information Systems (IS). This setup, called ViRXIS, may serve as an architecture for a variety of IS domains, such as a VR based Tourist Information System (ViRTIS) or a VR based Geographic Information System (ViRGIS).

Keywords

Tourist Information Systems, Virtual Reality, virtual worlds, real-time interactive 3D simulation, information systems, man-machine interface, object-oriented database management systems, spatial data access structures.

1. Introduction

The ever increasing computing power and storage capacity of low-cost computers and client-server systems enable the implementation of multimedia applications that integrate different media such as text, image, graphics, voice, music, computer animation or video for the presentation and manipulation of tourist information. At present, the user interface of such multimedia Tourist Information Systems (TIS) are mainly based on the 2.5D desktop metaphor and the direct manipulation paradigm. One of their strengths compared with classical means of sales support such as color brochures, catalogues or videos lies in their interactivity and dynamics concerning information presentation and manipulation. Progress in information visualization, human-computer interaction, sensing technologies, and the availability of integrated and workstation based simulation platforms allow the extension of existing computer graphics and multimedia technology to a new man-machine interface concept, called Virtual Reality (VR). Virtual Reality, as a first approach to conceptualize and implement such new man-machine interaction concepts, will enable the substitution of traditional 2.5D with new 3D user interface paradigms and metaphors. VR is considered an eneabling technology that may overcome typical shortcomings of todays information systems (eg. TIS or Geographic Information Systems (GIS)), such as limited space for information presentation and information exploration capabilities. Especially for tourism related data, characterized with its spatiality, VR may offer an essential extension and enrichment for experiencing information.

As a first walk-through application based on the ViRXIS architecture, the ViRGIS application prototype was designed and implemented. ViRGIS allows an interactive exploration of the Digital Elevation Model (DEM) of Switzerland [1], integrating two UNIX workstation platforms over a local area network (LAN) by a client-server concept. One platform is used for the visualization and navigation, the other for the data management of the DEM. In the following, the concept and underlying system architecture of ViRXIS will be described.

2. System Concept

Interaction with large vorlumes of multimedia type data puts high affordances to the underlying hard- and software resources. Because of main memory limitations, the design and implementation of a real-time interaction environment has to consider special data handling techniques to offer efficient and effective information presentation and manipulation conditions for the user. Most simulation environments use flat files instead of a DataBase Management System (DBMS) for storing and loading virtual scenes. Unfortunately, such techniques limit the possibilities for launching data queries to objects within the virtual environment. The underlying idea of ViRXIS was to develop a VR based generic information system architecture for intuitive walk-throughs and exploration of large-scale information spaces. Besides the the functionality of a real-time 3D interaction environment, mechanisms for complex object data queries were integrated. An object-oriented DBMS (ooDBMS) was chosen for the management of the entities within a virtual environment. The ooDBMS´s role is to serve the simulation environment with different types of multimedia information entities and store changes of entity attributes. To guarantee high frame rates for real-time interaction within the virtual environment, only object data beeing in the user´s primary focus of attention is loaded and kept in main memory. Additionally, the Level-Of-Detail (LOD) switching mechanism is applied to reduce and manage the graphics load on the rendering subsystem. Depending on the object´s distance to the viewpoint, field-of-view, viewport pixel size, and graphics stress factor only the perceptually relevant LOD (i.e. polygonal resolution) of a virtual object is rendered. The LOD concept assumes, that objects have to be modeled and stored or automatically generated in different geometric resolutions.

3. System Architecture

The ViRXIS system architecture consist of two main components: the ViRXIS-InterActor and the ViRXIS-ooDBMS. These two components are linked together over a LAN through a low-level networking interface. The objective of this client-server based approach is to distribute the work load over several system platforms and guarantee real-time interaction in a virtual environment. The ViRXIS architecture is shown in Figure 1.

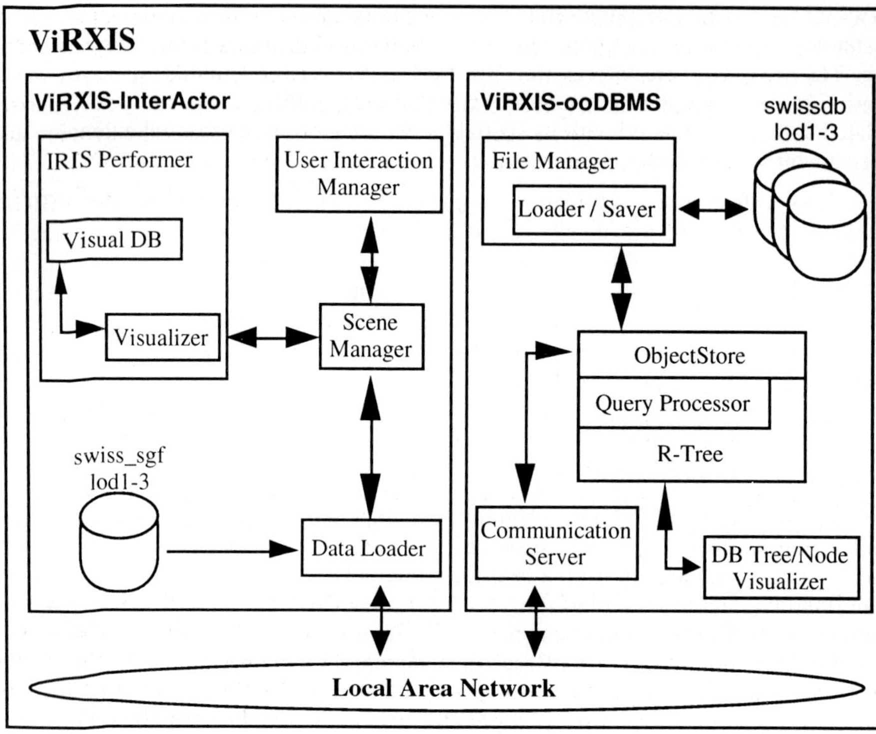

Figure 1: ViRXIS Client-Server System Architecture

3.1 ViRXIS-InterActor

The main task of the ViRXIS-InterActor, the component for interactive 3D visualization and navigation, consists in the processing of the user´s input, loading the required virtual scene data into main memory and visualizing them on the graphics display. The ViRXIS-InterActor runs on a Silicon Graphics Onyx RealityEngine2 with two raster managers using the IRIS Performer (Performer) visual simulation toolkit [2] [3]. Performer is a sophisticated toolkit that offers special mechanisms like multi-processing, auto-synchronization of application and rendering processes, LOD management functions and shared memory support for interactive real-time 3D simulation. Performer builds up a visual non-persistent database at run-time to store and manage object and attribute data of a virtual interactive environment.

The virtual scene is sub-divided into logical 3D rectangly organized patches that form the basic building blocks for a scene in the main memory on the simulation platform. Depending on the viewing frustum (defined by the user´s actual viewpoint, field-of-view, viewing direction and clipping planes) and navigation velocity, the corresponding LODs of the patches are loaded into main memory and the visual scene database of Performer. Only one LOD per patch is held in main memory to keep memory load at a minimum and have the opportunity to hold more objects in the main memory.

Responsible for the dynamic management of the actual scene is the scene manager. It traces the actual scene, inititates data load queries and deallocates no longer needed data. The data loader processes the data load query coming from the scene manager and sends either a query message to the ViRXIS-ooDBMS or loads the requested data from the local file system. After the reception of the requested data, the internal visual database of Performer is updated with the new data and automatically visualized. The user interaction manager handles the interactions, mainly mouse inputs and control panel manipulations, between the user and ViRXIS.

3.2 ViRTIS-DBMS

The ViRXIS-ooDBMS runs on a Sun SPARC Server 690 and uses ObjectStore from ObjectDesign Inc. as the underlying ooDBMS. The objective in chosing ObjectStore was to gain the advantages and features of a commercially available DBMS, such as data distribution, concurrency control, failure recovery, support of storing multimedia type data structures, persistency, and a virtual memory mapping architecture to guarantee referential integrity. ObjectStore uses C++ as the host language and offers several tools like a graphical schema designer to ease the design and development process.

The link between ViRTIS-ooDBMS and ViRTIS-InterActor is done over a LAN by BSD sockets. The communication server builds the link between the simulation and ooDBMS environment. It receives data load queries and sends them further to the query manager, where a corresponding data request is initiated to the ooDBMS. To filter the requested objects from the database as fast as possible, a sophisticated spatial data access structure in the form of an R-Tree [4] was implemented on top of the ooDBMS. To minimize the number of disc accesses and network transfers, the persistent neighbouring objects are stored physically in clusters. This is well supported by the ooDBMS including corresponding data access mechnisms. This offers the advantage, that only neighbouring relationsships need to be considered and spatial selectivity can be applied during information retrieval. The existing application prototype only deals with DEM related data and triangles that do not overlap in x/y-dimensions. Therefore only 2D range queries have to be processed.

4. Terrain Database

In ViRGIS, as the first application prototype, only topographical data are managed by the ooDBMS. This data consists of the DEM of Switzerland in a resolution of 250 meters between single vertices. The original data had first to be converted into the Silicon Graphics Object (SGO) data format to ease data transformation from ViRXIS-ooDBMS to ViRXIS-InterActor. On the ViRXIS-InterActor platform, dedicated routines allow an easy loading of SGO type objects. The DEM is stored in three LODs: 1.) 250 meters, 2.) 500 meters, and 3.) 1000 meters. To achieve better performance while transfering data from the ooDBMS to the simulation platform, the SGO data format was enhanced to the new SGF format. This enhancement reduced the amount of data to be stored and transmitted by 55% percent and offered a better data parsing and read technique for the simulation component.

5. Human-Computer Interface

The ViRGIS prototype uses a three-button 2D mouse as a navigation tool for the exploration of the DEM. The following navigation functions are currently supported: accelleration, de-accelleration, stand still and change of direction. Additionally, a Graphical User Interface (GUI) based control panel offers the possibility to manipulate system parameters, such as setting the view point, visualizing rendering statistics and modifying the rendering mode.

6. Application Scenarios for VR based Tourist Information Systems

As already mentioned above, ViRXIS may also serve as a software architecture for a VR based Tourist Information System (ViRTIS). By the help of sophisticated 3D data representation and interaction techniques, the user of such a ViRTIS may explore and experience tourism related data in a more intuitive and natural way. This new paradigm for man-machine interfaces offers potentials that go far beyond conventional 2.5D GUI based information systems.

Enabled by VR research results, telepresence and teleoperation platforms, based on high-speed and high-bandwith digital networks, offer the potentials to revolutionize the way communicative and collaborative work is done. Applying telepresence and distributed interactive simulation concepts to ViRTIS gives another very interesting and challenging scenario for Computer Supported Cooperative Work (CSCW) like application domains. A user may log-in into a remote host to prototype his next holiday trip. On demand, he can ask for a local tourist guide´s help to show him within the virtual world the interesting sights to visit while planning his stay.

Another interesting application may lie in the field of entertaining gastronomy by the concept of the "The Flying Panorama Restaurant". CAVE [5] or VET [6] like system, that are already available today, allow the setup of an immersive dining room, where guests of a restaurant may have a dinner while for example flying over the mountains of Switzerland.

Finally, ViRTIS could be applied at a Leisure Based Entertainement (LBE) park, at a World Expo or in the classroom of the future to experience exotic places on the Earth or Space in a game like way. CAVE or VET like installations may be linked together over wide area networks to allow users, staying physically at different places, to interact together in a shared virtual environment.

7. Conclusions

The ViRGIS project and the evolved ViRXIS architecture gave first insights in the development of real-time interactive walk-through applications. It became clear, that there has to be a focus on efficient data management and access techniques to fulfill the requirement for real-time performance within virtual worlds. Special techniques, such as R-Tree based data access structures, clustering of neighbouring objects, Level-of-Detail, parallel loading of scene data were implemented to maintain real-time performance and interactions within the virtual environment. The loosly coupling of ViRXIS-ooDBMS with ViRXIS-InterActor allows a flexible modification and extension of the database with new entities, that can be used by any other multimedia or VR based applications. The application of an ooDBMS offers the possibility to manage large amounts of data and launching data queries that go far beyond the capability of traditional file system based interactive simulation systems.

Adding VR technology to information systems, such as TIS or GIS, offers potentials to experience large volumes of complex data and allows a faster and more intuitive problem understanding. Benefits gained from such new intuitive and natural interaction paradigms have also implications to the reduction of information retrieval and manipulation costs.

8. References

[1] RIMINI, Das digitale Höhenmodell der Schweiz mit einer Maschenweite von 250 Metern, Bundesamt für Landestopographie, Wabern, 1992.

[2] Silicon Graphics Inc., "IRIS Performer™ Programming Guide", Silicon Graphics, Mountain View (CA),1994.

[3] Rohlf J., Helman J., "IRIS Performer: A High Performance Multiprocessing Toolkit for Real-Time 3D Graphics", Proceedings of ACM SIGGRAPH´94, in: Computer Graphics, Annual Conference Series, ACM SIGGRAPH, August 1994, pp.381-394.

[4] Guttmann A., "R-Trees: A Dynamic Index Structure for Spatial Searching", Proceedings of the ACM SIGMOD, International Conference on the Management of Data, Boston, 1984, pp.47-57.

[5] Cruz-Neira C., Sandin D.J., DeFanti T.A., "Surround-Screen Projection-Based Virtual Reality: The Design and Implementation of the CAVE", Proceedings of ACM SIGGRAPH´93, in: Computer Graphics, Annual Conference Series, ACM SIGGRAPH, August 1993, pp.135-142.

[6] Donelson A., "Drafting Boards and Blueprints Give Way To Interactive Design", Virtual Reality World, Nov./Dec. 1994, Mecklermedia, Westport (CT), 1994, pp.7-8.

[7] Maffeis S., "A Flexible System Design to Support Object-Groups and Object-Oriented Distributed Programming", in: Guerraoui R., Nierstrasz O., Riveill M. (ed.), Proceedings of the ECOOP´93 Workshop on Object-Based Distributed Programming, Lecture Notes in Computer Science 791, Springer, 1994.

[8] Digital Equipment Corp., Hewlett-Packard Corp., HyperDesk Corp., NCR Corp., Object Design Inc., Sun Soft Inc., "The Common Object Request Broker: Architecture and Specification", Rev. 1.1, OMG Document Number 91.12.1, December 1991.

"Virtual Travel: Promoting Tourism to Unfamiliar Sites Through Pre-Trip Experience"

Authors

Christian Bauer
R2 - Funware GMBH
Etrichgasse 18
6020 Innsbruck
Austria
Tel. +43 512 361441
Fax +43 512 361442
Email: chris@well.sf.ca.us

Dr. Robert Jacobson
Worldesign Inc.
5348-1/2 Ballard Avenue NW
Seattle, WA 98107-4009
USA
Tel. +1 206 781 5253
Fax +1 206 781 5254
Email: bob@worldesign.com

Abstract

The authors propose the construction of an immersive Virtual Reality system, to promote unfamiliar sites to tourists through a pre-trip experience. The Virtual Reality system should give the potential customer an idea on how the several traveling sites will look like. The provider of such a system should understand this as a tool for attraction and as a means for product promotion.

1 Introduction

The tourist travels in space, moving from one place to another. Virtual worlds are computer-generated images that can represent places. In a virtual world environment - an integrative, highly-convincing computer-communication medium - it's possible to apparently move from one place to another. In the process of "Virtual Travel," the tourist can visit places at little cost in time or money. The increasing availability of virtual worlds technology for generating persuasive simulations of potential tourist destinations creates new opportunities for stimulating tourism in unfamiliar places.

The usual tourist has at his or her disposal a number of means for planning future excursions. These include books, magazines, newspapers, brochures, films, videos, multimedia presentations, materials from tourism offices, and last but not least, consultations with a travel agent. Even so, the tourist is left to synthesize these sources of information - which can rapidly go out of date, especially the print materials - on his or her own, without much context. The tourist has every chance of missing important information, getting wrong or misleading information from the media he or she does acquire, and especially misinterpreting even true information as it passes through his or her cultural filter.

It is the lucky tourist who chooses wisely a new place to visit! Plagued by inadequate context within which to evaluate the plethora of information available to them, tourists choose "safe" destinations: places that friends, acquaintances, or they themselves have visited before; well-publicized "tourist traps"; or sites on a package tour that require no prior evaluation.

Some travelers, it's true, prefer to venture out in ignorance, the better to have unexpected adventures; but they tend to be a minority, often young people with limited financial resources who must go where free or cheap transportation will take them.

Figure 1, The CAVE - developed by the Electronic Visualization Lab of the University of Illinois at Chicago

As a result, many places remain starved for tourism, even places with fine attractions, even places located near well-traveled routes. This is especially true of locations in the Third World or the newly opened East that do not benefit by significant travel-press attention or well-financed tourism bureaus.

2 Virtual Travel

It is relatively easy, however, to build virtual worlds, spatial representations of these places, and so give tourists a chance to "experience" these places without inconvenience or expense. Virtual Travel enables tourists to travel to unfamiliar sites and plan extensive trips among these locales. In an immersive shared environment, several persons can simultaneously have these experiences, checking their impressions against one another's and confirming travel decisions on the spot.

Importantly, virtual worlds can be designed by worldbuilders employed in the service of these places or by the inhabitants themselves -- capturing in three dimensions the soul of a place, as other, less involving media cannot. Sight and sound both can be spatialized to heighten the verisimilitude of a Virtual Travel experience. Remarkably lifelike representations of physical locations can be generated by computers. It is more difficult to synthesize human beings in a virtual world, but still and moving images can be imported as digital signals that are compatible with a virtual world's computer graphics.

Figure 2, A scenery near the village Nassereith of Tyrol - a part of the project "ÖMV Wunderwelt"

Virtual worlds used for Virtual Travel have another important characteristic: they can include information that is not immediately apparent, in visual or aural form, but which can be "called up" from the computer(s)' memory to supplement natural images. For example, in traveling through a virtual world of Khazakstan, we might use a hand-held device to "click on" or point to an indicated orchard and then be treated to an additional textual or multimedia exposition on the history of the apple, a Khazakstani original. Virtual Travel can also be used to learn more about places which the tourist already knows, but about which he or she wants to know more.

Virtual Travel currently relies on one or more powerful computer workstations driving a stereoscopic headset or the increasingly popular "CAVEs" (Computer Audio-Visual Environments) and VETs <tm> (Virtual Environment Theaters <tm>). The latter are small theaters able to envelop from four to 20 individuals in a projector-defined visual space.

By mid-1995, personal computers equipped with more powerful processors and graphics components will be substitutable for workstations, lowering the cost of traveling virtually to a fraction of what it is today. Software to build virtual worlds is getting better and cheaper, too. In the near future, it will be possible to automatically build landscapes in virtual worlds from computer-stored GIS (geographic information system) data, and buildings from CAD (computer-assisted design) models.

The construction of a CAVE or VET in itself is not difficult, although cheaper materials -- particularly lower priced display technology, to replace expensive video projectors and screens, and more powerful PCs to replace workstations -- will certainly be welcome. The most engaging part of Virtual Travel, and the most challenging, is building the virtual worlds, the dynamic, interactive "portraits" of places to be experienced within the CAVE or VET. For now, the work is highly skilled and performed generally by designers and programmers who collaborate with clients to craft worlds. Tools for easier world construction are now becoming available, so that worldbuilding will soon be more accessible to anyone with basic computer skills.

Figure 3, Screenshot from the "ÖMV Wunderwelt"

How one of these systems will be best deployed and used is still to be seen. Some may be located in tourism bureaus and commercial travel agencies. Others may themselves tour, as
promotional systems taken from market to market. Still others may be collocated with other attractions, pointing the way from busily traveled sites to those less well-known. Ultimately, as global telecommunications networks evolve, it should be possible to virtually travel in the Net itself, calling up places and attractions and then "inhabiting" them in one's own home, library, school, or workplace.

3 Technical Requirements

The system basically consists of one fast Personal Computer and three graphics accelerators that have to be build into the PC. The graphics accelerators are connected to three videobeams who backlit projection screens. Wearing LCD Shutter Glasses, the user is surrounded and immersed by the projection screens. These glasses provide a stereoscopic vision when looked at the screens. Through devices for motion-tracking, the movement of the user is traced and can be fed into the computer, who then can calculate the proper perspective. The expensive part of this system are mainly the projectors: Three projectors cost about US-Dollar 60.000,-- the rest about US-Dollar 30.000,--.

Figure 4, Screenshot from the "ÖMV Wunderwelt"

A high-speed grafical workstation could improve the display quality by assuring a constant frame-rate of 60 Hz with high resolution, anti-aliasing and high polygon count. Such systems are available starting at US-Dollar 200.000,--.

But in order to use such a system, Virtual Environments have to be build. The cost for a complete modeling of a specific site depends on the level of detail, availability of data of the region and the objects and other factors. The modeling of a site like shown with the "ÖMV Wunderwelt" ranges between US-Dollar 30.000,-- up to 100.000,--.

4 Conclusion

Through increasing speed in grafical computation and the lowering of the cost factor, Virtual Reality can be used as a marketing tool in promoting unfamiliar sites to tourists. The system will only reach a certain degree in realism and can only offer a limited number of 3D-digitalized environments. But the potential customer will appreciate - and therefore consume - any means in planning his timely limited vacation and he will be attracted by the new and fascinating medium, that represents one important factor of vacation: fun.

References

1. Horx, Matthias: **Trendbuch** - Der erste große Deutsche Trendreport. (1993); Econ Executives Verlags GmbH
2. Moravec, Hans: **Mind Children** - Der Wettlauf zwischen menschlicher und künstlicher Intelligenz. (1990); Hoffman und Campe Verlag
3. Bormann, Sven: **Virtuelle Realität** - Genese und Evaluation. (1994); Addison Wesley (Deutschland) GMBH
4. Waffender, Wolfgang (Hsg.): **Cyberspace** - Ausflüge in virtuelle Wirklichkeiten. (August 1991); Rowohlt Taschbuch Verlag GMBH

5. Jacobson, Linda: **Garage Virtual Reality** - The Affordable Way to Explore Virtual Worlds. (1994); Sams Publishing
6. Rucker, Rudy; Sirius, R.U.; MU, Queen: **Mondo 2000** - A User's Guide to the New Edge. (1992); HarperCollins Publishers, Inc.
7. Naisbitt, John, Patricia Aburdene: **Megatrends 2000**: Zehn Perspektiven für den Weg ins nächste Jahrtausend. (1990); Econ Taschenbuch Verlag
8. Rheingold, Howard: **Virtuelle Welten** - Reisen im Cyberspace. (1992); Rowohlt Verlag GMBH

A European Electronic Market Place for Tourism

P.F.Byerley & J.Ewers

DeTeBerkom, Volta Strasse 5, 13355, Berlin

Gregory Lella & Gianluca Lo Reto

Saritel, SS 148 Pontina km 29.100, 00040 Pomezia

Uwe Zobel

Lufthansa Informationstechnik und Software

The TIM & MNET projects are providing prototype services for a trading environment, in a way which matches the specific needs of the customer. The application is sector generic, but the projects focus on tourism. In tourism, the customer could be a holiday maker, travel agent, or the original supplier of a product such as accommodation, a cultural event or a sports activity. The trading environment enables a pan European electronic market place for tourism.

1.0 Introduction

There are two unifying concepts for the tourism trading application, corresponding to "marketing", and "selling" tasks.

For marketing, the concept required is for "multimedia marketing information". PoO sites need to market their products in the way that they want, and, in apparant contrast, PoS sites require the flexibility to selectively present and view the marketing information in a manner consistent with an efficient sales process. In addition, automatic integration of multimedia updates to the distributed database system requires marketing information "objects" which are clearly defined and manageable in a consistent way across all PoO "authors". At a detailed level this concept is not sector generic since it would contain the attributes of typical sector objects e.g. holidays. However it is possible to define a concept which is appropriate for describing typical sector objects but which has generic features. The TIM project has decided to use the concept of a "**folder**". The folder concept satisfies the user requirements for flexibility in marketing and selling, but is sufficiently standard to enable data base management. A more rigid concept, such as the multi media "document", would have been both more restrictive and more complex for authoring and viewing. A document concept may, however, be appropriate for other applications, e.g. marketing automobiles. A folder in TIM is similar to the normal paper folder concept. It is a container for information, which also has some information displayed on its front cover. When a folder is retrieved from the database the user will be presented with the front cover. The front cover will contain a picture (image or graphic design), some text, and a list of the contents of the folder. These contents can be text, picture, sound, and video, and can describe particular facilities e.g. the bedrooms, or a more complex "slide show" presentation constructed by the PoO. The user is able to selectively view/listen to the contents, thus giving flexibility at PoS.

For selling, the concept required is for "product packaging". The requirements for this concept are the representation of a multi vendor collection of different travel/holiday products in a form suitable for purchase. Within the tourism sector the "**package**" concept is familiar. For TIM this can be defined using the concept of a diary of product selections and transport arrangements. In other sectors the package concept may be more rigidly structured, for example the mutually dependent components of a machine for spare part purchase, or the preconditions for the purchase of a house, or hardly structured at all, for example a "shopping basket" of consumer goods.

1.1 The User Services.

With the two application concepts the following TIM pan European user services have been implemented:
Creation of folders. (PoO). Original material can be digitised and edited at every PoO using the media specific editors. The folders must then be defined by the PoO user against the data base search attributes that will be used at PoS. A typical folder contains pictures, text, video, speech and sound, and is approximately 10 MB. The schedule of folder creation is specific to and controlled by each PoO user.
Distribution of Multi Media files of the folders. (PoO).The multimedia files for the folders can be distributed from PoO to specific database locations which will minimise the cost of retrieval for targeted customers at PoS. Integration of new information and updates into the database is automatic. The schedule of distribution of is specific to and controlled by each PoO user.

Viewing of folders. (PoO & PoS). Folders can be searched for by "dropping down" through layers of maps, or by directly specifying the folder type. An electronic note can be made of any product the viewer finds interesting. All folders are known and are accessible from all PoS and PoO, irrespective of location of storage of the multimedia files for the folder.
Packaging.(PoS). A multi vendor package of products can be constructed during the sales process from the available offers promoted by the folders. The package is structured as a diary. The electronic "note pad" created under the Viewing Service is available for transferring offers directly to the diary. Each product can be checked for availability and purchased via a variety of on-line reservation systems, but through one standard booking user-interface.
Administration. (PoO & PoS). These services provide the basis for the users to manage the application. PoO users can request feedback on the use that has been made at PoS of their marketing information. PoS users can request integrated access to customer records.
PoO-PoS Negotiation. (PoO & PoS). Direct marketing services will create many occasions where discounts and commissions need to be negotiated. In addition there may need to be direct requests to PoO to amend a product line or the marketing information. These will be principally conversational and messaging tasks.

1.2 Operation and Evaluation of the Services.

There are two major operation and evaluation periods of the TIM services, April-December 1994, and January-July 1995. The first period consists in installing and testing at user sites, and consequent debugging and software modifications. The second period consists in as realistic as possible "commercial conditions" trials. Evaluation in both periods is supported by additional data which will be made available from the TEN IBC Programme. Under TEN IBC the MNET Project will evaluate the TIM services over 8 international ATM links between November 1994 and February 1995. The locations of the user sites are given in Figure 1.

2.0 The Definition of the Application- User Company Requirements.

The User Requirements and Business Analysis work in TIM, excluding operation and evaluation of the system, was allocated 20% of the total project budget. Four types of work were conducted.
Firstly, an analysis of the position of each user organization within tourism was undertaken so that they could assess the impact of investment in communication services on profitability. This was done in the context of the Five Forces Model (Porter (1985))[1]. In addition the project needed to understand the sequences of strategically important activities (Value Chain) within each organization which lead to design, production, marketing and support, each of which may require communication . These analyses provided an initial basis for the choice of applications for which evaluation of new communication services were appropriate. These analyses pointed to the need for direct trading relationships, for targeted marketing, for user driven updating of offers, for competiveness based upon product differentiation, for greater and more cost effective exploitation of the individual rather than the standard mass tourism product.
Secondly, the chosen applications were then defined in terms suitable for service analysis. This requires describing an allocation of tasks to available humans and machines, which will create a requirement for cooperative work and communication services, such that the objectives of the application, understood from the first type of analysis, will be satisfied. (The result of this second type of analysis is termed a Reference for User Services (Byerley and Bruins (1992))[2]. Each communication task can be defined as an example of, conversation, send, or retrieve. Groups of these can also be identified as mutually dependent within the task allocation, and can be nominated as instances of generic applications, such as; retrieval and forwarding, collaborative retrieval, conferencing, etc. This task allocation provides a partial definition of the jobs of each of the end users.
Thirdly, the services which would enable the task "network" to operate need to be defined. The services need to be described in terms which make sense to the customer. This could be done by referring to familier service products (standard telephony), or, if this is not possible by using a service structure which relates directly to the communication tasks described above (conversational service integrated with a retrieval service providing for joint viewing of high quality video).
Fourthly, the user interface to the system must be defined for each user type. The tasks allocated to each end user need to be broken down into subtasks until they are sufficiently simple for service design. Then for each subtask an Enabling State (Byerley (1993))[3] of the system is specified. An Enabling State is a state of; the end-

1 Porter (1985) Competitive Advantage. Free Press

2 In: Byerley P. + Connell S. (1992) Integrated Broadband Communications: Views from RACE: Usage Aspects. North Holland

3 Byerley P. + Barnard P. + May J. (1993) "Computers Communication and Usability" North Holland

user, the service, and the object (on which the subtask acts, e.g. a multimedia file needed for editing), which enables the execution of the subtask. The state of the end user will include the task skills needed, the state of the service will include user interface attributes, and the state of the object will include its availability to be acted on by the user. For each enabling state the tasks which can create that state (Enabling Tasks) are defined. These tasks can include, provision of help or training, call-set-up and control procedures, and object retrieval procedures (eg alerting the other party by ringing their phone). In general the system will be more usable if the enabling tasks are automated or made very simple. In TIM special attention has been paid to design human machine interfaces which are **simple** and relevant to each user's main tasks, to simplify tasks such as setting up calls, and to remove unnecessary functions and to hide unnecessary information. The Enabling States Approach supports the design of work systems which give control to the user over their goal tasks, but for which enabling tasks are removed or automated. The screen dumps shown in section 5 illustrate this feature of the user interface design in TIM.

Figure 1 Locations of TIM & MNET Users

3.0 Architecture for the TIM Services

The requirements on the TIM architecture were: Multimedia marketing material produced locally, and possibly cooperatively, at PoO sites and then distributed at user determined times across Europe to user determined locations. Access at PoS sites to potentially all multimedia material for retrieval and the production of individualised multi vendor packages which could then be purchased with one action. The architecture also had to be affordable to the TIM partners, consistent with sector trends, and scaleable to eventually a much larger number of users.

The solution is essentially a distributed database with local database nodes at all PoO and PoS sites. Direct trading relationships are supported by local node to local node transmission of multi media data. All the local databases are accessable from all TIM terminals (if the user has the access rights). A global supervising node administers and monitors data base updates and system use, it does not act as a central store of the multi media marketing data. When the system is scaled up multi media data will be held on more levels, for example, private customer databases, and local nodes and regional nodes accessable from all TIM terminals.

The local architecture is an Ethernet local area network, with one or more terminals, local node of the database, and a router. When the system is scaled up the data transmission capacity of the local area network will be increased. At PoS sites access to transaction systems, international or remote local booking systems, is made via a modem and X.25 to a central TIM Gateway. The TIM Gateway provides a standard transaction interface to TIM users, whatever the particular services or networks the transaction systems use.

4.0 The TIM PoO and PoS Terminals

The h/w for both the terminal, and global/local database nodes is 486 PC, with the database running Microsoft SQL Server under Windows NT, and the terminal Windows for Work Groups. The objective was low cost and conformity with tourism sector developments.

Figure 2 indicates that the top menu bar for both PoO and PoS human machine interfaces shows to the left only the services for the main goal tasks of the user, and to the right help/training and exit services. Pulling down any menu item reveals services for the subtasks of the particular main goal task. In general all non essential services are removed e.g windows are full screen, and resizing and overlapping of windows is not possible.

PoO	VIEW	CREATE	DISTRIBUTE	COMMUNICATE	ADMINISTRATE		HELP	EXIT

PoS/PoI	VIEW	PACKAGE	COMMUNICATE	ADMINISTRATE		HELP	EXIT

Figure 2 *Top Level Menu Items for PoO and PoS*

All occasions of language use in the interface are language customisable. The services for folder creation (Create), retrieval of folders, (View), distribution of folders, (Distribute), and creation and booking of a product package (Package), are illustrated in more detail below.

The user interface will be illustrated with a description of the **Package** Service

The subtasks here are Create a new package, and Modify an existing package.

These subtasks are potentially the most complex of the users tasks since the services provided enable **customer specific** packages to be created and purchased, rather than just predefined packages to be selected.

The requirements on the package concept are; each element of the package should be consumable or usable, e.g. it should be possible to get from one product location to another in time, and each element should be available, it should be possible to vary arrangements and to complete the package when in the destination region. The chosen concept is the familiar one of a diary, with associated travel arrangements. The customer can be given a print out of their diary, and in addition can be provided with an electronic version which can be completed or amended at a TIM terminal when in the destination region.

The first sceen dump shows that during the completion of the package the Note Pad (filled out under the View service) is available for transferring product names directly to the Diary.

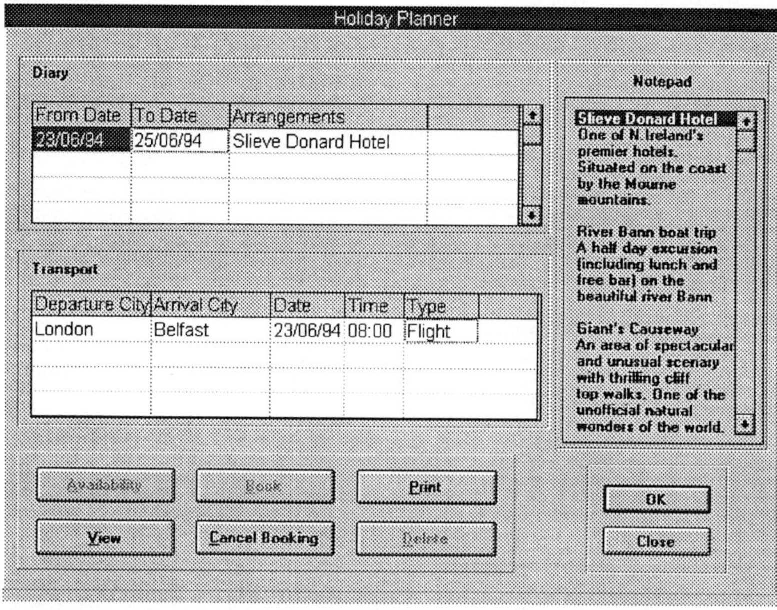

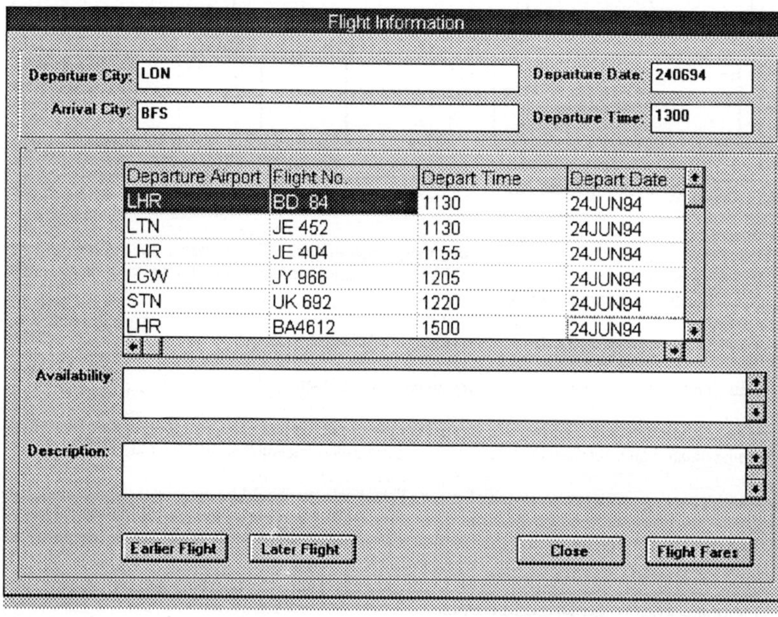

A multi-vendor package can involve a range of international and local booking systems, which will have different human machine interfaces, and often complex codes and abbreviations. The second screen dump shows, that for every product type, availability checking and booking is done via simplified, standard TIM interfaces. It is however not intended in the first evaluations of the system to allow the customer to use this PoS interface. This interface is designed for operation by sales staff with customers. A further simplified interface for stand alone use will be derived from the View, and Package services.

5.0 A Distributed Database for Supporting International Trading Relationships.

The requirements on the database design are **transparent support** for the international trading tasks described in the previous section. The PoO, & PoS users will not be required to undertake any of the "enabling" tasks associated with the maintenance of an up-to-date and consistent database. This can be illustrated via the concept of a database "operation". An operation is the basic unit of database activity. It can be defined by; who has initiated it, when it occurs, which nodes of the database it involves, on what database object it acts, what the type of the operation is, and what the result of the operation is. The database services which support the operation are; session control (e.g. managing the initial requests of the user), resource management (e.g. security management), operation management (controlling the ongoing operation), command execution (executing the users tasks such as creating, searching, deleting, distributing etc.), and finally logging the operation for later statistical analysis requests. The management of the operation takes place at terminal, local node and global supervising node level. Each operation executes a command with respect to an object.

The main object types in the database are; Folders, Inserts, Maps, and Packages.

Operations on a folder e.g.creating, deleting, searching for folders for retrieval and viewing, requires that the folder is described by a standard set of attributes. In order to support the creation of individually appropriate packages, folders need to be easily distinguishable and therefore they need to be described in detail. TIM standards, therefore, needed to be defined which are detailed and applicable across Europe. These standards were supplied by the TIM User Group. For the Folder type there are the following main classes; Country, Region, City, Accommodation, Tour, Event, Activity, Place of Interest, Transport, Food & Drink, and Shopping. These are then further subdivided, for example there are 130 sub-activities. Some attributes which measure grade/quality are country specific, grades of accommodation for example. The TIM project has not proposed European standards in these cases, but rather has implemented a Help service on both PoO & PoS interfaces which provides an explanation of the different gradings used.

Although the Operation Management of the system can be largely removed from the users there are some tasks which cannot be. Features which the PoO users of the system are responsible for are the quality and validity of the multimedia information. This issue is being tackled by the Standards Workpackage in TIM during the remainder of the project.

6.0 Communication Networks for Marketing and Booking.

The requirements on the communication networks concern three classes of task; distribution and retrieval of multimedia objects (folders), checking for product availability and booking, and operations management of the database. All these tasks include international communication. TIM supports these tasks with services that can operate and interwork over a variety of network platforms, (X.25, ISDN, MAN, ATM), in the context of a development path that combines exploitation over ISDN and continuing research for ATM issues.

6.1 The Distribution and Retrieval tasks

These are integrated within marketing and selling processes. This provides requirements for the maintenance of high quality, sound, images, video, and a responsiveness of the system which is "real time". In addition, marketing and selling is individually user driven, and unpredictable. Finally, the TIM application is one of "thousands communicating with thousands", in other words it is a "desk top" application which requires an extensive network and a network which is cheap to use. The commercially available network which provides the minimum performance for these requirements is ISDN (Integrated Services Digital Network. This network has a basic access of 64KBit/s). However, one folder which contains video sequences (5 MBs in size) will take a few minutes for transmission from one part of the distributed database to another over ISDN. Transmission of text and still image takes only a few seconds. Retrieval from a user´s local database to their terminal is in seconds even for folders with video inserts. In consequence, if the access to the TIM system is over ISDN then retrieval of folders with video which are not on the user´s local database cannot be "real time". Although the TIM services can be provided and used in a way over ISDN which makes commercial exploitation feasible, ISDN is obviously not an ideal choice either for speed or transmission cost. For this reason the TIM services are also being evaluated over the ATM pilot international services

Thus the international network over which the user services are being evaluated is a hybrid of ISDN and IBC. The design of the application is such that either network can be used. For commercial exploitation a clear evolution path is being drawn between the use of ISDN, and IBC.
A schematic of the current hybrid network is given in Figure 3. The next section provides more detail on the ATM links.

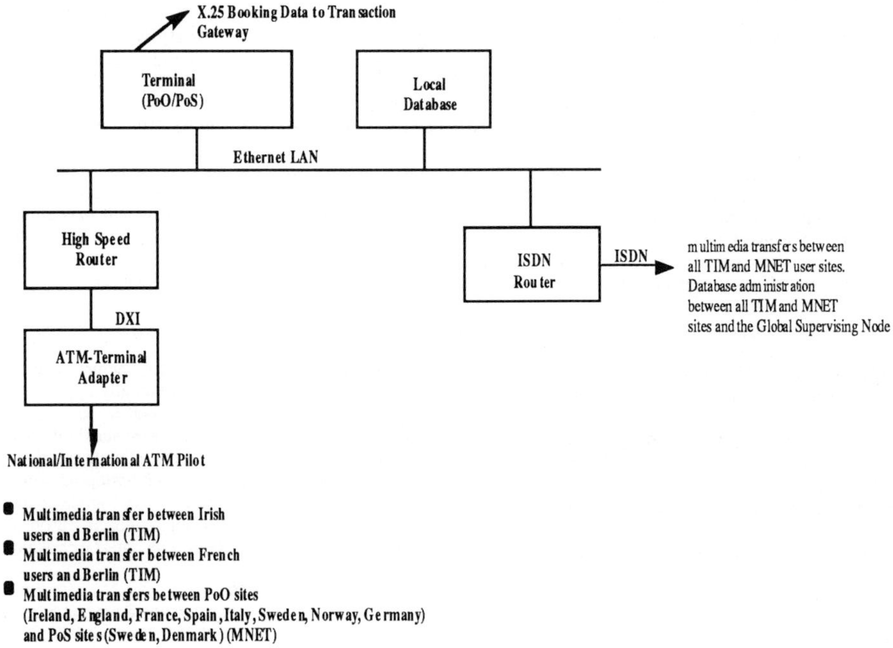

Figure3 The Hybrid TIM Network

6.1.1 ATM Services and Interfaces in MNET.

Within the MNET project ATM services are being evaluated as a replacement of ISDN for multimedia file transfer between local nodes of the distributed database. The ATM services are being provided by public network operators under the International ATM Pilot. The ATM links being evaluated by MNET are principally between Barcelona, Rome, Dublin, Belfast, Martlesham Heath (BT Research Laboratories), Berlin, Oslo, Paris, and Copenhagen and Malmö. The ATM services are, for the most part, 34 Mbit PDH. Complete uniformity of end user ATM interface equipment is not possible, however some interoperability problems are solved because DeTeBerkom for the Berlin site can provide several different ATM interfaces. This allows a two step link via the Berlin local node, if a one step link is not possible. We shall now briefly describe the major concepts of ATM.

ATM (Asyncronous Transfer Mode) was developed for multimedia communication. It splits data traffic into short segments or cells. The ATM technology, also known as fast packet switching, cell switching and cell relay technology, is based on a switching technique, in which cells are routed to their destination without regard to the content. At the boundary of a network, adaptation processes pack or unpack the cells and deliver digital information in its original format. Therefore, information of discrete media (text, graphics etc.) as well as digitised audio and video information can be transferred over networks with ATM technology, encompassing narrowband speeds (up to 2 Mbit/s) and broadband speeds (from 34 Mbit/s up to 600 Mbit/s). Broadband ATM segments information into 53 byte cells, of which 48 bytes are used for the data and 5 bytes for the header, including address information, generic flow control (GFC), virtual path identifier (VPI), virtual channel identifier (VCI), payload type (PT) and header error check (HEC).

All worldwide major standardisation bodies have recognised cell relay as the base switching technology for Broadband Integrated Services Digital Network (B-ISDN). ATM, a cell relay technology, has been standardised by ITU-TS in the Recommendations I.361, I.362, I.363 and I.432 as part of the B-ISDN Reference Model. The lowest layer of the B-ISDN Reference Model is divided into sublayers:

- bit transmission layer: combination of the physical medium (PM) and the transmission control (TC),
- ATM sublayer: communication service independent cell formating (I.432 and I.361),
- ATM adaptation layer (AAL 1..5): communication service segmentation and assemblation of the cell (I.362 and I.363).

Different classes of services are defined in the B-ISDN Reference Model:

- connection oriented line emulation with constant bit rate and constant end-to-end delay,
- connection oriented with variable bit rate and constant end-to-end delay (e. g. for audio and video with variable bit rate),
- connection oriented with variable bit rate and non constant end-to-end delay (e. g. for connection oriented data services like X.25 and frame relay),
- connectionless with variable bit rate and non constant end-to-end delay (e. g. for connectionless data services, LAN interconnection).

The access to the trial network depends on the preference of the network operators. It is made in one of two modes :

a) Native ATM over an SDH-STM/1 or PDH interface. This is the preferred access mode for the highest quality and flexibility. Most countries use this form of access. The ATM data stream is available in 34 or 155 MBit/sec. This service is also known as permanent or reserved Virtual Path (VP) service.

b) A connectionless service, e.g. SMDS, for an easy interface to a LAN. British Telekom and France Telekom are promoting this interface. The SMDS frames are transformed into ATM cells by an interworking unit that is managed by the network operator. A second alternative to SMDS is a frame relay protocol. There are still a lot of co-ordination and specification problems connected to this service.

There are several methods to connect to the VP sevice / native ATM :

a) A terminal adapter or DSU that translates between a DXI interface and the ATM cell stream. It is defined by the ITU and uses the AAL 3/4 mode. The DXI interface connects to a high speed router. The router provides the final interface to a LAN, e.g. ethernet, token-ring.

b) A private ATM switch connected to the public ATM network. The private switch provides low cost interface to end systems, e.g. workstations and servers. The switches that are now available support the AAL 5 transmission mode. A low-cost router can be connected to the switch. The router interfaces to a LAN.

c) A direct interface integrated into a workstation. Several companies are developing such an interface for PC-compatible computers or workstations.

The user equipment that is selected for MNET and that is based on the TIM project can be connected to any of the above mentioned interfaces. For the trial, the first variant has been chosen as primary solution and will be supported by most of the network operators.

6.2 The "availability and booking" tasks.
These are, in the ideal and typical TIM case, communication tasks with computerized reservation systems (CRS), so that products can be booked with no intervention needed from a human operator at the PoO. These systems may be international, such as Amadeus, Galileo, and Sabre, or local, such as Gulliver, Bokser, Bettenbörse. The TIM system contains a central Gateway for communication with both types of booking system and "real-time" performance can be achieved with standard data networks such as X.25. For cases where products are not on reservation systems the availability and booking tasks can be conducted directly via fax from the TIM terminal, using the telephone, or would have to rely on pre-allocation with the PoS. Local booking systems are rapidly expanding in Europe, and a major factor influencing the choice by PoS of PoO suppliers is the ease with which products can be booked.

6.3 Database operations management tasks. These tasks concern, for example, communication between the local nodes of the database and the Global Supervising Node. These communications are essential for maintenance of an up-to-date and consistent database, however this is "machine to machine" data communication which is adequately provided for by international ISDN basic rate access.

7.0 Integration of International Marketing and Booking.

In the previous section reference was made to the booking of products. The customer specific "package" which can be built using the TIM services will in most cases be multi-vendor, with the vendors (PoO) residing in one or more destination regions. A major requirement arising from this is that each element of the package should be easy to check for availability and to book. This requirement is however not met simply by the product elements residing on a computerized reservation system because each reservation system could present to the PoS user a different interface with different commands and codes. Thus multi vendor packages could present a large skill and training problem to the PoS.

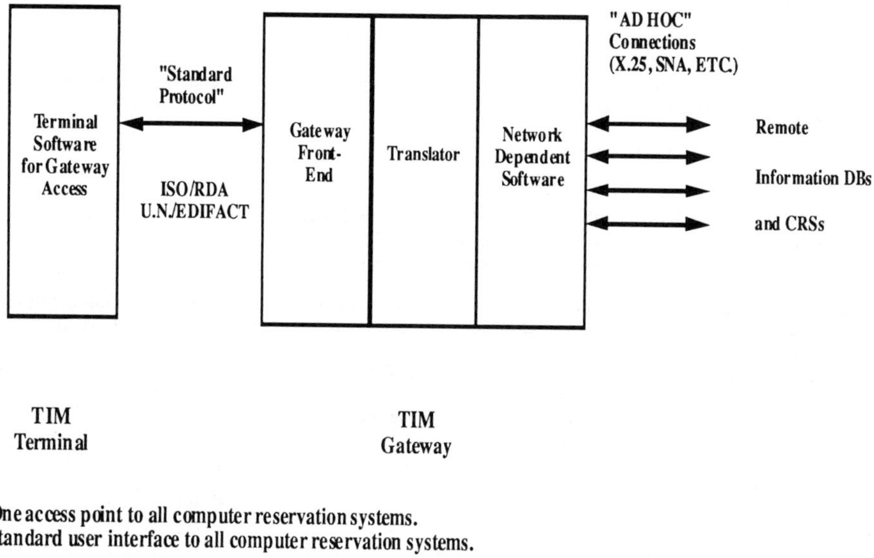

Figure 4 The TIM Gateway

This problem is solved in the TIM system by the provision of a central Gateway as illustrated in Figure 4 . The Gateway hides from the PoS user all differences in service and network between the reservation systems. The TIM user interface at PoS presents a series of screens which are standard for each product type, and which avoid the use of codes. The TIM database holds the information on which reservation system the product resides, and this information is passed to the gateway for the transactional tasks.

The implementation of the CRS specific components of the Gateway and the operation of the Gateway depends completely on the cooperation and collaboration between the TIM project and the CRSs. The TIM project has established research agreements with the CRSs; Galileo, Amadeus, and SABRE, on the basis of mutual exchange of information.

8.0 Operating and Evaluating the Prototype Services.

In order to support local training, computer based training programmes have been integrated into the PoO and PoS systems. These simulate the real systems and conduct short interactive training sessions for each of the user´s goal tasks. (These CBT programmes are publicly available, on request, from the project management).

The evaluation of the TIM services requires some constraints on operation in order that all aspects of the services are operated and evaluated. The Evaluation work is divided into; PoO, PoS, and Technical Evaluation.

The PoO applications that are being evaluated are the creation and distribution of folders of; tours, all non tour products, and regions (including cities, and countries). In addition the statistical services are being evaluated. Ten user companies have been involved in the evaluation of the creation of folders. This initial evaluation focussed on the usability of the system, and in general simply the feasibility of giving user companies responsibility for doing their own multi media publishing. All users were able to create and edit their folders, and found the system easy to use. There were a number of recommendations for improved functionality, for example the opportunity to use a text processor of the user´s own choice, the opportunity to move easily from the editing environment to the customer viewing environment so that presentation details can be improved. These have already been implemented.

The PoS applications that are being evaluated are; staff product knowledge training, retrieval of information during selling, construction of packages during selling, and, for Point-of-Information (PoI), supervised customer browsing of folders. The PoS evaluation begins with a Training Workshop on 12th-13th September.

For both PoO and PoS applications evaluation variables have been defined (e.g. support for the user´s goal tasks, time taken to learn, types of error, and subjective acceptability) many of which are automatically collected by the system.

Because of the hybrid nature of the TIM network, and because of the concurrent MNET trials the evaluation can make a direct comparison between TIM services carried by ISDN and the same services carried by IBC. This is particularly appropriate at those sites which have access to both types of network. The specific impact of broadband services are being examined for :

Folder Creation and Modification. For example; the preferred structure and use of text, image, video and sound, the preferred quantity of information in a typical folder, the rate of updating.
Distribution. For example; the number and type of targeted local databases, the latency and reliability of the distribution.
Retrieval. For example; the retrieval latencies, the type of information retrieved (text, image, video), the proportion of wide area network retrieval.
Packaging. For example; the product complexity and commercial value, the use of products from small companies compared to large operators, the mix of national/foreign products, the proportion of dynamic packaging.

The technical evaluation is using standard folders, and packages as reference materials for obtaining performance measurements of the terminal (e.g.media quality and retrieval latencies), database (e.g. internode distribution times), and network (e.g. internetwork comparisons), and gateway. For example, first results on response time using the gateway are shown in the table below

Function Name	TIM Gateway API response time	Galileo interface response time
Access	20 sec - 40 sec	0 sec
Connect	10 sec	17 sec
Flight	13 sec	17 sec
Fares	13 sec	25 sec
Flight_Reserve	20 sec	32 sec
Hotel	12 sec	6 sec
Hotel_Reserve	17 sec	45 sec
Encode	6 sec	3 sec
Decode	4 sec	2 sec
Earlier	8 sec	8 sec
Later	8 sec	8 sec

Although access time is inevitably longer, because it is necessary to reach Galileo via the gateway in Rome, the more complex transactions are realised more efficiently by the gateway API

9.0 SAMSON - a development following TIM

The starting point of SAMSON (Services for an Advanced Marketing System on Networks) is the final trials phase of TIM, in addition SAMSON will focus only on the German tourism market. In size and in user representation this project is highly significant within the German market. The objective of the project is to provide a greater degree of integration of the marketing services evaluated by TIM with commercial services and practises. It is hoped that the result of SAMSON will a development of a greater product range accessable from point-of-sale, with a reduction in cost of provision of customised products at point-of-sale. The tourism partners in SAMSON already represent an important part of the German market (including; START Telemtic, Thos. Cook, Berlin Tourismus Marketing, DER Tour, LTU), and this group will be expanded during the project via the formation of a Common Interest Group. The SAMSON project is financially supported by Deutsche Telekom via the DeTeBerkom company (the prime contractor of TIM). The prime contractor of SAMSON is Lufthansa Informationstechnik und Software, and the other technical partners are Alcatel SEL (also in TIM) and Optimal Systems.

The SAMSON I project began in October 1994 with a specification phase, and a short trial with the TIM-prototypes. The implementation phase and a trial with the SAMSON software (Marketing Support Center and Integrated Sales Environment) at about ten test-sites will begin in early 1995. Within the completion of SAMSON I a new proposal will be set up for SAMSON II, a project in which will involve over 50 test sites.

10. Conclusion

The use of advanced technology for tourism applications must be driven by a thorough analysis of the business requirements of the users of those applications. Purchase of the latest multimedia kiosk, or workstation without this analysis can quickly lead to disappointment. Multimedia needs to be used to improve business and reduce costs. The results from the analysis of user need undertaken in the projects mentioned in this paper point strongly to the use of communication networks for the production, distribution, and retrieval of multimedia marketing information. However the consequence of the freedom provided by flexible user driven systems for trading is the need for a greater degree of standardisation, not with respect to equipment, but within the tourism sector itself, for example for product description methods.

ISDN in the travel industry
A catalyst for change?

W.J.M. Teunissen

Rotterdam School of Management,
Erasmus University Rotterdam, The Netherlands

Abstract. The travel industry is long familiar with stories on future travelling destination searches: ranging from full-motion video to virtual reality, customers are expected to be given the opportunity to experience their possible destinations in every way but being there. Although some travel agents nowadays offer their customers to take home video cassettes on their destinations, we are still far removed from such 'high touch' applications, one of the main problems being the lack of a globally available, high bandwidth telecommunication infrastructure that will carry the large amounts of data involved. This paper focuses on the role the Integrated Services Digital Network (ISDN) may play in these developments. Even though it only offers medium bandwidths, this is compensated by flexibility, high availability, and a good price/performance ratio, thus providing the travel industry with an infrastructure to distribute products and services to the customer's home, fuelling changes that may even affect the structure of the industry.

1 Introduction

In Jarvenpaa and Ives [8] the following scenario is presented:

> '... *[During her flight to London] Tara Rodgers began to make arrangements for her stay in Oxford. Using a virtual reality simulator, she wandered into the rooms of the guest house she had been so delighted with during her last visit to Oxford. Being presented only with the rooms that were available to be rented that evening, she selected the one with the lovely pink wallpaper, ... She then booked a car to pick her up at Heathrow and transport her to Oxford. She could have looked at a short video segment showing where to meet the cab. ...*'

Scenarios such as this can be found in numerous treatments on travelling and/or telecommunications. Already information technology and telecommunications (IT&T) play an important role in the travel industry of which the computer reservation systems (CRS's) are the most familiar examples. More recent developments are destination information systems [5, 14] which in some cases go beyond the text-based interface into the new world of multi-media, where sound, video, data and text are integrated for a higher impact and a better impression of possible travel destinations.

The scenario presented also shows one of the trends in (leisure) travel: an increasing level of individualization. Other trends are [1, 2, 3, 12]: the absolute number of travellers is growing, they are increasingly experienced, and have more time and money to spend. One of the consequences of these developments is the increasing need for information on the possible destinations. To be able to make an informed choice between the hundreds of destinations, the customer must process a significant amount of information. Because most people consider selecting a travel destination to be a pleasant activity that offers them some holiday-feeling, much time is devoted to it. Numerous brochures and books are published to satisfy this need, complemented by TV-documentaries on destinations, all of which are enjoyed at home. With the advent of multi-media telecommunication, however, a whole new range of possibilities is created, allowing the customer to interactively browse through the vast amounts of data, in order to select and reserve a travel destination as well as provide the pre-travel thrill.

Reaching the travellers-to-be at their homes, or rather, enabling them to get at this information from their homes or anywhere else for that matter, will require a telecommunication network that has to be globally available, provide a standard interface, and allow high transmission capacities, all at an acceptable price-level. This paper presents the Integrated Services Digital Network (ISDN) as a - not really new - network that fulfils these requirements.

Following a brief technical introduction of ISDN, an indication will be given of the business changes that may be fuelled by employing a telecommunication infrastructure such as ISDN. Next, we will discuss some implications for the travel industry and its players.

2 ISDN: a new infrastructure?

The Consultative Committee for International Telegraph and Telephone (CCITT), defined ISDN as [9]:

> *'A network, evolved from the telephone network, that provides end-to-end digital connectivity to support a wide range of services, including voice and non-voice services, to which users have access by a limited set of standard multi-purpose user-network interfaces'*

Significant is the 'evolved from the telephone network' part: by replacing the original analogue transmission techniques with digital ones, ISDN is the natural evolution of the analogue public switched telephone network (PSTN). The new network combines the advantages of the PSTN - availability, flexibility, standard - with higher quality and throughput.

ISDN has already been around for some time, and in some countries such as Germany, Great-Britain and France there exists a large installed base of ISDN. In

The Netherlands, however, there are currently only about 2500 ISDN users. This is mainly because the national PTT was reluctant to implement ISDN before appropriate standards were defined [7, 16]. Since the establishment of the Euro-ISDN standard, the Dutch PTT is working hard to achieve national availability by the beginning of 1995. Complementing this effort, the ISDN Integration Centre was founded in the Netherlands at the beginning of 1994. A joint effort of some 20 suppliers of ISDN technology - both hardware and software - the Centre's goal is to promote ISDN to its potential users. Because ISDN has proven to be difficult to market only on the basis of its technical merits (ISDN lacking a so-called *killer application*), a different approach is taken in the Centre. A research was conducted among a selected set of users of ISDN in The Netherlands to investigate the ways in which ISDN influenced, or enabled, a more efficient way of working; other ways of doing business; or even changing the scope of the business. In the Centre, the results of this investigation are presented in a workshop structure, in which a selection of case material is presented to visitors. The visitors are then invited to make a translation to their respective businesses. This way the Centre hopes to increase the appreciation of telecommunication in general and ISDN specifically.

2.1 ISDN Features

ISDN comes in two flavours: *basic rate* with 2 channels with 64Kbit/s bandwidth each (the *B-channels*), combined with a 16Kbit/s signalling channel (the *D-channel*), and the *primary rate* with 30 (or in some countries 23) B-channels and a single (64Kbit/s) D-channel. The separation of B- and D-channels (known as out-band signalling) offers the advantage of availability by means of the switched D-channel, without having to interrupt a conversation, which runs via the B-channels.

Features of ISDN include (refer to [15] for a more complete overview of the subject):

- standard
  although there are several ISDN 'standards', Euro-ISDN being the accepted European standard, ISDN networks across the world will be interoperable;
- integration
  ISDN integrates communication of sound (of which voice is only one example), data, video, graphics, fax;
- general availability
  because ISDN builds on the already present telephone network infrastructure, installing ISDN only requires the installation of a small terminator box at the conventional telephone wire;
- flexibility
  as opposed to leased lines, there is no pre-determined communication partner;
- medium bandwidth (64Kbit/s to 2Mbit/s)
  the basic rate ISDN connection offers data transmission capacities of about 9 times the 14.4Kb/s that can be reached with current modems on 'good' telephone lines;

- fast call set-up
  an ISDN connection is established in less than 2 seconds, compared to 15 seconds average for the PSTN. This allows network-connections via ISDN to be temporarily disconnected (saving money) while the user experiences no significant delays in the access of remote network resources;
- several different ISDN terminals (fax, telephone, computer) may be connected to a single basic rate access connection
  the service identification numbers that are contained in the ISDN messages allow the message to be routed to (or rather picked up by) the proper terminal;
- subaddressing
  it is even possible to use subaddressing in order to attach two computers or two telephones and direct calls to one specific terminal;
- cost structure on the basis of use
  Apart from the subscription fees, one only pays for each second used, plus an added connection establishing fee. In contrast, the amount per second depends on whether the call is local or long distance. The cost of leased lines, for example, is directly related to the number of kilometres between the two end-points.

ISDN offers the possibility of *bandwidth-on-demand*. With the aid of a technique called inverse-multiplexing, ISDN's advantage of a fast call-setup can be used to modify the bandwidth of a communication channel by changing the number of ISDN B-channels used for the connection. With this technique, temporary peaks in data traffic may be effectively dealt with.

2.2 Application areas

As a telecommunication infrastructure, ISDN supports a wide range of applications which are not restricted to a specific functional area or industry type. Organizational changes enabled by ISDN therefore range from primarily cost-reduction - e.g. replacing leased lines with ISDN as a back-up for leased lines - to improving customer service, enabling the generation of new products, and facilitating co-makership relations. Below we give some illustrative examples of the use of ISDN as we found them during our research among Dutch ISDN users.

Audio-broadcasting. In The Netherlands, regional broadcasting companies are using ISDN to transport near-hifi sound between studios. Furthermore, interviews and live reports are transmitted to the studio using portable ISDN equipment. This has allowed a significant improvement of the quality of the recordings, but also a shortening of the planning period, because there is no longer a need for hiring temporary music-lines for higher quality.

The regional broadcasting companies exploit the integrative features of ISDN by using the network for telephone, for data-transport between their administrative information systems, and for centralised information system management.

Printing industry. The printing industry is rapidly incorporating ISDN as part of its communication infrastructure. ISDN is being used in a number of ways. One use is the delivery of computer-drawings (e.g. from CAD-software) of which a number of copies have to be made. Instead of copying a locally printed hard-copy, the information is directly transmitted from the CAD-software to the printer's shop for processing by a special plotter/copier. This has allowed a reduction in time (drawings need no longer be locally printed and physically transported to the printer's premises), but also in cost (no expensive high-resolution printer/plotter required).

ISDN is also found to enable printers and designers to change the way they communicate. They now transmit the voluminous Postscript files and subsequently discuss the result, editing it on-screen with the other person being able to see and comment on the changes, using the so-called screen-sharing and joint-editing features of ISDN. Cooperation rather than communication becomes the proper word to describe the relation between these organizations. In addition to compressing production-time, it is also found that the flexibility of ISDN allows each of the organizations to easily switch partners between projects, depending on the expertise required.

Health care industry. A similar application of cooperation may be found in the health care industry. Here, specialists can discuss a patient's medical file which can be examined by all using ISDN's screen-sharing and joint-editing features.

Other application areas are: multi-media tele-shopping, video-conferencing, querying multi-media databases, real estate marketing, distance learning, tele-working, but also 'low-level' applications such as LAN-LAN interconnections and back-up services for leased lines.

3 Travel industry: fertile ground for ISDN?

Coates has stated that the travel industry is an information industry and hardly anything else [3]. Distinguishing between pre-travel, travel and post-travel, he argues that in each of these three phases information plays a significant role. However, it is not limited to the usual information carried in computer reservation systems (CRS's) on airplane seats, meals, etc. It is about what to see, where to see it, why to see it, how to see it, and how to remember it.

In this paper we will primarily restrict ourselves to the pre-travel phase in which the traveller requires information on:

- where to go
- what one can see or do
- how to get there
- where to stay
- what it will cost

and subsequently be able to:
. make a reservation.

It must be noted that no distinction is made between the business traveller and the tourist because their questions are the same. They merely have different requirements. Therefore we assume that the information system that establishes the interface to the travel information database is sufficiently flexible to support both categories of travellers.

3.1 Drivers for change

Currently, travel information is mainly distributed by travel agents, tour operators, and tourist offices. Following a broad pre-selection of travel destinations, a process in which the travel agent may act as a consultant, the traveller must process the information and ultimately make a choice. This is generally done at home because of the amount of time involved, to allow discussion with travel companions, but also because for the fun of considering the different destinations.

The complexity of the (pre-)selection process is growing. The following reasons for this change can be identified [1, 2, 3, 12]:

. individualization of the product travel
  Travellers want to be able to compose their own holiday, possibly from a number of standard components, but the combination will their individual choice;
. growing number of possible destinations
  Travel agents will find it increasingly more difficult to be adequately informed and assist their customers;
. increasingly knowledgable travellers
  The former problem is exacerbated by the fact that the customers are becoming more knowledgable and require more detailed information on very specific travel destinations.

This situation may be improved by providing travel agents with information systems enabling them to navigate through the information intelligently, enabling supply of and demand for information on travel products to meet electronically, creating an electronic market [4, 10, 13, 14]. In the pre-selection process the travel agent would then take on the role of *computer operator*, translating the demands and wishes of the customer into commands for the information system to come up with a number of suggestions.

Taking this one step further, the customer could be put in charge, as he or she could sit behind a computer terminal and type the commands. Since the role of the travel agent would be minimal, if at all present, the terminal need not be located at the travel agent's premises. It could be, for example, at the traveller's home....

3.2 Home-shopping for travel information

Home-shopping is not a new phenomenon. Already all kind of products may be ordered by pressing just a few buttons on your telephone or the remote control of your TV set. For travel sales, for example, two pilots are conducted in the USA where cable-television customers can call up airline tickets and fares and order tickets from a local travel agency [6].

The following general advantages of home-shopping can be identified:

. customers will be able to shop 24 hours a day;
. the customer can take his or her time while considering the alternatives;
. environmentally friendly, travel is reduced.
. the telecommunication infrastructure operator will sell 'ticks';
. the information providers could benefit by charging the users, with the possibility of a discount when reservations are made.

In the specific case of travel information, home-shopping may

. become an activity on its own, when the multi-media material is 'sufficiently entertaining';
. provide valuable marketing-information for the travel industry.

However, home-shopping has its limitations:

. except when offered toll-free numbers, the customers will have to pay for information that is now free;
. there is a significant danger of information overload [6];
. people may fear social isolation;
. a responsibility issue must be resolved: can and should the customer be held responsible for making erroneous reservations? (Every computer user will realise that confirmation messages are more or less ignored when they come up for the second or third time.)

Home-shopping in the travel industry will not be an automatic choice, because of

. no access to on-line services, due to a lack of knowledge or finance;
. advice/consultancy is required.

This would require that the 'old' structure be continued.

3.3 Information requirements

The demands on the information, that will form the basis for the travel information system, are formidable. Firstly, for travellers to take the medium serious, access should be provided to information on as many travel destinations as possible. Considering the number of possible destinations this requires significant technical and organizational skill. Secondly, because of the perishable nature of the travel information, regular - possibly daily - updates are required on seasonal information and on rates, opening hours etc [14]. Adding reservation capabilities will require an on-line connection to e.g. the hotel or airline reservation system as to guarantee the accuracy of the information.

Because the accuracy of the information is so all important, careful consideration must be given to the question who is to be made responsible for the information. Considering that the stakeholders of the database are the suppliers of the information, such as the owners of the restaurants, hotels and parks (possibly represented by local tourist offices who may implement additional quality control procedures [14]) in the destination information systems as well as for example airline companies and the larger hotel chains, it seems reasonable that the responsibility should be placed in their hands.

Another issue to be resolved is who should pay for this electronic market, the information suppliers or the consumers, and how prices should be set. Relevant in this respect is that the information suppliers gain an additional marketing channel (see also the next section), which also can provide them with detailed information on customer behaviour. The customers on the other hand will be able to satisfy their demand for more information.

3.4 Technical requirements

Technically, there are several problems to be overcome. Firstly, the huge amounts of data must be prepared for access by the customer. This means that instead of the current databases which are mainly oriented towards the travel agent or some other intermediary making reservations, the data must be stored in such a way as to facilitate searches based on user queries. Secondly, a telecommunications infrastructure is required to get the information to the customer. Considering the features of ISDN as listed in the previous section, we feel that ISDN is the proper choice for such an infrastructure. It is capable of transporting the required amounts of data to and from the customer; it is standard and provides the flexibility and availability making it attractive for the travel industry to invest in applications that build on this infrastructure. Thirdly, the customer must be provided with a simple but powerful interface that will ask the right questions, facilitating the navigation of the information sea.

The last problem may not be as easy to solve as it may seem. Although an electronic market has many attractive properties, it is not very suitable as a marketing or selection tool for products or services that have many intangible features. Hotels, airlines, restaurants, for example, present themselves in such a way as to reinforce some image, be it low-budget or high-quality. Such an image is difficult to quantify and put in words. The electronic equivalent for the experience of holding a glossy brochure instead of some list of names of hotels, would be a 'glossy' user interface with lots of fancy features, nicely presented and containing all possible information. To integrate these different approaches in a manageable and usable fashion, lessons may be learned from existing global databases such as the Internet World Wide Web.

4 The position of the travel agent

Contemplating the possible impacts these information systems may have on the structure of the travel industry, a number of scenarios can be drawn all revolving around the position of the travel agent and possibly that of other intermediaries. Although the role of the travel agent may be expected to change, a complete disintermediation can hardly be expected. A statement from Naisbitt is appropriate here [11], in which he states that as technology increases in sophistication and capabilities, a commensurate increase in personal service may be expected, to balance the inanimate and often fearful nature of IT. Although it is not clear whether this precludes the personal contact to be via telephone or desktop video-conferencing, it seems that the travel agent may still provide added value when:

- assisting the customer when a quick decision is required
  When the customer does not have the time to go through all the proceeds to make his/her own arrangements, the travel agent could do it for him/her;
- the customer need to be made aware of his or her own preferences
  Such a function would effectively make a preselection, focusing the subsequent browsing and selection actions. Probably this function could also be performed by the system through a series of questions and answers from which a customer's profile may be compiled. This may even be stored for future reference;
- assist the customer in using the information system
  Because of the amount and complexity of the data involved, training and assistance may be needed by the users of such a system, irrespective of the availability of, for example, context-sensitive help facilities.

5 Conclusion

Relations between organizations in the travel industry are generally expected to change due to the deployment of IT&T, short-circuiting the relation between supplier and consumer, offering each more information on the other. As a standard, flexible, fully digital telecommunications infrastructure that is available now, ISDN may be one piece of the puzzle. Since the other parts of the puzzle may all be considered technically solvable, it is now time to put the pieces together.

Puzzles can sometimes be solved in more than one way. The solution to this particular puzzle will also evolve with time. As an example, with broadband network infrastructures becoming available in the not too distant future, ISDN is by no means to be considered the one and everlasting telecommunications solution. Replacing ISDN with broadband telecommunications will further spur changes in the travel industry, including virtual reality simulators as presented in the introductory scenario and maybe even Star Trek-like 'holo-deck' experiences. Hopefully this will not end the customer's appetite for the actual travel experience!

Acknowledgements

The author would like to thank Peter Vervest for his role in the realisation of the ISDN Information Centre and the insights gained, and also Ton Roodink and René Wagenaar for their valuable comments on earlier versions of this paper.

References

1. Archdale, G.: Computer reservation systems and public tourist offices. Tourism Management, February 1993, 3-14.
2. Bennet, M.M.: Information technology and travel agency. Tourism Management, August 1993, 259-266.
3. Coates, J.F.: The future of tourism: the effect of science and technology. Vital Speeches, vol. 58, no. 24, 759-763 (1992).
4. Ebner, A.: TIS - Tourimus Informations System - Tirol "Die Konsequenz Einer Idee". The Tourist Review, No. 2, 20-24 (1994).
5. Fesenmaier, D.R.: Traveler Use of Visitor Information Centers: Implications for Development in Illinois. Journal of Travel Research, Summer 1994, 44-50.
6. Glab, J.: A Remotely Threatening Idea. ASTA Agency Management, January 1994, 14-16.
7. Horn, A., Van der Veen, Y: ISDN: a new phase in the development of the telecommunications network (in Dutch). Studieblad PTT Telecom, June/July 1993, 354-383.
8. Jarvenpaa, S.L. & Ives, B.: The global network organization of the future: information management opportunities and challenges. Journal of Management Information Systems, vol. 10, no. 4, 25-57 (1994).
9. Knight, F.: CCITT's Director on the evolution of ISDN. Business Communications Review, Jan-Feb, 27-32 (1987).
10. Malone, T.W., Yates, J., Benjamin, R.I.: Electronic markets and electronic hierarchies. Communications of the ACM, vol. 30, no. 6, 484-497 (1987).
11. Naisbitt, J.: Megatrends: Ten New Directions Transforming Our Lives. Futura Publications, New York (1982).
12. Sahlberg, B.: The demand for new information systems in travel and tourism. The Tourist Review, No. 2, 20-23 (1993).
13. Schmidt, B.: Electronic markets in tourism. The Tourist Review, No. 2, 9-15 (1992).
14. Sheldon, P. J.: Destination Information Systems. Annals of Tourism Research 20, 633-649 (1993).
15. Stallings, W.: ISDN: an introduction. Macmillan New York (1992).
16. Wijbrands, R.J.: ISDN: digital access to information and databases (in Dutch). Studieblad PTT Telecom, June 1992, 313-335.

Mobile Computing in a Reservation Application

Ouri Wolfson*
EECS Dept. (M/C 154)
University of Illinois at Chicago
851 S. Morgan St., Rm. 1120 SEO
Chicago, IL 60607-7053
wolfson@eecs.uic.edu

November 17, 1994

1 Introduction

Users of mobile computers, such as palmtops, notebook computers and personal communication systems, will soon have online access to a large number of databases via wireless networks. The potential market for this activity is estimated to be billions of dollars annually, in access and communication charges. For example, while on the road, passengers will access airline and other carriers schedules, and weather information. Investors will access prices of financial instruments, salespeople will access inventory data, callers will access information about mobile resources (e.g. taxi cabs), route-planning computers in cars will access traffic information, and wearable ubiquitous computers will access a wide variety of databases.

Wireless communication is more expensive and less reliable than wire communication. We demonstrate that the way online data is allocated/replicated at mobile computers affects both, cost and data availability, and therefore data allocation has to change according to changing conditions, such as access patterns, users' location, etc.

Presently, the allocation scheme of a distributed database is established in a static fashion, when the database is designed. The allocation scheme remains fixed until the designer manually intervenes to change the number of replicas or their location. We show that this is an unsatisfactory solution, particularly in mobile computing.

The project we describe has three main objectives. First, we will develop, analyze and implement a set of algorithms for dynamic allocation of objects in mobile computer networks. Second, we will integrate these algorithms into a a comprehensive software system and software tools to provide dynamic allocation and replication. Third, we will evaluate the system using a commercial application

[1]This research is supported by NSF grant IRI-9408750

that serves travel agents. For this purpose we will collaborate with Talk About Travel, Inc. In the next three sections we provide details on each one of these objectives.

2 Develop, implement, and analyze algorithms for automatic dynamic allocation to mobile computers

The algorithms will determine which objects will be allocated to each mobile computer. Each algorithm will be implemented by software that resides on both, the mobile computer and the fixed network. Multiple algorithms are necessary since the appropriate one depends on the environment and on the requirements of the system. These requirements may change during system's operation, or from one object to another.

We will implement the algorithms, and then evaluate them analytically and experimentally.

3 Build a dynamic allocation and replication system

The system will serve the user of a mobile computer, and it will provide tools and language primitives for either automatic or manual dynamic allocation. Automatic dynamic allocation is provided by the algorithms discussed above, and it is transparent to the user. The dynamic allocation system will enable selection of a dynamic allocation algorithm, and parameterizing it.

The dynamic allocation system will also provide language constructs and primitives for manual dynamic allocation. Examples of such primitives are: "Create (delete) a copy of object O at computer x" or, "Retrieve the total number of objects stored at computer x".

Additionally, the system will provide tools for the user to specify three types of information, that will be used in selecting dynamic allocation algorithms. First, the the objective function and the cost structure. For example, the objective is to minimize communication cost, where the cost per message of length not higher than 55 characters is \$0.04; the cost per message of length between 56 and 109 characters is is \$0.05; etc. Second, the set of objects that are subject to dynamic allocation. For example, perform dynamic allocation on all the records for flights leaving Chicago on 12/13/93. Third, information about the access pattern to a particular object. For example, the reads and writes to an object O are Poisson distributed, with parameter λ; or, the read and write pattern today is expected to be similar to the read-write pattern on 12/12/93; or, the read-write pattern between 1pm and 3pm can be determined by observing the the read-write pattern during the first 5 minutes of the period.

The dynamic allocation system will also be incorporated with the transaction management and the data-dictionary of a distributed DBMS, e.g., Ingres. A distributed version of Ingres was built in the Database Information Systems Laboratory at the University of Illinois, Chicago.

4 System evaluation using a reservation application

We will evaluate the algorithms and system developed using a travel agency reservation system. The travel agency, Talk About Travel Co., needs to enable its agents to work (i.e., check availability, make reservations, etc.) while on the road (e.g. visiting clients). The agents could call their office computer via a cellular phone, but this is an expensive proposition since they would be connected most of the time.

The alternative option is to build, maintain, and update a local database on a portable computer. The local database will be built when the travel agent leaves the office, and it will contain the information the agent expects to use during the day. For example, suppose that the agent is working on a meeting in Chicago on 5/12/94 through 5/13/94. This means that the prospective attendees of this meeting throughout the country received the name and (portable) phone number of the agent, and they are calling to make reservations on flights to Chicago on 5/11/94 and from Chicago on 5/13/94. Then, before leaving the office the travel agent would download to his/her portable computer the information about all the flights to/from Chicago on the respective dates. Each flight-record is an object, and the downloaded information becomes subject to dynamic allocation. Changes in availability of each class of service, schedule changes, and other updates of this information will be received at the home (stationary) computer from the airlines. These updates will transmitted to the mobile computer either automatically (if the mobile computer has a copy of the object), or on demand, and the system that we will develop as part of this project will control, for each object, the switch between these two modes of communication.

During the day the agent receives inquiries and requests from customers on his/her cellular telephone. Inquiries that pertain to the flights to/from Chicago on 5/11/94 and 5/13/94 are answered by consulting the local database. Communication between the agent's mobile computer and the home computer will be by radio messages that will be transmitted by a carrier, such as RAM Mobile Data Co.

The End-User Acceptance of New Information and Communication Technologies in Tourism

by Walter Schertler, Matthias Maier, Sven Rohte

Department of Organization and Strategic Management,
University of Trier, D-54286 Trier, Germany.

Abstract: The paper shows the principal layout and design of an empirical study in Germany driven by the objective to learn more and to understand better the interface between new information systems technologies (IT) and the value of such systems that customers will identify in the tourism industry. The success of these information systems technologies in tourism depends directly on their`s acceptance by customers. The authors suggest a set of factors influencing the acceptance of these technologies. These factors serve as the basis of a framework which will be empirically tested in a study of the Department of Organization and Strategic Management at the University of Trier, Germany.

I Introduction

Press coverage of new information and communication technologies in tourism has been extensive in the past. Euphoria describes best the message of many publications relating to the new ways and new value that new technologies will create. However, past experiences with such technology-push-like efforts of the industry suggest that some reluctance might be appropriate, when trying to predict the future success of these technologies treated quite often as "nice to have" features or as "technology toys". Finally it is the customer, who will decide if IT in tourism will suffer the fate of the ("failed") German BTX or of the successful Internet.

II Objectives

The analytical approach chosen in this study is the following:
We strongly believe that innovators will handle IT completely differently than in the past and that innovation in tourism will be driven more by new ways of applying IT than by new products of the tourism industry.

When speaking of IT, we mean information systems technologies and their applications in terms of (i) destination information systems (DIS) and (ii) computer based reservation systems (CRS) with their specific booking, paying and handling procedures.

Our beliefs are based on one hand side on the criteria which constitute tourism as a service industry and as an information based business. Therefore we chose an information economy approach which focusses on the problem of information asymetries and the customer value constellation of the spontaneous availability of "just-in-time" information and the costs of professsional advices provided by third parties (e.g. travel agencies).
On the other hand we have to consider how IT changes competition and the whole structure, performance and strategic conduct of the tourism industry.

That means:

a) IT will allow producers to join forces with their suppliers,

b) IT will help producers to individualize their services for special customers (groups and individuals),

c) IT will help customers to get direct access to suppliers, to be better informed about value and prices and to foster customer`s experiences and competencies.

III Determinants of Customer Acceptance of New IT

Our research has shown that the precondition for customer acceptance of IT-based distribution and information systems is that it can create *additional value* for customers. If IT does not deliver either all-new services or traditional services that are significantly improved, customers will simply have no reason to use IT.

Then we have seen that the acceptance of IT by the customer depends on the following three parameters: (1) the degree of customer experience with computer based systems (experience and general attitude towards new technology as well as IT related experience), (2) the product specialization and the travel experience of customers, which is crucial for the intensity of professional advice that is necessary for the customer`s decision and selection of tourism products, and (3) the need for high responsiveness of information systems and the individual benefit of "just-in-time" information for the customer, operationalized through (improved) speed of information availability, faster access to market data and enhanced flexibility of the booking procedures.

1) *Customer`s experience with computer based systems:* The results of a represen-tative survey of general attitudes towards technology show that appro-ximately half of the German citizens are technology-adverse. This gives a strong hint that the acceptance of new IT-driven applications could be problematic. Probably the business community will be the first group of customers that will adopt the new IT -driven possibilities, because this group feels more comfortable with computer technology and can integrate it easily in the daily work.

2) *Product specialization and customer`s experience in travelling:* These two factors correlate and refer to the complexity of products in tourism and of course to the degree of travel experience of customers. The complexity of the tourism product determines the degree of additional information and professional advice that is necessary to design, book and consume the product.
Whereas standardized products like e.g. domestic flights can be distributed easily by ticketing machines, highly sophisticated products as e.g. adventure tours might well need intense information searches and individualized customer services.
Highly experienced customers, such as business travellers or frequent travellers, are well informed on destinations and know better to handle travel procedures. Experienced travellers could be "empowered" significantly by IT to use travel information and booking systems independently and improve their personal efficiency and competencies.

3) The third dimension is *the customer`s need of (high) responsiveness of information systems:* The quicker IT can answer a time-driven inquiery the more value IT can create for certain customer segments which put a higher premium on "just-in-time"- availability of information and products, e.g. flights, hotel reservation or a destination information, than other segments do.

That means that only tourism products that are *in* the systems and visible on computer screens will be accessible for such customer segments. To business travellers and their time-sensitive behaviour patterns these systems can create solid customer value.

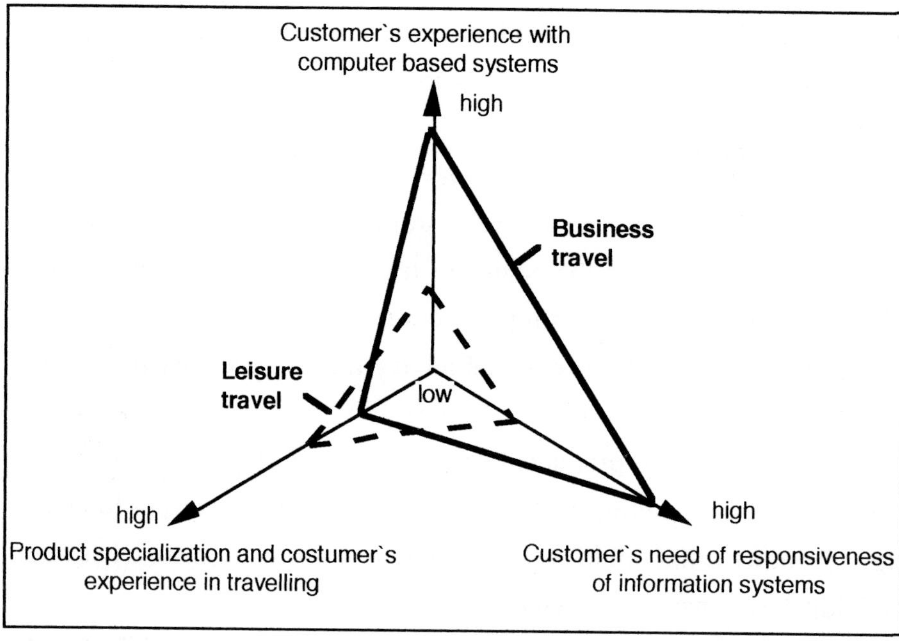

Figure: Determinants of customer acceptance of IT in tourism

This model not only shows the different aspects of customers acceptance which have to be tested in an empirical way but also different profiles of customer segments (leisure vs. business travel).

IV Empirical Study of Enduser Acceptance of New IT-based Distribution Channels.

An empirical study of the Department of Organization and Strategic Management at Trier University will analyse client´s attitudes towards IT in the tourism industry. The study will look for different rates of acceptance at different customer-related interfaces in the profit and non-profit sector of this industry.

In each of these areas we will evaluate representatively the attitudes of end users towards the introduction and use of IT-based information and reservation applications in the tourism industry, as e.g. booking or ticheting machines, multimedia information systems, interactive TV etc., distinguishing between the acceptance of applications with booking features (e.g. CRS), information features about destinations and a combination of both.

The empirical phase of our study aims at testing the following hypotheses:

- There are certain consumer segments that differ strongly in their attitudes towards the acceptance of electronic marketing.
- Frequent travellers are more likely to use electronic services.
- The more complex the product is the less it is suited to be distributed via electronic distribution channels.
- End users will rather accept electronic marketing for products where price advantage by "do-it-yourself" is paramount.

First results of tests with more than 600 interviews show[illegible]at the three determinants mentioned above are valid dimensions t[illegible]v more about customer segments and acceptance levels of IT i[illegible]ism industry.

References

Cash, James I. Jr. and **McFarlan**, F. Warren and **McKenney**, James L. *Corporate Information Systems Management.* Homewood, Illinois: Irwin, Third Edition 1992

Hammer, Michael and **Champy**, James. *Reengineering the Corporaion: A Manifesto for Business Revolution.* New York: Harper Business, 1993

Kanter, Rosabeth Moss. *Mastering Change.* In: Mobilizing Corporate Energies. Conference Proceedings for the 23rd International Manage-ment Symposium at the University of St. Gallen/Switzerland, May 1993

Norman, R. and **Ramirez,** Raymond. *From Value Chain to Value Constellation: Designing Interactive Strategy.* In: Harvard Business Review 7/8 1993, pp. 65-77

Porter, Michael E. *Competitive Strategy*. New York: Free Press, 1980

Schertler, Walter. *Tourism 2000: An Information Business.* In: Schertler, Walter et al.. *Information and Communications Technologies in Tourism..* Conference Proceedings of ENTER `94 Congress. Wien and New York: Springer, 1993

Schertler, Walter. *Impact of new information technologies on tourism industry and businesses.* In: The Tourist Review 2/94, pp. 2-8

Sheldon, P. J. *Destination Information Systems.* In: Annals of Tourism Research, Vol. 20, 1993, pp. 633-649

Skapinker, Michael. *Thomas Cook Launches Screen Booking System.* In: Financial Times, Thursday May 19, 1994

Stalk, G. Jr./**Hout**, T. M. *Competing Against Time: How Time-Based Competition Is Reshaping Global Markets.* New York, London 1990

Tapscott, D./**Caston**, A. *Paradigm Shift: The New Promise Of Information Technology.* New York 1993

Williamson, O. E. *Economic Organization.* New York 1986

Regional Integrated Computer Information Reservation Management Systems and tourism distribution channels

Dimitrios Buhalis [1]

Department of Management Studies, University of Surrey
Guildford, GU2 5XH, England

Abstract. Although Small Medium Tourism Enterprises dominate the international Tourism and Hospitality Industry, they are becoming vulnerable because of radical developments in new Information Technology and Computer Reservation Systems, and their inability to follow these developments. Therefore, the concept of the Regional Integrated Computer Information Management Systems is proposed as a platform of strategic tools which would enable SMTE to survive in the new challenging environment. The paper examines the different perspectives of the members of the distribution channel of tourism towards RICIRMS. In addition, it suggests that strategic usage the system can contribute to the SMTE and destination prosperity, in the contemporary business environment.

1 Introduction

Evolution in information and telecommunication technologies (ITT) and Computer Reservation Systems (CRS) have unquestionably altered both tourism industry practices and strategies. This paper elaborates the implications of ITT on the tourism and hospitality industries (THI) and specifically for the Small and Medium Tourism Enterprises (SMTE). A brief examination of the Computer Reservation Systems (CRS) demonstrates the effects on the operation of the SMTE, while the concept of the Regional Integrated Computer Information Reservation Management System (RICIRMS) is illustrated.

---

[1] The author would like to acknowledge Dr C. Cooper, and Dr J. Fletcher, DOMS, University of Surrey, for their valuable contribution to this paper. Financial support by the Surrey Research Group, ConTours Consultants, as well as, field-research sponsorship by the Greek National Tourism Organisation and the University of the Aegean, Greece is gratefully appreciated.

The paper is based on an on-going research, aiming to provide strategic solutions and reinforce the position of the SMTE [4,5,6]. It benefits from a field research survey which incorporated personal interviews and mail questionnaires in Greek Aegean Islands SMTE and in the European tourism industry. Useful inferences are also incorporated from the pilot application of the system AEGEO, a RICIRMS on the Greek Aegean islands. The emphasis in this research project is to observe the needs and responses, through the point of view of the different tourism distribution channel members (TDCM). It is beyond the scope of this paper to discuss technical terms and solutions. Thus, the users' requirements are analysed, based on the assumption that technology can offer almost every type of service required at a reasonable cost, at least in the long term, which in technology is assessed to be less than three years. The paper does not aim to offer a comprehensive quantitative analysis or statistically accurate results, due to the early stage of the analysis, but insights into the perspectives and needs of the TDCM. The ultimate aim is to conceptualise the requirements of each member and develop tools which can facilitate the prosperity of destination areas and SMTE.

2 Information and Telecommunication Technologies in Tourism

The ITT radical developments had profound implications for the Tourism and Hospitality Industries (THI), as they altered the best operation practices and yielded opportunities for business expansion in the geographical, marketing and operational sense. THI became flexible and more responsive to consumer requests, while operational costs are constantly reduced. The rapid increase of the reliability, capabilities and capacity of telematics, combined with the decrease of their cost has encouraged THI to adopt these new tools heavily. "A whole system of ITT is being rapidly diffused throughout the tourism industry and no player will escape its impacts" [19,29,20].

The globalisation of the THI is another driving force of the ITT penetration. The expansion of THI enterprises geographically, combined with strategic mergers, generates an enormous demand for accurate and timely information being available on line, in every part of the globe. Consequently, the operation of the global THI could never be handled without the support of modern ITT.

Moreover, the proliferation of computers in society and the fierce competition in the industry, forces enterprises to increase efficiencies by using new ITT [12]. As Poon [19] suggests "Tourism is a very information intensive activity. In few other areas of activity are the generation, gathering, processing, application and communications of information as important for day to day operations as they are for the travel and tourism industry".

The development of CRS is probably the most powerful of all ITT applications on THI, as it has transformed the best business practices worldwide. CRS facilitate the distribution of THI products and enable transportation/hospitality/entertainment enterprises to manage their inventory efficiently and profitably. Several types of CRS serve different types of THI enterprises. *Airlines* are pioneers in CRS development and have advanced their operations vastly since the 1970's. The growth of schedules and tariffs emerged from the air transportation deregulation in the USA, made airlines' planning and operation unbearable without CRS [24,27]. Additionally, *hotels* installed Hotel Information Systems and CRS in order to improve the management of their inventory, aiming to maximise both occupancy and average room rates [9,10,16]. Other members of the THI like *Rent a Car Firms, Ferry and Railways* Companies also developed CRS, while *Tour Operators* introduced systems where tourism packages are being held and distributed to the Travel retailers through VIDEOTEX networks [3,15]. Finally, the integration of most of the above mentioned CRS, on distribution platforms, based on Airline CRS, has generated *Global Distribution Systems* (GDS), which offer access to major THI firms worldwide. In this sense GDS are often regarded as "travel distribution supermarkets" [22,24,27]. The complexity of the CRS industry and the endless interconnections are demonstrated in Figure 1.

On the tourism demand side, a new/experienced/sophisticated/demanding traveller is seeking new and authentic destinations and experiences. Thus, travellers pursue a wide variety of distinctive information on areas' accessibility, facilities, attractions, and leisure activities at destinations. Timely, accurate and relevant information to the consumers' needs is often the key to successful satisfaction of tourism demand [28]. Therefore, the rapid penetration of ITT in the THI is driven by both the size and the complication of the tourism demand, as well as the expansion and sophistication of THI supply.

3 Small and Medium Tourism Enterprises and the implications of Information Technology

SMTE dominate the THI throughout the world, offering a very important contribution to local development, not only by providing tourists with direct contact with the character of the destination but also by facilitating rapid infusion of tourism spending into the local economy [7]. In Europe in particular, almost the entire THI is based on SMTE as 90% of hotels are small and family managed [12,6].

However, ITT and CRS pose a threat for the future of the SMTE. Hitherto, CRS and GDS are primarily serving the business traveller and thus incorporate scheduled airlines, chain hotels and multinational rent a car firms, often due to the availability of sophisticated technology and standardised procedures within these enterprises [18,21,2]. Go and Welch [12] fear that SMTE can be "left out in the cold by the rapid advantages in modern hotel technology, especially in the area of reservation systems". Recent research on the Aegean Islands demonstrated clearly that SMTE are unable to follow the ITT developments and capitalise on potentials, due to lack of expertise, understanding of the market and capital.

Fig. 1: CRS Interconnectivity and complexity

NOTE: Only a few names of CRS are provided to demonstrate the interrelations. Source: Buhalis, 1994

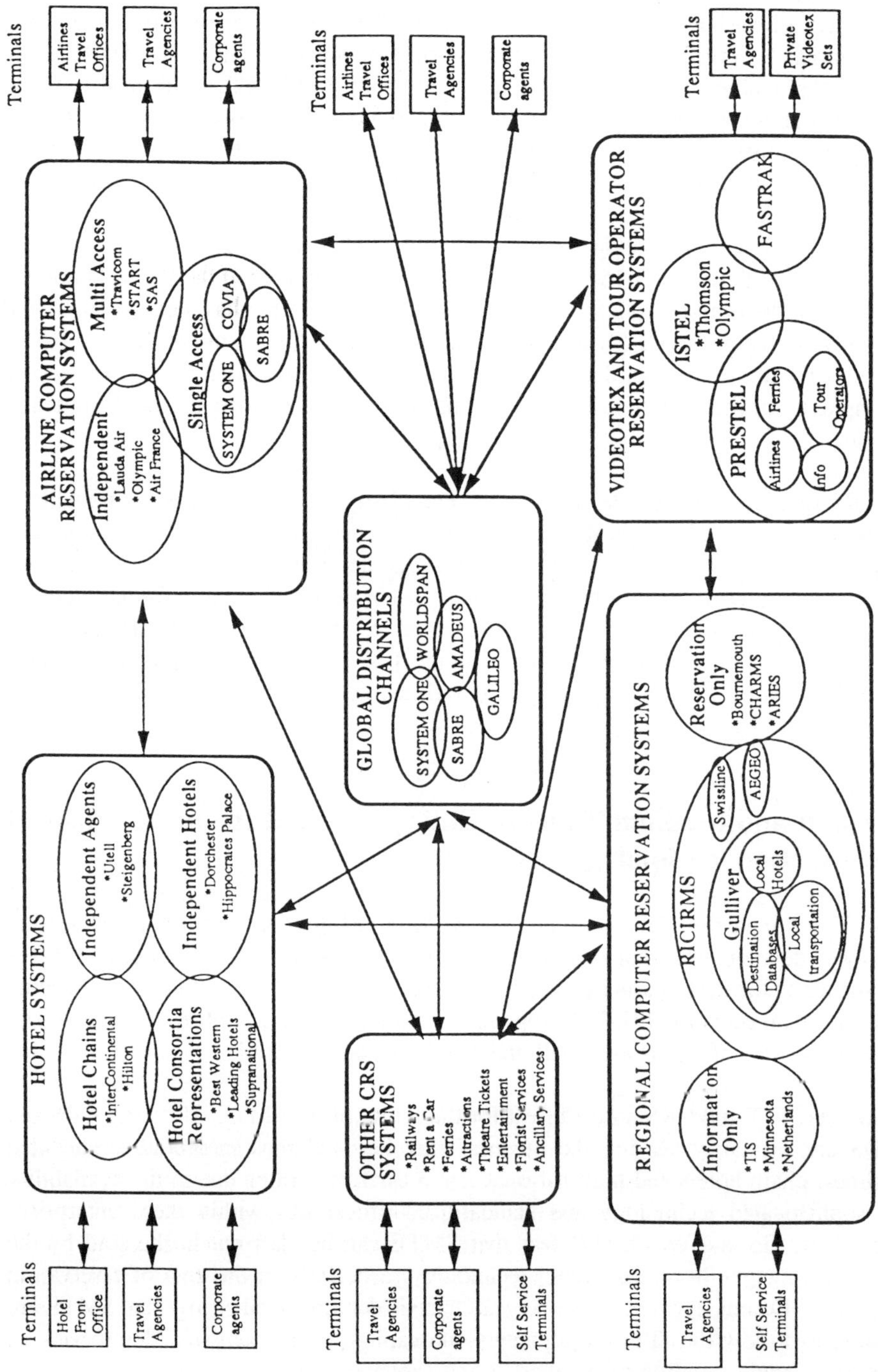

Thus, SMTE face a competitive disadvantage as Economist Intelligence Unit [8] warns that "while the independent property paradoxically may continue to offer the levels of personal services, they may at the same time find it much more difficult to remain in contact with their markets. If it becomes increasingly normal to use computerised systems to reserve and even pay for hotel space, there is the possibility that the small properties will be left out in the cold". Urgent action is, therefore, required in order to develop strategic tools which will reinforce the competitiveness of the SMTE and thus enable them to operate within the new market realities.

4 From Computer Reservation Systems (CRS) through Destination Management Systems (DMS) to Regional Integrated Computer Information Reservation Systems (RICIRMS)

Several destinations launched a process of developing destination focused information and reservation systems, in order to promote the local tourism enterprises and attractions. The ultimate aim is to attract more tourists, of higher spending power, for longer periods of time. In addition, destination systems can inform visitors about customs and environmental issues of the destination and therefore, offer "guidelines" which can minimise the social and environmental impacts of tourists on the destination.

Destination Management Systems (DMS) essentially promote leisure and sensibly priced products, with heterogeneous and customised attributes, primarily served by independent SMTE [6,2,18,21]. Although these systems are characterised by various names, such as Destination Information Systems [21]; Destination Management Systems [25,23,15]; Destination Databases [2,18,30] essentially describe a variation of the same idea, of a destination focused system. Vlitos-Rowe [25] quotes Haines [13,14] definition about similar systems: "A new breed of information technology that attempts to combine information and reservation by using artificial intelligence to link the two and, at the same time, derive a powerful marketing database with detailed customer preferences. These systems combine destinations' information and produce databases with enquiries or client databases and offer a combined information retrieval and reservation capability". A variety of DMS case studies are described in various documents [1,5,25,21,23,30].

DMS can be enhanced to the concept of RICIRMS, should a more strategic view be adapted, where the system is used for the entire range of information, promotion and reservations and management of a multi-integrated tourism industry [5,6]. At a *regional* level the system should incorporate the entirety of tourism services providers. Furthermore, *multi-integration* should be utilised, by coordinating SMTE and local firms of all economic sectors in order to maximise economic impacts of tourism on the area. In addition, integration of all available technologies would enable efficient and inexpensive operation of the system. Obviously, major benefits can only be achieved by a fully *Computerised* network, with the participation of all local enterprises at the destination. Reduction in ITT cost makes computerisation affordable, even to tiny organisations. RICIRMS should contain *information* for every potential enquiry about a destination, while it should facilitate *Reservations* and purchasing for the entire range of tourism products available. Finally, the system can also be used to provide a *Management* function for both the SMTE and the destination.

5 RICIRMS from the Tourism Distribution Channels Members point of view

The Tourism Distribution Channel (TDC) essentially links the consumer of the tourism products with the tourism services providers. In most cases it contains an Outgoing Travel Agent (OTA), a Tour Operator (TO), an Incoming Travel Agent (ITA) and several Principals, like accommodation establishments (ACC) or transportation [26,17].

In a recent survey the concept of the RICIRMS was examined by members of the TDC. In total 471 interviews/questionnaires were completed, with 304 ACC and 68 ITA at the destination area of the Aegean Islands in Greece, 54 European TO and 45 British OTA. As the project is still in the analysis phase, only aggregate results are presented in this paper. Since different members of the channel have distinct roles and interests, they tend to respond differently to the concept of the RICIRMS. A wide range of issues were examined from the point of view of each particular TDCM.

5.1 Need to develop a RICIRMS

Firstly, TDCM were asked whether a RICIRMS should be developed for the Aegean Islands. Table 1 presents that although the vast majority of the ACC supports the idea, the other members of the TDC are more reluctant. ITA have a fairly positive attitude, followed by OTA, while TO are obviously more negative on the concepts. Moreover, a differentiation between larger, mass TO in comparison with small, specialist TO is quite apparent. The first category could identify little need to develop RICIRMS, while the latter was more interested and could distinguish several benefits. A similar distinction can be made between OTA which belong to a multiple, promote almost exclusively tourism packages, and are associated with a large TO, in comparison with independent OTA, which normally serve the independent travellers.

Table 1. Should RICIRMS be developed for the Aegean Islands ?

	Hotels	ITA	TO	OTA
Yes	90.7%	75.4%	56.6%	66.7%
No	2.3%	13.0%	32.1%	20.0%
Do not know Do not answer	7.0%	11.5%	11.3%	13.3%

5.2 Major benefits perceived by the Tourism Distribution Channel Members

A wide range of benefits can be forecasted by the TDCM as demonstrated in Table 2. While *ACC* can primarily perceive a RICIRMS as a promotional tool, they can also see benefits like coordination at the destination level, distraction of isolation as well as improvement of tourism quality and reduction of dependency on TO. *ITA* also support most of these points, although they are more reserved in the perceived benefits. There is also a differentiation between ITA, which act as handling agencies for TO and independent ITA, who offer a wide range of services to independent travellers, with the latter being more enthusiastic.

On the other hand *TO* are the most reluctant TDCM to accept the usefulness of these systems. Larger TO have already an established network of information and reservations and can, therefore, see little benefits coming through the system. However, they value a RICIRMS for training of holiday consultants, who have not been to particular destinations. Smaller TO can see some more benefits, especially when they need to introduce a new destination or when they wish to organise a taylor-made package. They believe that a RICIRMS could save a lot of time and money in terms of ground research at a new destination. Finally, *ITA* are considerably more positive as they value the assistance a RICIRMS would offer in answering consumer enquiries and also having the opportunity to demonstrate images of the destination on a multimedia environment. They strongly believe that RICIRMS will be a selling tool for the future.

Table 2. RICIRMS major benefits perceived by the tourism industry

	HOTELS		ITA		TO		OTA	
	mean	s	mean	s	mean	s	mean	s
Provide Information for Tourists	4.48	0.89	4.30	1.05	3.68	1.29	4.34	0.68
Provide information to TO	-	-	-	-	3.59	1.34	-	-
Offer selling tool to consultants	-	-	-	-	-	-	4.17	1.06
Training of travel consultants	-	-	-	-	3.54	1.32	4.17	0.86
Promotion of destination	4.32	0.86	4.03	1.17	3.46	1.17	3.80	0.96
Reduce dependency on TO	3.48	1.49	2.64	1.59	-	-	-	-
Attract better quality of tourist	3.84	1.33	3.19	1.58	-	-	-	-
Coordination of local enterprise	4.03	0.99	3.46	1.41	3.44	1.25	3.69	1.02
Distracts isolation of islands	3.99	1.11	3.79	1.40	3.23	1.21	3.63	1.11
Facilitates reservations	-	-	-	-	3.68	1.42	4.03	1.01

Note: Likert Scale 1-5 (Very Unimportant - Very Important)

As it can be observed, most of the perceived benefits by the TDCM can only understood as contributors to the current distribution mechanisms. Thus, there is failure of the TDCM to perceive strategic benefits arising from RICIRMS in the long term, where the holiday decision and purchasing process will rely on the new realities of the technological environment. Therefore, it can be argued that the current players in the tourism industry suffer from a contemporary "marketing myopia".

5.3 Willingness to be involved

The willingness to be involved in a RICIRMS by the TDCM is presented on Table 3, where it is quite obvious that ACC and OTA have the most positive responses. On the one side ACC are interested to provide information and receive reservations, while they are quite positive that the system could enhance their profitability. On the other side, OTA which feel the trends of the tourism demand and the requirements of the modern tourists, have also a more positive attitude towards the reservations and information functions and they genuinely believe that their profitability can be improved, since they would be able to improve the service and offer more reservations in advance. ITA and TO are less prepared to use the reservations and information functions, while TO in particular can see little possibilities to increase its profitability by using a RICIRMS.

Table 3. Willingness to be involved with a RICIRMS

	HOTELS		ITA		TO		OTA	
	mean	s	mean	s	mean	s	mean	s
Interest in information system	3.54	1.44	3.24	1.55	2.94	1.38	3.40	1.43
Interest in reservation system	3.58	1.30	2.91	1.58	2.47	1.43	3.12	1.42
Possibility to increase profitability	3.99	1.05	3.67	1.33	2.98	1.32	3.50	1.27

Note: Likert Scale 1-5 (Very Unimportant - Very Important)

5.4 Willingness to invest on RICIRMS

Finally, the willingness of each member of the TDC to co-finance the development of a RICIRMS was examined, as presented in Table 4. Enterprises at destinations, ie ACC and ITA, were more willing to pay a proportional amount to their capacity or business generated; in contrast with TO and OTA, which were more reluctant to pay a contribution for the development of a RICIRMS. However, several respondents indicated the willingness to negotiate payment by a percentage of their benefits, ie commissions, should a RICIRMS provide additional business.

Table 4. Willingness to co-finance the RICIRMS Development

	Hotels	ITA	TO	OTA
Yes	13.0%	6.0%	5.9%	0.0%
Yes, under conditions	47.3%	46.3%	13.7%	15.9%
No	30.3%	41.8%	68.6%	47.7%
Do not know Do not answer	9.3%	6.0%	11.8%	36.4%

6 Conclusion

Despite their dominance in the international THI, SMTE are becoming very vulnerable in the contemporary, demanding business environment. Radical developments in ITT and CRS fields essentially mean that, unless SMTE find new co-operative approaches to regain and strengthen their competitiveness, they will be marginalised. Therefore, the concept of the RICIRMS seems to provide a platform of strategic tools which would enable SMTE to survive in the new challenging environment, while it allows destinations to integrate in order to maximise their economic benefits of tourism.

This paper describes the different attitudes of the TDCM towards RICIRMS. Since various members of the channel, namely ACC, ITA, TO, OTA, have distinctive commercial interests and functions, they tend to value the RICIRMS differently. Destination enterprises are, apparently, more positive and willing to participate, while TO and OTA tend to view RICIRMS with greater scepticism. ACC and ITA perceive RICIRMS as part of their promotional tools and therefore are willing to invest, according to their capacity or usage.

However, despite the broad horizon of business functions which can be supported by RICIRMS, the vast majority of the respondents failed to identify strategic applications for these systems. Instead they eliminated their perspective to comprehend RICIRMS as an aid to the existing methods of tourism product distribution. Further research and training should be employed in order to achieve the ultimate target of RICIRMS development which should be the maximisation of the long term SMTE prosperity; the satisfaction of the new/experienced/sophisticated/demanding tourists; and the enhancement of the economic, social and environmental benefits for the destination area and the host society.

References and Literature

1. Archdale, G., Stanton, R., Jones, C., 1992, Destination Databases: Issues and Priorities, Pacific Asia Travel Association, San Francisco.

2. Archdale, G., 1993, Computer Reservation Systems and public tourist offices, Tourism Management, Vol.14(1), pp.3-14.

3. Bennett, M., 1993, Information technology and travel Agency: A customer service perspective, Tourism Management, Vol.14(4),pp.259-266.

4. Buhalis, D., 1990, The new telecommunication technologies in the tourism industry of the Aegean islands, University of the Aegean, Research programme STAR, (in Greek).

5. Buhalis, D., 1993, RICIRMS as a strategic tool for small and medium Tourism Enterprises, Tourism Management, Vol.14(5),pp.366-378.

6. Buhalis, D., 1994, Information and Telecommunications Technologies as a strategic tool for small ad medium tourism enterprises in the contemporary business environment, in Seaton, A., et al (eds), Tourism-The State of the Art: The Strathclyde Symposium, Wiley and Sons, England, p.254-274.

7. Cooper, C., and Buhalis, D., 1992, Strategic management and marketing of small and medium sized tourism enterprises in the Greek Aegean Islands, in Teare, R., Adams, D., and Messenger, S., (eds), Managing projects in Hospitality Organisations, Cassell, London, pp.101-125.

8. Economist Intelligence Unit, 1992, International hotel prices and cost structures, Travel and Tourism Analyst, No 5, pp.66-83

9. Emmer, R., Tauck, C., Wilkinson, S., and Moore, R., 1993, Marketing Hotels: Using Global Distribution Systems, The Cornell Hotel Restaurant Administration Quarterly, Vol.34(6), pp.80-89.

10. Gamble, P., 1990, New developments in computer technology and their application on to the hospitality industry, in Cooper, C., (ed), Progress in Tourism Recreation and Hospitality Management, Belhaven Press, Vol.2,pp.222-231.

11. Go, F., 1992, The role of Computerised Reservation Systems in the hospitality industry, Tourism Management, Vol.13(1), pp.22-26.

12. Go, F., and Welch, P., 1991, Competitive Strategies for the International Hotel Industry, The Economist Intelligence Unit, Special Report No.1180, London.

13. Haines, P., 1991, Qualities needed by destination management systems, Proceedings of the International Conference on computer networking and the public Tourist organisation, Assisi-Perugia, Italy, 18-20 November.

14. Haines, P., 1993, Destination Databases: The Pacific Asia Travel Association Perspective, Paper No.6, PATA Occasional Papers Series, Pacific Asia Travel Association, San Francisco.

15. Hitchins, F., 1991, The influence of technology on UK Travel Agents, EIU Travel and Tourism Analyst, No.3, pp.88-105.

16. McGuffre, J., 1994, CRS development in the hotel sector, Travel and Tourism Analyst, No.2, pp.53-68.

17. Middleton, V., 1988, Marketing in Travel and Tourism, Heinemann, London.

18. Peroni, G., 1991, Problems and prospects for the renewal of public tourism marketing in the computer network era, Proceedings of the International Conference on computer networking and the public Tourist organisation, Assisi-Perugia, Italy, 18-20 November.

19. Poon, A., 1993, Tourism, Technology and Competitive Strategies, CAB International, UK.

20. Schertler, W., Schmid, B., Tjoa, A., Werthner, H., (eds), 1994, Information and Communications Technologies in Tourism, Conference Proceedings ENTER'94, Innsbruck 12-14 January, Spinger-Verlag, Wien.

21. Sheldon, P., 1993, Destination Information Systems, Annals of Tourism Research, Vol.20(4), pp.633-649.

22. Sloane, J., 1990, Latest developments in Aviation CRSs, EIU Travel and Tourism Analyst, No 4, p.5-15.

23. Sussmann, S., 1992, Destination Management Systems: The challenge of the 1990s, in Cooper, C., and Lockwood, A., (eds), Progress in Tourism, Recreation and Hospitality Management, Vol.4, Belhaven Press, London, pp.209-215.

24. Truitt, L., Teye, V., Farris, M., 1991, The role of Computer Reservation Systems: International Implications for the tourism industry, Tourism Management, Vol.12(1), pp.21-36

25. Vlitos-Rowe, I., 1992, Destination databases and management systems, Travel and Tourism Analyst, No 5, pp.84-108.

26. Wanhill, S., 1993, Intermediaries, in Cooper, C., Fletcher, J., Gilbert, D., Wanhill, S., (eds), Tourism Principles and Practice, Pitman, London, pp.189-204.

27. Wheatcroft, S., and Lipman, G., 1990, European Liberalisation and World Air Transport: Towards a translational industry, Economist Intelligence Unit, Special Report, No 2015, London.

28. Williams, P., 1993, Information Technology and Tourism: a dependent factor for future survival, in Ritchie, B., Hawkins, D., Go, F., Flechtling, D., (eds), World Travel and Tourism Review: Indicators Trends and Issues, Volume 3, CAB International, Oxford, pp.200-205.

29. World Tourism Organisation, 1988, Guidelines for the transfer of new technologies in the field of tourism, Madrid:WTO.

30. Yee, J., 1992, Proceedings from PATA Destination Database Conference, Singapore, December 9-10, PATA Intelligence Centre, San Francisco.

Marketing and Information Technology in the Hospitality Industry. A Strategic Approach

P. Desinano, C. Vigo

Centro Italiano di Studi Superiori sul Turismo e sulla Promozione Turistica, Assisi, Italy

Abstract. Marketing continues to be a rapidly changing discipline in regard to the power of scientific perspectives in aiding management performance. Some "hidden marketing" activities are often neglected and rarely intentionally supported by IT. Through value chain analysis a hotel firm can select the right technology and its application to achieve business goals. Management decisions about how to shape the product/service have to be based on market needs. The paper proposes to interface hotel offerings and value activities in identifying IT applications to gain competitive advantage.

1 Introduction

The aim of this paper is to discuss how IT can support and shape marketing issues in the hospitality industry. IT applications to marketing functions are well known and consolidated (e.g. guest history file, direct mailing and so on). Within a business organisation these activities are performed by the marketing function where this function is identifiable as a specific organisational unit on the organisational chart.

Management by process suggests a broader view in considering the marketing issues. It is possible to extend the marketing options to a large variety of business operations even to ones outside the traditional marketing domain. These marketing aspects are disseminated throughout the organisation and constitute a special management phenomenon which could be called "hidden marketing" or "spreading through marketing". This phenomenon particularly characterises service management and is a variable so critical that it becomes "strategic". Actually the large number of issues of "hidden marketing", their diffusion and significance make the real "marketing orientation" of an organisation. This is true especially for hospitality businesses such as hotels, restaurants, convention centres and so on. These aspects of marketing are often neglected and consequently are rarely *intentionally* supported by IT.

This overcoming of the traditional boundaries of marketing as a business function and its broader inclusiveness implies the rethinking of the IT application domain. This new way of thinking about marketing modifies the approach to the use of IT within the hospitality business. The authors intend to contribute towards reflection on this matter by offering some conceptual tools to use in planning IT with the various aspects of "hidden marketing" in mind.

The paper is divided as follows. In Section 2 the choice of the value chain approach for planning IT inside the firm is discussed. An adaptation of Porter's generic value chain to hotel businesses follows in the next section. The fourth point is focused on the link between guests' needs and the hotel offering. Section 5 correlates hotel activities, guests' needs and IT options. Some considerations conclude the paper.

2 Managing IT for competitive advantage

One of the best known methodologies for directing IT applications in business is the value chain model proposed by Michael Porter and Victor Millar in 1985 on the basis of a more comprehensive theory included in [14]. The value chain provides a method for analysing the business of the firm. This method allows the business to be desegregated into various concatenated activities - called "value activities" because they produce the value that the firm offers on the market. The specific strategy chosen by the firm is the guide-criteria for identifying the various value activities and their concatenation. A comparison between the value chain of the firm and the value chains of the competitors allows the identification of possible sources of competitive advantage.

Porter and Millar observe that in every product or service a more or less important information component exists. The same consideration is possible for each relevant strategic business activity. If IT can somehow manage those information components then this technology can assume a strategic relevance for the firm. When IT can support or shape either of these elements, it becomes a strategic weapon [20]. The results of the value chain analysis enable the chief information officer and his or her staff to start thinking about *what* technology to select and *how* use it to achieve business goals.

One point of strength of the value chain analysis is the close relationship that exists between firm system and market environment. Porter does not conceive of the firm as an island in the market "ocean". The firm is placed inside the value system, where it relates on one side with providers and on the other side with buyers. Moreover the firm and its providers and buyers exist inside the competitive arena where they interact with other competitors, providers, and buyers as well as new entrants and substitute products.

Another outstanding point of Porter's value chain concept is the characteristic of global consideration of the firm. The focus of analysis is on the core of the firm's business. All the relevant steps that implement the process of creation of value are identified and organised to obtain a global and clear framework. No activity is neglected even if at first glance it could be considered irrelevant. Every activity is a potential source of competitive advantage, directly or indirectly.

However the value chain model has been strongly criticised in recent years [11]-[13]. One object of criticism concerns the concept of a chain of activities in service business. Normann maintains that one outstanding characteristic in service businesses lies in the strong interaction existent between the client and the firm's personnel. Sometimes the client participates in the service becoming a *prosumer* (*pro*ducer + con*sumer*), according to Toffler's definition [17]. In this situation it is very difficult to delineate clear interfaces among the various value activities within the value chain. In [11] and [12] Normann and Ramirez specify that the core of new business is social innovation through the dynamic configuration of the relationships, the roles and the number of business players. The new post-industrial economy will be increasingly based on *reinventing* value and not on *producing* value. No longer a *value chain* but rather a *value constellation.*

Normann and Ramirez's criticism is well-founded but does not undermine the core of Porter's theory. Their concept is closer to sketching a "new type of business" rather than a "new logic of value". However such criticism is very valuable in reinterpreting the value chain approach applied to service businesses and therefore also to the hospitality industry. Normann and Ramirez's considerations have stimulated possible reconfigurations of the value chain for the hotel industry. The next section of this paper illustrates that proposal.

The value chain approach is very useful for our purposes because it allows the systematic recognition of each activity performed within the firm. This recognition serves to identify the points where possible hidden marketing issues can be applied and, consequently, to evaluate what IT options are applicable to increase the client's perception of value.

3 The value chain configuration in Hotel Businesses

The most important publications on marketing and management of service business and particularly on hotel business suggest the guidelines to attempt a reconfiguration of Porter's generic model. Fig. 1 illustrates this reconfiguration of the value chain adapted to the peculiarities of hotel businesses as discussed in [5].

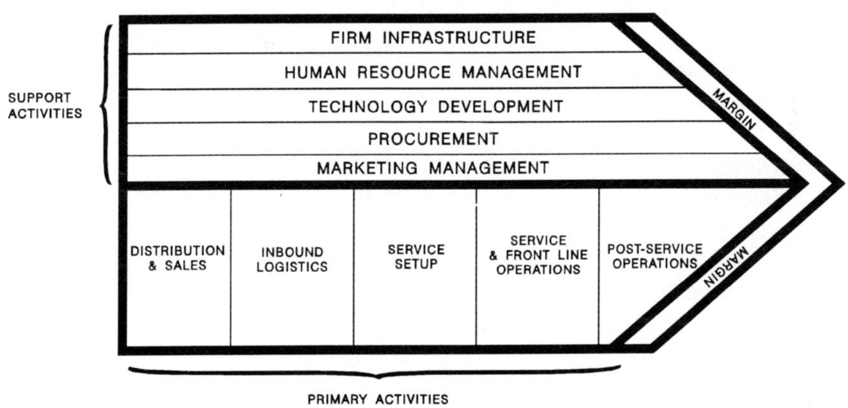

Fig. 1. The Hotel Value Chain [5]

The ideas at the root of a similar reconfiguration are as follows:

- the global consideration of the guest cycle
- the pervasive nature of marketing
- the typical distinction between front office and back office

The first concept provides a good base for identifying and organising the primary activities. The second one suggests transforming marketing management activity from primary activity to support activity. Finally the third idea allows the definition of service set-up activity (which includes every back of the house operation necessary to deliver the service) and service & front line operations activity (which includes every front of the house operation).

However, on identifying the strategic activities connected to this type of business, the value chain instrument permits a hotel business to gain a certain amount of margin in the competitive arena. Considering marketing a strategic activity affecting every other business activity rather than a mere organisational function, can lead us to evaluate and exploit the marketing power of IT applications in hotel operations.

The scope of marketing management has broadened over the last few years. A recent trend seems to be the addition of strategic planning and thinking concepts to the area of marketing strategy. Marketing management is one of the fundamental activities which in strategically supporting the various operations of a hospitality business, is involved not only with identifying needs and trends within the market place but also with the product concept, distribution and pricing strategies, the monitoring of competitors' activities, as well as control of internal and external operations.

The axiom that the firm must meet the needs of the client is true in relation to the value received, in terms of money, of customisation and of the uniqueness of the product/service.

A hotel business, which, like many other businesses in the service sector, must keep this cardinal element in mind, is conditioned in its productive choices in light of a market which demands more and more uniqueness and tailor-made service. It becomes strategic to determine optimisation processes for the various areas of production which come closer and closer to industrial production processes.

Marketing is the trait d'union to connect optimisation of productive cycles with cost control processes, on the one hand, and to find elements of strategic differentiation to satisfy the new needs of the market on the other.

The following process could accomplish these requirements:

1. Shaping hotel offerings according to the guest's needs (i.e. guest's value chain)
2. Identifying the value activities involved in satisfying the guest's needs
3. Choosing the most suitable IT options to support strategic value activities

4 Hotel offerings shaped by the client's value chain

With increasing competition in the service industry, many authors [6]-[8], [13], [16], and [19] advocate incorporating a marketing mentality in all the firm's management activities. The evidence suggests that marketing is the competitive cutting edge in many non-marketing oriented companies [10].

The marketing function should already have a part in all hotel operations [16] from the planning to the support of all activities. This consideration implies that an IT application is classified as a marketing application if it is placed inside the marketing strategy of the business. Effective IT applications to marketing can be represented by specific software to support various marketing issues. Moreover the design of the whole property management system must be oriented to support the marketing efforts that take place in every business activity.

Management decisions on how to shape the product/service have to be based on the market needs. This implies that managers must continually look for opportunities for product differentiation.

The essence of business is to deliver a product which satisfies a need and whose market value exceeds its cost [2]. In the transaction between buyer and seller, it is the product's value that the customer pays for. The product value concept is a business philosophy that recognises product value as the key concept to profits. It stresses competing on the basis of the satisfaction of customer needs with superior, higher value products. Value depends on the guest's perception of the product attributes, which are largely a function of the firm's technological, design, and manufacturing strengths and skills. The organisation whose driving force is market need, determines its products or services from needs in the markets or market segment it serves. Such an organisation will constantly look for new and different products to feel out these market needs.

Service and front office operations are "the moment of truth" for global hotel service because they directly involves the physical person of the guest. Service operations can be divided into those relating to the service personnel and those relating to the physical facilities and equipment. This allows the firm, through the service personnel, facilities and equipment, to deliver value service to the guest. Every deed, every action or performance is a potential source of quality enhancement. Each point of contact could also be a source of differentiation for the varied ways in which the service can be delivered.

The marketing activity indicates choices within the hotel business to configure all procedures aimed at obtaining the best performance in each operation. To determine the check-in procedures the planner must have in mind exactly what the customer wants and he does his best to plan every phase of the procedure so that the personnel or the machine involved can satisfy the guest.

In the planning the guest and his value are the focus of the operation. As in a mathematical formula, the guest is the independent variable and the procedures and the IT machines are the dependent variables for the satisfaction of the guest.

Starting from market preferences, marketing will be presumed the driving force for the choice of those variables (procedures, equipment, personnel behaviour) that lead to the best service to the guest.

For hotels the focus did not swing to business travellers until recently [9]. Independent hotels and hotel chains are now making big efforts to gain the business traveller market. Nowadays hotel managers must focus on other ways to influence booking for business travellers. In the past, hotels touted the traditional offerings: clean, comfortable guest rooms, inviting restaurants and lounges, and ample meeting and convention facilities. Now, to attract the business traveller, hotels try to make the guest's stay as comfortable as possible. One way to perform this is by offering "insider" services unavailable to (and usually hidden from) other guests.
For example, some chains provide special reservation number, preferential handling, room availability even on sold out dates, "spouse stays free" policies, late check-out, free local calls, personal check cashing, and automatic upgrades to the next level of accommodation when available, reservation for other hotels within the chain or the group. Electronic registration/checkout, business centres, health and recreational facilities have been provided by the major hotel chains to get competitive advantages. A few years ago, Marriott installed a in-room video checkout system in all of the chain's domestic hotels. At Hilton Hotels, guests are invited to use business centre equipped with a variety of office services, including computer work stations and personal computers are also available for in-room use. Westin Hotels provide free health club facilities that feature tennis courts, swimming pools and workout rooms.
An ongoing evaluation of guest satisfaction is extremely important to marketing and management decision makers. A survey can help decision makers determine which of the product or service qualities and values are most important to the hotel guest.
Examining the major aspects of a hotel operation oriented towards arousing the interest of business travellers, we can strategically select those promising high potential satisfaction [3]-[4] and [18] to design the guest value profile (independent variable). A well designed matrix can help us to understand which services are more valuable and what is the perceived value and ratings of satisfaction for a business traveller.
Value activities or procedures such as front office operations, check-in and check-out procedures (see the matrix) could hold the key to gaining competitive advantage. In such a light these hotel operations are the results of the assembling-delivering mix in choosing and designing physical equipment, organisational procedures and labour activities, interfacing of necessity with hotel guests to obtain the best performance.
Value activities or procedures such as front office operations, check-in and check-out procedures (see the matrix) could hold the key to gaining competitive advantage. In such a light these hotel operations are the results of the assembling-delivering mix in choosing and designing physical equipment, organisational procedures and labour activities, interfacing of necessity with hotel guests to obtain the best performance.
Value activities or procedures such as front office operations, check-in and check-out procedures (see the matrix) could hold the key to gaining competitive advantage. In such a light these hotel operations are the results of the assembling-delivering mix in choosing and designing physical equipment, organisational procedures and labour activities, interfacing of necessity with hotel guests to obtain the best performance.
The "give the guest what the guest wants" marketing philosophy becomes the starting point to develop the right operation and consequently put into effect the right choice.

If we select high satisfaction activities and interface the marketing management support activity with service and front office operations in the hotel value chain, we identify which services have to be delivered for high quality standards and where the firm must focus its efforts to gain or maintain the competitive edge.
Value activities or procedures such as front office operations, check-in and check-out procedures (see the matrix) could hold the key to gaining competitive advantage. In such a light these hotel operations are the results of the assembling-delivering mix in choosing and designing physical equipment, organisational procedures and labour activities, interfacing of necessity with hotel guests to obtain the best performance.

	Low	Medium	High
Easy booking			✓
A correctly handled reservation			✓
Convenient location			✓
Fast check-in procedures			✓
Smiling, courteous employees			✓
Sufficient supply of towels	✓		
Sufficient lightning in the room	✓		
Air ticketing and hotel reservation			✓
Efficient wake-up service		✓	
Excellent restaurant/bar			✓
Sufficient supply of hot water	✓		
Laundry and ironing services			✓
Fast check-out procedures			✓
Parking and shuttle bus services			✓
Secretary services			✓
Telephone, fax services	✓		
PC and printing equipment in the room			✓
TV set	✓		
Video rentals	✓		
Swimming pool, sauna and health club	✓		
Entertainment	✓		
Meeting room		✓	
Room service		✓	
Courtesy toiletries		✓	
Comfortable bed	✓		
Clean bedroom	✓		
Adequate lighting in the room	✓		
Credit card payment accepted		✓	
Automatic cash tellers			✓
Currency exchange and check cashing			✓

Table n. 1. Guest satisfaction matrix

Value activities or procedures such as front office operations, check-in and check-out procedures (see the matrix) could hold the key to gaining competitive advantage. In such a light these hotel operations are the results of the assembling-delivering mix in

choosing and designing physical equipment, organisational procedures and labour activities, interfacing of necessity with hotel guests to obtain the best performance.
The "give the guest what the guest wants" marketing philosophy becomes the starting point to develop the right operation and consequently put into effect the right choice. If we select high satisfaction activities and interface the marketing management support activity with service and front office operations in the hotel value chain, we identify which services have to be delivered for high quality standards and where the firm must focus its efforts to gain or maintain the competitive edge.
This focus will help the firm to follow the right procedures and undertake a correct organisational planning. Identifying such elements is a strategic tool for the firm for now it can concentrate its efforts on high potential activities in the hotel operation value chain.
The subdivision of service and front line operations determines groups of activities in the strategy of differentiation important for the choice of marketing management and technology development strategies.

5 "Hidden marketing" and IT

On the basis of the hotel value chain above proposed, the focus of the problem becomes identifying the right IT options for the above mentioned marketing management activity. To better develop this point one consideration is appropriate.
The transversal nature of marketing management activity along the hotel value chain suggests that marketing orientation is not one characteristic of a specific group of IT applications distinct from other IT applications (i.e. guest history file management rather than payroll file management). On the contrary, marketing insights are *diffused* among almost all PMS (Property Management System) applications. Under this perspective marketing becomes an inspirational principle inside the design process of IT application. Marketing orientation must become a skill of IT system analysts and designers and not only of the personnel and management of a hotel.
On the basis of this consideration it is very useful to have a method, or criteria for evaluating the impact of IT from a marketing management perspective. Indeed a similar method would provide management, IT analysts and designers with a tool for evaluating the "marketing orientation" of a specific IT application. The core of the proposal is the correlation of hotel offerings, value activities and IT options.
One good starting point to achieve that goal is Abell's proposal [1] about strategic definition of business. Abell states that to define a business strategy it is not enough to correlate products and markets. Instead it is necessary to correlate more comprehensively three dimensions: function, technology and target group. Reinterpreting Abell's scheme in order to accomplish the aim of this paper (which is quite different from Abell's one) we propose to add the dimension of IT options to the bi-dimensional matrix of the previous section. The following figure illustrates the new scheme.

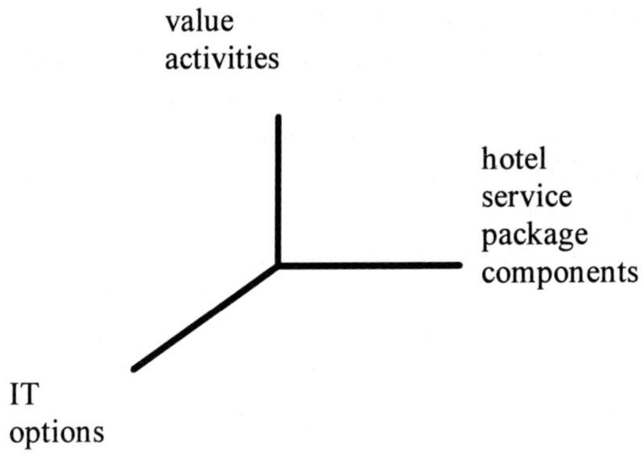

Fig. 2. The three dimensional matrix to evaluate IT impact

This grid makes it possible to evaluate the degree of difference between two or more hotel value chains regarding the IT options used to implement their respective offerings. These comparisons inform the firm management about *how* IT can contribute to decreasing cost or creating service differentiation.

Fig. 3 shows a typical service operation. “Currency exchange” is a service of hotels competing in a specific market segment. One hotel may choose to offer this service by involving the guest’s participation (self-service). Another hotel may offer this service throughout the figure of the concierge. These two different ways to satisfy a client’s need involve two different IT applications. The former requires the installation of ATM (Automated Teller Machines) inside hotel the latter requires the installation of a sort of data link between hotel and a rate exchange information provider.

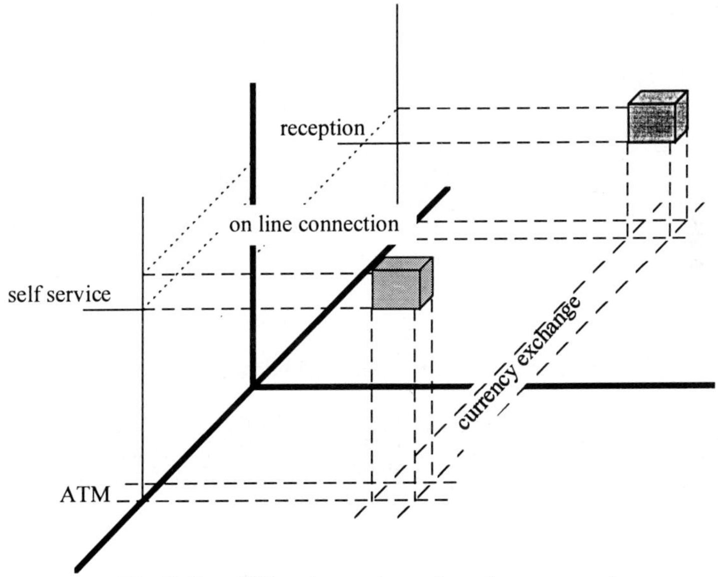

Fig. 3. Two different ways to perform the same service

This method allows hotel managers:

- *to IT application choices to be guided directly by the market segment*, because each IT option is directly linked to a specific hotel service.
- *to avoid buying useless IT products or services*, because each IT option is directly linked to a specific hotel value activity.
- *to evaluate the consistency of the global hotel offering*, in fact a wrong IT application choice can definitively alter the client's perception of the global service delivered.
- *to compare their IT application choices with the competitors' and, consequently, determine eventual sources of competitive advantage*; in fact we can position the IT options of various rivals firms in a single grid.

6 Conclusions

Marketing management in hotels is a very complex activity because other activities besides the traditional marketing activities may have marketing valence. IT can shape or support these activities but its applications must be carefully projected and Porter's value chain is a valuable tool to guide such projects. Our proposal suggests to represent hotel offerings, value activities and IT options in a three-dimension grid. On the basis of the configuration of this grid the firm management can decide *which* IT applications to set up to support marketing management to gain competitive advantage.

References

[1] Abell D.F.: *Defining the Business* (Prentice Hall: New York; 1980).

[2] Bennett R.C. and G. Cooper: The Misuse of Marketing: An American Tragedy (in P. Kotler and K.K. Cox (Eds.): *Marketing Management and Strategy*, pp. 36-48. Prentice-Hall: Englewood Cliffs; 1988).

[3] Bonini A.: *5 Case Histories nell'Industria dell'Ospitalità* (Franco Angeli: Milano; 1988).

[4] Bonini A.: *Hotel & Restaurant Marketing* (Pubblistampa: Milano; 1990).

[5] Desinano P. and C. Vigo: Developing Information Technology Options in the Hotel Industry. The Value Chain Approach (in A.V. Seaton (ed.): *Tourism: The State of the Art*. Wiley: Chichester, 1994)

[6] Eiglier P. and E. Langeard: *Servuction - Le marketing des Services* (McGraw-Hill: Paris; 1987).

[7] Kotler P.: *Marketing Management, 7th edition* (Prentice Hall International: Englewood Cliffs, NJ; 1992).

[8] Lovelock C.H.: Basic Toolkit for Service Managers (in Lovelock C.H. (Ed.): *Managing Services*, 2nd *edition*, pp. 17-30. Prentice-Hall: Englewood Cliffs; 1992).

[9] Martindale D.: The Changing Relationship (in P. Kotler and K.K. Cox (Eds.), *Marketing Management and Strategy*, pp. 287-293. Prentice-Hall: Englewood Cliffs, NJ; 1988).

[10] Michaels E.G.: *Marketing Muscle* (in P. Kotler and K.K. Cox (Eds.), *Marketing Management and Strategy*, pp. 21-35. Prentice-Hall: Englewood Cliffs, NJ; 1988).

[11] Normann R. and R. Ramirez: From Value Chain to Value Constellation: Designing Interactive Strategy (*Harvard Business Review*, vol. 71, n. 4, pp. 65-77; 1993).

[12] Normann R. and R. Ramirez: The value constellation is not about one kind of value (*Harvard Business Review*, vol. 71, n. 5, pp. 50-51; 1993).

[13] Normann R.: *Strategic Management Services, 2nd edition* (Wiley: Chichester; 1991).

[14] Porter M.E.: *Competitive Advantage* (The Free Press: New York; 1985).

[15] Porter M.E. and V. Millar: How Information Gives You Competitive Advantage, (*Harvard Business Review*, vol. 53, n. 4, pp. 149-160; 1985).

[16] Reid R. D.: *Hospitality Marketing Management* (Van Nostrand Reinhold: New York; 1989).

[17] Toffler A.: *The Third Wave* (Bantam Books: New York; 1979).

[18] Venison P.: *Managing Hotels* (Heinemann: London; 1983).

[19] Wind J., P.E. Green, D. Shifflet and M. Scarbrough: Courtyard by Marriott: Designing a Hotel Facility with Consumer-Based Marketing Models (in C.H. Lovelock C.H. (Ed.): *Managing Services, 2nd edition*, pp. 118-137, Prentice-Hall: Englewood Cliffs, NJ; 1992).

[20] Wiseman C.: *Strategic Information Systems* (IRWIN: Homewood, IL; 1988).

Simulation of the logistic and information infrastructure, applied in the value chain of tourist enterprises

Dick de Reus (*), Chris Meijs (**)
Department of Computer Science
(*) Eindhoven Universtity of Technology, currently working at a consultancy agency
(**) Wageningen Agricultural University, The Netherlands
e-mail: meijs@rcl.wau.nl

1 Introduction

There is a growing interest for arrangement issues regarding value chains, because optimization of the business processes results in increased efficiency and new opportunities for the involved businesses [Meijs94]. The tourist value chain is an area of enormous potential for integrating various systems but cooperating businesses require external integration. This shift spur on to look for improvements of the logistic and informational infrastructures. This paper will focus on the essential components that are needed for the construction of the computer-aided models, to simulate logistic an information systems. Therefore an in-depth analysis is conducted attempting to reveal answers on the following questions:

- What are the characteristics of logistic and information systems in the value chain of the tourist industry ?
- What are the essential components for simulating logistic and informational infrastructures in a cooperative way ?
- How can we optimize the logistic flows and services with the help of computer-aided models ?

To meet the changing demands of consumers of the tourist industry, enterprises need to offer a wide variety of products and services, in less time than previously and at competitive prices. The performance of enterprises and business units within the value chain of the tourist industry can be improved by using advanced information technology [Kosynski90]. It will be argued that for optimization of the logistic flow and information exchange, models, simulation and information systems are essential.

A case study at an airport will be included, that shows part of the constructed model, simulation results of 3 alternative logistic infrastructures and finally the conclusions of that study.

2 Aspects of the tourist value chain

We adapt the framework of figure 1 to indicate the aspects that will be considered in this study. This meta-model is suitable to deal with complex situations in the value chain. [Kokol93]

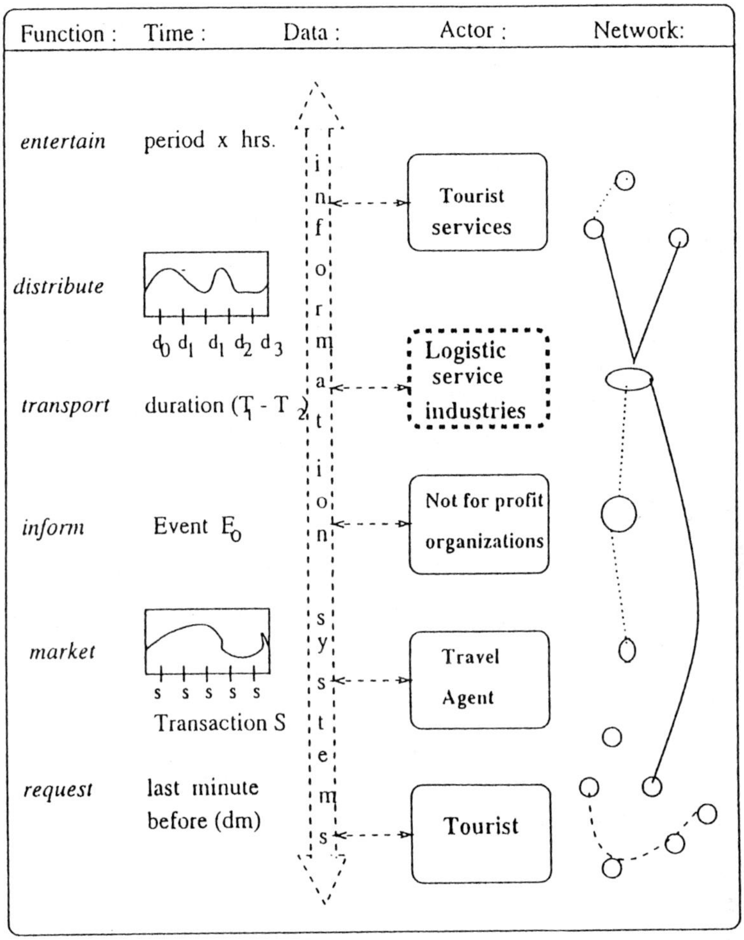

Figure 1: Aspects of the tourist value chain

A scenario for a project focussing an the logistical and informational issues of the tourist value chain might include:

- The function aspect that deals with the question how the core processes, transactions and coordination should be conducted.
- Temporal aspects are covered by looking at the triggering events, short time and long-term planning and the product-life-cycles.
- The identified actors in the tourist value chain. It should represent agreed alliances and how work is allocated at the organizational level. At a more detailed level the co-operation between software agents might be depicted.
- The data view shows what information about the tourist market, quality standards, regulations, goods and services are important.
- The network view focuses on distinct locations and units, their available capacities and the logistics.

Framework 1 might be extended by a third dimension showing the perspectives of involved stakeholders: people that have responsibility for (part) of the value chain, business owners and software engineers. The level of detail, scope and representing techniques might differ substantial, depending on their particular objective and task.

3 Modelling of integral logistic and information structures

The value chain in tourism represents how business functions of minimal 2 enterprises are linked to each other for the supply of information, goods, services, in order to satisfy the needs of the tourist. In order to optimize the logistic and information infrastructures of the value chain we think it is necessary to focus on several aspects. The major use of the resulting chain models are:

- analyse purpose and opportunities of the chain in order to tackle optimization issues.
- design of interorganizational information and logistic systems.

Some basic requirements on chain modelling are:

1. an integrated, structured design methodology
2. the ability to deal with complexity
3. the incorporation of relevant static, dynamic and organizational aspects

4. properties to highlight the perspectives of participating interest groups
5. reusability of specifications, e.g. for enterprises in the same line-of-business
6. the simulation of models
7. maintenance that enables fast adjustment

Therefore we apply modelling techniques in a metamodelling approach, where the resulting components of these techniques are adjusted, balanced and checked.

3.1 Optimization with computer aided models

Optimization seeks to redesign the infrastructure and related work processes in order to enhance the productivity and competitiveness [Meijs94]. Computer aided modelling supports the process of optimization in several ways:

making the model helps you to better understand the complexity of the structures

trial redesign of the structure can be 'implemented' without affecting the real life world, but with pinpointing potential problems of the redesigned structure, and of the process of implementing in the real world.

3.2 Modelling environment

At Eindhoven University a specification language, called ExSpect, has been developed. This specification language has been developed to describe complex discrete dynamic systems [Hee89]. systems. The ExSpect modelling tool is based on the fact that systems in general can be decomposed into subsystems. As a basis for the model of processes, we use a simple mathematical model called Petri nets. In essence, a Petri net consists of *actions* ('transitions') and *states* ('places'). Transitions and places are connected to each other by means of arrows. If an arrow points from a place to a transition, the place is called an input place for the transition. If an arrow points from a transition to a place, the place is called an output place for the transition. An action is *enabled* if all of its input channels contain *tokens*. If it is enabled, a transition may *fire*. This means that it takes tokens from all of its input channels and produces tokens for all of its output channels. In figure 2 and 3 shows worked out examples of Petri nets with client request, desk personnnel, reservations the tourist agents.

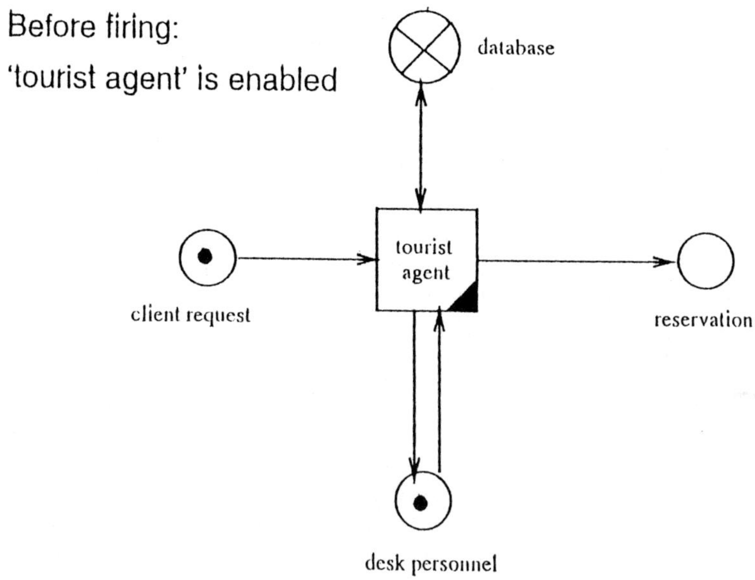

Figure 2: Example of ExSpect model. Before 'firing'.

Figure 3 represents the state after 'firing'. [Hee94] deals with the formal approach that underlies the modelling approach.

3.3 Reusable specifications

In paragraph 2 we stated that in order to optimize the logistic and information infrastructure, we may focus on the several aspects as given by our meta-model: data, function, network and time. We propose the development of domain specific libraries of reusable specifications. Using these reusable components instead of ad hoc descriptions depicted from scratch, results in a high-level specification with reduced complexity and size.

For large organisations, modelling in standard Petri nets becomes rather complicated. Therefore, we added some extra concepts to the standard model.

First of all, hierarchy is added. This means that you can select a part of your model, drag a box around it, and *fold* it into a system. From that moment on, you can use and re-use this system in your specification as often as you wish, without further worrying about its inside. Now it is possible to model both bottom-up and top-down. Furthermore, we enable usage of libraries. These can hold building blocks, so that the knowledge and experience in these blocks can be used in other system specifications.

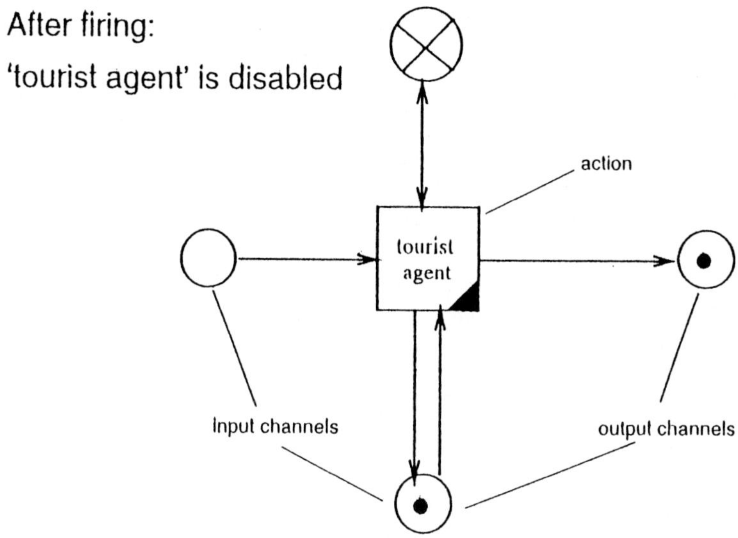

Figure 3: Example of ExSpect model. After 'firing'.

Second, we add values to the tokens. In this way, tokens get distinguishable. This means that we can base the actions on the value of tokens. Thus, tokens stand model for goods in a logistic model, or jobs in a workflow model.

Third, we add timing to the model. This is done by giving a certain delay to a token that is produced by a transition. During this delay, the token cannot enable any transition. This enables us to model timing aspects.

In the next section we first apply our approach to the flow of passenger at an airport.

4 The airport case

In the airport case, the airport direction was confronted with several facts:

- an extra departure hall for the passengers was needed
- new regulations were coming up stating that passengers travelling within the European Community would not have to cross any border.

Until then, the fraction of national passengers had been so small that the airport could afford to build a rigid border in their entrance and departure halls. With the internal design of the new hall not ready yet, and the new regulations coming up, this meant that a unique possibility occurred to implement a flexible border in the new hall.

Consider the departure hall of an international airport. Passengers arrive at the entrance of the hall with their luggage, in order to travel by airplane to certain destinations. Before the airplane takes off with the passengers and their luggage, several things have to be done by both the passenger and the airport. In general, luggage is stored in another place in the airplane than the passenger compartment. Because luggage handling companies are best at storing and administering luggage, they are glad to take over this task from the passenger. This means that at some place the passenger has to deliver his luggage to the company. Usually, this is combined with checking-in at the check in desk.

If a passenger will fly out of the country, border formalities have to be fulfilled. Also, a security check has to take place. In between al these processes, the passenger has to move from one location to another—e.g, from check-in desk to customs—or he has to wait because the airplane is not ready yet to receive passengers. Before he starts the procedure of checking in etc., he may want to say goodbye to accompanying persons.

The airport under consideration was building a complete new departure hall, and thus had the oppertunity to redesign its passenger and luggage logistics and processes. Besides, new regulations caused the fact that the number of non-border crossing passengers would increase significantly. Until then, this number was small enough in relation to the total number of passengers that they could permit themselves not to create special facilities for them. Because of the new regulations, they had to design the new hall such that non-border crossing passengers would not be bothered by a border, and that none of the processes was performed needlessly. The problem arisen essentially was the question of where to put the border.

Three possible answers were studied in more detail:

> The border can be put somewhere in the hall. This would mean that part of the hall was 'national', and part was 'international'.
>
> A border can be put at the entrance of certain piers. This would mean that some piers were international, and that most of the hall was international.
>
> A border can be put at the entrance of certain gates. This would mean that gates were international or national.

In the latter two cases, the border would have to be flexible at least partly.

4.1 Modelling and redesign

In order to gain insight into the effect of each of these possibilities, a simulation model was made. First the current situation was modelled, and verified with the real case. Next, the three alternatives were built into the simulation model, and they were run with estimated passenger numbers.

In the model, all the processes involved in passenger logistics were modelled as systems. Each system could be build up out of basic building blocks. It appeared that only a few parametrized building blocks were needed.
Furthermore, each passenger was modelled as a token. Thus, it was easy to measure the work load for each process, at each moment. Each passenger token carried with it all statistics of its personal throughput, i.e., delays.
Besides, each process maintained its work load at each moment.

Once the building blocks were made, it was possible to build the existing situation, and to experiment with possibly improved situations, simply by glueing the building blocks together in different ways.

The simulations showed that, technically spoken, the second solution was the best one: although there were transfer passenger that had to cross two borders, this fact could be minimized by putting connecting flights at the same pier.

5 Conclusions and further research

In this paper we presented a framework to identify the distinctive aspects of a complex environment. The presented methodology offers a clear approach to to analysis and design of logistic and informational infrastructures. Application of this approach, especially in the chain may lead to:
- reduction of complexity
- integration of static, dynamic and organizational aspects
- design of models for analyzing and also for (re)designing purposes.

References

[Hee89] K.M. van Hee, L.J. Somers, M. Voorhoeve.
Executable specifications for distributed information systems. In: Proceedings of the IFIP TC8/WG8.1 Working Conference on Information System Concepts: An In-depth Analysis; E.D Falkenberg and P. Lindgreen, eds., Namur, Belgium, 1989. Elsevier Science Publishers, Amsterdam, pp. 139-156

[Hee94] K.M. van Hee.
Information System Engineering: a Formal Approach, Cambridge University Press, 1994.

[Hopper90] M. Hopper.
Rattling SABRE new ways to compete on information. In: Harvard BR may-june 1990, p. 118-125.

[Kokol93] P. Kokol.
Metamodelling: How, why and what ? In: ACM Sigsoft, software engineering notes. vol. 18 no. 2 april 1993, pag. 25-26.

[Kosynski90] B. Kosysnki and F . Warren McFarlan
Information partnerships- shared data, shared scale. In: Harvard BR september-October 1990, p.114-120.

[Meijs94] C. Meijs , J. Trienekens
Optimization of the value chain using computer aided reference models (submitted for Proceedings IFIP WG7.6 Working Conference on Optimization-based computer-aided Modelling and Design, Prague may 1994)

[Uijttenbroek92] A. Uijttenbroek, P. Anthonisse, C. Meijs, B. Verdoes; Project management principles; Cap Gemini Publishing. Rijswijk, 1992.

Airline Hotel Reservation System Improvement: The Contribution of Value Chain Analysis

G. E. Haramis, Ph.D., G. J. Siomkos, Ph. D.

Department of Business Administration, University of Macedonia
156 Egnatia Ave., P.O. Box 1591, GR-54006 Thessaloniki, Greece

Abstract. The paper addresses the issue of improving the design of a hotel reservations system currently used by airlines. The improvement is based on the incorporation of the Value Chain developed by Porter. In particular, the paper incorporates Value Chain Analysis into the SAHARA System.

1 Short Description of the SAHARA System

SAHARA stands for SITA Airline Hotel Advanced Reservations Automation, and SITA for Societe Internationale de Telecommunications Aeronautiques.

SAHARA is an information system that gives an agent access to a world-wide data base of hotels. This data base provides hotel availability, rates and facilities and allows an agent to make bookings at these hotels all via the same reservation terminal that the agent uses to make airline seat reservations.

SAHARA has been developed with the active co-operation of both airlines and hotel groups.

Airlines access to SAHARA is by means of a "host to host" link which connects an airline reservation system to the SAHARA computer in Atlanta. This then permits an agent using any terminal connected to that airline reservations system to access SAHARA as well.

Several hotel groups have direct connections with the SITA Atlanta Data Processing Centre, where SAHARA is hosted and they have created and are maintaining a world-wide data base containing over 10,000 hotels.

Airline users of the system are able to access this data base and, if required, provide their own bias and/or supplement the common data base with their own information.

SAHARA display and booking transactions etc. are all query/response type transactions using "Type A" relecommunications facilities. The booking messages to

SAHARA at "End of Transaction (EOT)" are sent via airline teletype "Type B" facilities.

The System is comprised of the following two main areas:

- the structure of the data base, and

- the transactions available to airline users of the system.

The Structure of the Data Base

There are three sections within the system's data base (Fig. 1):

- the Common Data Base

- the Associated Data Base, and

- the User Unique Data Base.

The *Common Data Base* is available to all users. It is provided and maintained (with real time updating) by the hotel groups.

The hotels are grouped by city with up to 300 hotels listed for each city and an unlimited number of cities.

Location of each hotel may be categorised further by specifying whether it is in the city centre, at the airport, in the periphery, a resort hotel, etc.

The common data base also contains information about hotel availability-this is given by room type. A room type is shown as available, closed, on request or closed for arrival-sell through.

The type of hotel allows for further categorisation, i.e. whether the hotel is luxury, first class, tourist, etc. Rates may be given for up to six different room types at each hotel and a further six room types may be specified without rates. Up to 96 different types of rooms may be established in SAHARA including SGLB, DBLB, SGLS, etc.

Rates are given in local currency (although there is a transaction that converts one currency to another).

Each hotel has associated to it up to five pages of facility information. This includes information on the exact address of the hotel and points of interest nearby, deposit requirements, credit cards accepted, rates for additional beds, dining and entertainment facilities etc., plus information added by the airline user (optionally).

Information from the common data base is available to all users and since it is provided by the hotel groups, requires no airline updating.

Both the *Associated Data Base* and the *User Unique Data Base* are provided and maintained by the airline users of SAHARA on an optional basis. The information created by an airline in one of these data bases is available to that airline only.

The *Associated Data Base* allows an airline to bias the information given in the common data base. This bias allows a user to specify sales priorities for hotels and to have the system display hotels in any city in a specified order. If the associated data base is not used then hotels will be displayed in random order each time a display is requested.
The associated data base is also used to add airline specific facilities information to any hotel. One page of information is allowed per hotel.

The *User Unique Data Base* gives and airline the option of adding hotels and rates that are available to that airline only. The information in the user unique data base will only be displayed to the airline that created it, and is updated by that airline. It allows an airline to display information on hotels where, for example, they have special crew rates, etc.

The Transactions of the System

Transactions are used by agents to sell, confirm or request hotel space. The transactions create hotel auxiliary service elements in a Passenger Name Record (PNR) which reflect the status of the hotel bookings. At the EOT for the PNR a booking message is sent to SAHARA automatically by the airline reservations system. There it is indexed in the data base then sent from SAHARA to the appropriate hotel booking system.

The transactions are designed in such a way that gives unique user-friendliness and mission effectiveness; transactions in SAHARA allow agents to display hotel information, convert currencies, check city codes, make hotels bookings and retrieve guest records. The following information displays are available:

- Hotel City Display.
  This display gives a list of hotels associated to a specified city. The display can be made selective by use of a hotel category limitation such as type of hotel (luxury, tourist, etc.) and/or location, airport, city centre, etc.

- Hotel Availability Display.
  This provides informaion on room status, room rates, details about the hotel and city etc, so that, based on this information, a booking could be made.

- Hotel Facilities Display.

This gives all the information available about facilities offered at a particular hotel.

- Hotel Status Display.
  This gives a day by day availability status by room type for a specified hotel.

- Hotel Rate Display.
  This provides the various room rates over different rate periods. The system allows up to 12 rate periods per year.

- Hotel Bed Type Display.
  This provides a list of bed types associated with particular room types (for a specified hotel).

- Hotel Chain Update Display.
  Gives a free form text display of information associated with a particular hotel group, allowing the group to provide a type of sales and information quide to update the airlines. Up to ten pages of information are provided per hotel group.

- Hotel Guest Lists.
  This transaction is used to obtain lists of hotel guests for a specified hotel. Various parameters may be used to define this list including: first day of stay, last day of stay, confirmed guests, cancelled guests, etc. The lists may be requested for a specific day or a date range.

- Hotel Rate Conversion.
  This transaction allows an agent to convert an amount from one currency to another at the current bankes buying rate.

- Hotel Name / Code Display.
  This allows an agent to display a hotel name when the hotel code is known, or display the hotel code if the name is known.

- Hotel Locate City / Country Display.
  This allows an agent to find an applicable city code when knowing the country name, find the country when knowing the city code, or find the city code when knowing the city name.

- Guest Index Retrieval.
  This transaction retrieves a guest name index in SAHARA which gives the guest names together with the appropriate record locators corresponding to the associated PNRs in the airline's own reservation system.

Management Reports

SAHARA provides a daily booking statistics report that gives detailed analysis of all hotel bookings by city, hotel and group for a specific day and date range. This report may be generated on demand. This "on demand" report may be requested for any date currently held in the data base.

Additional reports available in the system include: a monthly booking report which gives an analysis of all bookings created by an airline in the system for one month. A monthly billing report is also available giving bookings and billing amounts. This report is used as the actual billable count by each hotel group.

Fig. 1. SAHARA System Overview Chart

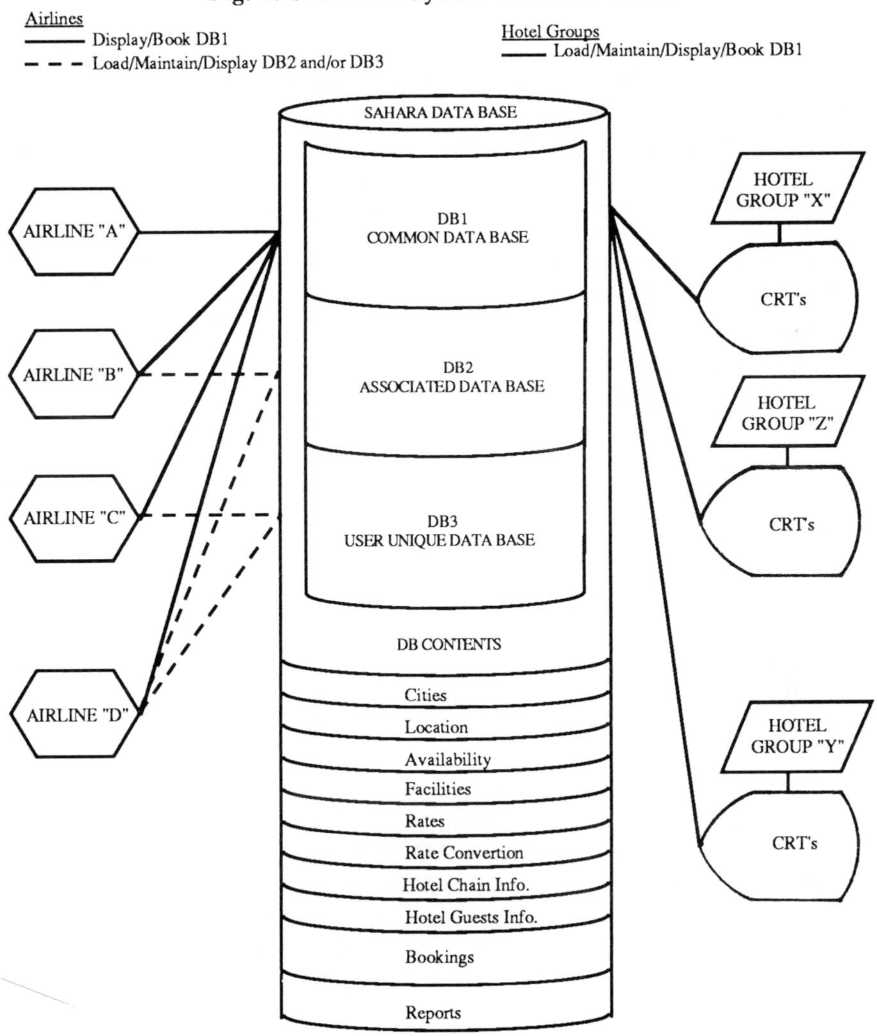

2 Porter's Value Chain Analysis Model

Value Chain Analysis is a major tool for identifying potential sources of value enhancement for an operation. In such an analysis, all of the activities for the organization are mapped into a value arrow with the two sides of the point refleting the total value in terms of revenue created by the organization and the total costs incurred to create the values or revenue. The difference between revenue and costs is the margin. In order for the organization to increase margin, it can either increase value or decrease costs. For that purpose, the Chain divides an entity into nine strategically relevant activities, which are further subdivided into support and primary activities. Primary are the activities which create value for the customers, and support activities are those that although do not directly create value, are required in order to maintain the operation.

Applications of the Value Chain Analysis Model by Rauch and Siomkos (1993) to the hotel industry leads to the identification of the nine value activities in a hotel. These include the four support areas which encompass the hotel's infrastructure, human resources, technology and purchasing, and the five primary areas. The primary areas are: reservations and check-in, hotel facilities and support, check-out, marketing and sales, and frequent use programs as a service of the hotel.

The Hotel Value Chain contributes to the hotel industry through the application of the primary activities in the chain, i.e., reservations system, luggage handling, and just-in-time check-in. The hotel's facilities and support should address the latest technological amenities available. Check-out should be swift and completed within the customer's room and include all relevant charges incurred at the hotel. The availability of frequent-use programs represents immediate reward for the customers' continued loyalty. A hotel's success depends on a constant loop between the frequent-use program and the check-in procedure.

3 The Lodging Customer

Value Chain Analysis reflects the perspective of the provider of the service, i.e. , the hotel. The other end of the service encounter is the lodging customer, the user of the service.

There are four major segments in the lodging market. They are (according to the American Hotel & Motel Association, with their corresponding shares in parentheses): 1. transient business travelers (25%), 2. conference participants (24%), 3. pleasure travelers (31%), and 4. pleasure/family travelers (20%). It is obvious that different factors influence the selection of lodging accomodations by these different customer/traveler categories (e.g., Lewis 1985). Research ha also indicated that different preferences - in terms of hotel accomodations and environment - exist between the two major lodging industry segments of business and pleasure travelers (McCleary and Weaver 1992; Taninecz 1990).

Specifically, it has been shown that approximately 40% of business travelers take 10 or more domestic business trips in the U.S. in one year. The same study (McCleary and Weaver, 1992) also indicated that business travelers prefer a comfortable, clean room and an environment that is favorable for work and relaxation. Taninecz (1990) has shown that business travelers also expect hotels to provide multiple facilities which pleasure travelers do not usually expect, such as fax machines, copy machines, special meeting rooms, etc. On the other hand, pleasure travelers tend to expect different facilities since they often travel with their families.

Sundaram et al. (1993) supported that different lodging customers (pleasure versus business, males versus females, frequent versus nonfrequent) use different information sources when selecting hotel accomodations. Both pleasure and business travelers consult with their past experience and opinions of their friends as the two most important sources of information. Business travelers consult mostly with colleagues and in the process gather information about lodging facilities at the destination. Apart from that source, business travelers also consider advertisements about lodging facilities as another information source. Business trips are planned and accommodations are done in advance, as opposed to pleasure travel. Therefore, pleasure travelers rely more on travel agent opinions than business travelers do. Nonfrequent, as opposed to frequent, users of lodging facilities are least likely to prefer staying at the first hotel encountered at their destination. Frequent users are more likely to consider advertisements about lodging facilities and relevant published articles, or rely on opinions of travel agents. As for female travelers, they are more likely than males to use opinions of relatives and pamphlets and brochures as sources of information. Males rely most frequently on opinions of friends.

4 The SAHARA - Value Chain Interface

Given the fact that different lodging consumers travel for different reasons, have different characteristics, and consequently have different lodging needs and preferences, it is appropriate to incorporate these elements in the SAHARA System.

Table 1 presents ten items which can be added to the Common Data Base. Their addition enhances the System by providing further detailed information which enables the airlines to successfully address the very specific customer needs. The items are explained in a more elaborated fashion, below.

Table 1

Items to be Added to the Common Data Base

[1]	Customs Regulations
[2]	Transportation Services (i.e., courtesy cars)
[3]	Automated / Immediate Check-In
[4]	Amenities
[5]	Catering
[6]	VCR, FAX, Voice Mail, Computers
[7]	Luggage Handling and Storage after Check-Out
[8]	Billing Procedures
[9]	Frequent Use Programs
[10]	Business / Pleasure Traveler

Information on customs regulations [1] would definitely help the traveler abroad. Several times traveling abroad may present a lot of unpleasant surprises for the uninformed traveler from the moment he reaches his destination.

Transportation services [2] offered by hotels (i.e., courtesy cars, mini buses, or vans) for picking up hotel customers from the airport, should also be indicated by the System, expecially of rcases of remote destinations.

Information on whether the hotel uses an automated/immediate check-in procedure [3] may also be of interest to the clients. The term "immediate" implies that the check-in system, besides being automated, has the ability to complete the check-in form and have it ready for the client upon his arrival at the hotel. In case that the client has made several hotel bookings on the same trip, this can apply for all apply for all of his destinations. However, it should be noted that here, we suggest that SAHARA should not simply provide information on this option, but also execute it. In other words, we recommend that the System itself does this for the client. For example, for multiple hotel bookings abroad by the same client, check-in forms can be automatically printed with the customer's passport number and other information, so that upon his arrival at the hotels, he will only be asked to sign the preprinted adn complete forms, thereby, minimize the required time for the check-in procedure.

Further useful information that the System could provide would be: the specific amenities offered by the hotel, both inbound amenities and amenities during-stay [4], catering services [5], available for private of business parties organized by hotel clients, and information regarding the availability of VCR's, FAX machines, Voice Mail equipment, and computers [6] for the use of hotel clients.

Of interest to many hotel clients is also information on luggage handling and storage [7] after they officially check-out of the hotel, in case that they wish to spend some more time in the city, before they depart for the airport.

A brief description on the billing procedures [8] and options available can prove useful, e.g., information on whether the client can get billed after his departure. The System currently supplies only information on the forms of payment (i.e., cash, credit cards).

Recently, however, many hotels offer "frequent-use" programs [9] with special rates that apply to those clients that frequently prefer the same hotel. This piece of information tends to become more and more important these days, expecially for business travelers.

Finally, the distinction between business and pleasure travelers [10] who book airline seats and hotel rooms through the System would prove useful as an elemetn for further analysis by the airline-user, as will be explained below.

Both the Common Data Base and the Unique Data Base should provide the function of generating updated bookings reports by type of customer (business or pleasure) and hotel, and with a time horizon of one month or one year and compile information for the most recent years. Besides statistical records, such an option will provide essential information to the airline. Specifically, statistical data can be presented in reports, broken down by hotel and customer type. Based on these reports, the airline-user can identify those hotels which were mostly preferred by its clients. These data could be used by the airline in negotiating better rates for its clients with those hotels. This, consequently, could also allow the airline to offer special complete packages or arrangements to business or pleasure (family) travelers. It could also allow the airline to better target categories of travelers that it is interested in, through more efficient marketing efforts (e.g., media planning, types of advertisements, sales promotion techniques etc.).

The benifits of the incorporation of these features to the SAHARA System lie with the availability of furthter detailed data describing specific hotel and traveler characteristics. The airline customer will better appreciate the provision of such data. The airline will be able to satisfy its customers' needs more effectively, in a "tailor-made" fashion, therefore adding value to its services.

References

1. Lewis, R.C.: Predicting Hotel Choice - The Factors Underlying Perception, The Cornell H.R.A. Quarterly, February, 83-97 (1985).

2. McCleary, K. W., Weaver, P. A.: Business-Traveller Survey Shows Guestroom Basics, Security Are Popular Selection Criteria, H&MM, July 6, 23-26 (1992).

3. Porter, M.: Competitive Strategy - Techniques for Analyzig Industries and Competitors, New York, The Free Press (1980).

4. Porter, M.: Competitive Advantage - Creating and Sustaining Superior Performance, New York, The Free Press (1985).

5. Rauch, R.A., Siomkos, G.J.: The Need for a Theoretical Framework and Professioal Expertise for Successful Hotel Operations, Proceedings of the Atlantic Marketing Association, pp. 311-315 (1993).

6. SITA: SAHARA System Overview.

7. Sundaram, D.S., Clinton, S.M., Richard, M.D.: A Study of Information Search Behavior of Lodging Customers, Proceedings of the Atlantic Marketing Association, pp. 406-410 (1993).

8. Taninecz, G.: 1990 Business Traveler Survey, H&MM, June 25, p. 29 (1990).

Changes in the Leisure Travel Market result in new Requirements for Tour Operator Systems

Marion Weber

Ploenzke Informatik, Business Unit Travel/Transport/Tourism,
Wilhelmstraße 48, 65183 Wiesbaden, Germany

Abstract. The leisure travel market will demand more flexible modular design products - *FIT products* - instead of predefined holiday packages. At the same time an increasing number of end-user reservation systems enable the customer to contract for these travel products directly with the service provider. Facing this situation tour operators must react to the customer's demand for flexibility. This requires changes in the organizational structure of the company as well as a new positioning in the market. To support the distribution of FIT components, aiso the tour operator's reservation system must be adapted to the new requirements.

1 Introduction

Traditional tour packages including a point-to-point return charter flight, a transfer between airport and hotel, a two weeks beach hotel accomodation and optional guided excursions meet the requirements of those travellers whose major interest is to relax and who prefer to rely on the organization of a tour operator rather than handling the travel arrangement tasks themselves.

Parallel with increasing travel experience and know how the expectation on holidays moves towards more flexible concepts where travel components may be individually combined by the customer. These modular holiday products are known as *FIT products*, where FIT stands for 'Foreign Individual Traveller' or 'Flexible Itinerary Tour'. The FIT concept allows for example to combine a scheduled flight to Sydney including a three days stopover in Singapore with various daily changing accomodations, a rental car and national flights in Australia plus a one-week stay at a beach resort on Fiji. More and more leisure travellers require this flexibility.

2 Technical Concepts meeting the FIT Traveller's Needs

Advances in technology provide the ability for the FIT traveller to directly access travel information from their homes. Not only company travel departments or business travelling employees themselves use the possibilities to connect their personal computer via public networks to travel service data bases as CRS or hotel reservation systems. The fast growing propagation of private PC combined with knowlege as well as readiness to communicate with external computer systems also enforce travel service distributors to introduce services for home-travel-shopping. Toll-free reservation numbers, fax or mail always existed to directly contact a service provider for information or reservation purpose. With electronic reservation systems the customer additionally gains the ability to easily compare offered services with regard to price and quality.

An experienced traveller may prefer to book his holiday arrangement via television, select the air connection by his preferred stopover destination by glancing through various CRS offers and pick up his ticket from an ETDN ticketing device. Further information which he would be given by a travel agent may also be retrieved from destination databases and government information services.

Main advantages for the customer are time flexibility and independency from travel agency preferences, which may be driven by overriding commission and incentive offers from specific providers.

For service providers the attractiveness of selling directly to the customer, bypassing travel agencies and tour operators, is the chance to lower their distribution costs.

3 The Role of Tour Operators

Tour operators offer holiday products which consist of services like hotel accomodation, air services and transfers which the customer alternatively could purchase directly from the service provider. The main value tour operators traditionally add to these individual travel services results from:

- combining them to holiday packages,
- providing access to information,
- handling reservations, payments and travel documents,
- offering better rates achieved through purchasing power and
- providing liability regarding claims against the service provider.

These services guarantee the market share for tour operators specialized on customer groups which will not use direct booking services and on products which cannot be substituted by FIT products. Examples are advice intensive products as study or adventure tours, niche products offered in combination with qualified and detailed information or exclusive high price products preferably booked face-to-face with an experienced reliable travel advisor, i.e. cruises.

The majority of travel products potentially allows to be substitued by more flexible component oriented services as the customer demands this flexibility. For these products the service of creating packages will loose its importance.

Distributing information and handling reservation will remain the most important service for a tour operator to provide. For the experienced customer user-friendly electronic end-user travel services giving access to booking facilities including payment methods and documentation for a large number of service provider's offers may become an alternative. If similar products are offered variety and quality of information, flexibility regarding the reservation, immediate confirmation and up-to-date availability may decide on the method to make a reservation.

Regarding these trends the tourism branch is facing a changing situation. Tour operators not specialized on niche products must move towards more flexibility by offering FIT travel components or multi optioned packages, otherwise they will experience a much smaller market in the future.

Modular-design holiday products require more changes within the tour operator company than refraining from creating packages. The positioning on the market place as well as the internal organization will dramatically change.

Tour operators have to move from being a 'production' company towards being a *marketing* company. As the FIT products themselves are less unique and much more comparable the way of marketing these products gains importance. The basic services have to be offered through various product lines giving them individual flavors and uniqueness. Each product line must clearly address a specific customer group and must be reflected by the individual overall appearance to the customer. Design and contents of the brochure is one of the most important, but not the only way to achieve uniqueness. A leather document case with the traveller's initials, an invitation to the airline's lounge and a fruit basket at the hotel room are some examples to underline the flavour of a luxury product line. Identical services may be offered through a product line focussed on young travellers by including a nightlive-guide and a complementary welcome drink at the hotel bar.

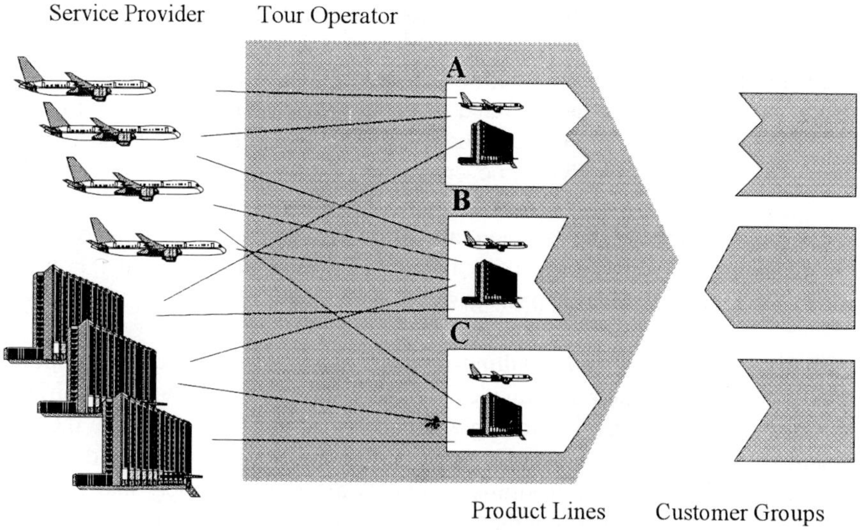

Fig. 1. Customer oriented Markting of FIT Components

Aside from changes on the marketing side FIT products require a new structure of the purchasing and contracting department as the price for each individual component becomes more comparable with the service provider's own pricing. Long term contracts and large purchasing quantities generally allow better rates. Specials offered by airlines, hotels and rental car companies depending on various conditions may still result in lower prices if these conditions are met. To prevent the tour operator's customer from paying higher prices than direct customers, immense flexibility is required for purchasing and pricing. Varying selling prices, a tour operator must take into consideration any legal restriction but should *not* be restricted by internal inflexibility. On the american market some tour operators already publish price ranges instead of exact prices in their brochures. The exact selling price being recalculated with each vendor price change is only available via the reservation system.

Tour operators which have undertaken these changes and have positioned themselves accordingly in the market have the chance to take over market shares from two sides:

- traditional package tourists demanding more flexibility without loosing tour operator liability and

- individual travellers who gain the advantage of contracting various products with one company without loosing flexibility.

If tour operator FIT products are also offered via end-user reservation systems the customer may honour having one common user interface and functionality for various different product types whereas most systems are very much service provider dependent.

4 New Requirements for Tour Operator Systems

Selling FIT products successfully requires a reservation system which fully supports the distribution of modulare travel components.

The functionality required depends to some degree on the individual needs and organization of the company and on the extent of product flexibility.

- Powerful yield management functionality,
- easy-to-handle user interface and
- multi language and multi currency support

are requirements which equally exist for package product reservation, whereas the functionality described below is specifically important for modular concepts.

4.1 Multiple Item Reservations

Unlike booking a predefined tour packages the reservation of FIT products requires the creation of multiple individual items. Each reservation item reflects one service (i.e. accomodation, flight service) and may have different dates and quantities as well as individual traveller association according to the customer's request. Additionally reservation status, advising, documentation and accounts payable requirements may differ according to the individual service provider.

Still the components of one reservation must be related to a single reservation file to allow the creation of one invoice and one set of documents.

4.2 Separation between purchased Services and offered Products

Vendor data should be stored for each purchased service. As the same service may be offered within different product lines only additional information should be stored for each product.

4.3 Validation and Combination Rules

As the user does not book a predefined product but combines the holiday-components himself, the reservation system should prevent him from errors due to non-matching items as well as violation against rules defined by the product management. To support this requirement the reservation process must consist of two steps:

- booking and validation of each individual service and
- validation of the complete reservation.

Checking the integrety of a reservation requires a hierarchical location concept for all services offered. Each product must be assigned to geographical locations or, in case of transportation services to transportation locations (i.e. airports, rental car pick-up and drop-off stations or harbours). If transportation locations are associated system-internally to the geographical locations they serve, the complete itinerary for each traveller may be validated by the system according to dates and locations each time a reservation file is to be stored.

Tour operaters offering FIT products still should not allow total flexibility in combining products. Examples for booking restrictions and combination rules are:

- Services with low profit per unit must not be booked except in combination with at least one high profit product, i.e. theatre ticket must not be booked without accomodation.
- Transportation services with limited capacity which serve destinations with risk allotments on accomodation are not offered as transportation-only products.

To allow the validation of the above described rules, relations between products have to be reflected in the product data base. A product can be associated either to another specific product or to a group of other products. The group of products may consist of serveral specific products or may be defined by the type of service (3 star hotel accomodation, appartment, rental car), the category (double room, convertable car, first class flight) and the geographical location.

The association must be further qualified by the *level* which specifies whether the combination is mandatory, restricted or optional (optional combinations allow pricing rules to depend on the combination) and the *quantity* to define the minimum number of units and/or the length of stay required to fulfill the rule.

The validation must also consider a maximum allowed discrepancy in dates for the combination rule to be met.

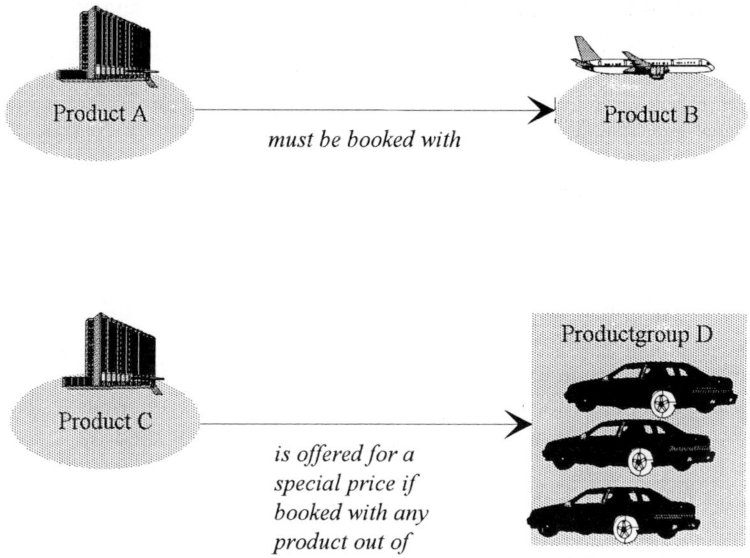

Fig. 2. Combination Rules

4.4 Flexible Fare Basis driven Pricing

Selling and vendor prices must be automatically computed depending on various rules. The pricing mechanism must be capable to reflect the tour operator's pricing structure as well as service provider's specials with regard to

- length of stay,
- booking dates,
- use dates,
- quantity of units and/or persons and
- person specific criteria (i.e. age).

This cannot be fullfilled by a set of predefined tariffs but requires flexible computation rules. The rules must allow a combination of the above criteria each resulting in added or subtracted flat amounts, percentage addons or discounts and/or base decrementation (i.e. pay 10 nights instead of 14). To define complex rules a basic understanding of logical operations is needed but they must not require programming knowledge. To achieve this the system should provide a user friendly 'language' comprising of predefined parameters and locigal operations.

The rules should relate to fare basis for which conditions may be defined which, if met qualify for the use of a specific pricing rule. Conditions may allow validation by the system i.e. stay over the weekend or may only be checked by the reservation staff. Fare basis should also be related to combination rules to support different pricing for the same product depending on other products within the same reservation.

4.5 Last Unit Availability

FIT product offered by tour operators should not lack up-to-date availability. As this information is available for service provider offers via their (direct) reservation systems, the customer may user other booking methods if a specific product he requires is not available via the tour operator's system. To achieve last unit availability a connection to the inventory basis is required. This may be accessed via fast online communication directly with service provider's internal system or via CRS. The so-called *Reverse Access* has been already established by some german tour operators, i.e. between DER and Worldspan and between Airtours and Amadeus. It provides the tour operator with the capability to

- automatically create PNRs containing flight, hotel and car segments,
- request availability,
- retrieve up-to-date flight schedules and other product information and
- use advance seat reservation functionality.

The quality of the availability information and immediate reservation confirmation depend on the access agreement between service provider and CRS. A tour operator may therefore use different availability sources, including internal stored allotment. Availability is taken depending on the priorities defined for each service.

To fully optimize the usage of contracted risk allotment or to provide availability in peak seasons the system should allow the combination of different sources for one reservation item. Of a two weeks hotel stay one week may be taken from internal allotment and the second week is booked via a hotel reservation system. This should not be transparent to the user.

4.6 Accessibility by local Agents

As FIT reservations are frequently changed in advance or during the stay, product data bases and external availability sources should be accessable by local handling agents. This may be supported by mailbox functionality, file transfer or online system-connection, depending on the amount of data to be transmitted.

Information system architectures and benchmarks for local tourist offices

C. Meijs (1) G. Dijks
(1) Wageningen Agricultural University, Dep. of Computer Science
Dreijenplein 2, NL-6703 HB Wageningen, The Netherlands
e-mail: meijs@rcl.wau.nl

1 Introduction

It has been continuing difficult to assess the benefits and impact of investments in the area of information technology. A challenge of major importance for the future is to enable organizations, to master the growing complexity associated with the effective and efficient use of information technology for their information-related tasks. To our opinion more attention has to be paid to the fitting of information-technology within an organization, based on the support of the involved management and end-users. Their judgement about business processes and the related products are emphasized in this paper. An instrument to make operational the setting of priorities for the selection of new information systems is presented. Therefore we need a clear description of the information system architecture. Information system architecture has yet no standard definition and much confusion surrounds the information architecture concept. This paper will focus on:

- the present role of management-information for local tourist offices in the Netherlands
- clarification of the context where various information system architectures are constructed and interact
- the way we make operational the setting of priorities of information systems

Because parties involved (managers, end-users, software engineers, consultants) in selecting and shaping information systems have different interests, views and favourite technology, the forecasting of the ultimate form and function of the relevant architectures for information systems requires examining these conflicting perspectives. Otherwise we run the risk that it becomes increasingly difficult to manage the vast inventory of information resources without a clear, global understanding of their existence, location and role as well as the dynamic relation among them.

2 The role of information at local tourist offices

Over 330 Local Tourist Offices (LTO) are more or less equally scattered around the Netherlands, each city or touristic region has its own local tourist office. Approximately 2.000 professional employees work in this branche. LTO's have the not-for-profit mission to market the local tourist product by representing the tourism industry and supply information for tourists, inhabitants and organizations. An LTO can be characterised as a business with:

- an intermediate position between two markets: the demand-market (tourists) and the supply-market (tourism industry in a region);
- a high service level because of the many offered services : information supply, sales promotions, consulting role, etc.
- a not-for-profit mission: the LTO mission has primarly a social, collective nonprofit goal taking into account that 40 % of the revenues are governmental funds
- a small scale, as the average LTO employs 6 professional full time equivalents of personnel.

2.1 Survey about management information

In a LTO study 4 classes of local touris offices were derived and two performance indicators were formulated [Dijks93]:

- the productivity of labour: the ratio of revenues (output) and the number of labour in fte (input: in full time equivalent) indicating the efficiency.
- the percentage of revenues from the tourism industry on the total budget. LTO's who can maximize funds from the local industry (hotels, camp-sites, retail trade et cetera) operate in an effective way, seen from the point of view from those stakeholders.

The data for composing these performance indicators were partly extracted from a meta information system that comprises data concerning the line-of-business. Regression-analyses show a significant interrelation of the two indicators, effective LTO's are usually efficient (Ry=0.56). In further research these two performance-indicators were compared to other aspects of management-information: the availability, the importance and the reliability. Management information in this context is data endowed with relevance and purpose to manage a LTO. A questionnaire was developed in order to survey the role of management information, the response was 86 % (N=44) [Dijks93]. In fig. 1 the global entities of this survey are depicted.

The data model corresponding to the questionnaire contains entities about *demand* including the attributes about the number of visitors and number of

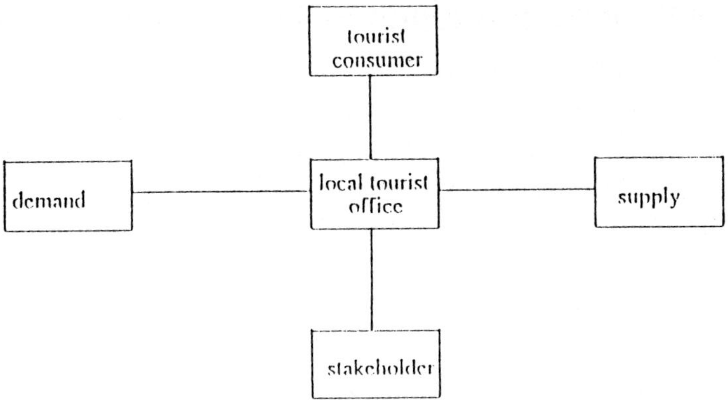

Figure 1: Global datamodel

hotel entries. *Supply* refers to accomodations and attractions. About the *customer* it is interesting to know: place of origin, kind of request, waiting time and number of complaints and compliments. *Stakeholder* encloses the members and their financial contribution. Other analysed entities refer to *personnel* and the numer of information requests of the *LTO*.

The outcomes in the next tables represent the judgement of interviewed LTO officials about two variables.

about Entities:	LTO city	borough LTO	country side LTO	LTO coast
demand	3.9	4.3	4.1	4.1
supply	3.7	4.3	4.1	4.0
customer	3.9	4.1	3.8	3.5
stakeholder	3.0	4.7	4.8	3.9

Table 1: importance of management information

Appraising the importancy was done was by assessment of mark in the range from 0 (not important) to 5 (very important). The judgement about the reliability was measured with mark in the range from 1 (exactly known) to 3 (not reliable).

about Entities:	LTO city	borough LTO	country side LTO	LTO coast
demand	1.8	2.3	2.3	2.3
supply	1.8	1.6	1.6	1.7
customer	2.0	1.8	2.1	2.0
stakeholder	1.5	1.1	1.4	1.3

Table 2: reliability of management information

2.2 Recommendations for improvements

The survey covers only a part of the LTO business information: especially information from the view of stakeholders and end-users (tourist) and the product information is lacking.

Because of the small scale of the local tourist offices and the changing environments, an approach using reference-information models joined with the object oriented approach [Wietrzyk94] is expected to be productive.

The results of the questionnaire made obvious that a lot of management information is not available, especially information about the demand-market is lacking. The average values of the availabilty come to 58 %.

The figures of the survey make clear that local tourist offices should pay more attention to information facilities and services. In the following approach it will be shown that balanced information system architectures are essential for this improvement [Meijs94]

3 Information system Architectures

For the introduction of information systems some obstacles may be noticed in general. A prime step for successes is the setting of priorities for projects, but this esthablishment is commonly hampered by:

- Long-duration of the planning and implementation of IT projects.
- Incompatibility of newly introduced systems with the existing computer infrastructure.
- Changes as businesses are pressed the to react because the ever-shorter product-life-cycles.
- Individuals carry their personal wishes through: users bypassing others or IT consultants driving their hobby-horse.
- Limited resources available for starting innovative IT projects.

A clear picture of the various architectues and their interactions will improve the planning and implementation of IT projects. We distinghuish architectures focussing on the business, information needs, the techology and on the systems.

3.1 Alignment of architectures

A business architecture establishes a clear understanding of the nature of the business and its main objectvies and activities. It provides a top level framework within which information systems, organizational units can be place in the context, with interrelationships clearly understood. Finally the organizational structure emphasizes the mutual dependencies between an organization and IT and the emergent properties derived from the interaction between them.

An information architecture is a personnel and technology independent profile of the major information categories used within an organization. It provides a way to relate business functions and data classes. Figure 1 shows some relevant data classes for a LTO and 2 represents a part of business functions of a LTO.

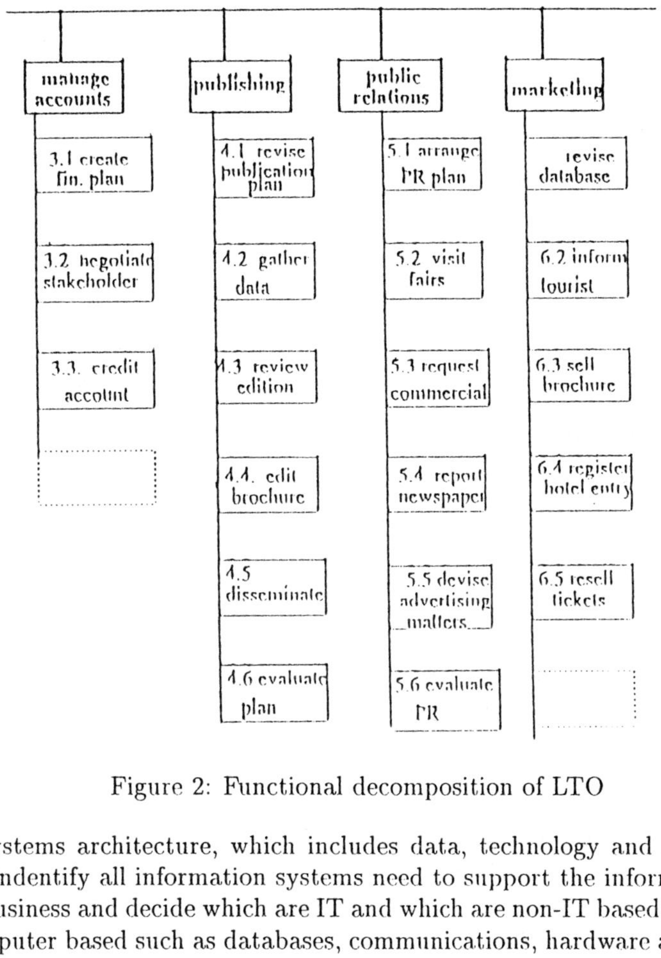

Figure 2: Functional decomposition of LTO

A systems architecture, which includes data, technology and applications, should indentify all information systems need to support the information needs of the business and decide which are IT and which are non-IT based, wheter they are computer based such as databases, communications, hardware and software, or non-computer based such as libraries, filing cabinets, microfilm, photocopiers and faxes.

The technology architecture consists of the computer infrastructure and digital networks that cooperate in providing computing support to the information needs.

Moreover, interactions among the activities of business architecture, information architecture, systems architecture and technical architecture takes place as feedbackloops and feed forward loops. Thereover they cannot be carried out sequentially but they must be done in parallel. An IS plan should be no longer be separated from the business plan and vica versa.

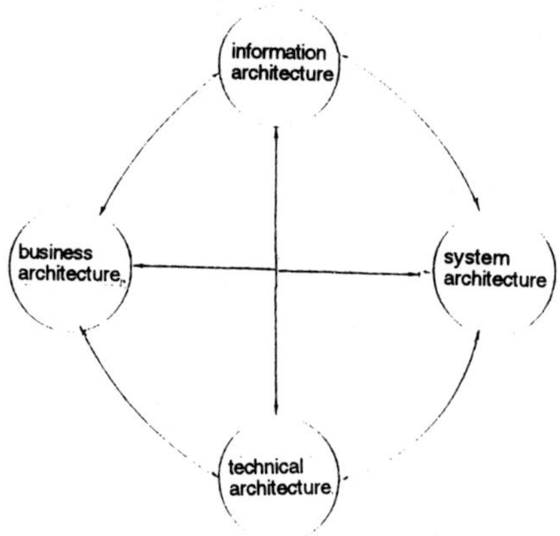

Figure 3: Alignment of architectures

4 Benchmarks

For the area of information technology we distinghuish three kinds of benchmarks:

- benchmarks of IT products: characteristics of IT products are determined resulting mostly in a short list for selection of a product.
- competitive benchmarks: some key ratio's are determined and compared with other organization.
- internal benchmarks: business functions within one organization are measured and compared.

In this paper we will mainly focus on this last benchmark [Meijs94] As the benefits of planned information systems are often difficult to quantify because there may be a lot of intangible factors there is a need for other instruments. Benchmarking has proven to be an adequate technique that can contribute to the improvement of decision processes [Lawrence93]. Benchmarking is a proces which measures the performance of some key elements of a business, in order to compare these measured results. The ways the performance of the business is measured include: (a) specifying and rewarding business processes and (b) identifying wheter appropriate results are obtained (see fig. 4)

Performance indicators define what data will be collected. The criteria are influenced by the management approach: e.g.

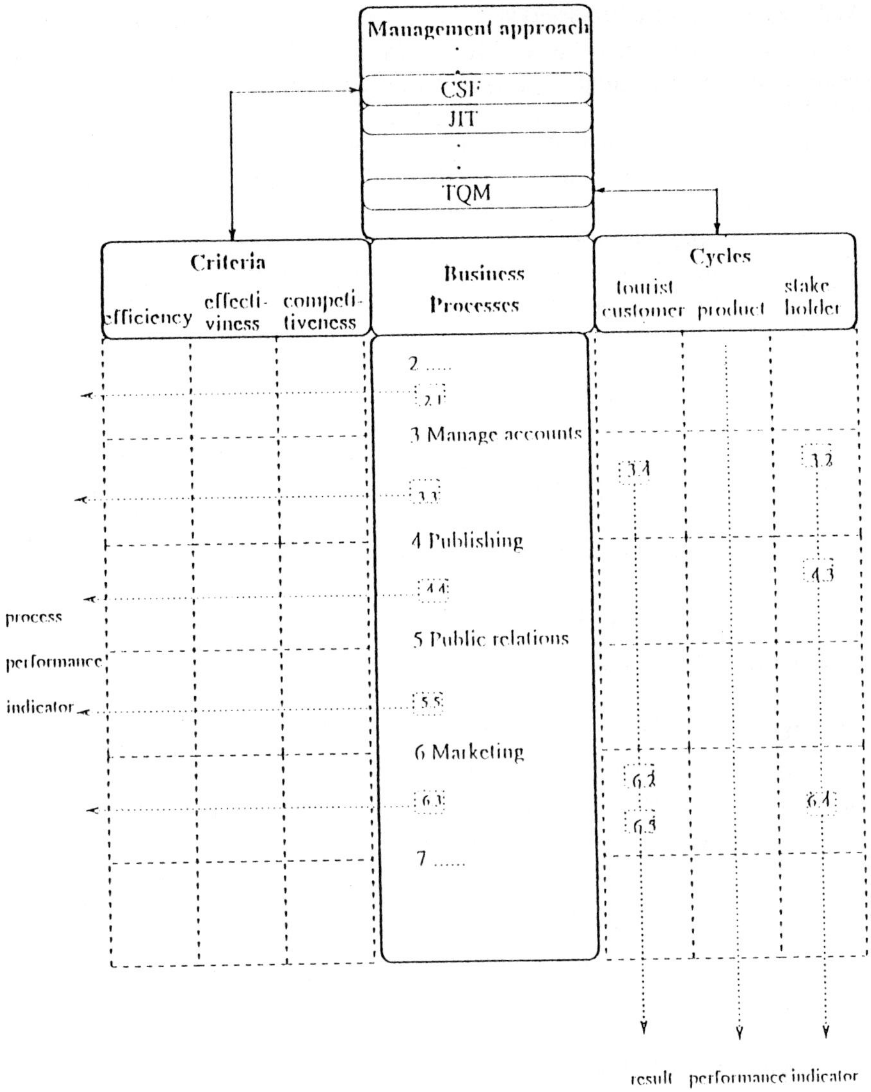

Figure 4: Benchmarks on basis of business functions

- Critical succes factors [Rockart79]
- Just in Time
- Total Quality Management
- etc.

A business may conduct all the processes of the functional decomposition very well but it may still be less competitive. This may be caused by processes which are not able to cooperate very well. Dynamic aspects can be taken into account by following the various flows in the business, cycles of the relevant flows seen from the view of a customer, stakeholder or product 4.

- tourist customer
- product
- stakeholder

Because measures are always approximations involving human judgement, taking measures involves inherent imperfections. Attention should be paid to protect against inappropriate manipulation of perfomance measures.

4.1 Setting of priorities

For the setting of priorities the business functions and additional questionaires are used for the benchmark. As these functions are on a more abstract level, there is no direct link to concrete tasks executed by individuals in the business. Therefore we have not experienced any hesitation or mistrust while doing benchmarks. Several steps can be identified within a benchmark study:

1. identify and research relevant data of the business
2. select the representatives
3. document the recognized business functions
4. create survey questions
5. introduce the functions and survey to the selected
6. customize spreadsheet for the specific benchmark
7. receive surveys and enter data
8. obtain quantitative raw data
9. analyse raw data and discuss results
10. format report with conclusions

5 Conclusions and further research

Reliable and actual information is a key issue for local tourist offices. This paper emphasizes in this era of all pervasive applications of information systems and technology the need for alignment of the various architectures. It was argued that the dynamic nature of local tourist offices should be recognized and should influence the adaption of the business processes and the selection of new information technology. The instument described , creates an join between market needs, business functions of tourist offfices and information technology. Lessons learned from conducted studies show:
- how to put into practice the selection of information systems, using the business functions as defined in the information architecture as a starting point.
- reference informationmodels decrease complexity and cost.
- communication and documentation should be well prepared, attention has to be paid to training and understanding of the involved tourist officials
- the verification processes for nonfinancial measures, such as tourist satisfaction and innovation should be furter developed.

References

[Dijks93] G. Dijks
Professionaliteit als succesfactor van VVV's (in dutch)
ANVV, Amersfoort 1993.

[Lawrence93] S. Lawrence and S. Katz
How benchmarking goes wrong (and how to do it right). In: Planning Review, jan. 1993.

[Meijs94] C. Meijs
Information systems architecture, creating links in the chain with IT, Proc. 1st Int. Conference on Agri-chain management, march 1994, Wageningen.

[Rockart79] J. Rockart;
Chief executives define their own data needs. In: HBR March 1979, p. 81-93.

[Scott Morton91] M. Scott Morton
The corporation of the 1990's: Information technology and organizaional transformation, Oxford University Press, New York, 1991.

[Wietrzyk94] V. Wietrzyk;
Development of adaptable information systems in tourism. In: Information and communication technologies in Tourism, Spring Verlag, p. 254 -255.

Electronic Networks: New Challenges for Tourist Organizations?

Ronald Maier, Wolfgang Röckelein

Institute of Business Informatics, The Koblenz School of Corporate Management, Burgplatz 2, D-56179 Vallendar, E-Mail: maier, roeckelein@wi.whu-koblenz.de

Abstract. This paper discusses the possibilities of using electronic networks in the field of tourism. Different electronic network technologies are investigated in detail. The concept of customer closeness is adapted to the relationship between tourists and tourist organizations, so that these technologies can be compared with respect to the requirements for information channels in tourism. Live examples demonstrate the potentials of electronic networks in tourism. A set of recommendations is provided in order to help tourist organizations develop profitable future electronic network applications which are closer to the customer than the existing ones.

1 Motivation

Today customer closeness, in our case that means reducing the distance between tourist organizations and their customers, is one of the key success factors in tourism. Most of the time the information flow[1] from tourist organizations to their customers is still time-consuming, costly, unstructured, one-way, only indirectly influenceable and heavily dependent on the "communication mediators" (e.g. travel agents). On the other hand, new information technologies and especially communication networks are developed or refined respectively. Electronic networks, a buzzword just a few years ago, form important information channels which more and more organizations use to support their needs of information exchange. However, tourist organizations are still not making full use of the possibilities electronic networks offer, except for computer reservation systems and some promising approaches to regional information exchange (e.g. TIS [9]). The customer - or the customer-to-be - is still not very much integrated into the tourist communication network. The application of electronic networks could improve customer closeness by offering a fast, cheap, structured, two-way, directly influenceable and independent information channel.

2 Research Design

The aims of this paper are:

- to investigate some of the most promising electronic networks which are closer to the customer as traditional tourist networks like the well-known computer reservation systems;
- to critically reflect the potentials when applying these technologies;

[1]In this paper the terms "information" and "data" are used synonymously. For a detailed investigation of the meaning of these terms see [15].

- using live examples in order to outline the possibilities of these technologies with respect to the improvement of customer closeness in the field of tourism;
- to give a set of recommendations for tourist organizations that cover the step-by-step development of profitable future applications of electronic networks.

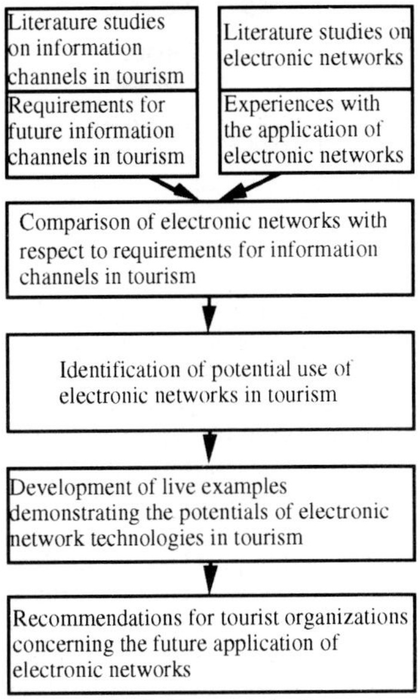

Fig. 1. Research design

Figure 1 describes the procedure the authors apply to achieve these aims.

The comparison of electronic network technologies requires literature studies, experiences with the use of electronic networks and the identification of requirements for future information channels in tourism. In a next step possible application fields are identified. For these application fields some live examples - partly existing, partly developed by the authors - are used to demonstrate the potentials of electronic networks in tourism.

Considering these potentials and the rapid growth of electronic networks, it is obvious that tourist organizations are facing new challenges. The recommendations outline what tourist organizations can do to cope with these challenges.

3 Electronic Networks

A few clarifications of the terms used below are necessary. Electronic network technologies can be divided into three stacked layers named basic, net and information technologies. The services concerning these layers are offered by PTTs[2] (basic technologies), service providers (net technologies), and information providers (information technologies) respectively. In this context tourist organizations would act as information providers.

3.1 Basic Technologies

The basis of all electronic networks are analog or digital telephone lines supplied by the PTTs. Wireless communication networks are a recent addition. While these all can be used for electronic networks, the future points clearly to digital lines which yield more bandwidth and are more reliable than analog ones. Data grade telephone lines are much cheaper in the US than in Europe [26] which is why a lot of developments in this area are first to be seen overseas.

---

[2] PTT=Postal, Telephone and Telegraph company

3.2 Net Technologies

The net technologies provide the framework for the electronic networks. You have to sign a contract with a service provider to participate in electronic networks either as a user or as an information provider. At present there are 3 main traits of net technologies. They will be outlined below together with a short glimpse into a possible future development.

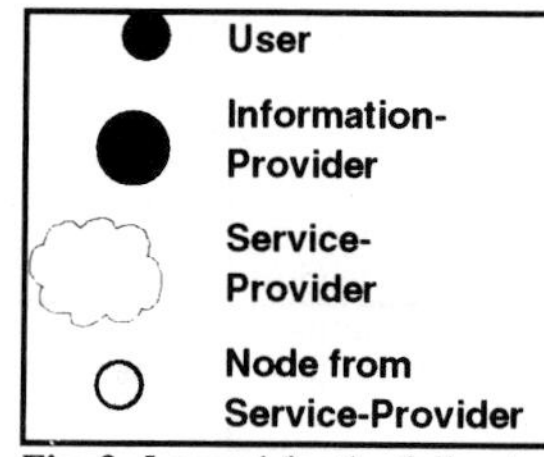

Fig. 2. Legend for the following graphs

Datex-J, Minitel and similar services: These systems are provided by the national PTTs. Therefore they have only national distribution as opposed to the international systems below.

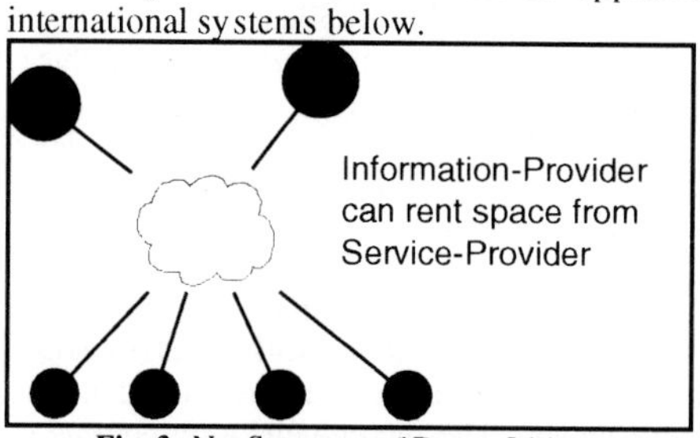

Fig. 3. Net Structure of Datex-J-like nets

In France the Minitel system has gained a significant number of users (more than 6 million [6]) while in other countries the progress is slow [5]. The cost for the users is low (starting with TV set enhancements); the cost for the information providers is middle. One major problem is the low bandwidth which makes these systems unsuitable for multimedia applications. That is why only few sophisticated information technologies are available on these systems. A major advantage for business use is the possibility to charge users. The amount is collected by the PTTs from the users and credited to the information providers.

CompuServe (CIS), Amerika Online (AOL), Prodigy, GENIE, etc. These systems are somewhat oversized Bulletin Board Systems (BBS) which have achieved nationwide or even international coverage. The companies running these systems are privately owned. They function mainly as service providers while also offering some information services themselves. They have attained a large number of users (CompuServe on its own has over 2 million users in 120 countries [3]), albeit mainly in the US. The problem of the low bandwidth as with Datex-J plagues these systems, too, although there are systems like AOL which have some multimedia capability.

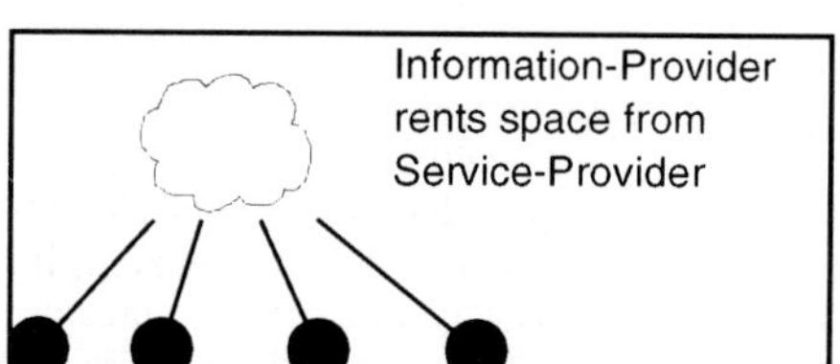

Fig. 4. Net Structure of CompuServe and similar Nets

The cost for the users are medium (a sub standard PC with a modem is sufficient) as they are for the information providers. Charging users is possible similar to Datex-J. The companies have started establishing gateways back and forth to the Internet. (see [4] as an example) Thus the destinction with regard to net technologies made here is beginning to blur.

Internet. The Internet is a large international network, which has already proven its great flexibility in the past.

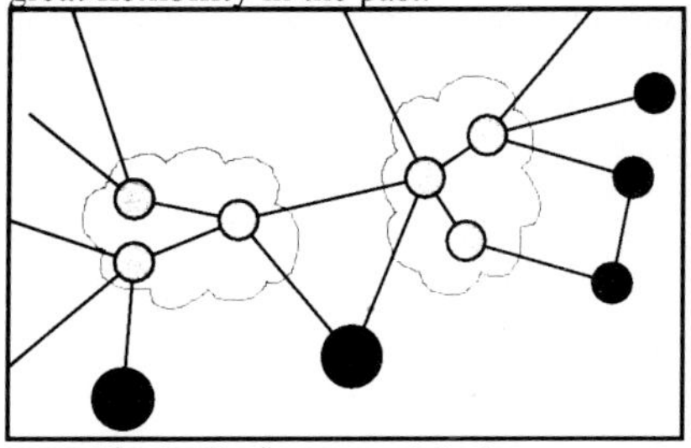

Fig. 5. Net Structure of the Internet

Its rapid development considering the number of hosts over the past few years is depicted in figure 6. Behind a host there can be from one to several hundred users, so the number of users is estimated as well over 20 million people worldwide today (see [19], p. xxi). Although the Internet has its roots in a university background the vast growth in the last years is due to the commercial area. In most countries there are several competing service providers (see [23], pp. 14-17 for a list of providers in Germany) which are connected with one another.

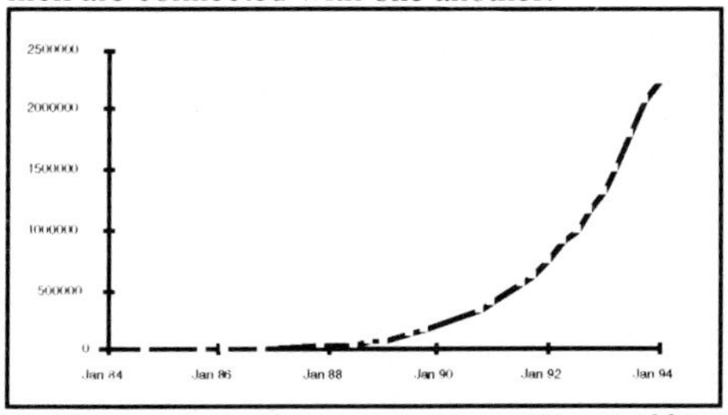

Fig. 6. Internet Growth (Number of Hosts) [22]

Bandwidth in Internet is merely a question of money as bandwidth up to several MBit/sec and more is easily available. The cost for the users is higher compared to the previous two examples, a fully equipped PC is necessary. However, the same configuration could serve as a starting point for an information provider, so cost on this side is low. Of course when offering large sophisticated multimedia applications to lots of users the equivalent computing power (e.g. UNIX machines) is necessary. Also there is no buerocratic hassle with the service providers when someone wants to act as an information provider. Instead you simply connect and start to offer. The Internet has now a wealth of information technologies available ranging from primitive file transfer protocols to sophisticated multimedia interactive protocols. The problems of the Internet at present are missing authentication and authorization mechanisms; charging and money-transfer schemes still are only in development [8,20].

Information Highway ("InfoBahn"). The Information Highway is a yet to be network linking private homes to a wide range of information providers (e.g. video rental stores, home delivery agencies, or newspapers). Some articles on this topic can be found in the BYTE March 94 edition.

It is promoted by a number of influential groups including the U.S. government. U.S. vice president Al Gore calls it "a network of networks" ([17], p. 46). Its net providers are supposed to be PTTs and cable TV companies, possibly under government control or supervision. Its protocols could be extensions of protocols used on the Internet today. On the user side a "set top box" on top of the TV would be the equipment necessary. These devices will be mass produced so they will be cheap. On the information provider side the necessary equipment will be similar to the Internet. The main new information technology will be video-on-demand which is kind of hybrid of video rental stores and pay-TV. Also the above mentioned problems of the Internet are supposed to be solved on the "Information Highway". The innovations in this area come mainly from the U.S. Therefore it is important to carefully watch these developments in order not to leave an important information channel exclusively in the hands of U.S. companies.

The main points regarding the net technologies are:

Table 1. Overview of net technologies

	BTX, et al.	CompuServe, et al.	Internet	Information Highway
Structure	central	central	distributed	distributed
Target audience	everybody	everybody	everybody*	everybody
Number of users	low to middle	middle	high	very high
Bandwidth	low	middle	high	very high
Cost for user	low	middle	high	low
Cost transparency	high	middle	low	?
Cost for supplier	high	middle	low to middle	low to high
Richness of info-technologies	low	low	high	very high
Multimedia	no	yes	yes	yes, even Video
Authentication	yes	yes	no	likely
Authorization	yes	yes	no	likely
Billing thorugh the service	yes	yes	no	likely

* in the past: Universities and Research centers

3.3 Information Technologies

The information technologies outlined below are taken from the Internet, as these are believed to be the models for future developments like the Information Highway. More detailed information can be found in [21, 13, 23].

Electronic Mail. With Electronic Mail one can write letters which will be delivered in seconds to the mailbox of the adressees. The recipients can retrieve them any time they wish to do so. In addition to simple letters multimedia documents can be sent, too. Cryptographic protocols already in use make it possible to encrypt messages and to verify the identity of the sender [27,28]. Having a list of E-Mail adresses one can easily send a letter to all members of the list with the push of a button, although the sending of unsolicitated mail is strongly discouraged on the Internet.

Newsgroups. Whereas Electronic Mail mainly supports one-to-one communication, newsgroups focus on many-to-many communication. In newsgroups the users can post questions or offer opinions, to which other people will respond. All communication is seen by all people participating. In order not to yield a babylonian confusion the newsgroups are divided into subject categories which are structured hierachically. Examples from the recreation subtree are "rec.climbing", "rec.travel", "rec.travel.marketplace", and "rec.travel.air".

Information servers. These servers act in a passive manner providing text, graphics, etc. to the people contacting them. For tourist companies they are the most interesting form of participation in electronic networks. There exist several different forms, which are detailed below.

a) **Passive Servers**: The relevant entries here are Gopher and World Wide Web (WWW). They both can provide text, graphics, film clips and all sorts of multimedia documents. For both graphical interfaces are available.

Gopher builds on a hierarchical information model ("tree") starting from an entry point just like hierarchical file systems.
Most servers provide links to other servers, so one starting entry could be enough. However, it is likely that users will collect their own set of "bookmarks" in the Gopher tree over the time. WWW uses the hypertext model. The information is provided in pages which can contain text, graphics (even embedded or inline), movies, etc. and links to other pages. These links are specially marked areas of text or graphics. With this model catalogs, maps, texts with references, etc. can easily be provided. The links can point to pages on other WWW servers or even to servers of other kinds such as Gopher (see above), FTP (File Transfer Protocol) Servers, WAIS (see below), etc. "Bookmarks" are available in the WWW, too.
b) **Database Server**: WAIS (Wide Area Information Server) are free text databases which can be queried with simple as well as complex search terms. Additionally already found documents can be included in the query with a hint to look up "similar" documents. For WAIS graphical frontends also are available.
c) **Interactive Server**: As a new development WWW provides a capability called "Forms". Using this addition, Graphical User Interface (GUI) elements such as text entry, buttons, check boxes, radio buttons, and drop-down-lists can be added to WWW pages. When the user pushes a submit button the server reads the user entries and decides on further actions e.g. recording the order, doing a complex search etc. Secure communication methods are developed in order to make the transmission of these user entries crytographically secure [11,18]. So critical pieces of information as credit card numbers can be sent, too.
d)**Value-added Servers** (e.g. intelligent agents, information brokers): The servers presented above could be further enhanced by intelligent agents which guide the user to additional entries he or she might be interested in, too. They could also provide help with entering appropriate values in forms ("Intelligent Help").
Apart from that special servers ("Information Brokers") could be developed which provide a frontend to other servers in order to refine and select the information from these servers.

4 Application in Tourism

The Target Audience/Time-Matrix is shown in figure 7. It is used to compare some well-known information and communication systems used in tourism with the above mentioned electronic networks. The systems are classified using the target audience and the phase of the communication with respect to the decision process of the customer. The target audience is divided into two groups: the tourist organizations and the tourists. The time-axis covers only the pre-holiday phase. Once the tourist has departed for the holiday resort, different types of information and communication systems are needed which are not addressed in this paper. The pre-holiday phase is divided into two parts: the pre-decisional and the post-decisional part.

4.1 Target Audience

Common information and communication systems in tourism (e.g. computer reservation systems like Sabre, Amadeus, Galileo, see [10,12]) traditionally address tourist organizations. The information providers are most often airlines, railway companies, travel organizers and the like. Travel agencies are the communication mediators between these tourist organizations and the customers. The tourist is not able to use these systems.

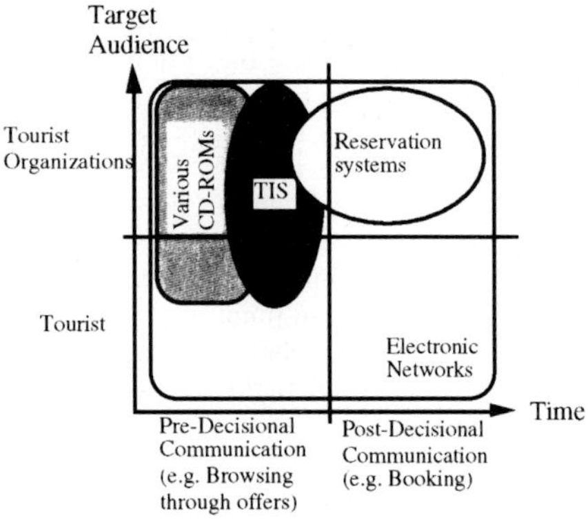

Fig. 7. The Target Audience/Time-Matrix

Recently, many local tourist organizations have begun to establish information channels that are closer to the customer. Examples are TIS and various CD-ROMs. However, these systems still mainly focus on supporting tourist organizations. Nevertheless, some companies, especially those running computer reservation systems, make attempts to extend their target audience to corporate clients (e.g. to support business travel needs) and to private customers respectively. Examples for these systems are SWISSLINE, START/Btx [25]. Furthermore the integration of multimedia and database information directly from elementary service suppliers are prime requirements for the extension of the target audience (this is a focus of already existing research projects e.g. the TIM-project [7]).

But unlike traditional tourist information systems various new systems (e.g. TIS) are already accessible to the customer and to all different kinds of tourist organizations (e.g. accomodation companies, camping sites, car rental companies, cultural organizations, leisure associations and organizations, restaurants, tourist centers, travel agencies and organizers, weather bureaus [14]) assuming that they are equipped with the necessary information and communication technologies. As opposed to these systems, the target audience of electronic networks consists of both groups, tourists and tourist organizations. In the near future the use of electronic networks will be affordable for almost anybody. The focus of this paper will be electronic networks that support the tourist as the target audience.

4.2 Time

The tourist market transaction is divided into two phases with regard to the decision process of the tourist: the pre-decisional and the post decisional phase. In the pre-decisional part the tourist needs information about the different holiday resorts (e.g. hotels, facilities, climate, general information, prices). In the post-decisional phase the tourist wants to book tourist services (e.g. flights, hotels, rental cars). Traditional reservation systems provide some of the information needed in the pre-decisional phase (e.g. prices, booking situation), but the emphasis is on the post-decisional communication (e.g. on-line booking).

As far as the pre-holiday phase is concerned regional information and communication systems only support pre-decisional communication (e.g. facilities provided, snow reports, booking situation). Moreover, these systems have only local (or nationwide) influence. Outside this area these systems are not accessible to the customer. Travel agencies are called in as communication mediators between tourist organizations and the customers. CD-ROMs address pre-decisional information needs as well, but in a more general manner (e.g. information about culture, landscape, activities).

Electronic networks are supposed to support both phases, the pre-decisional and the post-decisional phase. The communication between tourist organizations and tourists could be much closer than with the systems mentioned above. In the following, both, the pre- and the post-decisional communication support will be investigated in detail.

Pre-Decisional Communication. The tourist companies providing information can be divided into: (elementary) service suppliers, package producers (tour operators), travel agencies, local/ regional tourist offices [25].

From a structural point of view elementary service suppliers are a number of small companies (especially family businesses) and a few big companies (e.g. hotel chains). Therefore it is not surprising that the largest part of the information flow between elementary service suppliers and tourists (as the customers of the service suppliers) is mediated by package producers, travel agencies, and local or regional tourist organizations. The shift to a more direct form of communication between tourists and elementary service suppliers via electronic networks will result in remarkable changes for the business of travel agencies [1,16]. Furthermore as the tourist industry handles non-stockable goods (e.g. hotel-beds, flight seats) time is a critical factor in this business. For these reasons the tourist industry is characterized as being highly information intensive [25]; tourism is information business [24].

In the pre-decisional phase of the communication process the information needed by the tourist can be divided into static and dynamic information. In the following some examples are listed most of which can be found in electronic networks:
Static information needs:
- (general) information about the area in which the tourist wants to spend his or her holidays on different levels, e.g. geography, health/hygiene; history; people; transportation facilites etc. on the following levels: continent, country (and surrounding countries), state, region, city;
- general offers (from elementary service suppliers, package producers and so on, updated e.g. each season).

Dynamic information (and communication) needs:
- news (country, region, city), special events, current booking situation (considering the country as a whole, regions, cities), political situation, information about trouble spots (e.g. earthquake, floods);
- special offers (e.g. last minute offers);
- "cascade proposing": offers to support the tourists browsing through offers (e.g. when considering Australia, why not take a side trip to New Zealand);
- detailed individual information needs which cannot be foreseen and therefore need communication between the tourist and elementary service suppliers, package producers (tour operators), travel agencies and/or local/regional tourist organizations.

Post-Decisional Communication. The pre-decisional information flow is directed basically from tourist organizations to tourists (or tourists-to-be), except for individual questions which result in bi-directional communication needs. However, after the tourist has decided the information flow turns into a truly bi-directional one. The following functions are necessary to complete the tourist market transaction:

- **negotiation**: potential transaction partners are to be contacted; if not fixed conditions must be agreed upon;
- **booking**: the tourist services chosen and the tourists name, address and signature have to be transmitted to the transaction partners;
- **ticket transmission**: tickets (e.g. airline, railway, hotel voucher) have to be sent to the tourist);
- "**cascade selling**": additional offers could be presented (a function equivalent to "cascade proposing" in the pre-decisional communication phase);
- **payment**: the services have to be paid in advance in full or on account or at least the tourists credit card details has to be transmitted;
- transaction partners have to react to further **individual questions** or additional desires;
- further **individual information material** has to be sent to the tourists (e.g. travel routes, compiled information about special events in the resort chosen);
- **follow-up-activities**: the tourist can get individual compiled tourist information about the countries, states, regions or cities he or she is interested in.

These examples show the wide technical variety of different information flows a tourist market transaction triggers. There are technical, legal and social problems which have to be solved before these functions can be shifted to electronic networks like the Internet or the Information Highway whereas on Datex-J and CompuServe the technical problems seem to be solved already. Technical problems refer to booking and to payment: user authentication and credit rating are much more difficult to handle on decentralized electronic networks with public access (e.g. Internet) than they are on closed networks (e.g. automated teller machines in banking) or on centralized networks (e.g. Datex-J) respectively.

The payment problem creates further research needs to clarify legal problems e.g. with regard to safety issues of electronic currency. However, there are a lot of technologies in development which claim to establish safe electronic payment (e.g. DigiCash/ecash, NetCash and the like [8,20]). Social problems can be foreseen especially in the negotiation process. Today a lot of people simply refuse to negotiate with a computer. However, electronic networks can be seen as an additional communication channel which can be used by those people who are willing or even eager to accept this new form of negotiation.

Electronic networks are **ubiquitous** (7 days/week, 24 hours/day to any user anywhere in the world assuming access to a telecommunication network), **fast** (considering response time), **bi-directional** "media". Therefore electronic networks are suited much better for the dynamic part of the information needs than traditional tourist media (e.g. catalogues). However, the dynamic information often is needed while browsing through static information material. Therefore both, the static and the dynamic information should be provided together in one (electronic) media. However, today most of the tourist information provided in electronic networks is static. For this reason, the tourist companies using electronic networks cannot make a profit out of the advantages of this medium right now. The emphasis should be laid more on the dynamic part of the pre-decisional information needs.

5 Examples

The following examples show some already existing tourist applications in the Internet (for a detailed investigation in commercial applications see [22]).

5.1 Pre-Decisional Communication between Tourist Organizations and Tourists

A WWW-form is shown in figure 8 where a potential tourist to Nova Scotia can order printed information if the electronically provided information (from the other pages of this WWW-server) is not sufficient. As depicted in figure 9 a business tourist looking for accomodation can see the offerings of a hotel chain. He or she can take a look at the interieur of the hotel and can get information on the locations of all the hotels of the chain. Note that the tourist can navigate to a reservation page, too.

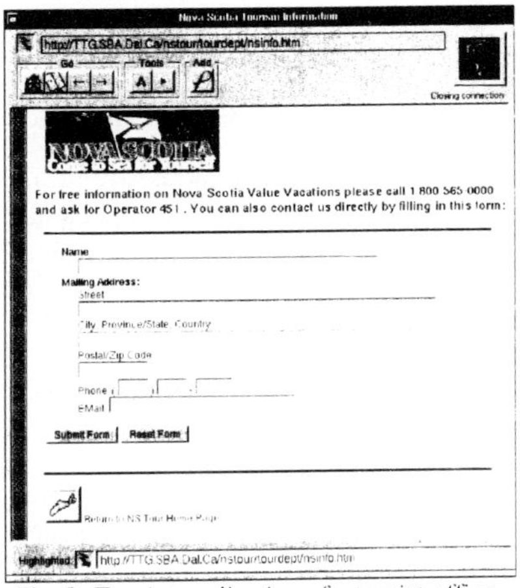

Fig. 8. Tourist application of a tourist office in Canada (source: http://TTG. SBA.Dal.Ca/nstour/tourdept/nsinfo.htm)

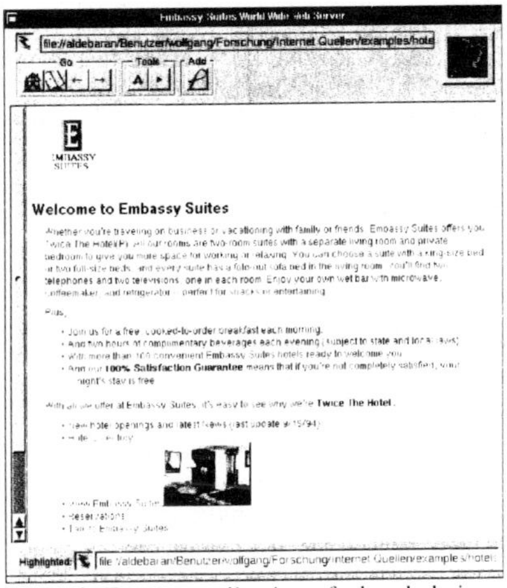

Fig. 9. Tourist application of a hotel chain (source: URL: htty://www.promus. com/embassy.html

5.2 Post-Decisional Communication between Tourist Organizations and Tourists

Figure 10 shows a page from AOL which enables a tourist to locate golf courses in the vicinity of his or her previously chosen holiday resort.

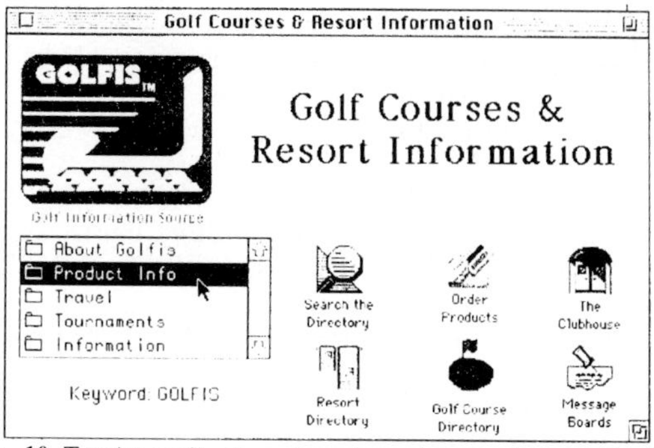

Fig. 10. Tourist application of an elementary service supplier [2]

6 Recommendations and Conclusion

In the following the authors provide some recommendations to tourist organizations concerning the challenges of electronic networks:

- Watch the technological, social, organizational and legal developments in products and services with regard to electronic networks carefully. The US-market needs special attention because at the moment the main innovations take place there.
- In order to accomplish this provide a member of your staff with access to the above mentioned electronic networks. Through the use of these systems know-how is gained. Moreover it will be easier to develop special expertise in implementing tourist applications because quite a lot of discussion takes place in these networks (e.g. in newsgroups like comp.infosystems.www.providers and in discussion lists like inet-marketing@einet.net).
- In a further step you can "test the water" by building a prototype application and measure the response from the customers. You can do thi s by yourself or you can contract it out to professional consultants (see the last paragraph of chapter 4).
- Electronic networks add a new possiblity to the traditional marketing instruments. Therefore you will have to re-arrange your individual combinations of marketing instruments (marketing-mix).

Because of the structure of the tourist industry not all tourist organizations can adhere to these recommendations. The big organizations (e.g. travel organizers, hotel chains) certainly do (or will do). Nevertheless, the smaller organizations need to gather information about the new challenges to avoid being pushed out of the market. As they might not be able (or willing) to cope with the additional costs of establishing these new services, they should cooperate to fulfill the above mentioned tasks (e.g. via tourist offices, associations or boards).

As there are already tourist organizations which react to the challenges of electronic networks, these challenges are real and the opportunities are enormous. Tourist organizations have to respond to them in one way or another.

Bibliography

1. Author unknown: Tourismus - Direkter Zugriff, in: Der Spiegel 9/1994, Hamburg 1994, 139-142
2. Author unknown: America Online, in: Internet Business Advantage - Online Solutions for Business Success, 3/1994, Colonial Village Lane (USA) 1994
3. Author unknown: CompuServe Overview, URL: http://www.compuserve.com/cserve_overview.html
4. Author unknown: CompuServce Overview, URL: http://www.compuserve.com/isd/press_release/enhanced_inet.html
5. Author unknown:Bildschirmtext: Aufschwung kommt nach zehn Jahren, SZ - Süddeutsche Zeitung, 22.02.1994, 24
6. Brasler, M.: Race for knowledge on super-highway, UK Times, 25.07.1994, 25
7. Byerley, P., Ewers, J., Entner, H.: Das TIM-Projekt: Gesamteuropäisches Direktmarketing im Tourismusbereich, in: Schertler, W. (ed.): Tourismus als Informationsgeschäft, Wien 1994, 347-388
8. Digicash Press Release: World's first electronic cash payment over computer networks, Amsterdam, 17.05.1994
9. Ebner, A.: TIS - Tourism Information System for the Tyrol, in: Schertler, W. et al. (ed.): Information and Communication Technologies in Tourism, Wien 1994, 35-42
10. Ellis M. A.: Elektronische Reservationssysteme, in: Newsletter des Kompetenzzentrums Elektronische Märkte, 3/1992, St. Gallen 1992, 1-2
11. Hallam-Baker, P. M.: Shen: A Security Scheme for the World Wide Web, URL: http://info.cern.ch/hypertext/WWW/Shen/ref/shen.html, 1994
12. Kropp, W.: Elektronische Reisevertriebssysteme: Von der Strichliste zum Global Ring, in: Roth, P., Schrand, A.: Touristik-Marketing, München 1992, 29-44
13. Maier, G., Wildberger, A.: In 8 Sekunden um die Welt, Bonn 1994
14. Maier, R., Galler, J.: Scenarios for CSCW Applications in Tourism, in: Schertler, W. et al. (ed.): Information and Communication Technologies in Tourism, Wien 1994, 186-194
15. Maier, R., Lehner, F.: Towards a New Perception of Data, Information and Knowledge, Research paper no. 16, The Koblenz School of Corporate Management, 1994
16. Mingay, L.: The TIM-System: Impact on Travel Agency, in: Schertler, W. (ed.): Tourismus als Informationsgeschäft, Wien 1994, 451-470
17. Reinhardt, A.: Building the Data Highway, in: BYTE, 3/1994, 46-74
18. Rescorla, E., Schiffman, A.: The Secure HyperText Transfer Protocol, URL: http://www.eit.com/projects/s-http/shttp.txt, June 1994
19. Resnick, R., Taylor, D.: The Internet Business Guide, Indianapolis, USA, 1994
20. Rickard, J.: NETCASH - Online Pocket Change, in: Boardwatch Magazine, 7/1994, 60
21. Röckelein, W.: Internet-Anschluß - Internet-Dienste, in: Signale 3/1993, Vallendar 1993, 39-40
22. Röckelein, W.: Neue Marketingmöglichkeiten in elektronischen Netzen, Research paper of the institute of business informatics, The Koblenz School of Corporate Management, 1994
23. Scheller, M., Boden, K.-P., Geenen, A., Kampermann, J.: Internet: Werkzeuge und Dienste, Berlin 1994
24. Schertler, W.: Dienstleistungseigenschaften begründen Informationsgeschäfte - dargestellt an Tourismusdienstleistungen, in: Schertler, W. (ed.): Tourismus als Informationsgeschäft, Wien 1994, 17-42
25. Schmid, B.: Electronic Markets in Tourism, in: Schertler, W. et al. (ed.): Information and Communication Technologies in Tourism, Wien 1994, 1-8
26. Schneider, M.: Auf dem Weg in eine vernetzte Welt, SZ - Süddeutsche Zeitung, Wissenschaftsteil, 08.09.1994
27. Stallings, W.: Pretty Good Privacy, BYTE 7/1994, 193-196
28. Stallings, W.: Protect Your Privacy: The PGP User's Guide, 1994

Designing an interactive telematic system for small businesses and private households

Christoph Kuhn

Institute for Information Management, University of St. Gallen, Switzerland

Abstract. This paper presents the critical success factors for interactive telematic systems for small businesses and private households - both playing an important role also in the tourist industry. Introducing a system archictecture the technical, economical and organizational aspects of existing telematic systems are analyzed. The architectural concepts are founded on an empirical basis by implementation in a prototype using commercially available low-cost hard-and software components on the end-user side. The final goal is to outline a system which supports and combines all three phases of market transactions of electronic markets (EMs), hence linking the private customer into the electronic data exchange chain.

1 Introduction

Computer technology has reached the point where it is a commodity. The number of PCs in private households is growing steadily. This fact is underlined by a press release by Intel Corp., where they predict the annual sale of PC's to be larger than the sale of TVs in the near future [1]. Besides the declining costs in hard- and software, wide area networking is now also penetrating into the sectors of small businesses and private households. The recent pace and dimension of the prevalence of telematic systems is also due to government driven programs, like the National Information Infrastructure (NII) project in the USA.

Another issue is the growing popularity of the Internet. The Internet has now become a platform for wide area networking for commercial purposes and for private users through various Internet access providers. The announcements from Microsoft to bundle the TCP/IP protocol stack with their new release of MS-Windows make the internet services easy to use also for users running a PC.

In Europe, the fact that an advanced national information technology infrastructure can provide a competitive advantage for the countries that develop it as well as for the companies that operate in those countries has already been recognized around 1980, especially in France [2]. The first programs emerging from those strategic plans were the design and implementation of interactive telematic services based on the Videotex architecture [3]. Now, more than a decade later, some of those systems are undertaking a major organizational and technical redesign in order to fulfill altered demands of their participants. In Switzerland no changes have been made to the national Videotex system despite of the stagnation of growth in terms of services and users and a predicted profit loss for 1994 [14].

2 Home interactive telematic systems

In comparison to interorganizational systems (IOS) which are used by business partners in a professional way [5], a new class of system must be recognized named 'extra-organizational systems' [6]. Here attention is directed to *home interactive telematic* (HIT) systems [9], a subclass of the extra-organizational systems. Such systems differ in many aspects from classical IOS. Two major aspects are:

- One or more commercial organizations cooperate with other entities that are small enterprises or private households.
- The system is open concerning the participants.

2.1 The HIT system in the context of Electronic Markets

Following the definition by Schmid in [8] EMs in the *narrow sense* are '*market places put into action by means of telematics. They support all phases of market inter-transaction (information gathering, negotiation, settlement), including the formulation of prices for goods and services.*'

A HIT system is a subclass of an EM whereby

- the (end)-user is mostly a private household or a small business
- many suppliers interact with many users
- the supplier is a large or a small business
- professionals and non-professionals interact
- the system is conceptually open to anyone (in contrast to special EMs like stock markets, where only specialized users interact).

3 The system architecture

The system architecture comprises of a layer model which is used to analyze the functionality of the system and the organizational model describing the different participants (actors) in the system.

The underlying idea is to facilitate the design of new (or the redesign of existing) HIT systems [11]. The decomposition of functionality into the four layers allows an easy and flexible way of composition for new HIT applications. Applications and services of the various layers can be used as building blocks. The organizational view maps the different functions to the system participants.

3.1 The Layer Model

The layer model segregates the functionality into different hierarchical layers. Each layer represents a set of functions which generate added value to the layer above. Thus the top layers are closer to the user and are at the end of a value chain, whereas the lower layers perform basic tasks with a smaller value per unit. However, this layering resembles the layering model introduced by ISO-OSI to a certain extend: Applications are on the highest level while the hardware oriented layers mark the lower levels.

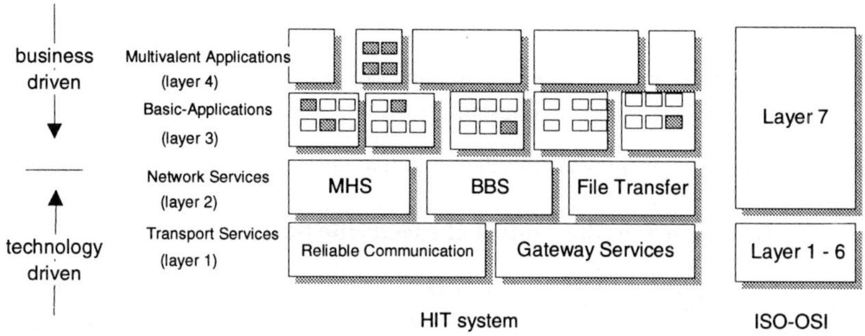

Fig 1. Layers of the HIT system architecture in comparison with the ISO-OSI layering (best fit basis)

3.1.1 Multivalent applications

In a HIT system the user has access to a vast array of electronic services which are provided by many individual suppliers. Theses services are assembled to *multivalent applications* of the HIT system and can be grouped into sets called *teleservices*, like telebanking, teleshopping, tele-entertainment, etc. The union of all the teleservices form a virtual *telemall.* In this context the individual service (multivalent application) is a shop in the telemall.

Multivalent applications ideally support the user through all phases of the market transaction. Sophisticated multivalent applications are emerging on the Internet based *Commerce Net.* Simple forms already exist in various telematic systems, like Videotex. There the settlement is done by charging the user's Videotex-account.

3.1.2 Basic applications

The basic applications provide their services to the multivalent applications. Typical applications in this layer are components of telebanking applications, e.g. electronic fund transfer, or airline reservation systems. However basic applications are also used directly by the end-user but in most cases they only support one phase of the market transaction.

3.1.3 Network services

The next layer consists of network services. These services enable reliable and secure data transportation and are generic and application independent. Furthermore services for data conversion are provided as well.

Typical network services are message handling systems (MHS), i.e. e-mail (inter-personal and inter-application), file-transfer, bulletin board systems (BBS) etc. But also services like WWW or Gopher which themselves comprise of different network-services. An important service provided by this layer are the security services (integrity, confidentiality, non-repudiation of origin, authentication).

3.1.4 Communication networks

Today's networking environment is heterogeneous. Different computers ranging from PCs to mainframes which are grouped into various sub-networks are connected through gateways, running off different network topologies and using different network protocols for communication. To circumvent this problem the *communication network* layer is introduced. The basic functionality is therefore to offer a reliable exchange of data between geographically distributed users within the system. Typical services are gateways, packet switched networking, protocol conversions (e.g. TCP/IP to X.25), high capacity lines, etc.

3.2 The organizational model

The organizational model describes the interaction between the participants in a HIT system. In order to allow small businesses to offer services on the one side and to enable the system to support all phases of the market transaction on the other side the concept of roles played by actors (participants) is introduced. Depending on the phase of the market transaction or the kind of service a participant offers, he must be able to switch roles. The three fundamental roles are those of the supplier, the intermediary and the user (customer).

3.2.1 The supplier and the user

The suppliers produce and offer goods and services to various customers in the system. The basic feature is that suppliers sell to customers which consume the services. Like suppliers who acquire goods and services to complete their products customers also resell goods. The HIT system must therefore enable a participant to act as supplier and as a user regardless of the economical size and type of business of the participant. The supplier offers it's services through multivalent applications and basic applications to the users.

3.2.2 The intermediary

For many reasons it is beneficiary for the user to interact with the supplier through an intermediary. The intermediary can provide services to both sides (user, supplier) in various forms which have a fundamental impact on the organization of the HIT system.

Intermediaries providing services on layer 1 and 2 are VANS (Value added Network Services) or VAS (Value Added Services). In this context clearing centers are also considered intermediaries.

On the layer 3 and 4 the functionality is more market-oriented: An intermediary can either act as a trader or broker between supplier and user or he can provide 'showroom' to the suppliers and group suppliers into categories, hence acting as a virtual mall. The latter role of the intermediary is very common for existing systems, especially those whose target market is in the domain of private users (e.g. Videotex, CompuServe, Prodigy) whereas the former versions of intermediaries which actually procure services is currently only implemented in special systems, e.g. FAST [12].

3.3 The design of HIT applications

The applications in the HIT system denote the users interface to the system as such and to a specific supplier. First of all, a supplier must be aware that his service must be integrable into the market transactions and secondly the service must be integrable by an intermediary, e.g. a virtual mall.

3.3.1 User interface

The user-interface does not only provide access to the application functionality in an ergonomically way it also reflects the identity of the supplier by showing corporate logos or characteristic layout features. However, suppliers must consider the path the user takes to access their service. Providing a unique user interface may contribute towards corporate identity. On the other hand, if the service is offered together with other services to the user through an intermediary, all services offered by the intermediary must adhere to the same look and feel in order to provide a consistent interface to the users. Unless the supplier cannot do without a special user-interface he should offer the services through an application protocol.

3.3.2 Application protocols

Application protocols define communication between user and supplier in a machine readable form. In an environment where the user accesses the services through a terminal (e.g. Videotex) the communication protocol between the two parties consist of an application independent protocol which carries visual information from the supplier (host) to the user (terminal) and keystrokes from the user to the supplier. In order to facilitate the processing of the data transferred from supplier to user it is preferable to use a specific application dependent protocol, e.g. UN/EDIFACT. This relieves the supplier from the chore of user-interface design and therefore he can offer his service to a broader clientele. In the case of telebanking for instance, the supplier (bank) can handle with the same suit of application protocols (PAYORD, DEBADV, CREDADV, etc.) retail and wholesale customers.

3.3.3 Component-Ware

From the users point of view, a HIT application is one amongst many applications he runs. Therefore the HIT application must be integrable with the existing software environment the user utilizes. Another side-effect of the integration is enabling the user to process the data from the HIT application in an enhanced way. In the case of telebanking, the user can add a cash management program as an *add-on component* to the telebanking software. The add-on software interacts with the HIT application through well defined application specific interfaces (e.g. DLL, DDE under MS-Windows). This way the user can create additional value to services provided by the HIT system.

3.3.4 Data security

In a commercial environment, data security is a prerequisite, especially when financial transactions are processed. Since the security requirements differ depending on the kind of service a parameterizable security service is desirable. Most of the existing HIT systems, e.g. Videotex, CompuServe, Prodigy, offer identification and authentication services but in first place for the accounting of their own services. None of the systems offers data encryption, probably because they were originally based on a terminal-host design. Future HIT systems must enable arbitrary trusted third parties to offer their services.

3.3.5 Client-server architecture

In order to fulfill the demands imposed on a HIT application it is advantageous to split the application into a client component and a server component. The client component is in charge with user-related features, i.e. application control, user-interface, etc., whereas the server component residing on the supplier-side provides the core functionality. The way client and server interact depends heavily on the design of the application protocol. The more application specific semantic is introduced into the protocol the more autonomy the client component gains. A well designed client-server HIT application minimizes communication costs by delegating a lot of functionality to the client.

3.4 System agility

The system agility describes how quick a HIT system can adapt to new changes in the environment. There are two diametrical facts which determine the system agility: standardization versus competition.

Standardization is a prerequisite for low cost production of goods and services because it contributes to the openness of the system. Therefore it would be most beneficial to build a system only from internationally standardized components. However standards have the inherent problem, that they conflict with competitive advantages and since the formation of (international) standards is a tedious and slow process they might lag considerably behind the demands of the user.

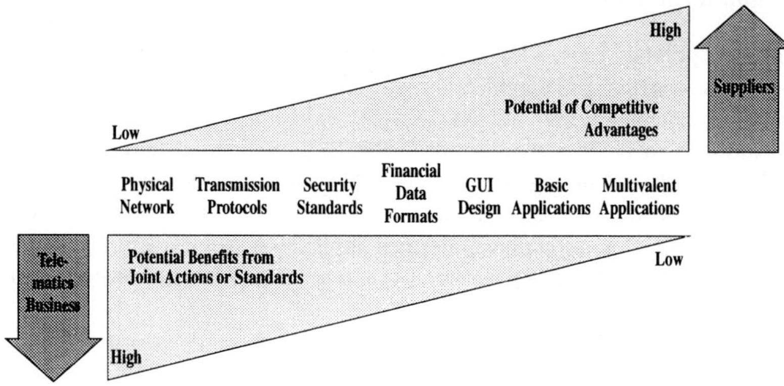

Fig. 2. Potential benefits from standardization (Source: [10]).

Figure 2 depicts the impact of standardization on the layers of the HIT system. As can be seen, standardization of the lower layers is beneficiary for the system, since it contributes to the openness. The enforcement of standards on the topmost layer can conflict with business strategies on the side of the service suppliers. In some cases it can deprive certain suppliers from gaining competitive advantages if the implementation of a new application feature would conflict with the current standard. Standards in the higher layers therefore diminish the system agility whereas standards in the lower layers contribute to the openness of the system.

From the organizational viewpoint an intermediary must have a clear business strategy: The traditional HIT system operators, (e.g. Videotex, CompuServe, Prodigy) provide services on all four levels of the HIT system architecture. In terms of system agility however the requirements of the layers 3 and 4 are business driven, where as the layer 1 and 2 are technology driven. This phenomena caused the Videotex service in Germany, Bildschirmtext, to separate the transport and network services (Datex-J) from the application oriented services.

4 Comparison of existing Systems

The following table compares a selection of existing HIT systems.

Intermediary	Videotex (CH, D, F)	Prodigy (USA)	CompuServe (USA, Europe)	Internet (worldwide)	Teletex (Europe)
Standards	CCITT	proprietary	proprietary	IETF	
Application design	Terminal-Host	Client-Server	Client-Server	Client-Server	Terminal-Host
Transport services					
Terminal access	Yes	No	Yes	Yes	TV
Packet Network	only for suppliers	only for suppliers	suppl. ok, for users Internet w. bandwidth restrictions (9600bps)	Yes	No. broadcasting from suppliers to users
Gateways (transport protocols)	No. Only CCITT protocols supported	Yes	Yes	TCP/IP to X.25	No
Network services					
File Transfer	partially	No	No	Yes	No
MHS (E-Mail)	Yes (proprietary)	Yes (SMTP)	Yes (SMTP)	Yes (MIME)	No
BBS	Yes (proprietary)	Yes	Yes (Forum)	Yes	No
Application support provided by intermediary					
User-Interface					
protocols	CEPT only, no style guide	Proprietary, with style guide	Proprietary / various terminal emul.	HTML (WWW), X-Windows, terminals	TV
System agility	low	limited	limited	high	low
EM features					
Information phase support provided by intermediary	only lists	keyword searching	keyword searching	Gopher, WWW	only lists
EDI support	none	limited	limited	Yes	none
Extensibility	difficult	limited	limited	excellent	none
Participation of users in value chain	low	medium	medium	high	none

Table 1. Comparison of existing HIT systems

5 The TeleCounter: A prototype application for a HIT system

Like in the tourist industry, the telebanking systems offered by the leading banks suffered in terms of compatibility. Especially their user-interfaces and set of terms for equal functions varied significantly from one another. The aim was to design a telebanking application for private users and small businesses using an attractive user-interface providing multi-banking features.

5.1 Implementation

Following the architectural model outlined in chapter 3.3, a prototype for telebanking was implemented. The client-component (the actual TeleCounter application) communicates on the application level via the internationally standardized UN/EDIFACT messages. This enables full multi-banking functionality, like consolidated account statements from different banks. The messages are transmitted to the bank via store and forward using the P_0 guidelines of transmitting UN/EDIFACT through an MHS and peer-to-peer security. Various mail systems (RFC 822, X.400) running off different VANS can be used for communication. Due to the client-server design the user need to be on-line only for the transmission of the UN/EDIFACT messages, thus saving communication costs.

The whole functionality was accessible over an easy-to-use graphical user-interface following the desktop-metaphor. With simple mouse interactions the user could execute payment transactions and produce an account statement tailored to the users personal preferences.

To keep hard-and-software components on the user side as low as possible the operating system of choice was MS-Windows (version 3.1). Add-On applications can interact with the TeleCounter software via Clipboard (Cut-and-Paste), DDE or DLL.

6 The tourist industry

6.1 The status quo

Unfortunately, most of the interactive telematic systems which are predominant in the tourist industry do not follow the system architecture as outlined in chapter 3, despite the fact that most of the businesses in the hotel and catering field have fewer than five employees [4]. The telematic systems are predominated by reservation systems operated by airlines (CRS), car rentals and large hotel chains [8]. The architecture of these systems is very hierarchical: The roles of user, supplier and intermediary is 'hard-coded' into the systems architecture and furthermore the systems are tailored to certain types of services (flight reservation, car rental, etc.). An integration of these systems with a telebanking application or with electronic train schedule software which runs on a PC (HAFAS in Germany, FINAJOUR in Switzerland) is technically difficult, since all information between supplier and user of the CRS is visual (Host-Terminal protocol, e.g. VT-100).

In Switzerland, last minute flights and package-arrangements offered from travel agencies are advertised over the Teletext [3] system. The advantage of this technology is it's availability in private households. Unfortunately this system only broadcasts the information *unidirectional* from intermediary (Teletext-provider) to the user. The user must communicate via telephone with the travel agency (intermediary) in order to make a reservation.

6.2 Potential benefits for small businesses

Like for telebanking, both small businesses and private users can benefit from the HIT application structure. The largest potential lies first of all in the client-server architecture where the client component provides interfaces to third-party add-ons (i.e. add-ons not provided by the supplier).

The new UN/EDIFACT standards (RESRSP, RESREQ, etc.) for reservation systems [13] will allow travel agencies to create multi-branch reservation systems in the way the TeleCounter application enables multi-banking.

7 Conclusions

Toady's HIT systems make a clear distinction between suppliers, intermediaries and users. Although the trend is to move from the terminal host architecture to the client-server metaphor the client component is from the technological viewpoint still tightly coupled with the intermediary and unfortunately, the intermediaries themselves have proprietary standards. This forces user and supplier to participate in more than one system which is very costly for the suppliers since they have to maintain different versions of their application.

One of the largest potentials, i.e. the processing capabilities at the side of the user is poorly exploited by the client software which is usually provided by the intermediary. The latest innovations were focused on new flavors in the graphical user interface and in off-line processing capabilities in order to save communication costs. However, there was little effort made of the level of extensibility and thus the user, i.e. the private households, are not integrated in EDI and therefore not fully linked into an EM at this point of time.

Future systems must allow the private user a more active role in the electronic value chain. Furthermore they must give better support on the level of an intermediary in the meaning of a trader/procurer, e.g. by providing more support in the information phase with market-like coordination mechanisms. A first migration step could be realized with text retrieval facilities which could be later-on complemented by quantitative market-like mechanisms. If intermediaries think they could gain competitive advantage by building fancy proprietary virtual malls instead of diversifying and encouraging the integral support of all phases of an EM they might be doomed to oblivion in the vast and ubiquitous Internet.

Acknowledgments

The author acknowledges the financial support granted for this research project by the Competence Center TeleCounter under the Information Management 2000 program of the University of St. Gallen. I wish to thank Richard Dratva, Paul Mausberg, Hans Meli and Hans-Dieter Zimmermann who helped in discussions leading to this paper and Andreas Göldi for the implementation of the prototype.

References

1. Süddeutsche Zeitung: Bald werden mehr PC als TV-Geräte verkauft. In: Süddeutsche Zeitung 21.7.1994, p. 31.

2. Cats-Baril, W. L., Jelassi T.: The French Videotex System Minitel. In: MIS Quarterly, March 1994.

3. Tanenbaum, A.S.: Computer Networks (2nd ed.) pp. 574. Prentice Hall International, Engelwood Cliffs, N.J. 1988.

4. Ruisz, J.: Change demands on hotel management. In: ENTER 94: Proceedings of the International Conference in Innsbruck, Austria, 1994. Springer-Verlag Wien, 1994.

5. Cash, J.I.; Kosynski, B.R.: IS redraws competitive boundaries. In: Harward Business Review No2/1985.

6. Clarke, R.: Extraorganisational Systems - A challenge to the software engineering paradigm. In: Working paper Australian National University, Canberra, 1992.

8. Schmid, B.: Electronic Markets in Tourism. In: ENTER 94: Proceedings of the International Conference in Innsbruck, Austria, 1994. Springer-Verlag Wien, 1994.

9. Zimmermann, H.-D.: TeleCounter: A case study on integration of private households in telematic systems.

10. Dratva, R.: WWW Based Home Banking in Switzerland. In: Proceedings of the 2nd international WWW, Volume 1. Chicago 1994. URL: HTTP//:www.ncsa.uiuc.edu/SDG/IT94/IT94Info.html

11. Dratva, R.; Kuhn, C.; Mausberg P.; Meli, H.; Zimmermann H-D: Abschlussbericht CC TeleCounter. Working Paper. University of St. Gallen, June 1994

12. Neches, A.-L.: FAST: A Research Project in Electronic Commerce. In: Electronic Markets, No. 9-10, Oct. 1993. University of St. Gallen.

13. Henry Schlieper: Introduction to UN/EDIFACT messages. November 1993; 7th ed. IBM Germany, Stuttgart.

14. Videotex Zeitung 9/91 p. 17: "Dabei muessen wir auch daran gehen, aus dem Viedeotex eine kostendeckende Dienstleistung zu machen. Wir sehen vor, Videotex bis Ende 94 kostendeckend zu gestalten."

Virtual Tourism – a Realistic Assessment of Virtual Reality for the Tourist Industry

Ivor Benjamin & Maggie Cooper

Centre for Human-Computer Interface Design, Department of Business Computing, City University, London EC1V 0HB

Abstract. This paper suggests that the hyperbole of virtual reality goes well beyond its capabilities now, and its likely capabilities in the medium-term future. The practical application of virtual reality centres on its ability to model places, buildings and information in three dimensions. We argue that the commercial use of virtual reality in tourism will be closely linked to developments in the use of broadband telecommunications and tele-media technology for sales and marketing, not as a substitute for travel itself.

1 The Hype – We Can Create It For You, Wholesale

The desire to travel somewhere without the trouble of actually going has long attracted the fantasies of writers and journalists, as well as anyone who has ever waited for hours in a crowded railway or airport terminal. Back in 1966, Philip K. Dick wrote of drug-induced vacations:

> " 'You'll know you went, alright,' he said. 'You won't remember us, won't remember me or ever having been here. It'll be a real trip in your mind; we guarantee that. A full two weeks of recall; every last piddling detail. Remember this: if at any time you doubt that you really took an extensive trip to Mars, you can return here and get a full refund. You see?' " [1]

But it is another technology that is currently engaging our imaginations. The popular press regularly suggest that at some undefined point in the future, tourists will travel the world from the comfort of their living rooms, with the aid of Virtual Reality Machines. Imagine putting on a headset, they say, and experiencing Fall in New England any time of the year, the Northern Lights of Lapland any time of the day or night ... Visit Tahiti – or even Ancient Rome, or Mars ... This is not entirely fanciful, either; the virtual resurrections of Dresden's Frauenkirche (by IBM Germany and the Research Triangle, USA) and the Abbey at Cluny (by Medialab), both now sadly destroyed in the real world, bear testament to the possibilities of virtual reality. And broader political issues have been used to further fuel the hype:

> "But will it be thought wrong to holiday in developing countries ... on the grounds that we are subverting traditional cultures? ... And from

> the tourist's standpoint why queue for hours to visit churches or museums, get crushed in airports, squashed in tourist class and run a real risk of getting stomach trouble, robbed, mugged or worse? The point will be made that with Virtual Reality, you don't need to go anyway." [2]

As the technology behind virtual environments matures, so must the consideration of its applications and the effects they may have. Predictions about the impact of new technologies are strikingly unreliable. Alexander Graham Bell thought that the telephone would prove useful as it would allow people to listen to musical concerts without having to travel great distances; Thomas Edison thought the phonograph, a recording device, would prove useful sending messages to homes from the telegraph office [3]. In fact, their applications are reversed. It must not be assumed that the principal area for concern in the introduction of a new technology is the novelty of the technology itself; of equal importance is how it may be integrated into existing human systems and how it will affect human attitudes.

2 The Reality – It's Almost Working ...

2.1 Virtual Reality and Multimedia

To process a virtual image in enough detail for photo-realism requires more computing power than is currently a marketable proposition. Most commercial virtual reality outside of government-funded research relies on limited resolution, local processing and dedicated programming. This will change, probably faster than we can estimate. Tapscott and Caston predict the convergence of technologies capable of handling distributed virtual reality applications as less than six years away [4]; initiatives for real-time multimedia telecommunication networks across Europe are receiving major funding as we write. The latest UK Department for Trade and Industry report on Telecommunications concludes:

> "In the medium term the plans of the operators suggest that UK infrastructure will continue to develop at a rate to keep it abreast of its competitors. In the longer term much will depend upon the rate of development and adoption of new broadband multimedia applications, and the ability of the operators to continue to keep abreast of developments and provide the infrastructure and services required to support the applications and encourage their ongoing development. There is a view held by some in the [telecommunications] industry that a clearer shared vision of the future would help ensure that the industry was able to do so." [5]

Nevertheless, the requirements for credible virtual worlds lie beyond the medium-term planning of the tourist industry. Where we suggest virtual reality is likely to have its impact over the next decade is in assisting the continued restructuring and re-marketing of tourism.

Currently, multimedia systems are beginning to make the transition from information provision to virtual point-of-sale for tele-shopping. Weintraub International Consulting have developed Interactive Video Sales (IVS) using examples of luxury cruise tours and airline seat sales [6]. Thomas Cook (UK) have pioneered multimedia point-of-sale in a few of their major outlets, though they do not currently allow direct booking. Oracle Ltd. (UK) have already shown prototypes of tele-shopping database systems, including video links to sales personnel, and such systems are already in use the USA. In the context of information provision, the use of virtual reality may be considered as a natural extension to multimedia systems generally, of changing from solely text-based information to the merging of text, images and sound, as media technologies converge. In addition, virtual reality systems offer interactive three-dimensional information to the user in two distinct modes:

- **immersive**, where the user is placed "in the picture" through the use of head-mounted displays (HMD) and three-dimensional sound, and

- **non-immersive**, where the user interacts with the image "through the screen", or in some other way that does not involve sensory substitution.

Both modes require the use of 3D interaction tools. In general, we consider current immersive systems to be of more use in creating a dramatic effect [7]. At present, non-immersive systems are more used for design or demonstration purposes, owing to the limitations placed on visual definition by current HMD design and the equivalent limitations in the simulation of movement in virtual environments. It is widely expected that non-immersive systems will eventually be superseded by better immersive technology [8].

Via networking, virtual simulations can become part of a broader system of information provision to include operations for selection and navigation – a significant development from teletext information services. Designs which make use of local processing and shared environment databases can speed up the real-time elements of virtual reality systems and allow them to be accessed by multiple users at varying levels of detail [9]. Such systems can and will make use of the growing global telecommunications network to allow two-way communication, as well as information provision for single users; even serious-minded commentators are seduced by the potential:

> "The real power of VR is in networking. Networked VR could ultimately steal market share from the travel industry as people choose to "travel by computer"; this is good news for the environment and of course for the telephone company ... Most industry

commentators agree that the future of databases lies in their global availability via broadband networks, the kinds of telecommunication links that will be widely available by the turn of the century." [10]

2.2 Tele-media

Tele-marketing is still a relatively new phenomenon. Only 2.5 – 3 million homes in the UK have satellite television access, a similar number (with some overlap) have cable access, though this figure is expected to rise to 5 million by 1995 [11]. BSkyB already promote their Sky Travel Service via their daytime satellite Travel Channel. Any estimates of success for tele-media sales must wait until both technology and usage mature enough to provide a kind of critical mass of take-up and use in the home. At first, such systems appear to be appropriate to high street sales outlets, or to television "shopping channel" operations. But tour operators could also realise the potential of such systems developed for direct sales.

2.3 UK Tourism

The UK tourist trade is one of the most advanced in the world, with a highly developed package and charter business worth over £5 billion per year. Customers expect big discounts and easy late purchasing. Tour operators generally rely on travel agents for sales and customer requirements and information. There is little incentive or opportunity to expand tailor-made holidays from their current niche market, though as in other markets, diversity tends to be led from the bottom via smaller independent companies. In mass-market package provision there is a long and almost unchallenged tradition of booking via brochures, which provide almost all customer information. Brochures must be produced and distributed in a time-scale where lead times further inhibit tailoring. Late and impulse booking, where holiday are bought as known and (usually) reliable commodities, also act as a strong market counterweight to tailoring. The Thomas Cook multimedia information systems at the point-of-sale are experimental: it remains to be seen how popular this "added value" marketing will prove. Moreover, the penetration of information technology to point-of-sale has been slow; it is the larger vertically integrated businesses who are investing in PCs and networking, rather than the high street independents, many of whom continue to use viewdata terminals – and at the end of 1993, 95% of the Association of British Travel Agents members had three sales outlets or less. (Figures courtesy of the Association of British Travel Agencies, quoted in [12].)

The Economist Intelligence Unit [13] identifies four principal corporate strategies within the tour operations industry:

- Core business of package travel only.
- Horizontally integrated travel business, including outbound package, incoming travel management and ground services, travel retail and business travel.

- Integration with an airline, a retail travel sales organisation, or both, to gain complete control of the domestic component of the package operation.
- Vertical integration from airline, through tour operator and travel agency to hotels, ground handling and possibly local airline investment at the destination(s).

All these strategies have the high street as the point of sale, where price, early programme launches and cost-cutting continue to arbitrate customer choice. Long haul travel may yet become more attractive if oil prices drop or recession recedes. In 1993, the UK was Europe's second largest purchaser of tourism (World Tourism Organisation). It is sometimes gloomily suggested that the limits of growth may have been reached, yet many Britons still never journey abroad.

3 Practicalities

3.1 The Status Quo

80% of UK holiday sales, for an estimated 4 million passengers, are through high street travel agents who charge tour operators between 10% and 15% commission (even sometimes as much as 17%). Such travel agency commissions are not passed on to the customer, further narrowing profit margins for tour operators in a highly competitive industry. Customers tend to associate holidays with the agencies, not the tour operators who provide them. While technology may have reduced the numbers employed in tour operation by up to half over the last 15 years [14], the current strategy of vertical integration appropriates the travel agency as part of the corporation. This may save commission costs, but adds the costs of high street trading, where large reductions are only made possible by cutting outlets, as most UK banks and building societies have discovered. Successful use of direct tele-media sales by tour operators could reshape the nature of the holiday trade by challenging the retail layer of the system. So let us posit:

3.2 A Future Scenario

In direct competition with the high street travel agencies, direct sale "home-booking" will provide detailed holiday information and purchase facilities as well as access to existing booking networks. Some customers will require no contact with sales staff; they will be guided by virtual travel agents; semi-intelligent software that can search, refine and customise choices based on selection criteria provided by the customer. These agents will make appropriate suggestions based on, for example, socio-economic factors, and prior experience of other customer selections, available to the agent via the system database and neural nets. For customers who need more personal assistance than a computer-based agent can provide, video links to their human counterparts will be necessary. Despite the American-led trend to maintain tele-sales as a centralised and closely monitored operation, UK tele-working sales staff will not be office-based, but, with a little trust and studio set-dressing, will work from home or small remote sites as part of a growing cottage industry for IT.

Direct tele-sales will also require comprehensive high-quality visual information, including video footage and virtual reconstructions of hotels, restaurants, resort facilities, excursions, local goods *etc.* Virtual reality systems will still not offer the apparent realism of video, but where even simple virtual representation will score over recorded media is in interactivity, allowing a customer to explore, investigate and compare resorts, hotels and facilities, just as the virtual reality systems of the mid-1990's allowed simple visual access to museum exhibits, or to architectural walk-throughs. Information can be regularly updated, and special events included at short notice. Of course such systems will be open to abuse; just as graffiti used to be air-brushed out of holiday brochure photographs, virtual walk-throughs might well dissemble about their actual counterparts. We expect that such virtual malpractice will find short shrift in a competitive market and that customers will expect and demand accurate information. It may be that a clearly independent, self-regulating body will be set up to verify virtual simulations, or offer an accreditation scheme – a kind of Virtual Egon Ronay, or Automobile Association.

Such systems will also facilitate the cross-referencing of holiday booking systems, maturing in much the same way as airline booking systems. In the early 1990's such arrangements existed between at least 17 US hotel chains using the Hotel Industry Switch Company (THISCO) [15]. Travellers seeking tailored holiday packages will be matched with similar would-be holidaymakers in numbers appropriate to economies of scale; single-flight charters, small-scale hotel bookings and excursion arrangements.

3.3 Assumptions

The scenario outlined here relies on key assumptions involving technology, provision, the industry and the market.

Technology

- The technology of virtual reality will improve to provide high-quality real-time graphic representation, if not photo-realism.
- The front-end technology will penetrate most households via cable and multimedia technologies.

Provision

- The roll-out of tele-media in international telecommunications will occur rapidly.

- The provision of on-line bandwidth will spread to keep up with the demands of new technology.

The Industry

- The costs of travel agency mark-up (or the maintenance of travel agencies by vertically integrated organisations) will continue to increase.
- Tour operators will need to find ways to facilitate longer-term booking and reduce discounting.

The Market

- A mature market will move away from holiday choice based on timings and costs, though it will still allow for late booking.
- A mature market will take advantage of more detailed and up-to-date information about destinations than paper brochures can provide.
- A mature market will prefer more independent and tailored holiday-making.
- Niche markets will give way to customised and personalised holidays; the package holiday will be repackaged.

4 Conclusion

We anticipate that the initial impact of virtual reality systems in tourism will be on sales and marketing. This is most likely to be provided by the satellite and on-line services industry, who are preparing for it NOW. If they are to be challenged in this arena, then it is the tour operators themselves who are best placed to sell directly to customers through tele-media and multimedia, and so reduce reliance on (and loss of profit to) high street travel agents. Where the travel agent owns the tour operator, or is part of a vertically integrated organisation, the same cost benefits can accrue if and when high street trading can be augmented by tele-media. At this stage there can be no guarantee that the extra revenue generated by direct sales will repay investment in tele-media systems. Nevertheless, the battle for control is now on; investment is required prior to the widespread introduction and acceptance of networked digital multimedia. In addition, such systems can offer added value to customers, reduce booking lead times by decreasing reliance on paper brochures, and help to reduce the current vicious circle of customer expectation of low prices and late booking as main measures of choice, with late discounting by the industry in return. Further work is required detailing actual budgets to validate this proposal.

5 Coda

The word "travel" is derived, via the Middle English "travail", meaning to toil, suffer and labour, from the late Latin *trepalium* – a three-pronged instrument or engine of torture [16]. It seems that travel was never intended to be easy. Evangelists of virtual reality would have us believe that virtual worlds will become "more real than real" – that people will holiday at home, happy and comfortable in their cybersuits. The reality is rather more prosaic. Just as television has not destroyed the brainstems of its viewers, so virtual reality is unlikely to stop people travelling in pursuit of all the benefits that virtual worlds can simulate, but not provide – suntan, surf, good food and drink, and sand in your shorts.

Acknowledgements

We should like to thank Caro Cook for her insightful advice on the tourism industry. Ivor Benjamin is funded by the Engineering & Physical Sciences Research Council, with assistance from the Centre for HCI Design at City University, London.

Contacts

Ivor Benjamin
I.D.Benjamin@city.ac.uk

Dr. Maggie Cooper
M.Cooper@city.ac.uk

Tel: 044 71 477 8405
Fax: 044 71 477 8586

References

1. Dick, P.K.: We Can Remember It For You Wholesale, Grafton/Harper-Collins. London, UK, 1991. (pp. 205-227)

2. Sherman, B. & Judkins, P.: Glimpses of Heaven, Visions of Hell: Virtual Reality and its Implications. Hodder & Stoughton, Sevenoaks, Kent, UK, 1992 (p. 131)

3. Vallee, J.: The Network Revolution, Confessions of a Computer Scientist, Penguin, Harmondsworth, UK. 1984.

4. Tapscott, D. & Caston, A.: Paradigm Shift: The New Promise of Information Technology, McGraw Hill, New York, USA., 1993. (p. 23)

5. Harrison, R.: Study of the International Competitiveness of the UK Telecommunications Infrastructure, Dept. of Trade and Industry, London, UK, 1994. (p .77)

6. Personal Correspondence, Weintraub International Consultants, Brussels, Belgium, (1994).

7. Cooper, M. & Benjamin, I.: "Envisionments: Constructing Dramatic Virtual Worlds", in: Singh, G., Feiner, S.K. & Thalmann, D. (eds.) Proceedings of VRST'94, Singapore, World Scientific, Singapore, 1994. (pp. 251-265)

8. Smets, G.J.F., Stappers, P.J., Overbeeke, K. & Van der Mast, C. "Designing in Virtual Reality: Implementing Perception-Action Coupling with Affordances" in: Singh, G., Feiner, S.K. & Thalmann, D. (eds.) Proceedings of VRST'94, Singapore, World Scientific, Singapore, 1994. (p. 97-110)

9. Fahlén, L.E., Brown, C.G., Ståhl, O. & Carlsson, C.: "A Space-based Model for User Interaction in Shared Synthetic Environments", in Proceedings of InterCHI '93, Amsterdam, ACM Press, 1993.

10. Travis, T., Watson, T. & Atyeo, M.: Human Psychology in Virtual Environments (1994), in: Macdonald, L. & Vince, J. (eds.): Interacting with Virtual Environments, J. Wiley, Chichester UK., 1994. (p. 53)

11. Harrison, R.: Study of the International Competitiveness of the UK Telecommunications Infrastructure, Dept. of Trade and Industry, London, UK, 1994. (pp. 44-45)

12. Richardson, D. "Rare breed that is going strong", in Carr, H. (editor), Travel Trade Gazette 40th Anniversary Issue, Morgan-Grampian PLC, London UK, Sept. 1993 (p. 43)

13. Bywater, M.: The European Tour Operator Industry, Special Report No. 2141 The Economist Intelligence Unit & Business International Ltd., London, UK, 1992 (p. iv)

14. Anon., quoting Roger Corkhill, (M.D. Cosmos Travel), in Carr, H. (editor), Travel Trade Gazette 40th Anniversary Issue, Morgan-Grampian PLC, London UK, Sept. 1993 (p. 46)

15. Tapscott, D. & Caston, A.: Paradigm Shift: The New Promise of Information Technology, McGraw Hill, New York, USA., 1993. (pp. 92-93)

16. Murray, J.A.H. *et al*, eds.: The Oxford English Dictionary, Oxford University Press, Oxford UK, 1933.

Explorative analysis for development of a GIS-based Tourisminformationssystem

G. Trichtl

Institut für Wirtschafts- und Sozialgeographie, Wirtschaftsuniversität Wien,
Augasse 2-6, 1090 VIENNA
Austria

e-mail: gerhard@wigeo1.wu-wien.ac.at

Document availible via FTP with following URL:
ftp://wigeo1.wu-wien.ac.at(137.208.13.10)/pub/doc/enter

Abstract: The following paper discuss an implementation of an GIS-Tourism-Informationssytem (TIS). The implementation was only in some cases to test the GIS-System for a TIS.

1.Introduction

You can see for a detail Introduction in the document with following URL: ftp://wigeo1.wu-wien.ac.at(137.208.13.10)/pub/doc/enter.

2. Architecture of the GIS-Tourisminformationssystem

The system consist of 5 moduls - Auswahl-Modul, Fremdenverkehrsgemeinden Modul, Räumliches Modul, Reiserouten Modul und Informationsnachführung.
The Auswahl Modul make transaction with the other moduls to choose one city for the holiday.
The Fremdenverkehrsgemeinden Modul illustrates in pictures, video, audio, text or other media the situation and infrastructure of the city.
The Räumliches Modul will generate 3D-Views of the City. You can choose the place and the direction you want to look.
The Reiserouten Modul calculates you the shortest path between different citys and display them on the screen.
The last modul - Informationsnachführung - will update the data for each city in the system.

Fig. 1. Structure of a GIS Tourisminformationssystem

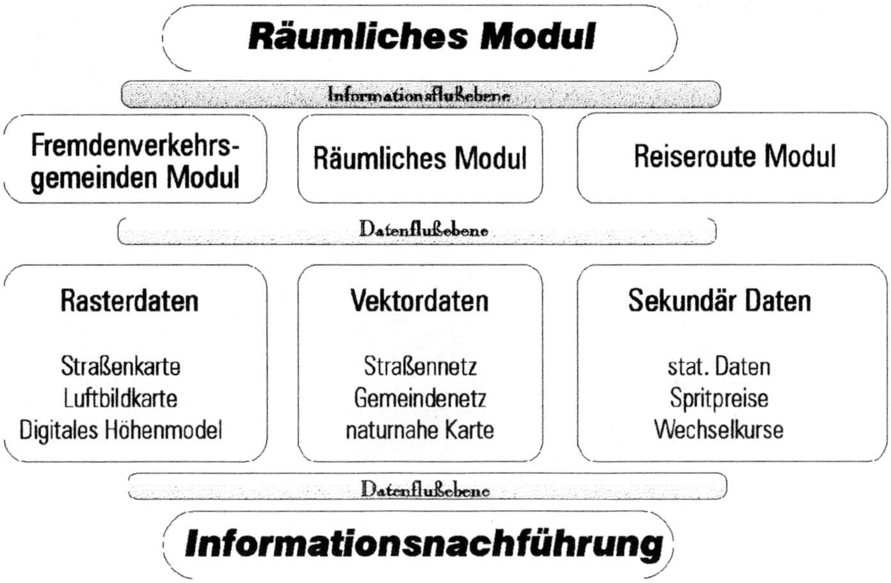

3. Output-Examples of the GIS-Tourisminformationsystem

Fig. 2 shows the textinformation of a city in the Fremdenverkehrsgemeinden Modul. Fig. 3 shows the example of a 3D-View of a city - in this situation from Mondsee to Schafberg - of the Räumliches Modul. Fig. 4 and Fig. 5 shows examples of output maps of the Reiserouten Modul - one with a pen-plotter and one with an image in the background.

Fig. 2. Example of a textinformation of a city

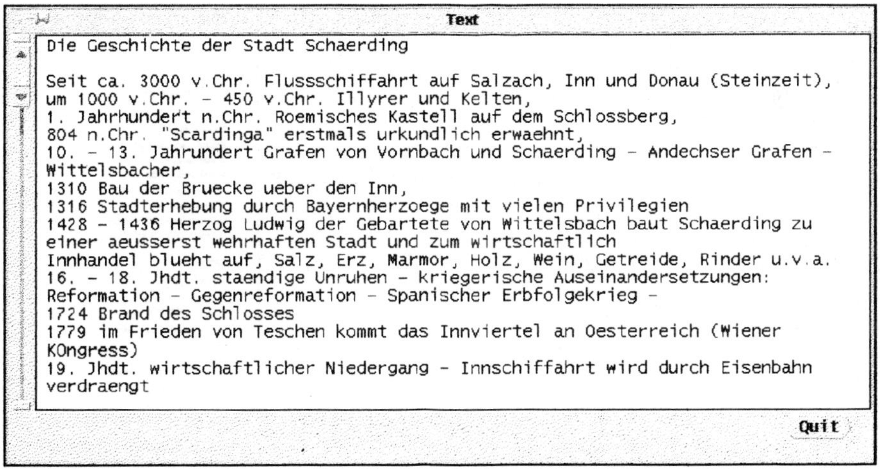

Die Geschichte der Stadt Schaerding

Seit ca. 3000 v.Chr. Flussschiffahrt auf Salzach, Inn und Donau (Steinzeit),
um 1000 v.Chr. - 450 v.Chr. Illyrer und Kelten,
1. Jahrhundert n.Chr. Roemisches Kastell auf dem Schlossberg,
804 n.Chr. "Scardinga" erstmals urkundlich erwaehnt,
10. - 13. Jahrundert Grafen von Vornbach und Schaerding - Andechser Grafen - Wittelsbacher,
1310 Bau der Bruecke ueber den Inn,
1316 Stadterhebung durch Bayernherzoege mit vielen Privilegien
1428 - 1436 Herzog Ludwig der Gebartete von Wittelsbach baut Schaerding zu einer aeusserst wehrhaften Stadt und zum wirtschaftlich
Innhandel blueht auf, Salz, Erz, Marmor, Holz, Wein, Getreide, Rinder u.v.a.
16. - 18. Jhdt. staendige Unruhen - kriegerische Auseinandersetzungen: Reformation - Gegenreformation - Spanischer Erbfolgekrieg -
1724 Brand des Schlosses
1779 im Frieden von Teschen kommt das Innviertel an Oesterreich (Wiener KOngress)
19. Jhdt. wirtschaftlicher Niedergang - Innschiffahrt wird durch Eisenbahn verdraengt

Fig. 3. 3D-View with the Luftbildkarte (ÖLK 10)

Fig. 4 Output of a Pen-Plotter

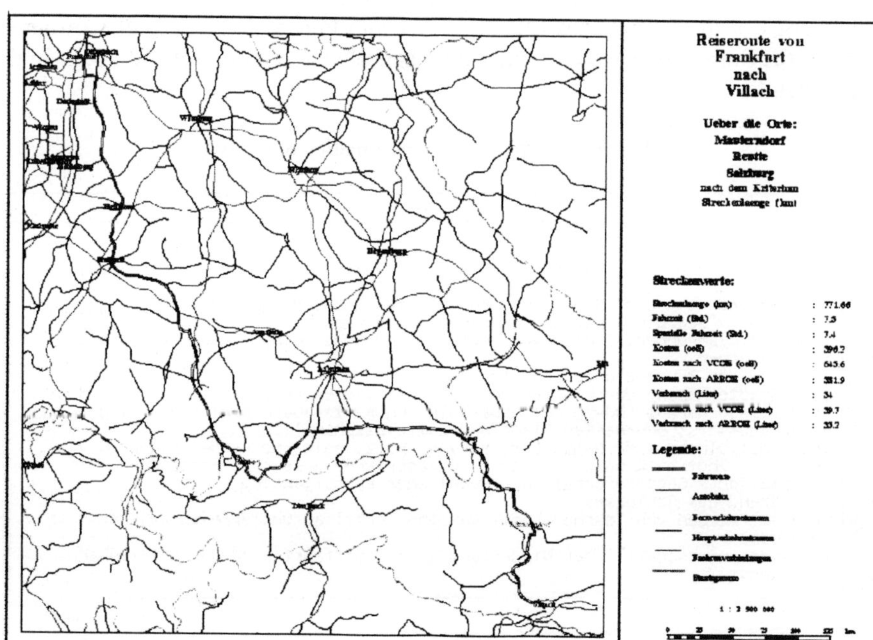

Fig. 5. Output with a background image

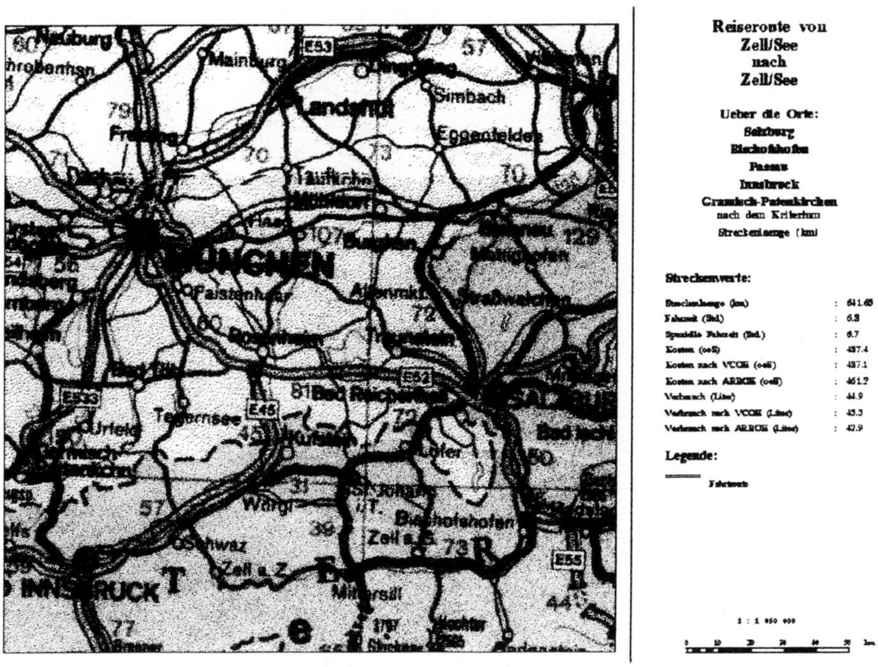

Fig. 6. Startup structure of the system

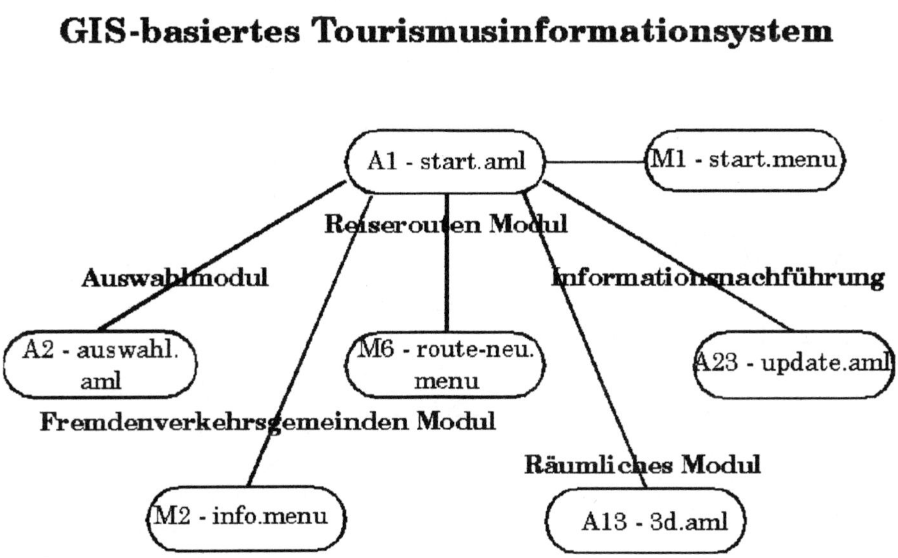

Fig. 7. Startup screen of the system

Fig. 8. Detail of the Räumliches Modul

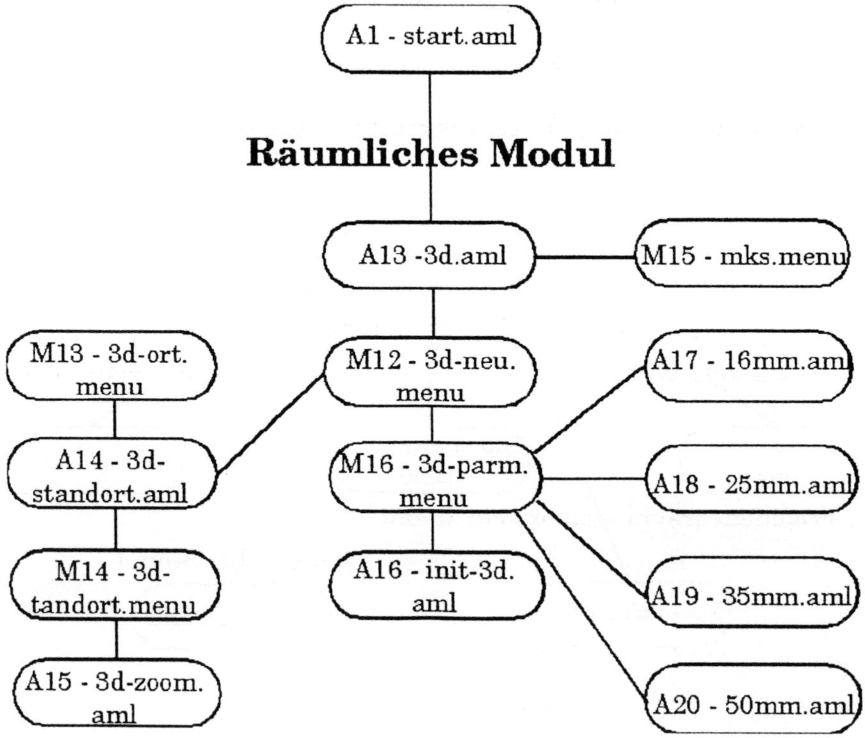

3. Implementation of the System

The System was developed with the macro-language of ARC/INFO the AML. It was programed with AMLs and Menus. Fig. 6 shows the startup of the system. Fig. 7 shows the startup screen. Fig. 8 shows a detail implementation of the Räumliches Modul.

4. Hard- und Software

The system was developed in 1992/1993 on the Institut für Wirtschafts- und Sozialgeographie on the Wirtschaftsuniversität Wien.

4. 1 Hardware

Hardware for running the program:

- SUN SPARCstation 1+: 64 MB RAM, 6 GB Harddisk; Entwicklungsmaschine für das Tourismusinformationssystem;

Hardware for development:

- APPLE Macintosh IIfx: 8 MB RAM, 180 MB Harddisk; for scanning picutres;
- HP DeskJet 550 C: for color prints;
- HP Laserjet IIIP: Laserprinter;
- HP ScanJet Iic: Scanner;
- PC 486-DX2 66: 8 MB RAM, 250 MB Harddisk;;
- SUN SPARCstation 1+: 64 MB RAM, 6 GB Harddisk;;
- ZOOM Faxmodem: V.32bis, 14.400 Baud; Modem.

4.2 Software

Software for running the program:

- ALCHEMY (1.6)
- ARC/INFO (6.1.1)

Software for development:

- ALCHEMY (1.6)
- Adobe Photoshop (2.0)
- ARC/INFO (6.1.1)
- CorelDraw! (3.0)
- Decodix (2.0)
- DeskScan II (1.5)
- HAFAS (3.40w)
- MS Excel (4.0)
- MS WinWord (2.0)

References

BILL, R. und FRITSCH, D. (1991): Grundlagen der GEO-Informationssysteme. Band 1: Hardware, Software und Daten, Wichmann Verlag, Karlsruhe.

DAROZI, Z. (1992): Von konventionellen zu multimedialen Geographischen Informationssystemen, Diplomarbeit, Institut für Wirtschafts- und Sozialgeographie, Wirtschaftsuniversität Wien.

ESRI (1992): **Network Analysis. Modeling network flow and path calculation**, ARC/INFO Manual, ESRI, Redlands.

ESRI (1992): **Surface Modeling with TIN . Surface analysis and display**, ARC/INFO Manual, ESRI, Redlands.

FISCHER, M.M. und NIJKAMP, P. (eds.) (1993): Geographic Information Systems, Spatial Modelling and Policy Evaluation, Berlin et al.: Springer Verlag.

FISCHER, M.M. (1994): From Conventional to knowledge-based Geographic Systems, **Enviroment and Urban Sytems**, vol 18(4), pp. 233-242.

GÖPFERT, W. (1987): Raumbezogene Informationssysteme, Wichmann Verlag, Karlsruhe.

HÄFELE, G. (1993): Herstellung digitaler Schräglichtschattierung mit GIS, in DOLLINGER, F. und STROBL, J. (eds.): **Angewandte Geographische Informationsverarbeitung V, Beiträge zum GIS-Symposium 7.-9. Juli**, pp. 81-88, in Salzburger Geographische Materialien, Heft 20, Institut für Geographie, Universität Salzburg.

KRIZ, K. und RIEDL, A. (1993): Konzept eines digitalen Informationssystems für den Dienstleistungssektor Fremdenverkehr im großmaßstäbigen Bereich, in DOLLINGER, F. und STROBL, J. (eds.): **Angewandte Geographische Informationsverarbeitung V - Beiträge zum GIS 7. - 9. Juli 1993**, in Salzburger Geographische Materialien, Heft 20, Institut für Geographie, Universität Salzburg.

MOELLERING, H. (1993): MKS-aspect™ - a new way of rendering cartographic Z surfaces, in MESENBURG, P. (eds.): **ICC '93. Proceedings, 16th International Cartographic Conference, Volume 1,** pp. 675-681, Bielefeld: ICA, DKT.

MOGOROVICH, MAGNARAPA, MASSEROTTI, MAZZOTTA (1992): Merging GIS with Multimedia Technologies - The Case-Study of an Information System for Tourist Applications, in HARTS, J., OTTENS, H.F.L. und SCHOLTEN, H.J. (eds): **EGIS '92 Conference Proceedings**, pp. 1085-1094, EGIS Foundation, Utrecht/Amsterdam.

RIEDL, A. (1992): INFO-MAP Niederösterreich. Exemplarischer Aufbau eines interaktiven visualisierbaren Informationssystems am Beispiel des Landes Niederösterreich; Band I, Softwaretechnische Realisierung, Diplomarbeit aus Kartographie, Institut für Geographie, Universität Wien.

SOB, M. (1992): INFO-MAP Niederösterreich. Exemplarischer Aufbau eines interaktiven visualisierbaren Informationssystems am Beispiel des Landes Niederösterreich; Band II, Datenermittlung und thematische Gestaltung, Diplomarbeit aus Kartographie, Institut für Geographie, Universität Wien.

TRICHTL, G. (1992): GIS und Multimedia, Seminararbeit aus Kartographie, Institut für Geographie, Universität Wien.

An Information CD on India

Anand Rao, Seema Sethi, Kamini Sharma

1. Introduction

The primary motivation for the project was to create an image of India and its culture in its entirety to the western world. It had been observed that the image of India projected was biased and stereotype. The current nature of reporting and the limited scope of the medium used have perpetuated this image. The inherent limitation of travel books, travel agents and news reporting have not been successful in breaking this image.

To counter this trend we took on a well known monument and tried to present it in an unbiased manner.

2. Theory

During our project we defined a theory which we call "Cross Cultural Communication". In this we wish to project the culture of country/area **A** to the culture / area **B**. We assume that the culture perception of country **A** is that which the natives of that country / area **A** hold.

Our complementary aim was to use the experiment and our observations from the test case to derive guidelines for more effective communication in future projects.

We have classified peoples perception of a culture in terms of music, design, and social environment. We assume that no other elements or older prejudices would disrupt the communication.

3. Assumptions

To begin the experiment, we further assume that there exists a team who understand and have experienced both culture **A** and **B** in terms of music, design, and social environment. The core team of Icon Softec consists of , a designer, a programmer and a project coordinator. The designer, qualified as a commercial artist, has been trained in Indian art and design and also worked extensively in advertisement and magazine publications. The programmer and project coordinator, both trained software professionals, have studied and worked in Western countries and during this course interacted with different age groups of the western culture. As a team they understand the subtilities of the western culture. In addition to this each member originates from diferent parts of India ranging from the Northern to Southern India and are thus able to create a more balanced image of India, free of inherited socio-inter-culture biases.

4. Target Audience

The target audience was determined as those who have an affordable media and constitute a large enough group to make the project economically viable.

Our target audience for the our first project are western people interested in learning about other places, who speak English and possess a Macintosh computer with a minimum of 5 MB RAM, a CD ROM with a datarate of 300 Kbs, a 14" colour monitor with a capability of showing 256 colours, and a Motorola 030 processor running system 7.1.

5. Project

The subject that we have chosen to implement our aims and objectives with, is theTaj Mahal.

The Taj Mahal is a widely publicised monument where as Agra, which was once the imperial capital of the Mughal dynasty and home to a lage number of beautiful monuments, is relatively unknown. Most people have a romantic notion of theTaj, but don't know much about the beauty of its architecture or the history To bring out its various facets, we decided to divide the information into 4 different sections:

The moods of the Taj
Footprints of yesteryears
Designed to Perfection
Beacon to Tourists

5.1 Moods of the Taj

Part of the beauty of the Taj is it's constantly changing appearance with the day and night. This section is a series of slides from sunrise to sunset, presenting not only theTaj but also the people that live in it's shadow. The accompanying music varies to enhance the mood of the slide show. The music uses different ragas (a sequence of notes played in a particular speed) depicting different times of the day. A number of interactivity features have been incorporated like, gallery, picture sequences, and photography information.

5.2 Footprints of yesteryears

A tourist is usually interested in the history of the place he is visiting.To give the user a cultural perspective, we have presented the development of art and architecture in Agra. History as we project it lends itself to two subheadings, the cultural development of Agra by the Mughal Emperors and the portraits of a few In the first section we deal with the influence of successive rulers on the culture of the city As there are many terms which are unfamiliar we have included a hypertext glossary.The second section narrates the biographies of some of the Mughals.

5.3 Designed to Perfection
Imparts detailed architectural information of theTaj and its complex. The architectural philosophy and construction concepts have also been highlighted. The 3 subsections dealing with the different parts of the Taj complex are, The funerary complex, The mausoleum, Space conception and development.Along with this tyhe plans and ornamentation have also been highlighted. Each section incorporates video, graphics, animation, and descriptive text.

5.4 Beacon for Tourist
The section provides information on accommodation; restaurants and the food ; how to reach Agra and local transport; other places of interest in Agra and what not to do in Agra. Food in India is very different to Western food. So to help the tourist we have not only given pictures and information of the type of food available in the city ofAgra, but also included recipes. In Accommodations, we have tried to represent the range of hotels available. Other places of interest includes tourist specific information for other monuments and places in Agra. The list of don'ts, are available to ensure that the traveller enjoys his stay.

6. Medium

The most effective medium for projecting a culture would require the involvement of all our senses that are required to create a real image.Virtual reality comes close, but lacks the sense of smell and touch. Multimedia computer systems lack the sense of 3D reality but are a more affordable media.

Multimedia has the potential of not only giving an audio-visual presentation but also can be interactive. If we are presenting the craftsmen of India, we can show the way the craftsman works with total user-interactivity. In this manner we can present not only places of interest but also show the whole environment through video and stillsAdding sound and music allows us to bring out the language and noises in the environment concerned. The interactivity makes the communication of cultures simpler as the audience can set there own pace of learning. It has been observed that retention power is also higher when one requests for information and views further details only when it is required.

Both digital video and sound require a large storage capacity. So for marketing the interactive multimedia presentation, the only media presently available that is also affordable is the Compact Disc. The CD not only offers 650 MB of storage space but is also robust.

As this was a private project and we had very limited resources, we were restricted on the choice of platform that we could use. Due to the facility of QuickTime and availability of inbuilt sound and video inputting capabilities we decided to use the Macintosh Computer as the production platform.

7. System Design Considerations

At all times our primary consideration was to keep within the 5MB limit, that is, 2 MB for the system software and 3 MB for actually running the presentation. Initially we did not paid much attention to the datarate of the final project which was a serious mistake Keeping the RAM into consideration, the design was finalised with a background screen covering an area of 640 * 480 pixels at a datarate of 300 Kbs.The elements placed upon the background average a datarate of 350 Kbs.As a consequence, the CD which runs on a CD-ROM with a datarate of 300 kbs, is perceptibly slow.

7.1 **Digital Video**

Bearing in mind the 3 MB limit, the lowest configuration of the Macintosh and the fact that QuickTime 1.6.1 does not play back video larger than 160 * 120 pixels smoothly, all our video was limited to the size of 160 * 120 pixels at 10 frames per second (fps). Initially the vos consisted of several special effects and long pan and zoom shots.Analysis of the QuickTime in Premiere 3.0 revealed an excessively high datarate.The effects were therefore reduced tremendously. To further increase the datarate and quality of playback, we used Cinepak compression [1] and reduced the frame rate to 90-100 Kbs. The size of the Quicktimes in the architecture section (Built to Perfection) of 121 * 80 pixels was a purely design issue.

The video was shot with a 8 mm Handycam and digitised with the inbuilt video-inputting capability of the 840 AV with monitor settings to thousands of colour.

7.2 Pictures

The still pictures shot were mostly slides due to their better quality in comparison to print film. Keeping in mind the minimum target configuration of 256 colours the pictures mode was changed from thousands to 256 colours.This sort of a conversion gives a very dithered look to the picture.To counter this we got photo CDs of our pictures and using Adobe Photoshop, we carried out colour corrections and changed the brightness and contrast of the pictures. However this has an adverse efect on the picture quality as with an increased contrast the dithering process creates a banding efect.

At all times the colour palette of the pictures was set to the apple system colour palette, a major limitation in terms of design. MacroMind Director could import diferent colour palettes but this would increase the size of the file and require much more memory

7.3 Sound

Both music and narration are vital elements of any multimedia project, as it is the music that brings out the mood of the presentation and narration the actual message. Language, is another barrier to cross-cultural communication.The simple language of English, most commonly spoken all over the world has diferent dialects. Just the fact that one knows English, usually is not sufficient to have a conversation with another English speaking person from a different country. Watching American and British films helps us to understand there terminology. India, in the same manner has built up a specific Indian-English terminology. To help the audience get accustomed to this we have tried to add as much narration as possible.

Music again is very culture specific. Though the 7 basic notes remain the same, their permutation and combination differ in different cultures. The basic rhythm of the music was based on Indian ragas which define the mood of the music. However western tunes were composed based on these ragas. To introduce the western world to Indian music we decided not to use pure Indian music, but fusion music played on Indian instruments. However, as the music is to be played on computers and there is a restriction on the quality of music that can be outputted from the computer, we had to ensure that the music recorded was within the 22 KHz range [2]. In this range the user would be able to hear the subtilities of the natural instruments and the whole mood of the music would sound flat. Therefore the music was created on synthesisers. Keeping the sound level of 22 KHz in mind, the instruments synthesised were flute, piano, sitar, chimes, Indian kettle drums, sarangi, drums and harp.

During the mix, the sound was monitored in Sound Edit Pro before actual sound Input. This allowed us to detect the high peakswhich were then normalised using Sound Designer.

Due to the base memory restriction of 3 MB, we had to create loop sounds of short duration's. To actually create a good loop sound, the sound should have at least two bits to it and run for roughly 12-15 seconds. Due to the memory and datarate restrictions we limited the sound to 7-8 seconds of loop sound.

8. Artistic Design

We begin the issue of design with a look at our perception of the two cultures in terms of colour, type, motifs, music and language.

In the west the colours used are generally cold blues and grays or pastel shades.The textures used are very limited. Bright colours are used primarily for young children and fun elements. The manner in which bright colours are used also suggest plain or inornate forms. Subjects of a serious nature are generally presented in blues and grays, with touches of bright colours to highlight certain issues.

Colour in Indian culture has derived its depiction from the use of colour in religion.The colours used are generally bright and vibrant and have very specific significance. Black and gray signify death, while red suggests life and purity of fire, and safron a holy colour. Browns and pastel shades are derived from the basic raw materials used for design and construction.

Colour in our project, was determined by the basic need to project the element of Indian design which is textured by hand-woven and ethnic designs.The colours are therefore composite. To bring out this effect, the textures were scanned in for the backgrounds and buttons. Indian textures appear appropriate for backgrounds, but were found inappropriate when scanned in.After several trials it was observed that the texture required depth created by texturisation. If the texture contained drastic or flat colors or the texture was uneven the scan would be inappropriate. The final backgrounds were then worked upon in Adobe Photoshop to soften the extreme effects of the texture and blend in the effect with non-traditional Indian colours. This gives the CD an overall Pastel shaded soft effect [Fig 1.].

Fig. 1. History Screen - uses silk texture n the background

9. Indian Art translated to computers

Modern western design presents itself as straight lines giving an angular and inornate appearance to the design. In stark contrast Indian designs are still very ornate, giving a soft look . If there are sharp edges and straight lines in the design, other elements present will counterbalance the effect. Motifs are primarily of design importance. In the design fusion process we first identified the essence of the Indian design in terms of motifs, design pattern, or design element. These objects were then applied to the backgrounds with western color, and line concepts using the Adobe Photoshop and Aldus Freehand.

Most of our screens have a base pastel texture. All buttons although rectangular, have been given slightly diffused boarders to maintain the angularity but at the same time offset its harshness [Fig 2].

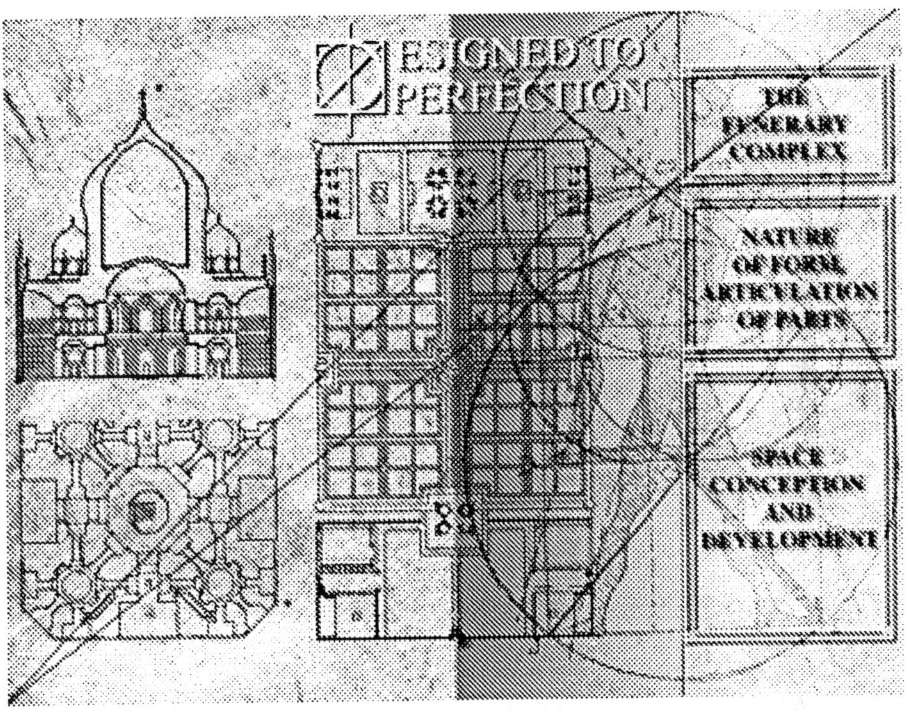

Fig. 2. Architecture Menu - uses an old parchment as a back ground, with butoons on the right

Inside the buttons, diffused patterns have been placed, to bring out the ornate curvature of design in Indian Art. Wherever bands were required, for boundaries etc.. , they have been decorated with motifs from real Indian design. Their size and proportion have been maintained in such a manner that they are unobtrusive and yet noticeable

Presented in its natural form, these aspects would not appeal to the western eye. The blurred, softened diffused, shadow effects bring about a subtlety in the design. Gently introducing these essential elements to the western eye.

For a topic like the Taj, the type noramally used has suggested a romantic and mysterious form. To break away from this stereotype and to suggest the information as well as practical nature of the CD, we have used mostly simple Serif fonts. Due to resource restrictions we did not wish to have to add any fonts onto the CD so we used only the system fonts available on the Macintosh. Where stylised elements were considered necessary, they were created in Adobe Photoshop and ported into the authoring package as a separate element.

The layout of the design screens and information was totally western. As one would format a publication, computer screen, or design an interface.

10. Conclusions

Based on the feedback from Apple Hong Kong, Apple Cupertino, and University of Atlanta we have arrived at certain conclusions. These conclusions have been derived from our analysis as the feed back is not precise. The feedback does not give detailed artistic or technical criticism to the different elements of the design. It only gives a level of user satisfaction in terms of user friendliness, understandability, visual effect, information depth, content relevance.

Upto the present day the general consensus is that the music loops were somewhat repetitive and consequently irritating after a period of time. The theme music for the panoramic section was good and took them through the slide show comfortably The music lacked the "typical Indian sitar music, piped music efect", this made the music bearable.

The visual effect was "stunning", they felt that it was subtle enough for western viewing, each screen was composed very well, but they did find it dificult to identify the buttons in the design.

Their was sufficient depth to satisfy a person just initiated to Indian culture, however it would not satisfy a person who was already aware of the culture. In sections like history Indian words were explained, but in the tourism section they were not. Tourism also lacked the level of depth that a tourist would require, maps, a variety of hotels and restaurants which were not included due to resource and information constraints. The architecture section required more knowledge of design than a novice would have and consequently the section was not as interesting to a large number of users. The narration in the history and tourism was easily understood.

Based on this feedback we can say that the formula or combination of elements was appropriate. But what has actually happened is that we have communicated the culture in a modified manner that it not actually how it appears when the individual arrives in India. The subtlety and color of our designs, the fusion of the music, the clarity of our accent and speech. Yes, we have succeeded in our aim to introduce Indian culture in terms of design, music and places to the user. They have responded in a very positive manner toward Indian culture. Our formula in terms of attracting western audiences is a success as it packages Indian culture in an appealing manner .

Our manner of presentation has been recognised by organizations and individuals that see the need for this very same type of packaging. Our up and coming projects include An information Kiosk for the Indian railways sponsored by the government of India.A comprehensive series of CD's on the Palace on Wheels that runs through seven cities of Rajasthan. The series covers each city. An information Kiosk and large screen presentation for Rajasthan State Tourism to be displayed at the Berlin Fair in march 1995.

Our complimentary aim was to derive guidelines for cross culture development.We still require more precise feedback, and need to carry out experiments with the same people but with variations of the formula of artistic design.We wish to experiment now with a totally different aspect of Indian culture, e.g.The temple architecture, and art of south Indian.

Reference

1. Miller Sam, Harris Arno: The QuickTime How-To-Book - For QuiickTime 1.0 & 1.5, systems 7.0 & 7.1: San Francisco Paris Duesseldorf Soest: SYBEX 1993

2. Jerram Peter, Gosney Michael, Verbum Inc and The Gosney Company Inc: Multimedia Powertools: New York Toronto London Sydney Auckland:Random House Inc.(1993)

Managing WWW Documents in Distributed Editorial Environments

Franz Burger, Siegfried Reich
FAW - Research Institute for Applied Knowledge Processing
Softwarepark Hagenberg
A-4232 Hagenberg - Austria
email: {franz, sre}@faw.uni-linz.ac.at

Abstract. Global on-line information services, such as provided by the World Wide Web (WWW) are an adequate and invaluable communication platform for tourist industry. The production of such electronic publications requires different information types to be handled and linked together in a sophisticated way. The task of hypermedia information handling even becomes more difficult if a group of people is working cooperatively on it. An application scenario for the production of WWW publications demonstrates how the HyDoMan Distributed Hypermedia Document Management System can be applied to cooperative development of hypermedia publication[1].

1 Introduction

The goal of this paper is to show the applicability of the HyDoMan Distributed Hypermedia Document Management System developed at our institute for the cooperative development of World Wide Web (WWW) publications for tourist information.

Section 2 discusses why on-line information services are of importance for tourist industry. The principles of the WWW distributed hypermedia system, the publication process and related issues are described in section 3. Section 4 presents an example scenario for the production of on-line tourist information using the WWW as delivery platform. Finally we give some information on future plans and conclude in section 7.

2 Potential Benefits of On-line Information for Tourist Industry

The overall success of tourist industry strongly depends on how successfully it can communicate marketing information. According to a study of the EU [8], travel and tourist industry is one of the largest information providers and may well exploit the strengths of electronic media.

[1] This work has been done within the European RACE project R2042 EUROPUBLISHING and has been funded by the Austrian Federal Research Foundation (FFF) under grant no. 2/310.

Compared to "traditional" media (e.g. broadcast, print) electronic media offer a number of unique features. Multiple information types (video, sound, animation, high quality color images) may be used together with text for communicating information more effectively. Interactivity and topicality are other characteristics of electronic media which make them appealing.

Electronic delivery of hypermedia information via international computer networks, such as the Internet, is an interesting alternative to traditional distribution platforms. The Internet provides tourist industry with a way to reach out to large, global audiences with marketing information that has to be updated steadily. It thus reduces the hurdles normally faced with hardcopy distribution (e.g. print, diskette, CD-ROM), such as high production costs and inaccurate information. Globally distributed hypermedia systems give end-users (the readers of hypermedia documents) instant access to the information provider's documents, such as maps, historical background and related information.

Due to its wide-spread and rapidly growing user basis distributed hypermedia systems, such as the WWW[2][5], may be successfully used as a complementary communication platform for marketing and information services of the tourist industry.

3 WWW Publications

The WWW project [4] which has implemented the concept of a globally distributed multimedia system uses the Internet for accessing and transferring multimedia documents.

3.1 Distributed Hypermedia

WWW's concept for multimedia document representation and exchange is based on the notion of structured documents using the Standard Generalized Markup Language (SGML) [1, 10] as specification language. SGML is a standard for defining structured document types, and markup languages to represent instances of those document types. For the purposes of WWW the Hypertext Markup Language (HTML) [2], being an application of SGML, has been developed. It describes the structure of hypermedia documents and specifies hyperlinks to multimedia objects in an application- and platform-independent way. An HTML instance is like a text file, except that some of the characters are interpreted as markup. The markup gives structure to the document.

WWW uses an Internet protocol (Hypertext Transfer Protocol, HTTP) [3], which allows transfer representations to be negotiated between client and server.

[2] There were 62 registered WWW servers in April 1993 compared to 1,248 servers in May 1994. The load on the WWW server at CERN doubled every four months between April 1991 and April 1994.

3.2 Production Process for WWW Publications

The design and development of high quality electronic publications requires the cooperation of several specialists like authors, editors, as well as designers. Usually, these people are working at distributed locations but intermittently consult and collaborate closely. The process in general is not a linear one but usually needs several iterations in order to develop high quality information.

Figure 1 gives an overview of the production process for hypermedia information:

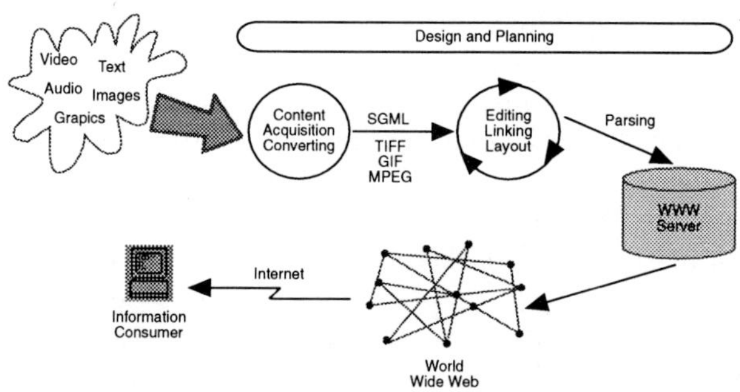

Fig. 1. Production of WWW Publications

The first task in a project is the planning and design of the hypermedia publication and the production steps needed for achieving the desired result. Thus, planning requires the definition of the target group, specification of the information content and structure, and definition of the media types (e.g. text, images, video, sound) to be used. Depending on the publication's specification, the necessary development and production tasks, the needed software tools and devices have to be identified. A workgroup for the project has to be recruited and responsibilities have to be specified. If this general design and planning task is complete, the actual work on the publication can start.

The next task has to deal with the creation and acquisition of the basic content. Different authors have to provide multimedia content like text, images and graphics, video and sound clips in electronic form. Within this task format conversions are likely to happen, since information sources usually are available in an application- or platform-specific format.

If the basic content is available, value adding by means of editing and restructuring of different multimedia information can start. The structure and content of HTML documents has to be specified. Specific HTML editors or general purpose SGML editors may be used for this task. The essential goal is to specify the hyperlinks between related chunks of information (also called "weaving" a web), so that a consistent hypermedia information space is the result. Testing of interim documents with an HTML viewer like *Mosaic* [13] allows the identification of errors occurred during authoring and previewing the result of changes.

Editing and manipulation of multimedia data (images, video, sound) has to be done at the same time. Note, that the task of editing may require several cycles to be completed.

Before making the newly created hypermedia web accessible by the world, validating the collection of HTML documents ensures that only syntactically correct information will be distributed. The task of validating HTML documents may be accomplished by parsing the documents with an SGML parser (e.g. sgmls [7]) against a valid HTML DTD. What has also to be done is analyzing hyperlinks that point to files or servers. Automated hyperlink validation programs like *html_analyzer* [14] may be used for exploring the relationship between hyperlinks and the contents of the hyperlink.

As soon as the documents and multimedia objects have been downloaded to the server the information is publicly available on the WWW and may be accessed by interested consumers via the Internet.

3.3 Issues in Providing On-line Hypermedia Information

In order to provide the information users want to get and an organization wants to provide several issues have to be considered.

The company's information management has to take into account the information needs over the long term and that hypermedia documents have to be managed on the media required by their users. Consequently the information management must face the task of the implementation of a document management system. The system must help address security and version control issues and provide hypertext links. Especially the version management is of main importance since organizations no longer have complete knowledge whether the correct versions are being released when information exists electronically and is available for access over the Net [16].

Hyperlinks are critical because they provide pointers to other related information in separate documents. The issue of maintaining the integrity of data is relevant within this context. As a consequence, building of document collections rather than simply displaying individual, unrelated documents to the Web, is gaining more importance. An adequate document management system will enable information providers to offer more comprehensive information.

An issue in producing hypermedia publications based on structured documents descends from the fact that structured documents provide only references to multimedia objects. Structured documents do not contain the actual multimedia data. This means that these objects have to be stored and handled somewhere on a file-system or in a database. Structured documents do not provide any functionality which assures that the referenced objects really exist, or exist in the right version or appropriate format. As a consequence the issue of data integrity is raised again.

4 HyDoMan

A Distributed Hypermedia Document Management System, called HyDoMan [6, 12], has been developed at our institute. Its overall aim is to support people cooperating closely during the design, content acquisition, and editing of hypermedia publications.

4.1 Aims of Distributed Hypermedia Document Management

The goal of a distributed hypermedia document management system can be described on several dimensions. One dimension is that of cooperative work. A document management system (DMS) has to provide functionality that allows multiple users performing different roles to cooperate in a common project. Thus a DMS must support distribution, access control, concurrency control and Versioning.

The second dimension of goals can be derived from requirements for structured hypermedia documents. These are handling of structured documents, maintenance of hyperlinks, and multimedia object storage and access.

Besides these specific goals a document management system must be able to operate in heterogeneous hardware environments and allow the usage of existing tools and applications for processing the document's content.

4.2 Features and Architecture

HyDoMan allows the storage, retrieval, and access to structured hypermedia documents, like HTML documents used in WWW, in a distributed way. A compound document model has been implemented for the management of several multimedia components (structured text, images, video clips, and sound). The document model helps to overcome the deficiencies of structured documents in maintaining hyperlinks and references to multimedia objects.

Basic groupware capabilities such access control, concurrency control and versioning are supported and allow secure and efficient cooperation among users.

The system architecture is based on a client/server model. Multiple clients may be connected to one or more document servers for accessing document information.

Client and server applications may run on different platforms (UNIX, Macintosh, or MS-Windows) due to their implementation in VisualWorks\Smalltalk. The usage of TCP/IP for communication allows the system to run in a heterogeneous environment.

The storage and access functionality for multimedia objects is realized by a set of autonomous object servers, which can be distributed to several locations.

For persistency of document information we make use of the ArtBase object-oriented DBMS which is fully integrated into VisualWorks\Smalltalk. This tool provides also services for concurrency control and transaction handling.

5 Application Scenario

The following section describes a scenario for producing hypermedia tourist information for the WWW by a group of people working together. The scenario follows the production process for WWW documents as described above.

5.1 System Configuration

A system configuration consisting of several client and server workstations shall demonstrate an example scenario for distributed production of WWW publications. Let us assume that people cooperating are located at three different sites

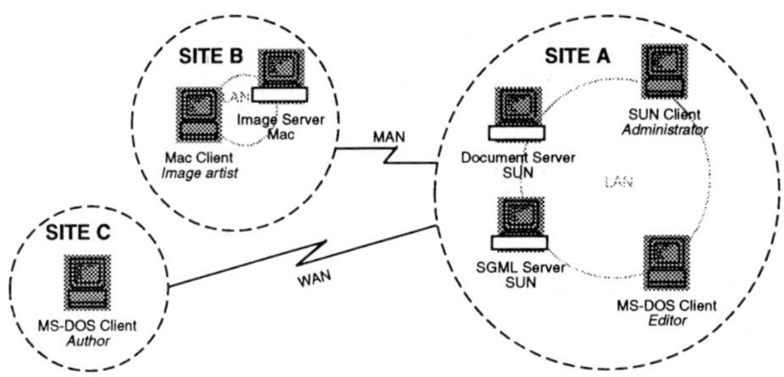

Fig. 2. Example Configuration

A, B and C. Site A is the location of a main tourist authority where the editor and the system administrator have their offices. The document server located at that site will be accessed by all users, whereas the SGML server is accessed by people (e.g. editor and authors) doing manipulation of text contents only. Both server applications run on UNIX workstations. The administrator uses his SUN-client for system set up and maintenance.

Site B is located in a town next to site A. An existing metropolitan area network (MAN) provides the network connection to the document server at site A. The image artist is responsible for capturing and editing images, photographs, etc. Both the client and the image server run on Macintosh computers. Because of frequent access to bulky image data the image server is preferably located at this site.

Finally, at site C, which is located at a third place, an author creates the basic text content for the publication. This site is connected to the editorial site via wide area network (WAN) (e.g. X.25 or ISDN). The author runs the client program on an MS-DOS computer for accessing the central document server and the SGML server.

5.2 Production of WWW Publications using HyDoMan

Configuration and set up of the Document Management System. An *Administration Tool* (see figure 3) is provided for specifying the publication's structure and various system settings.

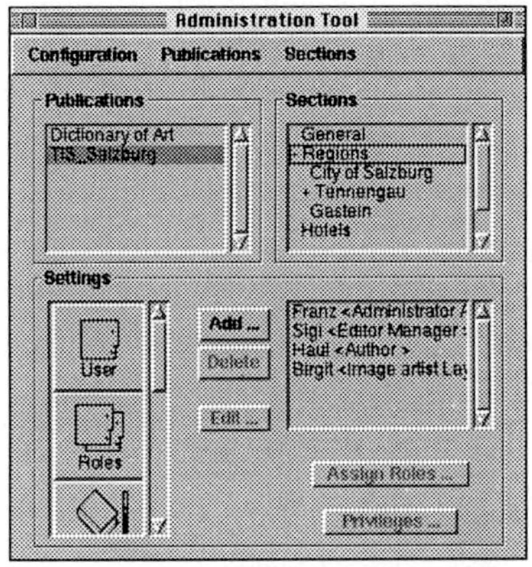

Fig. 3. Administration Tool

The organizational structure of a hypermedia publication consists of one or more sections. A section is structured into subsections or contains a set of documents. The specification of publications, sections and subsections establishes a hierarchical organization, which supports efficient storage and retrieval of documents. These hierarchies are also used for specifying access privileges of users and groups.

The settings part of the Administration Tool contains the parameters for system configuration. The following set of system parameters has to be specified: users and groups, roles, document status information, access privileges, information on document and object servers, document types, multimedia object formats, and specifications of component types.

Creation of Hypermedia Content. The skeleton of WWW publications is provided by text objects structured and encoded according to the HTML DTD. These text objects are created by means of an HTML editor (e.g. HoTMetaL, HTML Editor, etc.) [11] or a general SGML editing tool like Author/Editor [15].

Images and art work, such as logos or city maps may be created by using common drawing and painting tools. Photographs and pictures will be scanned and converted to an appropriate import format.

Audio sequences may be generated by digitizing analog audio information or captured from digital audio sources. Video clips can be created in a similar way.

Import of Hypermedia Content. In order to import an HTML document and its related multimedia objects the user creates a new document with the *Document Editor* tool and stores it under the respective section of the publication. A HyDoMan document has attributes like name, section, creator, creation time, last modification, version and status.

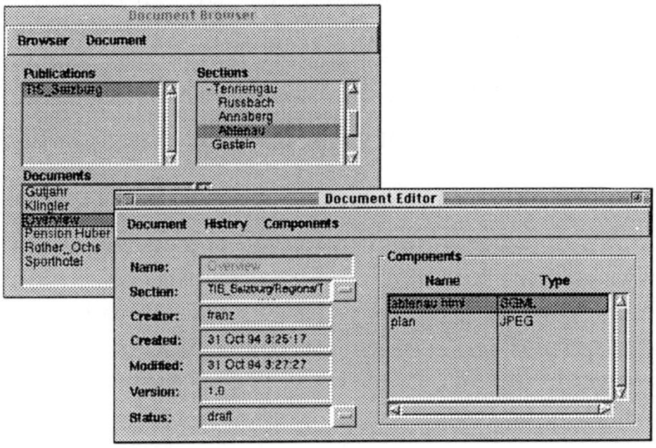

Fig. 4. Document Browser and Document Editor

An essential feature of HyDoMan documents is to contain a set of typed components for storing and accessing the content of a hypermedia document. For each specific multimedia object type there is one component type describing the general attributes (e.g. file format, DTD). For managing WWW documents the following set of component types is used: HTML-text, JPEG-image, XBM-image, GIF-image, TIFF-image, AU-audio, MPEG-video.

The handling of compound hypermedia documents requires to make a distinction between components which are *embedded* in the document and those which are *linked* to the document. Embedded components have a stronger relationship to the parent document in a way that they will be used by that document exclusively. On the other hand, linked components may be used by more than one document at the same time. Consequently, if the owner changes this object all other documents will point to the changed component too. For this reason it is necessary to allow versions of components [17] in order to avoid inconsistencies but also enable sharing of objects at the same time.

For each newly created component version the creator must decide whether he wants to share it with other documents or use this component exclusively. In the latter case the component must be marked as "private". Otherwise the component is "public" by default which means that other users having access to the respective publication may re-use the content of that component by referencing it or by creating a new version of the original component.

All major modifications on documents like creation, modification, and deletion of document information and components are recorded in the document's history list.

Value Adding - Editing of Documents. As soon as documents and multimedia objects have been created and imported into the document management system, the editorial work can start. For document retrieval a *Document Browser* tool is used. The browser allows the user to navigate on the hierarchic structure of publications. In addition to that documents can be renamed, moved, deleted, and edited. If an author wants to change the HTML-text component of a document he selects the corresponding document and launches a document editor. In the next step he selects the component from the editor's component list and opens a browser on it.

The *Component Browser* shows detailed information about the component and its versions. For doing any modifications on objects the author has to check-out the respective component version. If no other user is currently working on that version he will get a copy of the object transferred to his workstation. The check-out of a component version causes a lock on that object. Other users have read-only access while an object is locked. After the author has finished his task he has to check-in the component, in order to make the changes persistent and release the lock on that object. Instead of modifying the content of the component checked-out, the author could also create a new version.

Export of Documents. The exchange and transfer of publications to WWW servers and other applications is accomplished by export functionality. The user may select a document, section, or even a whole publication from the document browser and choose the export function.

The export function transfers the content of selected documents from the object servers to the specified destination on the file system. In order to store the information in an appropriate way, a directory structure according to the publication's structure is created automatically. All text components (=HTML objects) will be stored into this structure. For each multimedia object type a separate directory for storing the publication's multimedia objects will be created.

Distribution of Documents to the Web. The final distribution of the newly created tourist information requires that the existing home page of the organization is extended by a new hyperlink pointing to the root document of the new publication. distribute

An import issue to be considered when transferring the publication's content to the file-system of a WWW-server is path information contained in HTML documents. It has to be ensured that all references to documents and multimedia objects are valid and correct.

The HTML DTD foresees especially for this issue an element called BASE which specifies the document's location. The specification of the base address allows to make relative references to other documents and objects within this document. This feature eases the transferability of HTML documents substantially as only the BASE address of the document needs to be changed [9].

6 Future Plans

For the future we intend to provide support for parsing HTML document during document import. This feature shall allow interactive specification of components and component references for hyperlinks and multimedia objects.

7 Concluding Remarks

We have demonstrated an application scenario for producing tourist information for the Internet using a distributed hypermedia document management system. HyDoMan has originally been designed for supporting general electronic publication processes using an SGML-based document model. We have shown the most important features of our system in order to tackle important issues in producing hypermedia publications. The experience gained with this specific application scenario for the development of WWW publications has shown the general applicability of our system and will lead to future modifications and extensions.

References

1. *ISO 8879: Information Processing - Text and Office Systems - Standard Generalized Markup Language (SGML)*, 1986.
2. Berners-Lee, T. Hypertext markup language. Available in hypertext on WWW as http://info.cern.ch/hypertext/WWW/MarkUp/MarkUp.html.
3. Berners-Lee, T. Hypertext transfer protocol. Available in hypertext on WWW as http://info.cern.ch/hypertext/WWW/Protocols/HTTP/HTTP2.html.
4. Berners-Lee, T. The world wide web initiative. Available in hypertext on WWW as http://info.cern.ch/hypertext/WWW/TheProject.html.
5. Berners-Lee, T., Cailliau, R., Luotonen, A., Frystyk, H., and Secret, A. The world wide web. *Communications of the ACM 37*, 8 (August 1994), 76–82.
6. Burger, F., Quirchmayr, G., Reich, S., and Tjoa, A. M. Managing structured documents in distributed publishing environments. *Proceedings of the 5th International Conference DEXA '94* (September 1994), 83 – 92.
7. Clark, J. sgmls parser. Public domain parser; available via ftp from ifi.uio.no/pub/SGML/SGMLS/.
8. Commission of the European Communities, Directorate General XII, I. T., Industries, and Telecommunications. New opportunities for publishers in the information services market - executive summary. *Report EUR 14925 EN* (January 1993).
9. Connolly, D. W. Html elements. Available in hypertext on WWW as http://www.hal.com/users/connolly/html-spec/Tags.html.
10. Goldfarb, C. F. *The SGML Handbook*. Clarendon Press Oxford, New York, 1990.
11. Graham, I. Browsers, viewers and html preparation software. Available on WWW as http://www.utirc.utoronto.ca/HTMLdocs/intro_tools.html.

12. MÖHR, W., ET AL. Implementation of common publishing tools. Tech. rep., R2042 EUROPUBLISHING project, August 1994. Deliverable No. 16 - R2042/GMD/IPSI/DS/R/016/b1.
13. MOSAIC PROJECT, N. C. F. S. A. Ncsa mosaic. Available in hypertext on WWW as http://www.ncsa.uiuc.edu/SDG/Software/Mosaic/NCSAMosaicHome.html.
14. PITKOW, J. Html analyzer. Documentation available on WWW as http://www.gatech.edu/pitkow/html_analyzer/README.html.
15. SOFTQUAD, INC. *SoftQuad Author/Editor Version 2.2 for Macintosh*, September 1993.
16. TURNER, L. Publishing on the information highway: These are the issues. *Avalancher* (Summer 1994).
17. WEBER, A. Publishing tools need both: State-oriented and task-oriented version support. In *Proceedings of the 15th Annual International Computer Software and Applications Conference* (Tokyo, Japan, September 1991), pp. 633–639.

Legal aspects and security in electronic markets for tourism

Dr. iur. Bruno Wildhaber, CISA

r[3] Security Engineering AG, Zürichstrasse 151, 8607 Aathal, Switzerland
Email: wildhaber@r3.ch

Abstract: With the increased vulnerability of the information society, users have to be convinced that the systems they use are secure and therefore socially acceptable. There are several legal rules which demand secure systems. Base Line Security concepts will help to achieve an adequate level of security. Traditional procedures have to be replaced by more adequate ones, like the use of digital signatures as a new method of authentication. These procedures are currently tested in multinational pilot projects and could be used in tourism.

1 Introduction

1.1 Emerging technologies

New technologies are emerging and offer a large variety of opportunities how to achieve a more complete and comprehensive way of distributing information to any place in the world. These new technologies and concepts, like Open EDI, IN (Intelligent Network Services) [5,8,10], „Information Highway", Interactive Video etc. are bringing new dimensions into the life of every individual. With the fast expansion of these systems, everybody will be influenced by their positive and negative consequential effects.

1.2 Social acceptance of new procedures

With the increase of the *dependence* from these new systems, the society becomes more and more *vulnerable* in case technology fails [7]. In order to make new procedures social acceptable, people have to be convinced that the systems in use are working correctly, that their data will be carefully and confidentially treated and in case of failure adequate backup and recovery procedures exist. If the users do not trust into the systems, commercial success will be in question. Systems have to be built in a way, that they become socially acceptable [7,15]. In this respect, security has become an enabling factor for any new system that is to be planned and put into service.

1.3 The role of security and the law

There is a strong link between security and the law. These link is mainly based on three legal regulations [15]:

- Liability
- Secrecy

- Evidence

Although *liability* can be limited to a certain degree, dependable on national legislation and jurisdiction, there will always be the question whether the *necessary care* was taken to limit the possible damage to the acceptable degree. According to the legal system and the contractual agreements, limitation or exclusion of liability can be agreed upon [14,17]. However, in most of the European countries, exclusion of liability will not be allowed for gross negligence or intention. During proceedings at law, the question will be raised, whether *all necessary care* was applied to prevent or limit the damage to the proportional and adequate degree. To prevent this situation, every user of the system, enduser, service provider, clearing centers and PTTs must apply necessary security measures to reduce their risks to an acceptable degree. Measures and controls will be described later in this document (3.1-3.2).
Another source and connection factor between the law and security is *secrecy*, like professional secrecy for certain professions and people with a special position of trust, like lawyers or medical practitioners. Finally, all legal rules which are connected to procedures of producing *evidence* also demand for correct and integer information [15].

2 The legal framework

2.1 Telecom Law

Telecommunication is building up the backbone of most of the interactive systems used in tourism. Therefore, it will be important to know, which legal rules and regulations are affecting the users in a typical telecom environment. The following, simplified situation is showing the typical relations between *public and private law* in a third party network [14,16]:

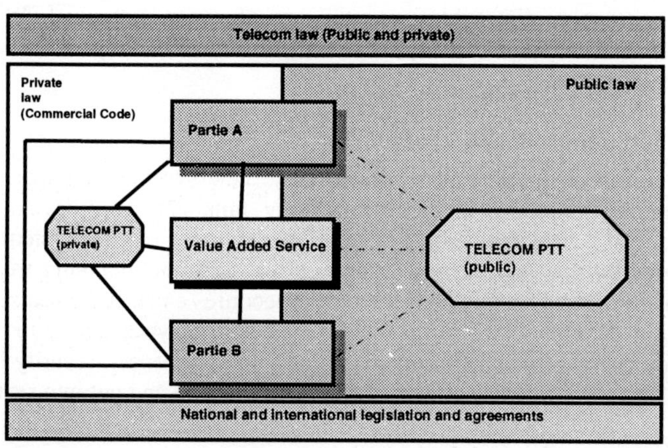

Fig. 1. Telecom Law

Although there are countries like Germany where the relations between the PTT are nowadays stipulated under private law, most of the key points, like the liability rules, are still based a public law and there is only narrow margin for private arrangements [3]. Telecom laws are already directly affecting electronic dataflow and related security measures (Switzerland: Fernmeldegesetz, FMG [4, 12]).

2.2 Secrecy

In Switzerland the *secrecy of telecommunications* (Fernmeldegeheimnis, art. 15 FMG) has been stipulated in Telecom law [14]. This is a peremptory rule and has to be applied to *everybody who is offering telecom services*, therefore applies also to the suppliers of enhanced services. It is therefore illegal to reveal any details about the contents, the parties and all other data in factual relation to the offered service. The supplier is even obliged to take all necessary care that the secrecy of telecommunications will not be compromised by any other party. There is no immediate indication in law, which measures have to be taken. There are some indications however, which allow to define the quality and quantity of security measures.

2.2.1 Liability

In swiss telecom law services are split up into the so called "Grunddienste" (*Basic Services*, art. 3 lit. f FMG) and "Erweiterte Dienste" (*Enhanced Services*, art. 3 lit. g FMG) [4]. Any processing of information which is more than normal transmission will be considered as enhanced service (art. 3 FMG). This separation of services is of main importance to the commercial user, due to the fact that the basic services, at current stage, will be reserved for the swiss PTT only. This will also have an impact on liability and diversification of risks. At current stage, there is a trend to contractually transfer the *liability to the enduser*. This is a very problematic procedure, due to the fact, that most of the enduser will not be able to estimate the risks they are forced to take over. There are different solutions to this problem, one would be to obligate the parties that they commit themselves to a defined security level (see 3.1).

2.3 Data Privacy

2.3.1 Legislation

In most of the European Countries, *Data Privacy* laws have been put in force. They are based on the tendencies *to protect the fundamental rights and freedom of natural persons, in particular their right to privacy, with respect to the processing of personal data* [13,17,19]. Therefore, the individual or all information and data about an indentified or identifiable natural person should be protected by Data Privacy Laws. The right of *information self-determination* is the central right concerning Data Privacy. Every indvidual should have the possibility to control the use of his/her data. To accomplish this, there are some basic principles which have to be set in legislation. Persons have to be *informed* that processing of personal data takes place, that they can *consult* the data and to object to processing whether they are manually or automatically processed. Processing of personal data in the public sector must be *lawful and adequate*. The data must not be excessive in relation to the purposes for which they are processed. The processing can only take place:

- with the *consent* of the data subject,

- if there is a *written legal basis*.

One of the main instruments for the individual is *the right of access* which has to be granted by the data owner.

2.3.2 Transborder data flow

One of the most controversial subjects in the EU is the question, to which degree data can be transferred to other countries. Basically, there will be a prohibition if the receivers country does not ensure an *adequate level of protection.* This level of protection will be extendend to either the private or the public sector. This is causing serious problems considering that certain countries, like the USA, do not grant comparable rights to their citizens. The US Data Privacy Law only guarantees the rights of citizens in relation to the public authority. This conflict is one of the main reasons why the EU Council directive on data privacy has not yet been passed.

2.3.3 Relevance for information in tourism

Most of the data in information systems for tourism will be related to natural persons, therefore, Data Privacy will be a main issue.

2.4 EDI contracts

Although tourism has not traditionally been an area where EDI has played an important role [17], this situation will change dramatically with the opportunities *Open EDI* or *Electronic Markets* will offer. In either case, EDI contracts will play an important role in structuring the legal relation between the parties. They have to describe the *control framework* which consists of the following points [20]:

Table 1

Definitions	Validity and Formation of Contract	Admissibility in evidence of Messages	Processing and Acknowledgement of Receipt of Messages
Security of Messages[1]	Confidentiality and protection of personal data	Recording and storage of Messages	Operational requirements for EDI
Technical specifications and requirements	Liability	Dispute resolution	Applicable Law
Effect	Modification, term and severability		

[1]Topics shaded have a direct link to security.

3 Security

3.1 Base Line Security

As previously mentioned, there will be a need for all parties involved to implement an adequate level of security. This can be accomplished by agreeing upon a certain degree of security, called *„Base Line Security"*. This would describe the controls and

measures which are state of the art in a certain environment. Examples for this can be found in [1,9].
In IS security, controls are more than just technical and organizational measures to secure *availability, integrity and confidentiality*:

> *Control encompasses the policies, procedures, practices and organizational structures that assure the adequacy of information asset management and the consistency and reliability of computer information systems activities [9}.*

This includes organisational questions like personal selection, IS management and change management to physical security like fire extinguishers and perimeter protection. Through the growing importance of global networking in tourism, telecommunication has become one of the most critical topics in security.

3.2 Security Services in Telecommunication

A number of security services have been identified which can be found in the ISO International Standard 7498-2: *Open Systems Interconnection Reference Model* - Part 2: Security Architecture, 1989. EDI or other communication services require the following security mechanisms [2,5,10,15]:

Table 2

Data or message (origin) authentication	The corroboration that the source of data received is as claimed
(Peer) entity authentication	The corroboration that a peer entity in an association is the one claimed
Non-repudiation service	The prevention of a denial by one of the entities involved in a communication of having participated in all or part of the communication

3.3 Authentication of Messages

3.3.1 Definition, Methods and Document classes

The classes of documents which require *authentication* and which are of main importance in the context of EDI and tourism can be listed as follows [17]:

- Company documents and forms,
- Bills of sale,
- Bills of exchange,
- Shipping documentation,
- Taxation declarations.

Authentication describes a form of proof that a document or a message is originated from an *identifiable* and *authorised* source. This concept requires at least the following qualities:

- Integrity and
- Non-repudiation (to deny having sent/received a message).

A *hand-written signature* is the most common form of authentication and is recognised in all EU states and EFTA countries. Usually the highest form will be the verification of a signature by a *Notary Public*. In civil law countries, a document drawn up in this way will be recognised as directly enforceable in court without additional formalities. There are some differences in case law countries, where there where still seals in use, however, recent English legislation has dispensed with the necessity of sealing by companies [17].

3.3.2 Hand-written Signature

In most of the examined countries *no legal definition* of "signature" exists. The most common form is the signature written with one's own hand. There are certain elements specific to a signature [6,11]:

1. *Hand-written* form (written with one's own hand), showing the signatory disclosing his or her identity, proof that the signed document is originated from an identifiable authorised person.
2. *Distinct and specific* to the identity of a person and that of the contracting party.
3. A firm *intention to be bound* by the contents of the document
4. *Verification* of the documents *authenticity*.

Any hand-written signature has several functions and characteristics which one should be able to reproduce when using electronic equivalents [6,11,15].

3.3.3 Electronic authentication

Different electronic equivalents to hand-written authentication exists. The most effective way of reproducing the above functions is the use of *Digital Signatures,* which allows to include the following security functions [6,11]:

- User identification
- User authentication
- Message content integrity
- Message sequence integrity
- Non-repudiation of origin
- Non-repudiation of receipt
- Confidentiality

The most typical and standardised way of applying a digital signature is the following. Each entity has created its own key pair consisting of a *secret* and *a public key*. The public key is distributed in some secure way to all other users. When an electronic document has to be authenticated by a particular entity, a *hash value* of the entire electronic document is calculated and encrypted (signed) by the *secret key* of its owner. The digital signature is then appended to the document. The receiver will verify this signature by performing the same procedure as the signatory, but using the *public key* to encrypt the message. If both signatures are identical this will be proof that the message is integer [6].

3.3.4 Hand-written vs. Digital signatures

We have seen the technical approach to produce a digital signature, but what are the real *differences* between this surrogate and its antipode, the hand-written signature ? We will have to compare the whole document, not only the signature. There is a fundamental difference between the two methods. A hand-written signature always looks the same, but is not "glued" to the document. An electronic signature depends on the content of the document; *a different document will always result in a different signature*. In addition to the document contents there will always be a time stamp added, to make sure, that none two messages look alike. Comparisons between the two methods can be found in [6, 16].

3.3.5 Verification of signature

When a paper document is called into *evidence*, witnesses may be called to identify the signature and an expert witness may be called for the verification of the signature. The electronic equivalent. e.g. the Digital Signature, provides a link between the message and the signature and even verifies the contents of the message. It will be necessary to use a third party to provide the notary function. This will be successful if this position will be held by a common and unconditionally *trusted third party* (TTP) [6, 17,18].

3.3.6 Legal situation regarding electronic signatures

There is *little consistency* in the different laws as to the need for a written document to evidence the existence of a contract between parties, although all countries require some form of consensus. There are *eighteen* (18 !) legal systems in Europe with varying requirements to the formality and authentication of paper-based contracts, therefore there will be no common approach for implementing harmonised EDI relevant legislation [17].
A minority of countries speculated that electronic signatures might be accepted as a legal form of "signature" (Italy, Denmark, Netherlands, Ireland, Finland, Switzerland, Spain). In others, other form than hand-written will not be accepted unless notarised (Germany). In a third group of countries, *custom rather than law* has allowed the use of digital signatures.
In fact a *legal vacuum* exists. There is no harmonised provision for the use or regulation of EDI. Therefore future legislations will have to make sure that traditional paper contracts can coexist with their electronic successor.

4 Actual projects in the EU

4.1 The FAST Project

The purpose of this project is to design and verify an european wide *operational secure EDI pilot* in which existing organisations/companies (institutions and private bodies) will define in detail their respective roles and set up the necessary facilities [18].

To limit the complexity of the project organisation, the project started in six European countries, namely Belgium, Denmark, France, Germany, Portugal and Switzerland, with the aim to extend it to other countries as soon as the feasibility is demonstrated and the critical success factor is achieved.

Within the scope of future development of EDI EDIFACT and its correlated need for security on one side and the explicit need for security services as stated in the new European Model for Interchange Agreements [20], the FAST project identifies clearly the role of the different actors.

In an intersectoral and transnational communication environment, the EDI EDIFACT Users (i.e. the message authors and receivers) and the transmitter must be clearly identified through a digital signature. Moreover, this *signature needs to be authenticated* and its legal validity certified by an independent local body acting as a *Certification Authority (CA)* and issuing the appropriate certificate. This function will be handled by the local Chambers of Commerce or their branch offices. The certifications performed by local CAs require a "guarantee" by a *Central Certification Authority (CCA) at national level*, acting as a moral authority and a guarantor of the respect of the rules of behaviour and of the certification procedures by the CAs. This function will be realised by the *national federations of Chambers of Commerce*. The national CCAs are, in turn, covered by an *International Certification Authority (ICA)*, acting as a moral authority and a guarantor of the compliance with the rules of behaviour and with the certification procedures by the CCAs. This function may be realised by the International Chamber of Commerce and/or by cross certification between countries.

The public distribution of the certificates is done by means of international data communications provided by the PTTs or other international carriers. By means of these data communications facilities the users have access to "*servers*" which are able to verify the validity of a given certificate.

Security Experts, VANs providers, hardware and software manufacturers provide the necessary expertise and systems in order that the FAST structure will function securely in accordance with the aim of the project.

The pilot project is a co operation between:

- Federation of Chambers of Commerce for the registration of users and the creation of certificates;
- PTT organisations for the on line distribution of certificates;
- EDI users in private and public sectors, some of which are involved through national organisations such as Siprocom;
- Security consultancy providing the necessary security tools;
- VANs providers, providing EDI services and systems integration.

The consortium will ensure close cooperation with other relevant TEDIS projects, such as EDIRA, E1 and E5 as well as legal aspects [20]. At the same time liaison will be ensured by membership of several partners to UN/EDIFACT SJWG, ISO/IEC SC27, EWOS SEC and Infosec projects which are relevant, such as the work on TTPs and the Green Book. Legislation will be considered and respected carefully, and the emphasis will be on the application of digital signatures.

References

[1] BSI, British Standards Institution: A code of Practice for Information Security Management, 1993.

[2] COOPER, JAMES ARLIN: Computer & Communications Security, Strategies for the 1990s, New York 1989.

[3] FANGMANN, HELMUT: Rechtliche Konsequenzen des Einsatzes von ISDN, Opladen 1993, pp

[4] FISCHER, PETER: Telekommunikation, in MEYER-MARSILIUS, HANS JOACHIM/SCHLUEP, WALTER R./STAUFFACHER, WERNER: Beziehungen Schweiz-EG, Kommentare, Zürich 1991.

[5] FUMY, WALTER: Sicherheitsstandards für offene Systeme, DuD 6 (1991), p 288f.

[6] GOEBEL, JÜRGEN W./SCHELLER, JÜRGEN: Elektronische Unterschriftsverfahren in der Telekommunikation, Wiesbaden 1991, DUD - Fachbeiträge, Bd. 12.

[7] HAMMER, VOLKER/PORDESCH, ULRICH/ROßNAGEL: Betriebliche Telefon und ISDN-Anlagen rechtsgemäss gestaltet, Berlin 1993.

[8] HERRIGEL, ALEXANDER/LAI XUJIA: Authentication and Authorization in the IN based on Symmetric and Asymmetric Techniques, 3rd Int. Conf. On Intelligence in Networks, ICIN'94, Bordeaux, Oct. 11-13, 1994.

[9] The EDP Auditors Foundation: Control Objectives, Controls in a computer environment: Objectives, Guidelines and Audit Procedures, Carol Stream, 1992.

[10] PFITZMANN, BIRGIT/WAIDNER MICHAEL, PFITZMANN ANDREAS: Rechtssicherheit in offenen digitalen Systemen, DuD 5 und 6/90, p 243 f.

[11] RIHACZEK, KARL: Das elektronische Unterschriftssurrogat, Rechtliche Aspekte und ihre technische Umsetzung, DuD 11 (1991), p 568 f.

[12] SCHWEIZER, RAINER J./LEHMANN, BEAT: Datenschutzrecht/Informatikrecht, Loseblattsammlung, Zürich 1988.

[13] TINNEFELD, MARIE-THERES/EHMANN, EUGEN: Einführung in das Datenschutzrecht, München 1992.

[14] WILDHABER, BRUNO: Electronic Markets and Security Requirements - The Legal Basis, Newsletter of the Competence Centre Electronic Markets, University of St. Gallen , April 1994, p 8.

[15] WILDHABER, BRUNO: Informationssicherheit, Rechtliche Grundlagen und Anforderungen an die Praxis, Zürich 1993, pp 53-57.

[16] WILDHABER, BRUNO: I4, proceedings

[17] TEDIS Phase II, B5: Report on Authentication, Storage and Use of Codes in EDI Messages, Vol. I- III.

[18] FAST: First Attempt to Secure Trade, EC Project, Project documentation.

[19] Draft European Parliament and Council Directive on the *Protection of individuals with regard to the processing of personal data and on the free movement of such data*, October 1994

[20] Draft recommendation of the European Commission on a "European Model EDI Agreement", October 1994

An Anonymity Service for Targeted Advertising

Nancy D. Griffeth James Katz

Bellcore
445 South Street
Morristown NJ 07960 USA

1 Introduction

Privacy concerns can hamper the tourism industry's efficiency in reaching targeted audiences through advertising[7, 8]. The same concerns might also decrease the likelihood that individuals can find interesting travel opportunities. We propose a novel method of providing personal information to tourism advertisers while simultaneously shielding the identity of the individual consumers to whom the information pertains. Thus tourism marketers can target their efforts more precisely, even on the basis of confidential information, without violating personal privacy.

We assume that a targeted advertising system involves at least the following functions:

- An advertiser submits a profile to an advertising delivery system. The profiles specify values of certain consumer attributes.
- Viewers matching this profile will be provided with the ad.
- The advertiser will be billed for the number of consumers that were provided with the ad.

The central requirement is to prevent leakage of private information due to the normal operation of the system. The most difficult threat to thwart is advertisers inferring private information about consumers by using the profiles together with the number of consumers receiving the corresponding ads. Methods for inferring information from a profile and the number of matching individuals in the database are described in [3].

We observe that the information can be protected, even while allowing advertisers to target consumers having selected values for confidential attributes, if it is not possible to identify the consumers having given values of the attributes.

For example, if an advertiser is told that 100 consumers out of 10,000 are interested in blue movies, the advertiser still does not know which 100 are interested. The threat to confidentiality is realized only if enough information is provided to identify which consumers they are. This can be prevented by partitioning the values of the publicly-known attributes so that individual consumers cannot be identified from information about them that is publicly available.

Our proposed system is one method of reconciling the apparent conflict of interests between advertisers and consumers. We describe a trusted profile filtering and ad delivery service that will neutrally serve the interests of all market participants, in this case, the tourism industry, advertisers, and consumers.

1.1 Example

We illustrate the privacy mechanism using an imaginary database of "frequent flyers", shown in Table 1. Given the popularity of such incentive programs, and the types of customer data generally found in travel agency databases, we think an example drawn from this area should prove germane. Specifically, one out of every ten U.S. citizens has registered in the American Airlines company's frequent flyer program, and so some personal information resides in this airline's database. This represents a significant type of data both for targeting and for privacy concerns. Our imaginary database contains the following attributes:

- Dietary restrictions - values are ordinary, low cholesterol, diabetic, diet, heart, kosher, phenylketonuric, low salt, vegetarian, and other;
- Gender - values are M (male), F (female), and unknown (U);
- Occupation - a 3-digit code indicating occupation
- Frequent flyer classification - values are ordinary, bronze, silver, and gold;
- Area code - 3-digit area code;
- Telephone number - 7-digit telephone number;
- Zip+four - 5-digit zip code plus four digits specifying block;
- Credit card number - 3-digit credit card number (shortened for illustration);
- Frequent flyer number - 1 to 5 digit frequent flyer identifier;
- Income level - percentiles, from lowest decile to highest;
- Education level - H (high school), B (college), M (master's or other non-doctoral graduate degree), P (doctoral degree)
- Name - frequent flyer name

Trav	Diet	S	Occ	FF Cat	Phone Number	Zip+Four	CC	Freq Fly Num	I	E
0000	ordi	M	284	silv	555-4705	8030-1021	420	43894	9	B
0010	ordi	M	807	silv	555-8000	8030-8610	525	36964	9	B
1000	ordi	F	920	bron	666-9459	7050-5700	561	32941	5	M
0000	ordi	F	807	ordi	555-9858	8050-0002	444	75556	5	H
0000	ordi	M	281	bron	555-6373	8010-4220	798	65809	7	P
0001	ordi	M	234	bron	555-6693	8040-1011	101	37990	2	B
0000	ordi	F	258	bron	555-5151	8010-1011	379	37576	2	B
0000	ordi	F	282	bron	666-4933	7020-4620	025	163	1	B
0000	vege	U	231	bron	555-6054	8010-1832	998	69067	9	P
0000	diab	M	234	ordi	555-3718	8040-4992	257	63865	3	M
0010	diet	F	807	ordi	555-6942	8030-4511	228	55963	3	M
0000	ordi	M	807	bron	666-3168	7040-2001	245	208	3	B
0001	ordi	M	256	bron	555-6330	8040-4851	828	55999	8	B
0000	ordi	F	801	bron	555-6185	8010-4238	383	4456	4	M
0000	ordi	F	807	ordi	555-4272	8030-4313	493	10504	5	H
0000	chol	M	807	ordi	555-4272	8030-4312	272	27253	3	H
0000	chol	M	807	ordi	666-5136	7040-3413	575	32896	6	B
0000	ordi	M	285	bron	666-4684	7020-5123	883	262	8	M
0000	diab	M	259	bron	555-9766	8040-1322	876	47476	8	M
0000	chol	M	807	ordi	666-5547	7040-2205	965	280	9	B

Table 1: Sample Frequent Flyer Database. Attributes: Trav=Travel History, Diet=Dietary Request, S=Sex, Occ=Occupation, FF Cat=Frequent Flyer Category, CC=Credit Card Number, Freq Fly Num=Frequent Flyer Number, I=Income Level, E=Educational Level

Most of the data in Table 1 is bogus (e.g., credit card numbers and frequent flyer numbers), but because the names and some other information are from a real database we have left out the names.

2 Background

Long-standing concerns about protecting individual privacy have been exacerbated by the storage of large databases of information on computers. The privacy of individuals in demographic database for targeted advertising requires protection from at least the following threats:

- Direct release of raw data about an individual.
- Deduction of information about an individual from knowledge of who received an ad corresponding to a given profile; and
- Deduction of information about an individual from knowledge of a series of profiles, together with the number of individuals that received or would

receive the ads corresponding to those profiles.

Protection from the first two attacks follows the method of Loeb and Yacobi used to protect the identity of recipients of information from an information filtering system, described in [6].

The nature of the third attack is subtle. It could arise through the billing of an advertiser for a sequence of ads. Each ad is sent to a collection of individuals satisfying an advertiser-provided profile. Subsequently, the advertiser is billed an amount depending on the number of individuals receiving the ad. Alternatively, it could arise through a "what-if" facility provided to support advertiser planning. In this scenario, the advertiser would submit profiles and the response would provide the number of individuals satisfying each profile.

There are several methods commonly used for protecting the privacy of individuals' data from this kind of attack. The best-known mechanism restricts the size of the responses to queries, so that the answer is not given or is given as "less than (greater than) B" if the size of the response is less than (or greater than) some bound B. Unfortunately, this does not protect against "tracker attacks" described in [9], where it is shown that even for bounds close to half the number of records in the database, it is possible to compromise information with a simple tool called a "tracker".

Trackers are a special case of linear system attacks, which involve solving a system of equations

$$HX = Q$$

where $h_{ij} = 1$ if $j \in C_i$, $h_{ij} = 0$ otherwise, and q_i is the sum over some attribute of the number of records in the response to the ith query. Dobkin, Jones, and Lipton proposed restricting query set overlap in [5] to prevent this kind of attacks, but implementing such a control is probably infeasible since before releasing a statistic the database would have to compare the latest query set with every previous one.

There are also methods restricting potentially compromising statistics. One such method is the "cell-suppression" technique, in which statistics that would reveal sensitive information are never released. Cell suppression applies best to 2- and 3-dimensional tables, however, rather than arbitrary queries, so it does not appear applicable for our problem.

Another approach, which is close to that used here, is to partition the database into disjoint groups[11, 1]. The properties of the partitions developed in these methods are not useful for targeting ads, and so we develop a different partitioning below.

Mechanisms that add noise, such as by adding or subtracting a random number to the result, are appealing in their simplicity, but not entirely satisfactory since the result provided to the advertiser is inherently inaccurate. One potentially useful of the noise-addition approaches would be the *random sample query* approach[2], in which responses to queries are based on random samples of the population rather than the entire population. Dalal has also developed a method for protecting confidentiality of data by permitting respondents to lie about the true value a certain percentage of the time[10], but this would mean that targeted ads would be sent to the wrong audience a certain percentage of the time. For products that send different messages to different audiences, this could be a serious problem. Another issue is raised by the existence of a variety of noise removal methods. One or more of these may be applied to removing the noise, thus destroying confidentiality.

All of the methods described above were developed primarily for protecting the data in statistical databases and do not fit the targeting advertising scenario particularly well, because either they do not permit exact targeting on the basis of the values of the confidential attributes, or the response is not precise as to the number of such individuals. Our method does permit both, by introducing uncertainty about the identity of the individuals having those values, rather than by introducing uncertainty about what the values are. It should also be useful to investigate combination of this method with other methods.

3 Architecture of the Privacy Mechanism

The privacy mechanism is summarized by figure 1. It guarantees that an advertiser cannot deduce, through the normal functioning of the system, by the methods described above, the values of certain attributes of an individual that are considered private.

The entities appearing in Figure 1 are:

- the consumer, who provides a profile describing his or her attributes and preferences;
- the advertiser, who submits advertisements and profiles describing members of the desired audience for an advertisement;
- the filtering entity, which determines which consumers should be in the audience for a specific advertisement; and
- the ad delivery entity, which knows the network addresses of the consumers and sends the ad to them.

There are four parts to the method:

- The advertiser is separate from the ad delivery entity, so that the advertiser does not know who receives the ad and thus cannot deduce who satisfies a given profile from the delivery addresses.

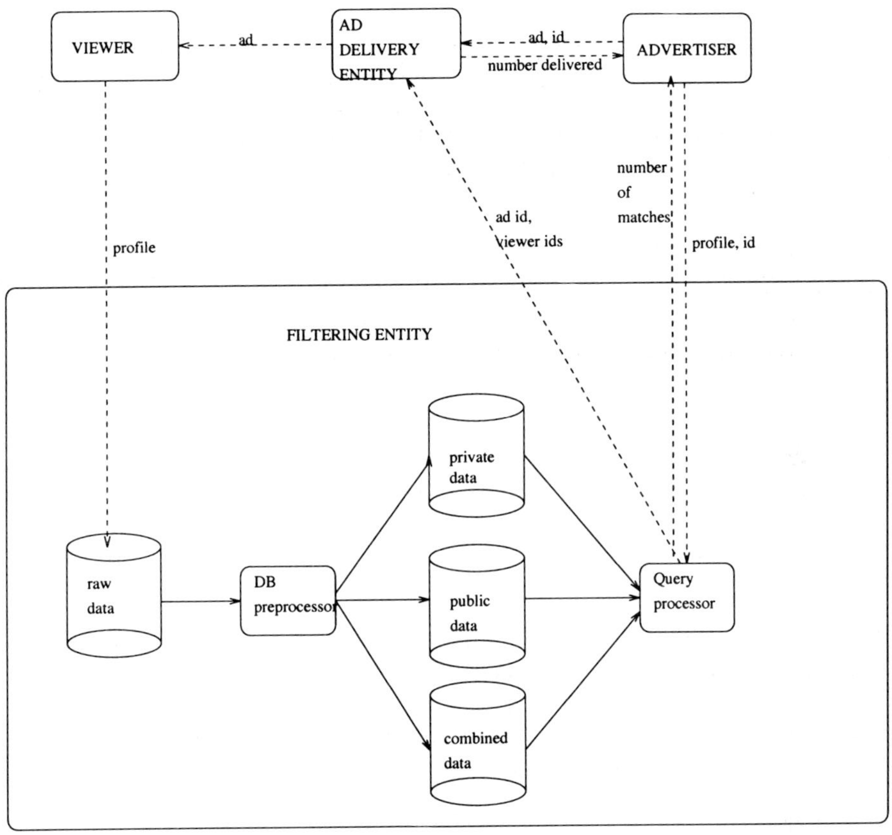

Figure 1: The profile filtering and ad delivery system.

- The advertiser and the ad delivery system are separate from the ad filtering entity, so that neither of them can determine who has a given profile.
- Attributes are divided into *private* attributes and *public* attributes. The private attributes are those whose values individuals can be expected to keep private, and they cannot be determined by ordinary methods of data collection and without assurances of confidentiality. We expect that the values of the public attributes (such as name, address, and so on) are widely available.
- The database is processed by a pre- and post-processor in such a way that a certain level of uncertainty is introduced as to which values of private attributes go with which individuals, so that it is impossible to say with certainty that an individual has a given value of a private attribute. The level of uncertainty can be controlled.

In the example database, the private attributes are: income level, dietary restrictions, frequent flyer classification, and travel patterns. The remainder are public attributes.

In subsequent sections, we describe the way we pre-process and query the profile data without violating the privacy of individuals.

4 Processing and Querying the Data

4.1 The data model

We assume here that all of the profiles are collected in a single repository at a central location. The profile is defined by asking an individual to enter the value for each attribute in a defined set $\{A_1, ..., A_n, P_1, ..., P_q, ID\}$ where the A_i are the public attributes, the P_i are the private attributes, and ID is a unique identifier for an individual consumer.

We require that only one value be entered for each attribute. If it is necessary to use multi-valued attributes (in the example, the travel history is such an attribute) then the attribute will take on sets as its values, and we treat each possible set of values as a single value.

Note that we assume that there is only one row in the database for each individual, but we do not assume that there is any combination of attributes other the ID that uniquely identifies an individual. Thus it is possible that many different individuals will have exactly the same values on the public attributes. Furthermore, the ID will never be used in targeting advertisements; it will be used only for the consumer to update the profile.

Trav	Diet	S	Occ	FF Cat	Phone Number	Zip+Four	CC	Freq Fly Num	I	E
0000	ordi	F	210	bron	829-4692	7040-3032	353	72550	1	H
0000	ordi	U	210	ordi	829-4692	7040-3032	251	39250	3	B
0000	kosh	M	210	ordi	829-4692	7040-3032	268	61813	4	M
0000	ordi	M	210	ordi	829-4692	7040-3032	285	67888	4	M
0000	ordi	M	210	ordi	829-4692	7040-3032	302	72271	4	B
0000	ordi	M	210	ordi	829-4692	7040-3032	319	74233	4	B
0000	ordi	M	210	ordi	829-4692	7040-3032	438	35605	5	B
0000	ordi	M	210	ordi	829-4692	7040-3032	455	62524	5	M
0000	ordi	F	210	silv	829-4546	7040-3032	506	69517	8	B
0000	ordi	M	210	silv	829-4938	7040-3032	421	4744	9	B

Table 2: Sample Frequent Flyer Database. Attributes: Trav=Travel History, Diet=Dietary Request, S=Sex, Occ=Occupation, FF Cat=Frequent Flyer Category, CC=Credit Card Number, Freq Fly Num=Frequent Flyer Number, I=Income Level, E=Educational Level

We require the advertisers to specify which attributes (both public and private) are most important for targeting. To illustrate the operation of the algorithm, we will assume that the advertisers have specified the the attributes Sex, Occupation, Zip+Four, Income Level, and Educational Level are the most important attributes. The advertisers will be able to specify the values of these attributes to the creates degree of certainty.

Finally, we require that allowable levels of uncertainty K_i be specified for each private attribute P_i. In the illustrative example, these will 3 for Travel History, 3 for Diet, 2 for Frequent Flyer Class, and 3 for Income Level. Thus, since there are 10 distinct values of Diet in the database, an individual's actual value for this attribute could be determined only up to 3 of the values.

4.2 Pre-processing the data

The pre-processing of the data is used to introduce uncertainty about which values of the private attributes correspond to which individuals. The measure of uncertainty about a private attribute is the number of values of that attribute that could apply to that individual. K_i denotes the minimum uncertainty that is desired for private attribute P_i.

We want to enforce the following uncertainty property:

Uncertainty Property For each individual in the database, if the public attribute values are $A_1 = v_1$, $A_2 = v_2$, ... , $A_n = v_n$ for that individual then for each private attribute P_i, there are at least K_i distinct values appearing in rows having the values $v_1, ..., v_n$ of $A_1, ..., A_n$.

For example, suppose the database has the rows shown in Table 2. Even if an advertiser is able to determine that a particular individual has Occupation 210 and Zip+Four 07040-3032, it is possible to deduce only that the Income Level is 1, 3, 4, 5, 8, or 9. As a result, the privacy of any such individual's Income Level is safe from queries involving Occupation, Zip+Four, and Income Level.

However, some values of private attributes may deducible. For example, if there are no other rows in the database with Occupation 210 and Zip+Four 07040-3032, then we see that only two values for Diet are possible: kosher and ordinary. Since the uncertainty level specified for Diet was 3, the privacy of these individual's Diet choices are not safe (at the specified level) from queries involving Occupation, Zip+Four, and Diet.

To achieve the required levels of uncertainty, our mechanism uses two kinds of operations:

1. Combine values of an attribute.
2. Remove tuples from the database;

The first operation allows us to camouflage individuals by disguising the attribute values that make them distinct from other individuals. The second operation allows us to remove tuples corresponding to individuals that are easy to identify and hard to disguise by the first means.

Pre-processing method.

1. For each private attribute P_i:
   (a) **Determine which rows of the database are already safe for P_i.** Create a set F of safe tuples and a set R of unsafe tuples:
      i. Sort the database on values of the important public attributes. Within that, sort on the values on P_i.
      ii. Count the number of distinct values of P_i that occur for each tuple of values $\langle v_1, ..., v_m \rangle$ on the public attributes. If this is more than K_i, then these rows are safe; otherwise, they are not. Add safe rows to the set F; unsafe rows to the set R.
   (b) **Compute collections of attribute values to combine to make rows in R safe.** Repeat the following steps for important public attributes A_j, in decreasing order of the number of values of A_j appearing in the database[1], using the resulting database on the subsequent iteration, until enough tuples are safe:

[1]The same attribute may be used repeatedly if it has more values after this step than any other attribute

Pass	Number of Values of Zip+Four	Number of Values of Occupation	Attribute Used in Pass	Safe Tuples After Pass
-	1669	45	Zip+Four	1914
1	391	45	Zip+Four	3993
2	191	45	Zip+Four	4780
3	99	45	Zip+Four	5546
4	53	45	Zip+Four	6277
5	31	45	Zip+Four	6949
6	31	19	Occupation	7257
7	20	19	Zip+Four	7653
8	13	19	Zip+Four	8159
9	13	4	Occupation	8406

Table 3: Results of Successive Passes of Database Pre-Processing.

i. Create a file containing all tuples in the database having a value on the public attribute A_j that appears in an unsafe tuple (this can be done by projecting R onto A_j and joining the result with F).

ii. Sort this file on the values of the important public attributes *excluding* A_j.

iii. For each tuple of values on the important public attributes other than A_j, find rows containing K_i distinct values of P_i. Combine the values of A_j appearing in these rows.

In this step, each value of A_j should be used in only one combination of values. To avoid using it again, maintain a list of previously combined values and ignore rows with those values subsequently.

(c) **Create a new database of tuples in which the individuals having specified values of P_i cannot be identified.** Select a representative value from each collection of values defined in the preceding step (perhaps the first value added to the set), and substitute it for each value of A_j appearing in the original database.

2. For each remaining public attribute: Combine the values occurring with each fixed value of the important public attributes.

Table 3 illustrates the effect of these steps on a sample database of the type described in section 1.1. The sample database contains 8464 tuples. We will protect the value of the important private attribute "Income Level".

Income Level. The number of safe tuples in the original database is 1914; the number of unsafe tuples is 6550. Table 3 summarizes the results of running the algorithm.

Since Sex and Education Level have so few values (3 and 4, respectively), they were never candidates to be used in a pass. There are still 258 tuples in the database whose values of income level could not be protected. These tuples represent unusual individuals in the database.

4.3 Querying the database

If a new database containing only the combined values of attributes are stored, then queries can be executed against this database without modification. However, the queries should refer to the combined values rather than the original values of the attributes.

Alternatively, a record of the partitioning of attribute values that is computed by the above procedure can be maintained instead of building a new copy of the database. The query processor can then either reject or modify any queries of the following form:

The query specifies values of both public and private attributes, in such a way as to violate the partitions of values defined in the pre-processing step. We say that a query violates a partition of an attribute A if the partition contains values v_1 and v_2 and the response would include a row in which $A = v_1$ and not an otherwise identical row with $A = v_2$.

To determine whether this is the case, the response can be computed and then the rest of the database checked to see if any such rows exist.

To modify such a query, the query processor would include the rows that would violate the partition instead of leaving them out. This amount to modifying the query and the advertiser should be informed of this.

5 Conclusion

In conclusion, the tourism industry, like so many other information-intensive activities, is confronted with the dilemma of working efficiently without endangering important social attributes, such as privacy. Yet both consumers and vendors can gain if accurate personal information is used in the aggregate without threatening the privacy of the individual concerned.

To serve this end, we have proposed a mechanism separating public and private attributes so exact values of private attributes can be used in targeting ads or other information without revealing the identity of individuals having those values. Our mechanism expands and improves upon mechanisms proposed by others for protecting confidential data. In further contrast, ours does not require introduction of noise into the values of apposite private attributes.

As powerful information delivery technologies become available, it is vital for societal and individual well-being that important values, exemplified by privacy, be preserved. We believe our mechanism promotes this end.

References

[1] F. Y. Chin and G. Ozsoyoglu. Security in partitioned dynamic statistical databases. *Proc. IEEE COMPSAC Conf.*, pages 594–601, 1979.

[2] D. E. Denning. Secure statistical databases under random sample queries. *ACM Transactions on Database Systems*, 5(3):291–315, September 1980.

[3] D. E. Denning. *Cryptography and Data Security*. Addison-Wesley, Reading, MA, 1982.

[4] D. E. Denning, J. Schlorer, and E. Wehrle. Memoryless inference controls for statistical databases. 1982.

[5] D. Dobkin, A. Jones, and R. Lipton. Secure databases: Protection against user inference. *ACM Transactions on Database Systems*, 4(1):97–106, March 1979.

[6] S. Hardt-Kornacki and Y. Yacobi. Securing end-user privacy during information filtering. *Proceedings of the Conference on High Performance Information Filtering*, 1991.

[7] J. Katz. Social aspects of telecommunications security policy. *IEEE Technology and Society*, 9(2):16–24, Summer 1990.

[8] J. Katz. Privacy in der telekommunikation: Trends und probleme. *Technikfolgenabschdtzung in der Telekommunikation*, 1991.

[9] J. Schlorer. Identification and retrieval of personal records from a statistical data bank. *Methods Inf. Med.*, 14(1):7–13, January 1975.

[10] S. L. Warner. Randomized response: A survey technique for eliminating evasive answer bias. *Journal of the American Statistical Association*, 60:63–69, 1965.

[11] C. T. Yu and F. Y. Chin. A study on the protection of statistical databases. *Proc. ACM SIGMOD International Conference on the Management of Data*, pages 169–181, 1977.

Multiperspective hypermedia representation of customs and rituals: implications for tourism

H. Lukas, J. Stockinger

Institut für Völkerkunde, University of Vienna
Universitätsstraße 7/4, A-1010 Vienna, Austria

Abstract. Models for a multi-perspective hypermedia representation of rituals are discussed with the help of examples from Southeast Asia (reburial ritual of the Toba-Batak of Northern Sumatra, funeral rites of the Toraja of Sulawesi, Thai everyday rituals). The long-term objective is the development of a Virtual Book on Cultural Etiquette and Manners for tourists, businessmen and women and diplomats. As a distributed hypermedia system the World Wide Web could act as an ideal carrier. In the framework of collaborative writing contributions from all over the world on behavior specific to cultures should be collected and coordinated.

1 Introduction

The average touristic consumer who wishes to learn the correct manners, the emotional models and the forms of behavior specific to the culture of his "target country" usually has only a limited amount of reliable sources of information at his disposal. Normally the interested tourist preparing for a journey into a foreign culture must make do with guide books, slide lectures, travel magazines, brochures etc. Adequate and well-researched "books on cultural etiquette and manners", reliable descriptions and interpretations of foreign cultures, which are comprehensible for the lay mind, too, either do not exist, or if they do they are not available for the general public. Among the subjects dealt with by books on cultural etiquette and manners should be everyday rituals as well as dramatic ones. Rituals as we understand them are formalized social procedures and events which recur in their specific context. They comprise (1) spectacular, dramatic rituals as well as (2) everyday rituals (common customs such as the eating and drinking habits, the forms of greeting, etc.). Ideally, after these preparations, the prospective traveler should convert the following guiding ideas into practice:

In a certain sense each culture forms a singular world of its own. Consequently this foreign culture should not be measured with outside standards. Each culture should be described and evaluated through its own categories. Thus different perceptions of reality, society and the world are in circulation in the different cultures. This is a fundamental basis for the differences between the diverse socio-cultural systems of our planet. One perception is as good for certain purposes as another. It is thus impossible to give an evaluation of a picture which is commensurate with reality, without having relativized it before by means of a different perception (moderate cultural relativism). Figuratively speaking one must stand on the outside of a landscape to get a general panoramic view. It isn't until one has learned the cognitive concepts and values, which are regarded as important, real, correct and adequate by the members of the culture being visited, that one can think and act like a member of this culture. The cultural differences are not only based on cognitive but also on symbolic orders of the world and of the discourses. In addition the members of a culture are rarely conscious of its fundamental axioms. Thus it is important and unavoidable to concentrate not only on the cognitive orders which can be communicated by means of speech and writing, but also to deal intensively with another culture's symbolic orders situated mainly in the non-verbal sphere. All this shows that dramatic rituals as well as everyday rituals are very suitable for getting to know the cognitive and the symbolic orders which constitute the differences between cultures. Everyday rituals grant an excellent approach to the foreign ways of thought and perception as well as social manners. Examples from Southeast Asia shall demonstrate how patterns of reasons and explanations for frequent behavior can be related from the viewpoint of the people of the host country.

2 Rituals as a key to understanding foreign behavior and conceptions of life

In analogy to Hall's suggestion [9] to view literature as a key to perception, we suggest rituals to be regarded in this fashion (especially when dealing with ethnic groups who have no literary tradition at all, or not a very long one). Rituals which express social conceptions of order mainly in symbolic form and less in a conceptual one, give a condensed demonstration of the actors' idealized models on their social structure, the fundamental values and adequate behavior [10]. In this context one must consequently give special attention to the fact that it is generally very difficult to verbalize rituals. But like any customary behavior rituals can be interpreted as "a kind of speech, a mode of communicating behavior"[11]. The decisive point is that this is a way of saying things, where the focus of attention is not centered on the words but on the symbols. Here the possibilities of incorporating drawings, pictures and video sequences offered by hypermedia proves to be extremely helpful, especially when, in a kind of interaction, the user is called upon to react appropriately to certain situations and gestures. This "cultural quiz" should not be restricted to a purely mental duplication of the behavior specific to the culture, but should also stimulate bodily imitation. For the interested tourist the dramatic rituals are more than just "authentic" material for getting to know another culture. In case the rituals have been fundamentally transformed and reshaped in the course of their touristic exploitation, the visitors from afar can recognize the part they themselves have played in them; thus the exotic ritual from "over there" would turn out to be the result of a world-wide interaction between different cultures. Thus we have distinguished between authentic and unauthentic (dramatic) rituals: (1) "Authentic" rituals are a cultural medium which orientates according to the needs of the participants and expresses them. They could (in spite of a permanent process of reshaping and reformulating), as self-determined products of the natives, become the object of a "fact finding" tourism. (2) "Unauthentic" rituals on the other hand are products of a complex interplay of the natives, the tourist industry and the tourists.

2.1 The secondary funeral of the Toba-Batak of Northern Sumatra (Indonesia): An authentic ritual

It is only on condition that they are a native medium in the actual sense of the word, that rituals represent an ideal picture which a society draws of its social behavior and its relations. If one wishes to learn of the rules controlling the behavior in a condensed form, the most adequate way to do so is to observe and study the dramatic rituals (weddings, funerals etc.) in which the actions of the members of a larger community must follow an exactly prescribed plan and where clearly defined rules of behavior and forms of expression must be obeyed. Although the dramatic rituals hardly offer any help for learning the concrete rules for correct behavior in everyday life, nevertheless they convey the conception of the world without which these rules of behavior could never be understood. An almost classic example of an authentic dramatic ritual is the reburial ritual of the Toba-Batak of Northern Sumatra. Although a large part of the population had converted to Protestantism and in spite of the rapid modernization setting in with Indonesia's independence (1949), the Toba-Batak of Northern Sumatra still adhere to the worship of their ancestors and the reburial rituals connected with it. As in almost all the first and secondary burial rituals of the Indonesian cultural sphere, which reaches from Madagascar to Northern Luzon, in these festivities status and power are expressed and manipulated by means of the public display of sacrifices and the distribution of meat. Although since 1975 the conservative center of the Toba-Batak country, Samosir Island, has developed into a destination of national and international tourism, the reburial rituals held annually during the high season, they have never been discovered as tourist attractions by the industry. By means of a multi-perspective representation (proceeding from a holistic approach) of ritual sequences, including interlinks with different realms of the socio-cultural system (kinship system, house and settlement structure, music, religious concepts etc.) the hypermedia user is presented in a comparatively uncomplicated fashion with the social structures and the conception of life of the Toba-Batak. Different scenes from the ritual show objects, individuals and actions, which, if isolated, would be absolutely incomprehensible for the foreign observer (fig. 1). The TONDONG hypermedia system[1] offers the opportunity to call up the social relations between the actors as well as the spatial arrangement of the festivity grounds (fig. 2) and by relating them to the seating arrangement during different stages of the ritual (fig. 3) to gain information on the social structure and the concept of space.

2.2 The ritual of the dead of the Sa'adan-Toraja of Sulawesi (Indonesia): A pseudo-traditional ritual

The Sa'adan-Toraja living in the highlands of Sulawesi Island (Celebes) are counted among those Indonesian societies in which the political power in pre-colonial times lay exclusively in the hands of the heads of the genealogical groups, or their local segments. Their archaic religion is predominantly an ancestral cult with complicated and materially substantial death rites. In Indonesian state affairs the Toraja still play a rather inferior role, as do the members of ethnic groups of the same type (such as the Dayak of Kalimantan/Borneo).This part of Indonesian society is confronted with

Fig. 1. TONDONG picture browser

Fig. 2. Spatial Arrangement

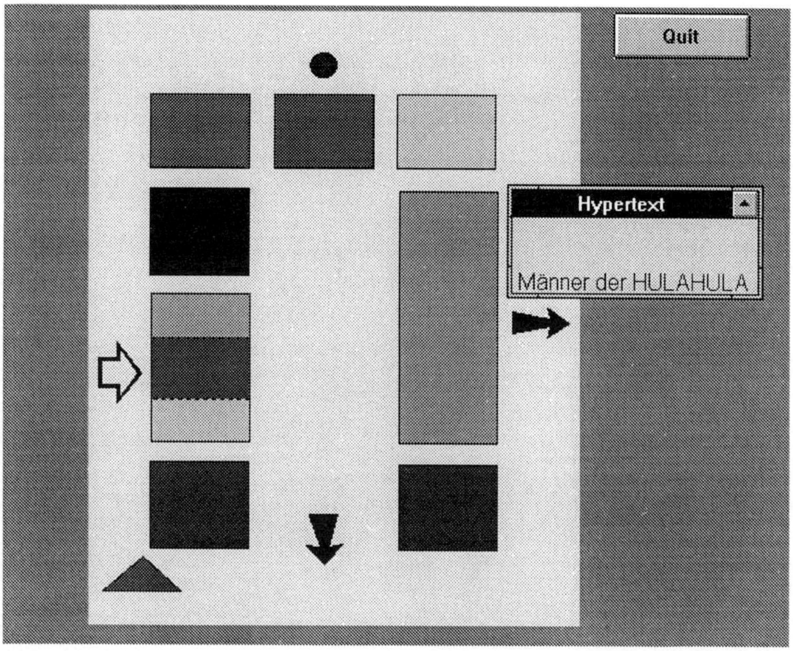

Fig. 3. Seating arrangement

the following problem: How much of their traditional way of living can and should they preserve as members of a nation whose objective is the creation of a modern and uniform culture? The Sa'adan-Toraja were subjugated by the Dutch in 1906 and it wasn't until the 1920s that they were missionized by the Dutch Reformed Church. In a certain sense the Dutch mission succeeded in imposing their distinction between ADAT (custom, tradition) and ALUK (the native religion) on the Toraja. They decided which aspects of the ritual were purely customary (secular, social) and which ones were "really heathen" and thus had to be rejected. Fundamental changes were brought about by the Second World War (especially by the Japanese occupation, 1942-1945) and a guerrilla warfare conducted by Islamic rebels from Southern Sulawesi after the declaration of independence (1949). But in spite of the transformation of religion and ritual through the Christian missionization and the dramatic outmigration setting in after 1965, the sixties brought a revival of the traditional religion (ALUK), which, in a cleansed, rationalized and theologized version, was finally recognized by the Ministry of Religious Affairs in Jakarta in 1969. It was no coincidence that tourism was to play a decisive role in Indonesia's first five-year plan: Indonesian government and travel industry "discovered" that Torajan rituals were a marketable commodity [15]. Side by side with the already world-famous culture of Bali the Sa'adan-Torajans' sumptuous rituals for the dead were intended to draw a stream of international tourism into the country. From time to time these rituals, which create and express a social hierarchy, bring together hundreds and thousands of Torajas from their homes scattered throughout the mountains. Some of the largest funeral services with a great number of participants often last up to seven days and follow a strict plan which corresponds to the status and wealth of the deceased person's family. In the course of these great rituals ceremonial edifices and stands were erected for the numerous guests. The sacrificial slaughtering of a multitude of pigs and water-buffaloes are especially impressive, as are the many dances, chants and processions. The first ritual of the dead which was attended by hundreds of foreign tourists took place in 1972. This event was documented by the international media, among them a film crew accompanied by the former Beatles-member Ringo Starr. In a short time the Toraja land became a main destination of international and national ethnic tourism. This ethno-tourism commercialized strange customs of indigenous and often exotic peoples such as the Esquimos, the San Blas Indios of Panama, the Toraja or the Papuans. The attractions of this kind of tourism are the opportunity to visit the villages and homes of the natives, the performance of dances and ceremonies and the shopping of traditional and exotic goods. While there were only 50 visitors registered in 1971, their number soon rose to 50.000 per year! [4, 16]. Step by step the ritual of the dead, which had been reduced to a tourist attraction, was adapted to the standardization, assembly and serial production of the tourist industry. This fact, i.e. that the rituals, like any other cultural forms of expression, are in permanent flux and that their transformation, which has greatly accelerated during the last decades, are closely connected to their touristic commercialization is not mentioned by the guidebooks. Studying this ritual (which includes the comparison with the model of a reconstructed ritual) clearly demonstrates to the visitors, how their own behavior as tourists (as involuntary co-actors of the ritual) can have a great influence on the culture of those they visit.

2.3 Everyday rituals in Thailand

Everyday rituals comprise behavior controlled by the rules and norms specific to culture. The presentation of everyday rituals must not be confined to an enumeration of technical rules. To grant a flexible and intelligent application of the maxims of behavior the rules of good deportment must always be complemented with - or, to be more exact, be derived from - the axioms of the symbolic and cognitive order. A good case in point is Thailand's WAI: The WAI does serve as a greeting, but beyond that it represents a culturally demanded tribute of respect: The farther the brow is lowered to meet the hands folded as in a prayer, the deeper is the respect expressed in this fashion. Thus the WAI is (1) a form of greeting, (2) a ceremonial gesture of respect and (3) the most significant of the many social actions preserving Thailands social structures. The WAI is the expression of the inequality pervading the entire Thai society and presents a sharp contrast to the barbarian custom (from the traditional Thai point of view) of the European handshake. So the WAI must be seen in the context of the hierarchic social system and the principle of avoiding conflicts. This becomes apparent in the rules concerning the return and the initiation of a WAI: In case of a great social distance the higher ranking person does not have to return the greeting at all. So when a small child greets a grown-up, it will at best be answered with a smile or a nod. Thus a waitress who expresses her thanks for a tip with a WAI must not be answered with a WAI in return. One should never initiate a WAI towards persons of a distinctively lower status (servants, workers, children). If one is greeted by a person of low status with a high-set WAI, one answers with a lower one. Here again hypermedia offers an opportunity to supply the necessary informations concerning the different forms of the WAI and its appropriate return, which are quite difficult to convey verbally, via drawings, photographs, sound and video sequences which invite you to imitate and exercise. Beyond that the Thai socio-cultural background and their concept of life, without which an understanding of the rules concerning the WAI would not be possible, can be conveyed by means of graphical illustrations and comments.

3 The development of the books on cultural etiquette

Books on cultural etiquette, which treat everyday behavior and the intercultural communication in Southeast Asia, are a relatively recent phenomenon and still quite rare even today: Due to the decisive military importance of the minorities living in the densely wooded and hardly accessible mountains of Vietnam ("montagnards", 10% of the overall population, 65% of the entire territory!) the U.S.-Army commissioned studies to be carried out which, besides describing the culture, social structure and religion of the respective tribal groups, treated the following subjects: civic action considerations, paramilitary capabilities and suggestions for personnel working with the tribes [3]. Since the Vietminh and the Vietcong also had a certain success in gaining the sympathies of parts of the minorities, the American army also tried to introduce a kind of code of manners to its personnel via instructions, brochures and leaflets [13]. It wasn't until the 80s that books on cultural etiquette were developed for businessmen working in Asia.

Changed economical conditions and an increased self-confidence of the respective developing countries enforced a change in thinking: As international business relations present a special form of culturally overlapping interaction and communication, the often ignored or underestimated cultural factors play an important role side by side with the economic and political factors. Businessmen and managers who maintain business relations with countries of the so-called "Third World" must, whether they like it or not, strive to identify, understand and interpret the cultural powers of their host country. The realization that an understanding of the cultural characteristics of a foreign country, especially of the values, attitudes and patterns of behavior of its inhabitants, are the indispensable precondition for an intercultural encounter without conflicts has first won recognition in the Anglo-American world and later also in the German-speaking countries [1, 6, 12]. The reasons for the development of books on cultural etiquette for tourists in Southeast Asia [2, 8, 14] are the quantitative increase in long-distance tourism and the concept of soft tourism which appeared in the 80s: In contrast to the usual travel guides, which describe what one is going to see in a certain country, the aim of the books on cultural etiquette is (1) to acquaint the travelers with the perceptions they will sense, (2) to help them overcome the insecurities regarding the correct ways of greeting, hospitality, dress codes, table manners etc., (3) to help them to get over the culture shock and (4) to enable them to learn foreign manners, ways of thinking and perception (= adjusted behavior).

4 Model for a Virtual Book on Cultural Etiquette and Manners

After an intensive study of the information which are filed on the World Wide Web (WWW) concerning the subject of tourism, we had to face the fact that the development on the Web has taken a similar course as that of the printed literature on travels: Thus one finds a "Virtual Tourist" and a "Virtual Traveller" for example, or GNN's travel Center [7] and a lot of other information, but as yet no book on cultural etiquette and manners. Yet the WWW, due to its structure offers excellent opportunities for a holistic interlinking of informations (fig. 4). The Virtual Book on

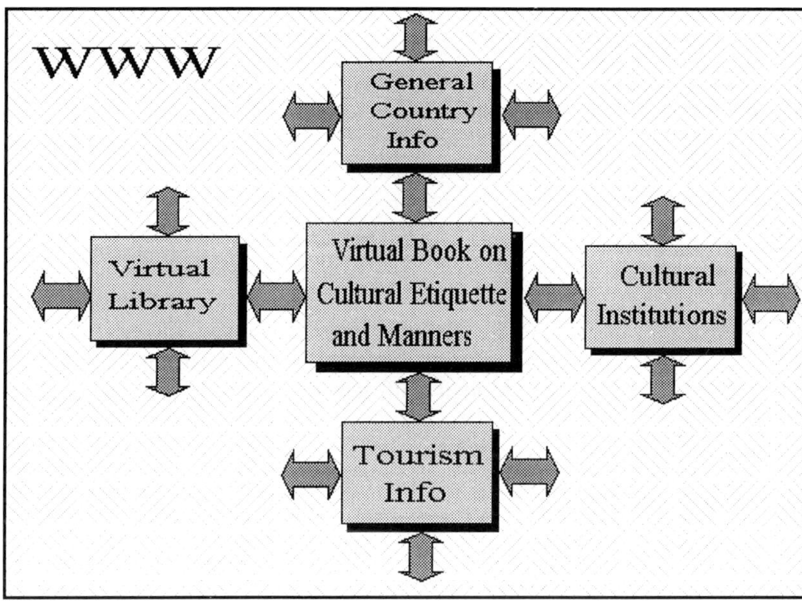

Fig. 4. Virtual Book on Cultural Etiquette and Manners

Cultural Etiquette and Manners should offer links to other informations on the Web. A meaningful complementation and enrichment of information filed elsewhere would be a contribution to global knowledge. As Deemer remarks the World Wide Web is an international phenomenon, "...suggesting an emerging holistic organization of knowledge" [5]. As a distributed hypermedia system the World Wide Web offers a good condition for the interlinking with other informations: Apart from collaborative writing the multi-media capabilities open up the possibility of the presentation of rituals. The problem of access (especially to publish on the WWW) must also be considered in this context: "The flip side of a global electronic democracy is an aristocracy of learning where only the fortunate (those who qualify by location or wealth or standing) are given access to the new electronic networks of information - and by access are given power" [5]. Especially cultural minorities would be in danger of being excluded from access to the data highway. Perhaps international cultural organisations could take corrective measures in this respect. The webbed structure of the WWW-information conditions a certain reciprocity and symmetry in the acquisition of information: if we want to have access to a foreign culture's book on cultural etiquette, we must at the same time inform ourselves on our own cultural norms. The possibility of collaborative writing allows the comparison, or the interlinking respectively, of self-view and outside view: If, for example somewhere in the world data on rules of behavior in Austria is filed in a tourist information system, these informations could be complemented and/or contrasted with other viewpoints.

5 Prospects

Beyond the production of individual systems of rules of behavior specific to cultures, the long-term objective should be the development of books on cultural etiquette for tourists, businessmen and diplomats on the basis of hypermedia, using the world Wide Web on the Internet. Yet one important precondition is still lacking: a binding model for the standardized collection and presentation of data concerning the modes of perception and thinking as well as the manners specific to cultures.

Notes

[1]This ethnological hypermedia example was developed under the name of TONDONG in the course of a project, financed by the Austrian Federal Ministry for Science and Research, which dealt with terminological issues in the social sciences.

References

1. Andres, T.D.: Understanding Filipino Values. A Management Approach. Quezon City: New Day Publishers 1981.

2. Cooper, R., Cooper, N.: Kultur-Knigge Thailand. Köln: Hayit Verlag 1990.

3. CRESS (Center for Research in Social Systems): Minority Groups in the Republic of Vietnam. Ethnographic Study Series, Headquarters: Department of the Army Pamphlet No. 550-105, Washington 1966.

4. Crystal, E.: Tourism in Toraja (Sulawesi, Indonesia). In: Smith, Valene L. (ed.): Hosts and Guests. The Anthropology of Tourism. Oxford: Basil Blackwell 109-125 (1978).

5. Deemer, C.: Humanities in Cyberspace: How the Internet is changing teaching and scholarship in the humanities. INTERNET, URL: http://www.teleport.com/~cdeemer/humanities.html, 1994.

6. Devine, E., Braganti, N. L.: Asia and Australasia. How to converse, bargain, dine, dress, make friends and conduct business. London: Sidgwick & Jackson 1987.

7. Dougherty, D., Koman, R.: The Mosaic Handbook for Microsoft Windows. Sebastobol, CA, 1994.

8. Draine, C., Hall, B.: Kultur-Knigge Indonesien. Nördlingen: Simon & Magiera 1988.

9. Hall, E.T.: The Hidden Dimension. Garden City, New York: Doubleday & Comp. 1966.

10. Leach, E. R.: Political Systems of Highland Burma. A Study of Kachin Social Structure. London: G. Bell & Sons 1954.

11. Leach, Ed. R.: "Ritual". Eintrag in: International Encyclopedia of the Social Sciences. New York: MacMillan & Free Press 1968.

12. Lukas, H.: Cultural Background for Economic and Business Relationships with Indonesia. In: Busch, Georg (Coordinator): The Indonesian Economy and its Relations to Austria. Study by the Austrian Institute of Economic Research (WIFO), sponsored by the Austrian National Bank.Vienna: WIFO (February) 87-117 (1994).

13. Mole, R. L.: The Montagnards of South Vietnam. A Study of Nine Tribes. Rutland/ Vermont & Tokyo: Charles E. Tuttle Company 1970.

14. Roces, A., Roces, G.: Culture Shock! Phillipines. London: Kuperard 1992.

15. Smith, V. L. (ed.): Hosts and Guests. The Anthropology of Tourism. Oxford: Basil Blackwell 1978.

16. Volkman, T. A.: "Visions and Revisions: Toraja Culture and the Tourist Gaze". American Ethnologist, vol. 17, nr. 1, 91-110 (1990).

Beyond ISO 9000: trends in the standardization and certification of the quality of information systems development

G.J. van der Pijl, Tilburg University
J.G. Verrijdt, Rabobank Nederland
G.J.P. Swinkels, Rabobank Nederland, University of Amsterdam

POB 90153, 5000 LE Tilburg, The Netherlands, tel. 31-13-662138
E-mail: PIJL@KUB.NL

Abstract. ISO 9000 and the Capability Maturity Model are two ways by which software developers try to guarantee the quality of there software products. Users and buyers of software, surely in tourism where most software is bought from third parties, should know what the relevance of quality certificates according to these two models is. This paper illustrates the usefullness of both methods, explains the differences between them and demonstrates that still much can be done to assure the quality of software.

1. Introduction

If a company wants to maintain its strategic position it can be necessary to improve the quality of its business processes and to communicate these improvements to the customers. In European countries the ISO 9000 standards and accompanying certificates are becoming a more and more popular way to do this. The ISO 9000 standards [ISO87] are also used by software houses and software development departments within companies that try to get their quality systems certified. More specifically for systems development the ISO 9000-3 [ISO91] standard has been specified. A growing number of information systems developers use standards as a way of implementing their quality systems.

There is, however, a lot of discussion on these standards and the certificates accompanying them. Many companies seem to be eager to get the certificate because of market pressure. This often means that a minimum set of procedures and quality handbooks is set up without a quality system really being implemented, or quality awareness being created among the employees. In those cases the possession of the certificates does not guarantee the quality of the software production process or a reasonable price/performance ratio for the products delivered to the client. Even if a company maintains a quality system according to the standards of ISO 9000, the quality of the final product can never be guaranteed. And worse still: adhering to strict software-quality standards can in some circumstances be counterproductive because in many cases the software development process has to be attuned to the specific type of system that has to be produced and the specific systems development environment in which the production takes place.

In this paper we discuss the use of standards in the control of the quality of the information systems development process. The ISO model, which is the most popular standard in Europe and Japan, is compared with the Capability Maturity Model (CMM) [Hump88], [Hump89], [Paul91], [Paul93] which is becoming the main de facto standard in the USA.

When looking at standards like these, we have to realize that they serve a dual purpose. On the one hand they can be used to provide guidance to organizations installing quality systems that help them to produce goods and services of the desired quality. On the other hand they are the basis for certification of quality systems. Quality certificates are meant to give buyers of goods and services an impression of the quality of the suppliers and thus indirectly of the quality of the products and services supplied [Rugg93]. It is in this respect that ISO 9000 and CMM are relevant for the tourist industry. Problems with standards can arise in either these fields.

We show that CMM solves some of the problems of the ISO model. But CMM also has shortcomings. Therefore we indicate the direction in which software quality assurance and software quality standards have to develop in order to improve the quality of the information systems delivered by the development process.

2. The ISO 9000 standards

The set of international standards ISO 9000-9004 describes how companies can implement quality systems in their organizations. Once a quality system is in place the organization can have it certified by an independent institution. The certificates can then be used to show the customers that the company adheres to externally verified quality standards.

The philosophy of the standards is consistent with the developments in the theory on quality management [Jura88]. The focus is shifting from controlling the quality of the final product to controlling the quality of the production processes from which the product arises [Pijl94]. The essence of the ISO 9000 standard is that a company should visibly control all aspects of the business in order to guarantee a minimum level of quality of its products. Visibility is realized by describing the quality system in a Quality Handbook. The standard does not describe what is the most effective and efficient way of controlling the business processes. It just demands that the organization maintains sets of quality procedures and guidelines without exactly specifying them. This is both the strength and the weakness of the standard. The open character makes it applicable to many different production processes. But for producers of goods and services it makes it hard to decide on the specific type of measures to be taken in specific situations. And for purchasers it means that a quality certificate does not necessarily indicate that the suppliers' quality system is well attuned to the specific product and market situation. This is the main reason for the development of more and more specific versions and interpretations of the standard for different types of industries.

For systems development we have the ISO 9000-3 standard: 'Guidelines for the development, supply and maintenance of software'. In this standard the life-cycle of information systems is taken as the process to be controlled. However, it remains a very general description of the procedures and guidelines for quality management.

ISO 9000 is very popular both in the United Kingdom and in the Netherlands and the number of applications in Germany is rising. There is, however, a lot of criticism. This criticism stems partly from the fact that companies try to get ISO 9000 certificates for reasons of marketing rather than for reasons of (total) quality management. But even if we accept that companies use standards to really improve their production processes, it is possible to be critical of the contents and construction of the standards. Important criticisms concerning the use of ISO 9000-3 for systems development are:

- The general nature of the standard makes it necessary to translate it into specific quality measures in each organization. The standard only demands that quality procedures are installed. It does not, however, indicate what the *correct* procedures are. Thus the standard cannot be used as a detailed blueprint for the construction of quality systems in practical situations. It is also hard to use the standard as a norm when judging the appropriateness of quality systems in specific situations. This implies that possession of the ISO 9000 certificate is only weak proof of the quality of a software supplier. In many cases additional audits will be necessary to properly assess this quality;
- The standard is specified on the level of quality systems for systems development organizations and gives only limited attention to quality measures on the level of specific development projects;
- ISO 9000 recognizes only one certifiable level of quality while in practice different quality levels may be advisable for different situations. It is quite possible that, within a company with several systems development departments, not all of these have to operate at the same quality level because they are developing different types of products. Levels of quality would also be useful to indicate the stages along a growth path that a systems development organization could follow in improving the quality of the work. It is also possible that buyers of information systems do not look for the same quality level for each and every information system they buy;
- The emphasis on strict procedures and the documentation of these in manuals easily leads to a bureaucratic type of behaviour instead of a growing awareness

of the importance of quality for the organization. Attention for new insights and methodologies in systems development may be hampered. A good example is Boehm's "spiral model" [Boeh88] that tries to cope with uncertainty in systems development but thus clashes with the rules of ISO 9000-3;

- In some cases throughput-time may be of more importance for the development of information systems than superb quality. Quality standards leave very little room for the principles of rapid application development.

3. The Capability Maturity Model

The CMM as put forward by the Software Engineering Institute builds on the 'maturity model' presented by Humphrey [Hump89]. The maturity model presents a growth theory according to which the quality level of a systems development organization can grow along a given growth path. The gist of the model is that several quality levels for the systems development process can be recognized. An organization can go from one stage to another and thus grow from a situation with no quality management to a mature situation with a very high level of quality control, as described in exhibit 1.

level CMM	description
1. "initial" processes	- ad hoc, sometimes chaotic processes - project succes not guaranteed
3. "defined" processes	- process documented - process standardized - tailored standards used for each project
4. "managed" processes	- process understood - process measured - process controlled
5. "optimizing" processes	- focus on process improvement - focus on rapid technology updating

exhibit 1: The quality levels of CMM

Each level is determined by a set of key process areas which in turn consist of sets of key practices [Webe91]. By measuring which key practices are implemented the maturity level of a systems development organization can be measured. A structure for such a measurement is given in exhibit 2. As shown there, each key process can be judged as being sufficiently (S), partly (P) or insufficiently (I) implemented. The total set of key practices is specifically aimed at the systems development organization and is much more detailed than the prescriptions of ISO-9000, thus leaving much less room for interpretation.

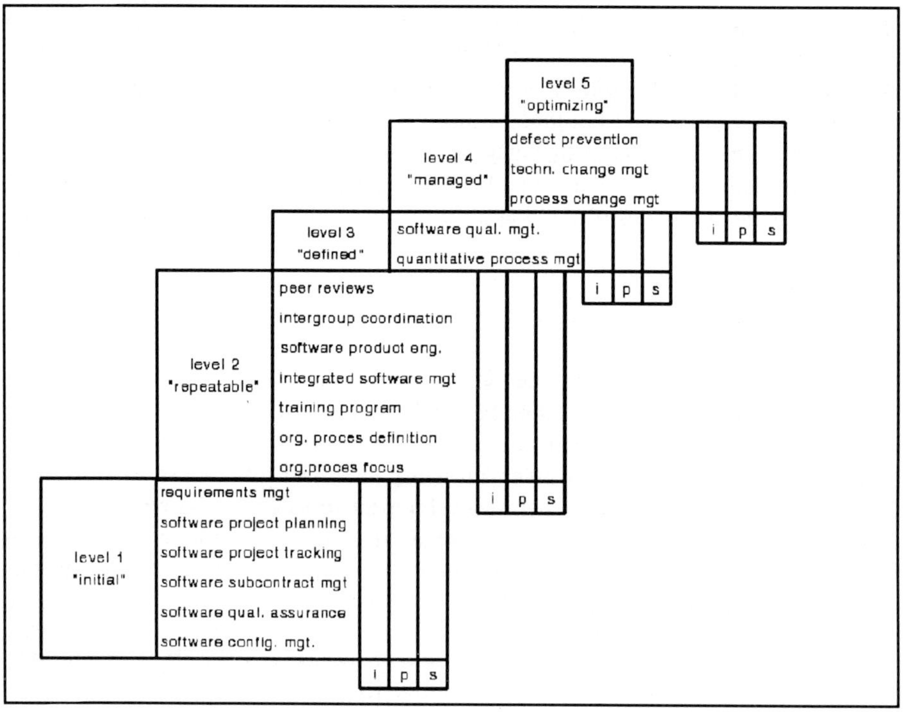

exhibit 2: assessing the quality level of an organization

Each quality level can thus be seen as a well-defined stage on the way to a mature organization. From each stage a set of well-defined small steps leads up to the next higher quality level. Of course the leading thought behind the model is that a higher degree of maturity leads to better results in terms of defects, costs, throughput times and quality of the systems delivered. Recent research [Dreh93] shows that the CMM's quality levels cannot exactly be found in the real world. Possibly a more gradual pattern of growth would be a more realistic hypothesis. This does not, however, fundamentally change the idea of CMM as an elaborate example of how to install quality management in systems development in a series of consecutive steps. It might, however, influence the idea that quality of a software suppliers development process can be assessed by looking at a detailed set of key processes and key practices and assessing at which stage of the CMM model the supplier is. There may be other possible growth paths that also enable suppliers to deliver software of the desired quality. The quality of these suppliers would not be recognized if their business processes are only compared to the levels of CMM.

4. Comparing ISO 9000-3 and CMM

Both ISO 9000 and CMM are widely accepted standards. CMM is a de facto standard in the USA. In Europe and Japan the number of companies using CMM is growing. ISO 9000-3 is recognized all over the world. Both standards can be considered stable in the sense that they have widely been used for a number of years and "teething troubles" have been cured. There are possibilities for computer-supported use of both standards but they are not very well developed. Our research [Verr93], in which the demands of ISO 9000-3 are compared with CMM's key practices, shows that there is much overlap between the two approaches. This becomes clearest at the second and third levels of CMM. Almost all articles of the ISO standard can be translated into key practices at these two levels. Implementing CMM up to the third level and completing it with only a few additional items (5.2.2 "contract items on quality"; 5.8 "acceptance"; 5.9 "replication, delivery and installation"; 6.2.4 "document changes"; 6.8 "included software") from ISO 9000-3 make certification according to ISO 9000 possible. However, there are also important differences between the approaches:

- CMM is specially aimed at software development. It models the development process in a much more detailed way than ISO 9000. The quality characteristics of the levels in CMM are described in much more detail than the quality characteristics of ISO 9000-3. Therefor it is much easier to use CMM as a guideline for building quality systems in software development.
- At the higher levels of CMM differences between software projects are explicitly taken into account. Accumulation of statistical data on success and failure factors on the project level makes it possible to attune the quality system to the project at hand.
- The ISO standards prescribe one fixed level of quality management. CMM points out that different levels are possible but does not prescribe which level a systems developer has to choose. The idea is that this is determined by the specific situation in which the systems development takes place. The levels 4 and 5 of the CMM model clearly stand for higher quality than does ISO 9000-3.
- The structuring of the quality characteristics in CMM makes it easier to discuss quality matters.

From the description above it will be clear that CMM solves some of the problems associated with ISO 9000. The more detailed specification of quality characteristics makes it much easier to use CMM as a blueprint for quality systems in systems development organizations. Because of the explicit attention to the relevant aspects of systems development it is also much easier attune it to different circumstances. Quality assessment on the basis of CMM, therefore, gives the purchaser much more certainty that the quality system is well attuned to the demands of the situation. The fact that CMM recognizes "maturity levels" for quality systems makes it possible for software development organizations to improve their quality programs progressing from one maturity level to the next. Organizations that have reached the third maturity level of CMM (the "defined" stage) comply in most aspects with the ISO 9000-3 standard (see exhibit 3). But CMM permits one to stop at a lower level or to aim at higher levels of process quality. Thus it can be more easily attuned to different circumstances. On the other hand purchasers can select systems development organizations with a quality level fitting their purposes.

Since it is not completely clear that the growth path to quality that is indicated by CMM is the only possible growth path for reaching quality, one should be careful to use CMM as the exclusive basis for certification. It might very well be that organizations following a different growth path also deliver good quality software [Boll91].

5. Expected trends

In our view we should focus on the quality of the development process itself and not only on the quality system. The quality system is an integral part of this process. The measures that ensure the quality of an information system that has to be developed, have to be tuned to the characteristics of that system and to the circumstances under which the development takes place. Software projects have to be analyzed in relation to the strength and weaknesses of both the development organization and the user-organization [Giel92]. This analysis determines the specific set of quality measures to be taken. But if the set of measures to be used can differ from project to project this makes it very difficult to use a standard quality assurance system. We will have to find a balance between specifying a set of minimum requirements valid for all projects and leaving enough room for the particularities of individual projects. In finding this balance we will have to take account of a number of aspects that we will discuss briefly.

- A complete quality system takes into account all factors that explain the quality of the final product. A variety of aspects, such as the quality of the people involved, the methods and tools used and the commitment of the management, influence the result. Empirical evidence shows that we do not know all the factors and causal relationships that explain the final results [Cape86]. Only a limited number of factors is taken into account in the standards. In order to develop good quality software, however, we have to take all factors into account.
- Measures to improve quality are very divers (preventive, detective, corrective) and can partly replace one another. If, for example, not all members of a project team can be instructed in the use of a method, we will have to pay more attention to testing the final product and feeding back the results of the tests to the project members.

- Measures taken for a specific project can conflict with the normal standards. Using a standard method has the advantage that all the members of the organization are familiar with it. But using several methods makes it possible to take care of the specifics of the project involved. Differences in steps and deliverables make it difficult in that case to compare projects and thus gain experience.
- The more quality systems are implemented in organizations the more probable it is that there are projects in which several parties have there own quality systems. Taking into account all the requirements of these different systems will often be very complicated and costly.
- The present quality standards are mainly oriented towards standardizing activities and procedures. In practice, however, projects are also controlled by controlling deliverables and the capabilities of members of the project team. The specific mix of control mechanisms is determined by the circumstances.
- Project- and organization-specific quality systems can only be implemented and certified if products and processes can be measured with a clear and widely accepted set of metrics. Though work in this direction is going on in the ESPRIT-AMI project, there is no such generally accepted set of metrics.
- Information technology and methods of information systems development are changing quickly. International standards generally develop at a much slower pace. Thus it is a problem to continually include new insights and developments in the standards.

There are a number of trends that support the growing importance of quality assurance such as outsourcing and facilities management, fixed price, fixed date, but also fixed quality contracts between purchasers and developers of information systems, service level agreements etc. There are also some trends that support the development of more situation specific norms, such as norms for specific areas (e.g. detachment), development of quality metrics (e.g. using function points) and specifying software quality [ISO 91.1].

For the time being most software developing-organizations can still improve their quality by using the existing standards wisely and adapting them to the needs of specific situations. This also means that buyers of software should realize that adhering to the existing standards (that is: what is certified by a certificate) is not always the best thing do. Well founded deviations from the standards should be accepted. Furthermore we have to keep in mind that standardization of processes is not the only way to guarantee quality. Other coordination mechanisms like standardization of skills, standardization of outputs and communication between all concerned must also be used [Pijl90].

The specification of a quality system is a matter of weighing costs and benefits, on the level of organizations as a whole as well as on the level of specific projects. Important questions are:

- Are our clients obliging us to comply with standards (such as, for example, AQAP-norms for the military sector or Lloyds for the steel industry)?
- Does a certified quality system result in a growing turnover because of its commercial importance?
- Does such a formalized approach fit in the culture of the organization?
- Does a well-balanced quality system on the project level make it possible to offer our clients better contracts with lower risks (e.g. fixed date, fixed price, fixed quality)?
- How certain is it that we can profit from our investments in quality systems in the future?
- Does reduction of the number of errors reduce costs (for example because of a smaller number of fixes or lower insurance premiums)?

Advantages and disadvantages of improvements in the systems development process have to be weighed against each other and against the costs of implementation [Dion93]. Conclusions can differ for different parts of the organization.

In the long run efforts have to be directed at formulating more specific standards for specific situations. An alternative could be to develop standards that contain substandards relating to different circumstances.

6. Summary and conclusions

At present there is a conflict between the desire for better quality systems resulting in measurable improvements of the systems development process and the way in which this is implemented by means of standards. Quality certificates can thus give a wrong impression of the real capabilities of an organization. This should not lead, however, to an abolition of standards, as is suggested by some authors. The majority of organizations can improve by making (sensible) use of the standards. But there is a need for improving the standards.

In the short term the quality of systems development can be improved by an approach that is specially constructed for assessing systems development environments, which supports measurable improvement of the development process and which supports the choice and implementation of actions. Although not perfect, CMM offers more possibilities in this respect than does ISO 9000-3.

In the longer term standards and certificates will have to take into account the diversity that exists in the real world. Standards and certificates will have to be attuned to this diversity. We think that this process will take some time and that therefore we will have to carefully assess the value of quality certificates in different situations.

references:

[Boeh88] Boehm, B.W., A spiral model of software development and enhancement, *Computer* 21 NO.5, P.61-72, 1988.

[Boll91] Bollinger, T. and McGowan, C., A critical look at software capability evaluations, *IEEE Software* July 1991, p. 25-41.

[Cape86] Capers Jones, *Programming productivity*, McGraw-Hill, 1986.

[Dreh93] Drehmer, D. en Daklava, S., Measuring software engineering maturity: a Rash calibration, *Proceedings of the fourteenth internationational conference on information systems*, Orlando, December 1993.

[Dion93] Dion, R., Process improvement and the corporate balance sheet. *IEEE software*, July 1993.

[Giel92] Gielen L.J.M.W., Swinkels G.J.P., Kwaliteitsbeheersing bij de ontwikkeling van informatiesystemen via knelpuntenanalyse (Analysing strengths and weaknesses as a means of quality assurance for the development of information systems), *Handboek A.I.V.*, November 1992.

[Hump88] Humphrey W.S., Characterizing the software process, *IEEE Software*, march 1988

[Hump89] Humphrey W.S., *Managing the software process*, Addison Wesley, 1989

[ISO87] *ISO 9000-9004 quality management and quality assurance standards*, 1987

[ISO91] ISO 9000-3, Quality management and quality assurance standards, part 3: *Guidelines for the application of ISO 9001 to the development, supply and maintenance of software*, 1991

[ISO91.1] *ISO 9126 Software Product Evaluation-Quality Characteristics and Guidelines for their Use*, International Organization for Standardization, Geneva, 1991

[Jura88] Juran, J.M., *Juran on planning fot quality*, McMillan, New York, 19988.

[Paul91] Paulk M.C., Curtis B., Chrissis M.B., *Capability maturity model for software*, Software engineering institute, CMU/SEI-91-TR-24, DTIC Number AD240603, august 1991

[Paul93] Paulk M.C., Curtis B., Chrissis M.B.,Weber C.V., *Capability maturity model for software*, Version 1.1. Software engineering institute, CMU/SEI-93-TR-24, august 1993.

[Pijl90] Pijl G.J. van der, Weterings P.L.M., Standaardisatie in systeemontwikkeling (Standardization and systems development), *Maandblad voor bedrijfs-administratie en organisatie*, December 1990.

[Pijl94] Measuring the strategic dimensions of the quality of information, *The Journal of Strategic Information Systems*, vol. 3 nr.3, 1994

[Rugg93] Rugg D., Using a capability evaluation to select a contractor, *IEEE Software*, July, 1993.

[Verr93] Verrijdt J.G., *Het beheersen van kwaliteitsverbetering: groeien van Murphy naar Humphrey* (Controlling quality improvements: developping from Murphy to Humphrey)

[Webe91] Weber C.V., Paulk M.C., Wise C.J., Withey J.V., *Key practices of the capability maturity model*, Software engineering institute, CMU/SEI-91-TR-25, August 1991.

Database Support for PC Software Configuration and Version Management in the START Network

S. Auerbach *, A. Buchmann†, I. Buchmann *, T. Kudraß †, K. Lange *, C. Lier *, K. Weidmann *

* START Informatik GmbH
Mainzer Landstr. 341 , D-60326 Frankfurt

† Technical University Darmstadt, Dept. of Computer Science,
Database Systems Division, Frankfurter Str. 69a, D-64293 Darmstadt

Abstract. Configuration management problems are discussed in the context of one of Europe's largest wide area networks, the START travel services network. Problems are caused mainly by the size of the network, its heterogeneity, its growth rate and the availability requirements of day-to-day operations which are stretching the current file-based configuration management system that is used to control the remote update of software on the point of sale PCs. A database solution for support of a new configuration and version management process is presented and two pilot implementations, one relational and one object-oriented, are discussed.

1 Introduction and Environment

Travel services, ranging from airplane, rail and ferry tickets to tour packages, car rentals and tickets to special events are offered by a variety of service providers. To make the services of railways, airlines and tour operators readily available to the public through the travel agencies and to allow for the appropriate payments and accounting, START operates a wide area network with more than 26.000 terminal nodes worldwide at the point of sale, facilitates the interoperability among service providers and supplies the necessary back-office functionality. The nodes at the point of sale are PCs equipped with a special purpose networking board and may run under either SCO UNIX, XENIX or OS/2. Because of equipment amortization laws and the logistics of replacing and installing such a large number of PCs, at any given point in time there may be a variety of hardware configurations in the field, ranging from low-end Intel 80286-based machines to powerful pentium-based LAN servers. To make the situation even more complex, travel agencies often require additional software that is installed directly by the user on the PC. The heterogeneity in hardware and user preferences is also reflected in the multiple versions of the operating systems that must be supported on the machines in the field. At the center of the WAN are two powerful Siemens H120-S mainframes running above 200 transactions per second with a third mainframe, an H130-E for backup. The mainframes provide the interoperability between the PCs in the travel agency and the more than 70 hosts of the service providers and carry out the necessary accounting.

In 1993 more than 5.3 million direct tour bookings were handled through the START network alone in Germany. It serves also as a gateway to the Amadeus reservation system routing 30.5 million bookings to Amadeus in 1993. The network, currently one of Telekom's 10 biggest customers, is being converted to packet switching technology. Figure 1 illustrates schematically the configuration of the START WAN.

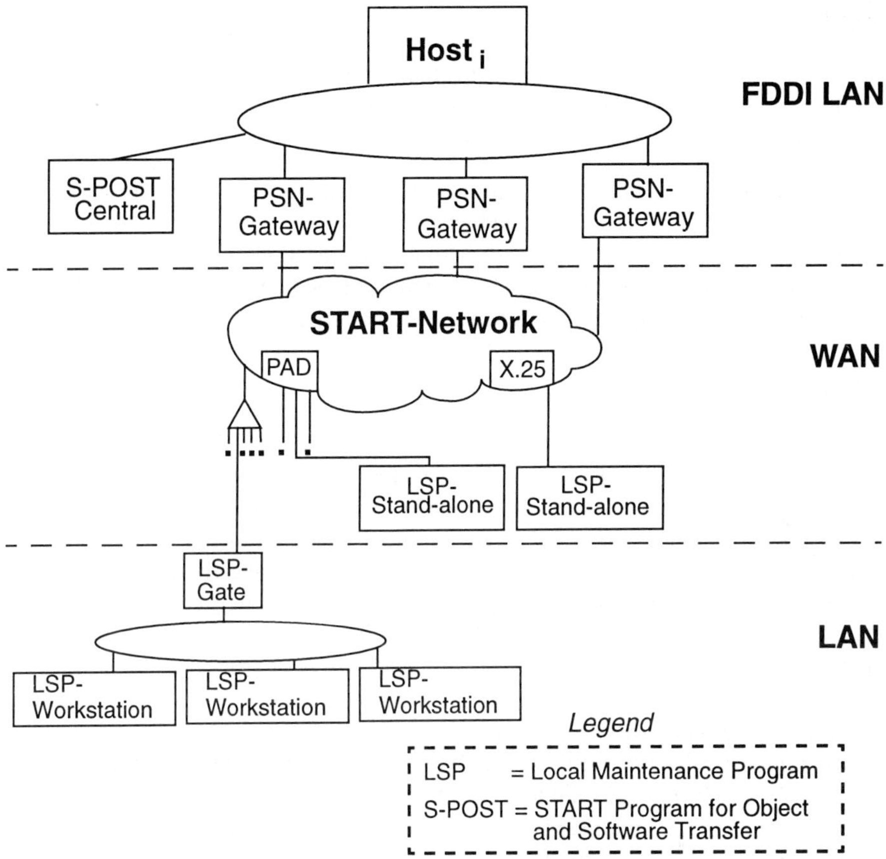

Fig. 1. Configuration of the START WAN

2 The configuration management problem

To maintain a network of this size and heterogeneity running with acceptable level of reliability is a difficult task. New software, updates and bug fixes must be installed in the point of sale machines with a minimum of disruption for the user and the day-to-day operations on the host. Further, users should not be burdened by the installation of software, a task that would be too taxing for the less sophisticated users and could thus lead to a loss of network reliability. Therefore, software is installed automatically mainly during off-hours under careful load-control by the hosts to avoid service degradation due to the transfer of large software packages over a low-bandwidth WAN.

Scheduling of software updates depends on the status of the machines in the field, information about new sales or lease agreements, new software releases and compatibility information among the new software, the specific PC's capabilities and possibly with third party software known to be installed on a particular PC. For example, it may not be possible to upgrade the version of some customized software in a given operating system environment, because a given software module it uses frequently is not yet available for the new OS version.

In addition, many special situations must be handled. These include the limited release and distribution of new software to pilot customers, special handling for teaching and demo equipment, and software customization for some of the larger clients.

The huge task of maintaining, controlling and providing the configuration management of such a network is compounded by the possibility of component or network failure and human error, which may range from disconnecting a PC overnight to inadvertently damaging a file necessary for communication between the PC and the host, or not updating the configuration information after a repair.

3 The current system

At present, software maintenance is carried out through the ASP system ("Automatische Software Pflege"). This system consists of a host-based portion that initiates and controls the software maintenance process and a local counterpart (LSP) on the PC that establishes the communication and carries out the installation locally. The information necessary to control the software update process is kept in the form of files that are periodically updated and compared and from which extracts are used to drive the software actualization process. Because of the file-based nature of the current system and a cumbersome input and output process, combined with a lack of consistency enforcement capabilities, the quality of the configuration management data kept on the central ASP suffers both in consistency and timeliness. As the WAN expands at a rather brisk pace and more service providers offer their travel services through START, the existing system will slowly reach its limits. Therefore, a new system is being developed in which the critical data handling problems for controlling the configuration management process are addressed. The remainder of this paper describes the new system, its design and pilot implementations that were realized in conjunction with the Technical University of Darmstadt.

4 S-POST - The New System

To address the handling and consistency problems mentioned in section 3, a new system called S-POST (START Program for Object and Software Transfer) was designed [1]. Since most of the data handling problems arise on the host side, a new central component was conceived based on a relational DBMS. Figure 2 shows an outline of the schema. The information handled can be roughly grouped into terminal and network information; information describing the properties of software packages; maintenance, version and transient status information; and special requirements information.

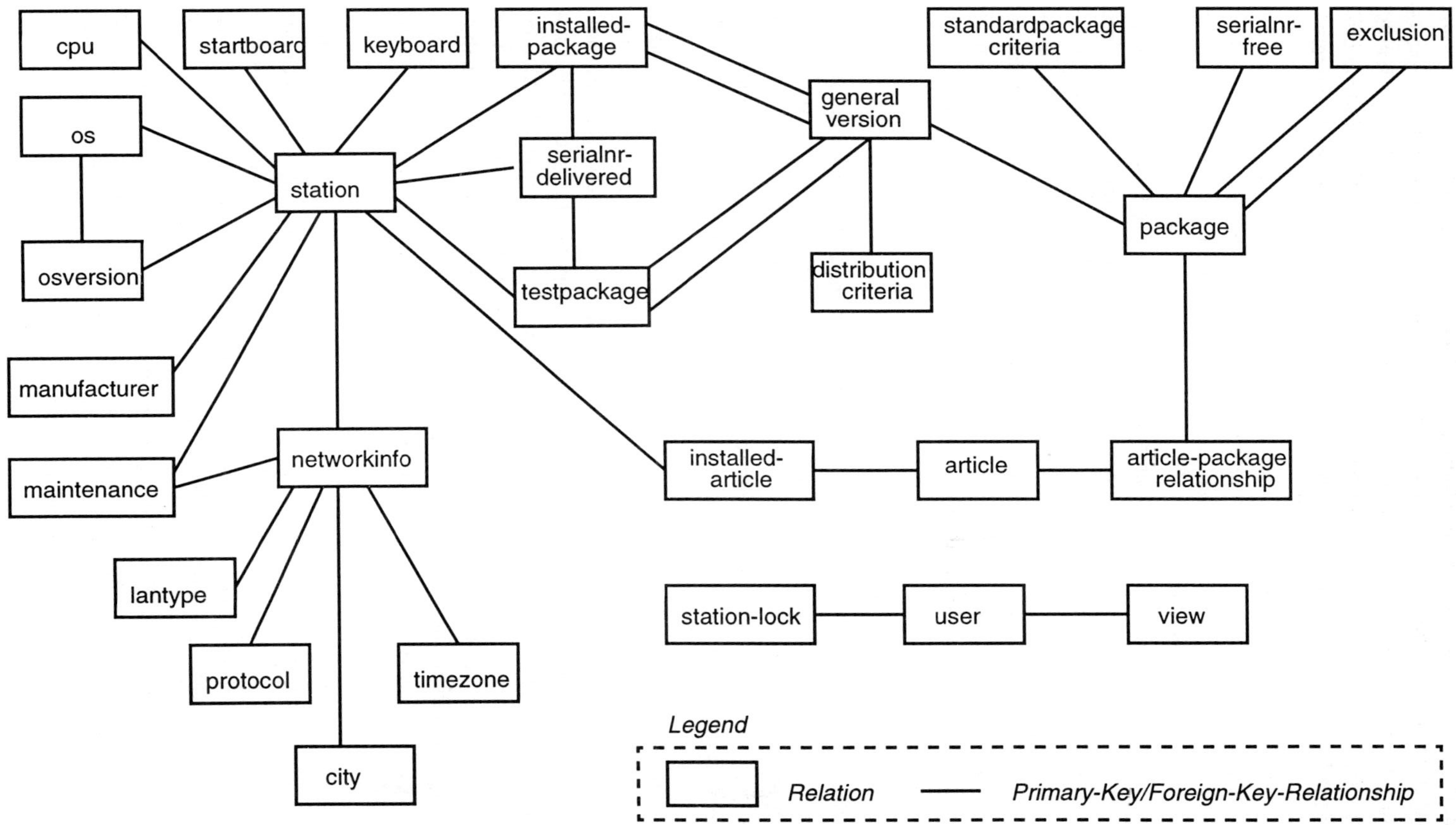

Fig. 2. The Schema of the S-POST Database

Terminal equipment and network information (also considered as core data) comprises all the hardware data, such as type of CPU, whether a system is standalone or part of a LAN, whether it is a gateway, the type of LAN, communication protocols, location, serial numbers, operating systems and its version, etc. Core data further comprise all the basic software that is installed once and not updated or changed remotely.

Software Information describes the configuration of a software product, its versions and its packaging into files for distribution. Each software product may be configured differently according to hardware capabilities, operating system and kind of service required by a customer. In many cases, other software products may depend on a particular feature of another product. If this feature is not available in the basic configuration but only in a larger configuration, the system must ensure that the minimally required functionality is always installed. Similarly, exclusion dependencies may exist. These dependencies among software products are important and must be tracked. They may also be transitive and the formation of any cycles must be detected. It is further necessary to document carefully in the database how a given software product is broken up into packages for distribution and the order in which these packages must be distributed and installed.

Maintenance, version and transient status information comprises all the operational information that is needed for day-to-day operations. It includes all the information about the software maintenance process proper, the recent version history at each node and such transient status information as reachability of a node or the necessary locks that must be placed on a system while the software maintenance process is under way. The whole set of core and maintenance data is referred to as base data.

The special requirement information is important to provide much of the flexibility needed to handle special cases. This information is defined by the user (in this case user refers to someone responsible for day-to-day operations of the START network) according to special criteria. For example, if a new software product is released it is not installed on all PCs across the board, but in a controlled form. Therefore, distribution criteria that may comprise certain cities or selected clients acting as test-sites must be defined. These testing criteria may also have a certain validity interval, after which they should be removed. In the S-POST system, different distribution or locking criteria may be specified. The distribution and locking criteria are stored in the database in the form of SQL-like selection predicates that are parsed and executed.

Finally, one of the major requirements of the new system is to assure data consistency in a far higher degree than is possible under the current file-based solution. This can be achieved by exploiting the consistency enforcement mechanisms of the DBMS, such as key uniqueness, foreign-key and domain specifications. More complex consistency criteria can be realized through triggers offered by today's DBMS.

The database of the S-POST system provides commonly used data for all components of the new system. The automatic maintenance module is responsible for periodically checking all PCs, and when new software needs to be installed, it sends the corresponding information to the PC and starts the local maintenance program which brings the PC up-to-date. To be able to track the update process and do trouble shooting, a separate supervision module is implemented. This module allows the supervisor to look at all the data und provides the tools to generate statistics and reports.

A number of daily check jobs update the base data and look for error situations and inconsistencies.

Introduction of new versions, exclusion dependencies and distribution criteria is done by a database administration program that allows to manipulate the data interactively.

5 The Pilot Implementations

Two pilot implementations of sizeable portions of the S-POST system were realized by teams of students at the Technical University of Darmstadt. Within these pilot projects the schema was designed using a variant of the Coad Yourdon methodology [2], leading to a refinement of the original system specification [1]. The object-oriented design was mapped both into a relational and into an object-oriented schema. During this mapping the existing operational experience and information about access patterns were heavily considered to guarantee a good performance. The relational schema was implemented in INFORMIX-Online Version 5.0 [3] while the ObjectStore Release 3.0 [4] was used for the object-oriented implementation.

In the relational realization the configuration and distribution information is defined by the network administrators in a manner that is conceptually close to a view definition. This approach allows the use of the same basic maintenance procedures to all systems rather than having different processes for normal distribution, pilot system distribution, training software etc. This unified handling results in an easy definition of new patterns or exception handling capabilities without one special-purpose module undoing what was done by another. However, it means storing the view definitions (which are typically metadata) as data in the configuration management database and processing these data in the same applictions as the base data. To do this efficiently, a parser was developed that translates the stored view definitions into dynamic SQL statements and translates the external names into the corresponding internal names to avoid or speed-up the joins.

Consistency may be violated either by modifying the base data or the configuration and distribution criteria defined over them. Consistency among base data is enforced immediately after updates on them using the trigger mechanisms provided by Informix. Consistency between the base data and the selection criteria defined over them cannot be enforced with Informix's trigger mechanism since the trigger mechanism does not allow dynamic SQL statements in the action part. Therefore, a hybrid solution had to be chosen in which the insert, delete and update operations were embedded in C functions that implement the consistency checks.

Object-Oriented DBMS are often touted as being ideally suited for supporting software engineering applications in general and configuration management systems in particular. Therefore, it was interesting to compare the facilities offered by the relational system and those offered by a typical C++-based OODBMS. The OODBMS proved much more powerful for expressing typical aggregations, such as all the software that needs to be installed on a certain node or a LAN consisting of a gateway, non-gateway nodes, printers, etc. The OODBMS also supports better the ordering relationships and dependencies. On the negative side, the lack of a powerful query language with which to define views dynamically made it more difficult to express in a flexible and user-friendly way the distribution criteria. On the interface side, currently available OODBMSs require much more ad-hoc implementation than the relational systems.

6 Outlook

Several trends can be recognized in the development of software in general and the software for the tourism industry in particular that will effect the version control strategies.

- The increase in computing power of the PCs at the point of sale is forcing a shift of the functionality currently handled by big mainframes to the PCs. A typical example are consistency checks during the input process instead of shipping inconsistent data and verifying them on the mainframe. This means that certain sets of data, particularly those that are relatively static, such as the list of airports and railway stations, must be shipped with the software to the terminal nodes.
- The growing popularity of graphical interfaces and the increased functionality of the software running on the PCs has lead to much larger files needing to be transferred.
- The growing number of service providers and the diversification of services offered makes it difficult to guarantee immediate and universal distribution of every service and the corresponding software and data to every PC. Therefore, the possibility of on-demand transfer of certain software and/or the associated data may be necessary.
- The emergence of lazy vs. eager update strategies in database systems and the triggering mechanism to enforce them may lead to new strategies for version control.

These trends must be balanced against the capabilities and costs of the underlying communication network. The new S-POST system considers many of the above trends and provides the means for a flexible version and configuration management. Special emphasis was placed in the easy definition of distribution criteria and the description of the packaging process of the software into distribution units.

Acknowledgements

The authors wish to acknowledge the enthusiasm and many hours of hard work of the students who implemented the pilot solutions.

References

[1] Auerbach, S., Buchmann, I., Merhazion, E., Stöck, S.: Das START-POST Projekt. Systemspezifikation Version 1.0., START Informatik GmbH, 1994.

[2] Coad, P., Yourdon, E.: Object Oriented Analysis; Prentice Hall, 1991.

[3] Informix Software, Inc.: The Informix Guide to SQL: Reference, Sept. 1992.

[4] Object Design, Inc.: ObjectStore Release 3.0 for UNIX Systems, Dec. 1993.

Electronic Market Support for the Tourism Industry: Requirements and Architectures

M. Merz, K. Müller, W. Lamersdorf

Depart. of Computer Science - Hamburg University, D-22527 Hamburg

email: [merz|kmueller|lamersd]@dbis1.informatik.uni-hamburg.de

Abstract: Recent advancements of global communications networks allow for distributed office transactions - as, for example, information gathering or reservations functions in tourism industry applications - to be provided and executed easily and efficiently. In corresponding electronic market systems, frequent changes of the economic environment require new on-line information services - together with underlying infrastructures - to be highly flexible and adaptive in order to adequately reflect dynamically changing requirements of service providers and their individual client applications.

This contribution presents applications requirements and innovative system support for a *Common Open Service Market* (COSM) as a distributed open information service infrastructure. The corresponding COSM system software allows independent and autonomous clients and service providers to cooperate in an Electronic Market System and to let market demand and supply depend on the price mechanism in a more flexible form as in existing centralized information service systems.

1. Introduction

This contribution discusses the increasing influence of customer-accessible information services on future developments of the tourism market. In the tourism industry, there are both service suppliers and consumers in high numbers - such that a high potential for perfect competition is given. However, perfect competition as a microeconomic model is usually considered an unrealistic simplification for real markets due to general transaction costs and - specifically important in the tourism field - due to costs for information search and acquisition for the individual customer [1]. In order to reduce such costs, travel agencies play the role of contracting agents between customers and service suppliers. They mainly benefit from information advantages and from economies of scale in their respective roles as immediate clients of, e.g., electronic reservation systems.

In the tourism market, individual goals of various actors are generally in conflict with each other: For example, suppliers (e.g. hotels and airlines) may aim at raising capacity utilisation and charges, whilest consumers (travellers) try to minimize the price/performance ratio as well as support for service selection and reservation. Value added resellers (e.g., travel agencies, package tour organizers, reservation systems) on the other hand, may live on reducing high search costs and, therefore, promote standardisation and substitutability of services, and may also gain from economies of scale.

Taking pattern from the definition given by Schmid [2], an *electronic market* (EM) is a medium that realizes market coordination at any time and place and increases transparency for all subjects involved in market transactions. It should reduce transaction costs in all three transaction phases: information gathering, trading, and settlement. *Electronic market systems* (EMS) provide the computational infrastructure required by EMs. In this contribution, the EMS concept is restricted to systems that are not specifically designed to electronically support one single market segment, but rather assumes an arbitrary market variety of on-line services across a multitude of business fields. Such a generalized EMS has not been realized yet, since existing ones do not support *all* transaction phases. Nevertheless, several research projects focus on distinct aspects and components of such an EMS like, e.g., electronic currency representations [3], notary services [4], or specific support of information gathering [5].

This contribution first identifies critical success factors for customer oriented information and reservation services. It then analyzes existing information service architectures with regard to their suitability as EMS platforms. The third section presents our own EMS architecture and prototype system, COSM (Common Open Service Market), motivated by a scenario from the tourism field. Finally, conclusions are drawn for further development of EMSs.

2. Success factors for electronic market systems

Information service *infrastructures* generally support interaction and cooperation between both of their possible user types, clients and servers. Specifically, they provide various *auxiliary services* such as connection support, billing, or directory services. In open systems environments, client and server cooperation can only be initialized if the server's address and functionality is known to the client and both customer and supplier trust in each other's reliability.

In order to separate the "real" market sphere from the electronic medium, the most important terms are defined here as follows:

- *Client*: the software component allowing access to servers.
- *Customer*: the user of a client software component.
- *Server*: software component accessible via a communication network.
- *Supplier, provider*: the person or company providing a service via the server.
- *Infrastructure service*: the communication function which provides not only server access based on an EMS-specific protocol. The infrastructure might either be realized by the mere communication network that supports transparent server access or, additionally, by a logically centralized provider organization.

Before examining existing information service infrastructures for their suitability to establish a general electronic market system, some critical success factors for such a system shall be considered. Afterwards, existing information systems are classified according to their fulfilment of the following goals and requirements:

- Reduction of *search costs* for clients [6] - and therefore transaction costs - to a lowest possible scale. Search costs result from a lacking transparency of supply.
- Reduction of *switching costs* [7] which arise when, e.g., customers plan to examine other services than the currently accessed one(s). High switching costs may restrict clients from evaluating these services or gathering new ones. Switching costs comprise billable costs for accessing new service providers as well as costs that arise from familarization with a new service's functionality. To give an example, current on-line image databases are so heterogeneous with regards to user interface and database functionality that clients are required to install, maintain and use individual client software for *each* service used.
- Reduction of *adaptation costs* concerning both client and server. Such set-up costs arise at the EMS infrastructure providers and comprise, e.g., fixed subscription fees, service offer fees for providers, software purchase and installation costs for clients or servers, etc.
- Adequate *standardization*: Communication standards are vital for open systems communications, but the more standardization involves application-level aspects the more restrictions have to be imposed on service individuality. A distinction is therefore made between *representation standards,* which rather prescribe syntactical aspects of data exchanged, and *content standards,* which address service semantics. If, e.g., "car model" is a standardization subject for rental services providers, they are obliged to adhere to the model palette specified. Thus, specialized "one-of-a-kind" services become impossible because their offer is not classifiable by such a restrictive standard.
- *Dynamic emergence of value chains*: In a scenario of 100000+ on-line services offered world-wide there is a rising demand for transparency, selection support, and service evaluation [8]. The EMS architecture should allow or even encourage the existence of value-added services (VAS) to customize, enrich, or combine existing ones and to flexibly close occuring gaps between supply and demand. VASs act on behalf of their clients and provide indirect access to other services for their clients.
- *Decentralization level* of the EMS infrastructure: Despite of physical decentralization, EMSs may be logically centralized in the sense that they are involved in each single market transaction as a central control unit. Auxiliary services are then provided exclusively by the central infrastructure provider.
- *Security, and trust* [3]: Both cooperating parties, client and server, establish a legal contract when, e.g., a reservation is made. Beyond fundamental security requirements, a *trusted* auxiliary service is required to assure the identity and reliability of the respective contracting partners. This service may either be provided by the EMS infrastructure itself or by specific third-party services playing the role of a notary.

System infrastructures like the BTX service of German Telekom are based on logically centralized accounting and billing. Anonymous user activities are thus impossible. However, this does not reflect market transaction in real life where, e.g., theater tickets are anonymously purchased. However, additional clearing and accounting services such as banks may be involved in the trading process if, for example, payment has to be effected in a traceable way.

Apart from transaction cost reductions, flexibility in mapping real world activities to an electronic market system appears as a fundamental factor for the success of EMSs. Current commercial infrastructures like BTX or CompuServe lack this ability: *Every* transaction involves distinct parties: the client, the actual service provider, and the infrastructure provider. Current developments in research, however, rather focus on a peer-to-peer oriented communications infrastructure [9,10] where auxiliary services may only be *optionally* involved and selected from both contracting partners. One of the most obvious aspects of these systems is that auxiliary services (e.g. directory services) are not an infrastructure component but have to be realized at the 'application' level (Fig. 1). In principle, these services can thus be provided by third parties and are therefore allowed to evolve more rapidly in order to respond faster to changing market demands.

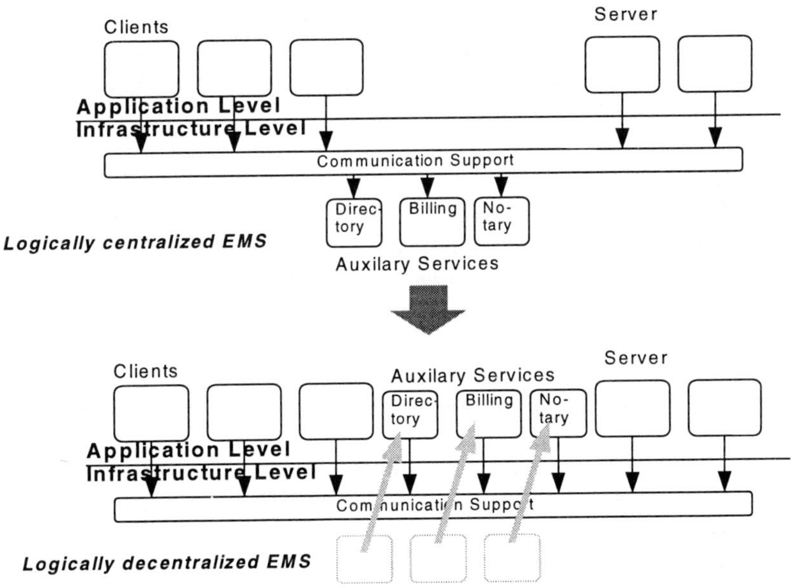

Fig. 1. Lifting infrastructure services to the application level

Finally, EMSs should not be restricted to single market sectors. The tourism market field, however, can be considered as a highly relevant and representative testbench, since real services are easily mapped to their electronic counterparts and the tourism field shows sufficient heterogeneity for an open decentralized environment.

The following section presents "COSM" as a recent research prototype system to support EMS application in open distributed systems in the more general framework of the COSM/TRADE (Common Open Service Market / TRADing Environment) research project [5].

3. The COSM project: Assumptions and architecture

3.1. COSM architecture

The COSM infrastructure allows service providers in open EMSs to offer newly created service without previous content standardization [10]. (When such innovative services have gained maturity and coherence among competing providers, an a-posteriori standardization based on a uniform service type may take place later.) The specific advantage of the COSM architecture lies in increased *autonomy* of service providers and clients: Service providers are not obliged to adhere to existing service interface standards for their own operational interface.

To give a tourism-related example, an "innovative" car rental company may provide the end-users with an on-line reservation service which allows to browse interactively through the car models offered and to inspect various rental conditions. This car rental service may provide a world-wide unique interface: From a technical point of view, the operational service interface of the respective server software can vary substantially from service to service as a consequence of the multitude of providers within this business field. Customers are confronted with severe problems of such heterogeneity if they want to reserve a car at any arbitrary supplier. This motivates the need for (value adding) *mediating services* which hide such interface heterogeneity from accessing users.

The architectural model of COSM has the following main components (see Fig. 2):

- The *Generic Client* (GC) supports (client) users in service discovery, service access, and binding, and in the inspection of service descriptions at run-time.
- A common *Service Representation* (SR), which contains several descriptional components (defining the operational service interface, the GC's user interface layout, the interrelation between user interface and remote procedure invocation, human-understandable descriptions of service functionality, billing information on the charge of procedure invocations, a description of the order of operation invocations, etc.).
- *Service providers* (servers) implement dedicated functionalities and are accessible on-line in the COSM network. They supply their respective SRs to their potential users (possibly via GC or mediating services).
- SR *Browsers* and *Repositories* support users to inspect and store service descriptions.
- *Traders* identify appropriate service suppliers more efficiently by automating the search for best suitable services based on given service description criteria.
- Finally, *Mediation services* provide application specific tasks like, e.g., collecting news articles for their customers.

When binding to a server, a GC receives the SR and generates the corresponding user interface automatically (see Fig. 2). The user can then inspect the information provided by the SR and familiarize with the described service functionality. A binding to the server can then be established (or released if this information does not describe the kind of service the user was looking for). In COSM, the user interface representation of a remote services site is standardized at the GC, layout and content, however, may vary from service to service. This interface enables users to execute remote operation calls just by filling out forms and pressing corresponding buttons automatically.

A sample prototype as presented in [10] allows clients to first select a car model for a distinct time period. After the selection operation is executed, an offer is sent to the customer. Finally, the customer either accepts the offer by pressing a "selection button" or rejects it by releasing the connection.

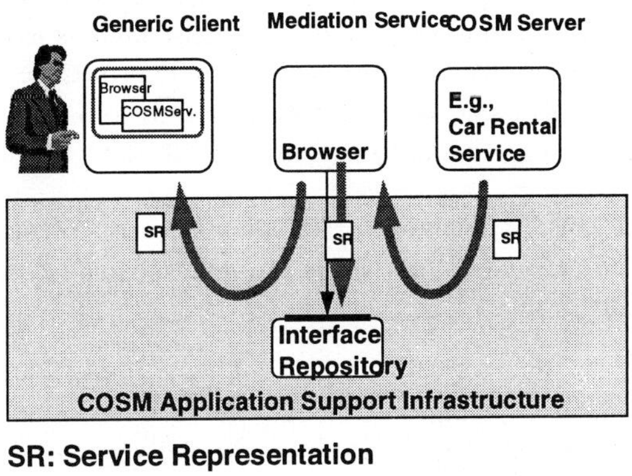

Fig. 2. Accessing remote services in COSM

Service references are data values which can be transferred across the network. On this basis, dedicated COSM services are enabled to act as directory services allowing servers to register their service representation and clients to obtain detailed information about the requested services. Such mediation services may act on behalf of their clients to evaluate the quality of services offered, or they may act on behalf of servers to "advertise" registered entries.

In a commercial environment, interaction with remote servers frequently implies a contract establishment as well as a payment flow for service utilization. Therefore, current research also focusses on the integration of an anonymous electronic payment component as suggested by [3]. Accordingly, servers may charge their clients either on a connection basis, by operation invocation, or by the amount of data transferred. Mediating services may thus charge either service registration operations (advertising services) or service reference look-up (directory services). In the first case, service look-up is free of charge for clients, in the latter interface registration access for servers [8].

Despite of the fact that COSM servers are defined by their operational interface, they constitute a hybrid system consisting of the on-line accessible software part and human users who take part in a server's response activity. Mediators which evaluate remote services therefore carry out their task by letting users access remote servers for testing purposes and making this information available for client afterwards.

3.2. Characteristics of the COSM approach

This section reviews the COSM approach in the context of the requirements of section 2. Three basic assumptions are made when comparing information services:

- Any information service infrastructure that is widely accessible imposes communication costs on customers. Since these costs are not specific for architectures and generally decreasing over time, they are considered negligible in this context.
- In addition, the ubiquitous availability of a common communication infrastructure, like the Internet, for private households is assumed. Only at this scale value-adding services become commercially profitable.
- Furthermore, a sufficient communication bandwidth (e.g. >=30 kBit/s) is required for accessing clients to support smooth data interchange with up-to-date servers.

A comparison of COSM with the information service platforms *World Wide Web* (WWW) [9] and *BTX* reveals first some few but substantial differences between COSM and the WWW:

1. COSM allows to interactively access *software applications* whilest WWW supports *document exchange.* Although interactive forms are supported by WWW, "operation calls" only result in the delivery of a further document. Restrictions of WWW apply when results of previous operation calls are used as parameters for further ones (statefull servers).
2. The second difference concerns possibilities for *chaining* service providers to allow value chains to emerge. Since COSM servers present an operational interface, they allow for specific client software that *automatically* executes operation calls. This software does not provide a user interface but may act itself as a COSM server. In addition, in order to let client calls directly pass-through to the back-end server, such front-end servers may carry out specific computations on parameter and result values.

Both, COSM and WWW differ from centralized system like BTX in several points:

- *Autonomy*: In BTX, service providers are strictly required to register at the infrastructure provider that additionally charges such service offers; i.e. the mere accessibility imposes costs on providers. In WWW and COSM, servers can emerge at any time and be accessible via the Internet without additional registration or administration effort. Instead, service providers are expected to care on their own for the registration at existing directory or mediation services. BTX thus poses higher adaption costs on service providers.
- *Accounting and billing* as auxiliary services are provided by the infrastructure provider, BTX. Therefore, both BTX clients and servers have to adapt to the provided payment policy. Customers are thus not capable to anonymously access remote services.
- *Decentralization*: In WWW and COSM, connections are immediately established between communicating peers. Service access does not require registration at any central unit.

Architecture	**BTX**	**WWW**	**COSM**
Infrastructure provider	German PTT	No provider	No provider
Cost structure for clients	Connection costs, Subscribtion fee, costs based on connection-time and service charge	Connection costs, free service access	Connection costs, servers (mediators, etc.) may charge fees
Cost structure for servers	High	Low	Low
Standardization requirements	Access protocol, page layout, interaction schema	Syntactical and graphical representations of documents	Syntactical and graphical representations of interface descriptions
Emerg. of value chains	On a referencial basis	On a referencial basis	By reference & chaining
Centralization of administration	BTX host is a logically centralized control unit	No central administration	No central administration
Security, trust	Central server handles billing, information servers may not provide service as demanded	Billing is completely excluded from information service (e.g., by credit card), no quality guaranty for services provided	Privacy and trusted third-party services can be optionally involved in client/server contracts

Table 1. Comparison of information service infrastructures.

3.3. Value chains in COSM

In real markets, value chains supply abstraction, sophistication, and transparency to their respective consumers. End consumers are usually not involved in mining raw materials, manufacturing parts, assembly, or packaging of the goods they purchase. Accordingly, package tourists are not willing to be involved in time consuming service selection, evaluation, and combination processes - they preferably rely on the specialization of dedicated firms like travel agencies, tour organizers, or organizations such as the "better business bureaus". Transformed into the context of the COSM approach, an important infrastructure design goal is to facilitate the emergence of *Value-adding Services* (VAS) which are built on pre-existing ones. The only precondition for a reliable use of COSM VASs is a stable interface of the underlying services over time: Servers are allowed to introduce additional operations, to accept additional parameters, or reduce the number of result values, but syntax and semantics of previous interface versions must be preserved.

Applied to the tourism field example, VASs may realize a search function for, e.g., the best offer for a given car model within a regional scope. Such services hide confusing details of the heterogeneity of implementations from various service providers from the customer. Current research focusses on how to support dynamic transaction-based service access to a *group of servers:* The user is initially asked to select a group of servers such that the succeeding interaction with them is considered a single transaction which can either be committed by the user, or aborted if one of the operation calls does not return the expected result. For a common example, the combination of hotel, flight and car reservation can thus be bracketed by a single transaction. Such a VAS then acts as a transaction monitor, that routes operation invocations to servers and provides roll-back mechanisms for the case of failure (Fig. 3).

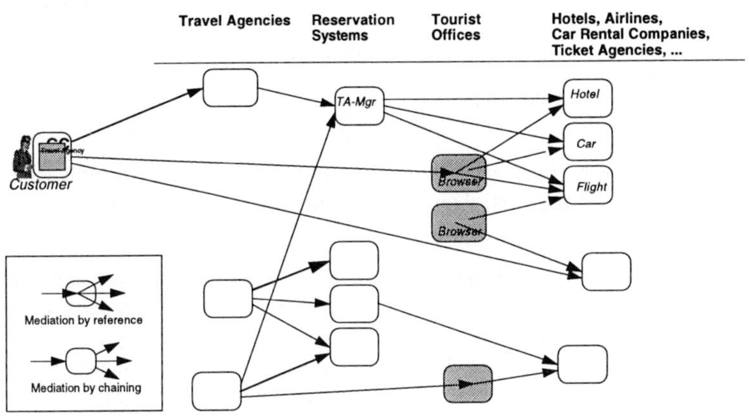

Fig. 3. Chaining COSM servers.

4. Concluding discussion

Future developments in global communication networks allow individual access to remote services at any point in time and space. In such an environment, restricted proprietary or nationally provided on-line information services (that rely on gateway functions between one another to let customers access services across borders) do not appear to be appropriate for a tourism industry that is itself heterogeneous and distributed at a global scale. The current dramatic expansion of the World-Wide-Web information service illustrates the demand for a greatest common denominator at this global level. WWW supports information gathering and rudimentary form-based interactions such that information kiosks or visitor information services are feasible already today.

However, due to pure document exchange the WWW infrastructure still lacks support for arbitrary and individually callable network services. Assumed that there exists a WWW-like infrastructure allowing such services to emerge, a tremendous potential is given for a shift from exclusive large-scale tour organizers and travel agencies to alternatives of small and innovative service providers with comparably low operating costs.

The COSM project proposes an architecture for supporting arbitrary client/server interactions in open distributed environments. First practical experiences have been made with a corresponding COSM/TRADE infrastructure prototype implementation of a decentralized collection of services. It comprises system support tools like the Generic Client as well as Browsers, Repositories, and Trading services (like ODP-conform trader). As a consequence, the reduced effort to make existing program libraries or "legacy systems" available for external access decreases set-up costs for service providers. The resulting lack of a centralized cost-intensive infrastructure nexus is compensated by reduced transaction costs and the possibility to involve auxiliary services like, e.g., notary services if both customer and supplier agree.

Generalized EMSs will not be established in the tourism field unless they satisfy the requirements described in section 2 and unless they do not conflict too severely with the goals of all participating roles. Otherwise, either customers or suppliers will not be ready to use the new emerging EM medium soon. Currently evolving open system infrastructures (like the COSM/TRADE prototype system) provide flexible means to support unrestricted interactions of autonomous client/ server components in world-wide distributed electronic markets (like in the tourism industry) for the benefits of both customers and service providers.

5. References

1. Williamson, O: Markets and Hierarchies, Free Press, New York, 1975
2. Schmid, B.: Electronic Markets. Electronic Markets, No. 9/10 (Oct. 93), Vol. 3, pp. 3-4
3. Medvinsky, G., Neuman, B. C.: Electronic currency for the Internet. Electronic Markets, No. 9/10 (Oct. 93), Vol. 3, pp. 23-24
4. Merz, M., Müller, K., Lamersdorf, W.: Trusted third party services in COSM. Electronic Markets, No. 12, (Sept. 93), Vol. 4, pp. 7-8
5. Merz, M., Müller, K., Lamersdorf, W.: Service trading and mediation in distributed computing systems. Proc. IEEE 'International Conference on Distributed Computing Systems' (ICDCS), L. Svobodova (Ed.), IEEE Computer Society Press, Los Alamitos, 1994, pp. 450-457
6. Malone, T.W., Yates, J., Benjamin, R.I.: Electronic markets and electronic hierarchies: Effects of information technology and market structures on corporate strategies. Communications of the ACM, (30:6), June 1987, pp. 484-497
7. Bakos, J.Y.: A strategic analysis of electronic marketplaces. MIS Quarterly, Sept. 91, pp. 295-310
8. Miller, M.S., Drexler, K.E.: Markets and Computation: Agoric Open Systems. In: Huberman, B.A.: The Ecology of Computation, Amsterdam, 1988, pp. 133-176
9. Computer Networks and ISDN Systems, Amsterdam-Lausanne-New York, Vol. 27, No. 2, November 1994
10. Merz, M., Lamersdorf, W.: Cooperation support for an open service market. Proc. 'International Conference on Open Distributed Processing' (ICODP'93), IFIP-Transactions C: vol. C-20, Elsevier Science Publishers B.V. (North-Holland), Amsterdam London New York Tokyo, 1994, pp. 329-340

Adaptable object-oriented distributed system integrating multimedia resources

Vlad Wietrzyk, Venkat Ramaswamy*, Athula Ginige*

University of Technology Sydney, Computer Science, Po Box 123
Broadway NSW 2007 Australia. vlad@socs.uts.edu.au
* School of Electrical Engineering

Abstract. This paper is concerned with the integration of two important areas, namely distributed systems and multimedia computing. We introduce a distributed system which provides extensible as well as integrated environments for users and application programs to access and combine distributed resources conveniently. The system is based on the concept of object-oriented service bases. On the other hand, in this kind of distributed environments, the numbers and types of data available to users are being expanded, users may have troubles to access and manipulate these data. Application programs, functions provided by computers, operations on multimedia data are becoming more complicated. Therefore, it is necessary to use an uniform method to manage these distributed resources and to provide convenient and integrated high level services to the users.

1 Introduction

Computer networks are the basis for building distributed applications from a set of cooperating application components running on different physical nodes [1]. Although the advantages of distributed applications are well known and widely recognized many questions are still open, especially adequate abstraction mechanisms which provide appropriate and user-friendly specification and implementation techniques. Still missing is a high level approach to support the development of distributed applications, enabling a constructive approach for the integration of all aspects, which have to be taken into consideration. Recently, developments in networks, especially the high bandwidth and high speed networks (for example, ISDN and LAN), make the sharing of multimedia data in a distributed environment available and practical. In our model we distinguish between the application-oriented, management-oriented and the communication-oriented aspects of a distributed application. Rapid access to information is one of the key ways in which telecommunications can contribute to the effectiveness of a business operation.

I now describe multimedia information access in a travel/tourism industry where the visual capabilities of multimedia can be used extensively.

For example: audio/video sequences of selected travel destinations are displayed to clients in travel agencies. This can be used to introduce a personalized element into travel planning, for instance by booking the client into a specific hotel room that he/she has selected from images of the room and the view from the window.

2 Modelling

2.1 Aspects

In terms of the ODP model our approach covers the computation and engineering viewpoint. However, we have concentrated onto a clear separation of communication, application and management-oriented aspects, Fig. 1.

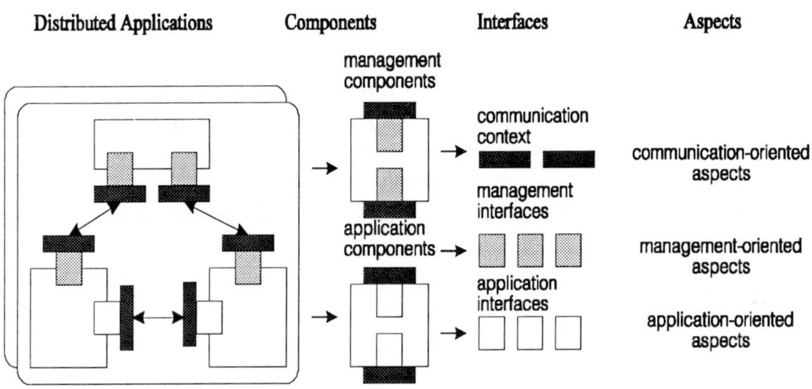

Fig. 1. Integration aspects in distributed application development

2.1.1 Communication-oriented aspects

A communication service is needed to support the interaction between the application components of a distributed application which may reside on different machines within a computer network. Our approach for the specification of communication requirements is based on the concept of a communication context which could be assigned to each interface.

2.1.2 Management-oriented aspects

In order to enable management activities, each application componenet must provide management interfaces which define operations for the control, maintenance and monitoring of application components. In our approach management is realized by management components, which are special components providing only management functions, i.e. they are constructed from a set of management interfaces Fig.1. Administration is performed by interaction between management components and the application components of a distributed application via management interfaces.

2.1.3 Application-oriented aspects

The interface concept provides configuration independence because there is no direct naming of other application components. From the application-oriented perspective a distributed application is composed of a set of application components. In order to support the specification of a configuration of interconnected application components a configuration language is needed, which is also useful to generate the executable distributed application.

2.2 Computational model

The computational model supported by our model defines the rules for the behaviour of computational objects that can be supported by our model. Only those computational objects (and by extension, distributed applications) that conform to this model can achieve the full benefits offered by this model: transparent distribution, transparent fault-tolerance, portability, independence from platform, etc.

The model is based on the support of language-level computational objects. Since D-Quelle [2], is a prototype SE-ODP (Support Environment for Open Distributed Processing), the computational model primarily concerns the interactions between computational objects.

In the black-box view, a distributed application is viewed from the outside; the computational objects are seen as black boxes, which interact via defined interfaces. This is the view of, say, an application designer. The programmer's view is of one computational object, from inside that object; other parts of the system are seen only by the interfaces used for interaction. This is the white-box view, and concerns the programming of a computational object in such a way as to conform to the computational model.

2.3 Computational objects

From the computational viewpoint, a distributed application consists of a number of (language-level) program modules, which can interact with one another. The important feature of this computational model is that the program modules are computational objects; each computational object encapsulates some (data) and the operations on that data. From the computational viewpoint, these operations provide the only means whereby other computational objects may read, or cause changes to, the state encapsulated by a computational object. Direct manipulation, by one computational object, of the state of another computational object is not permitted, and, in the ganeral case where two interacting computational objects are executing on distinct host machines, will not be possible. The implementation of the object's encapsulated state, and of the operations supported, is not visible to other computational objects.

2.4 Service interfaces

Object interactions are based on the offering and invocation of services, via clearly-defined interfaces. The set of operations supported by a computational object (and made available for invocation by other computational objects) constitutes the interface to that object. In many cases, these operations fall into a number of distinct sets, and it is convenient to treat such a set of operations as a dostinct interface, referred to as a service interface. The distinct service interfaces supported by a computational object give different "views" onto that object. Different service interfaces may be made available to different groups of users. Fig.2, shows the elements involved in the interactions between two computational objects A and B. Object A is the service user; object B is the service provider. This interaction is constrained by a particular service interface; the only interactions supported are the operations and responses defined by that interface.
A given coputational object may, of course, be both a user of some services and a provider of other services; the terms "service user" and "service provider" refer only to their relationship to the particular service interface, and not to the computational object as a whole.

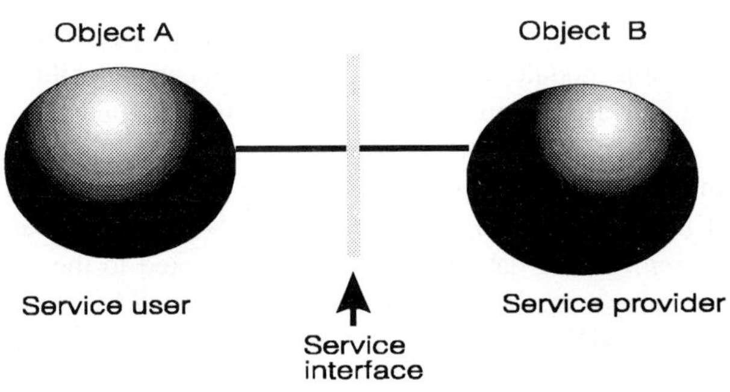

Fig. 2. Simple object interaction

3 Object management framework

All objects within our approach consist of a simple or complex data structure with associated operations stored on a distributed network. An object can contain internal dependent objects which are not duplicated or remotely accessed independently. All objects are strongly typed; a type specifies the operational interface, the data structure, and the operation implementation of similar objects. This information is also used to guide format conversions for object transmission purposes. Objects are identified by systemwide unique identifiers. If an object is created at a node n, the identifier consists of the unique address of this birthnode n and of a number which is unique within the context of that node. An application accesses local and remote objects in a uniform, location-independent way via method invocations. Each node maintains an object table which maps object identifiers to local storage addresses if a referenced object is local. For references to remote objects, the object table contains a location hint entry instead of a local storage address. A location hint entry comprises the address of the node where the referenced object is assumed to reside. A remote object can be accesses by sending a message (which includes its unique object identifier) to the location denoted by the address of the node where the referenced object is assumed to reside (location hint). If an object has moved several times, the location hint may not be accurate any more. The access massage has then to be forwarded to the next location etc.

We structure the service base (including the interface) as a collection of object. The directory classifies all objects which can be used though this service base. The query analyzer object is responsible to handle the queries sent from users or application programs, and to perform mapping between different views. The communication module object provides communication interface between objects in different nodes. Inside the service base of a node, communications between objects are supported by object communication mechanism of the language which implements the service base. Communication between objects which exist in different nodes is supported by the communication module. After the source object sends a message, control is passed to the communication module. In other words, objects inside a service base are not directly communicate with objects in other nodes. Therefore, it is not necessary that the language which implements our system is a distributed language. In the communication module, two kinds of communication facility are provided: remote procedure call (RPC) and message passing. For example, in our system, to execute a service is to combine objects which are related to this service. When the operations of an object are local and the data of the object are remote, the data are fetched to local machine through message passing. When the operations are local and the data are remote, the data and control are migrated to the remote machine through RPC. In our system, the communication module will be imolemented by the socket promitives in UNIX. The socket function covers protocols under session layer.

4 Integration with relational dbms: a quick view

A directory is used to classify resources. For each resource, a class instance (object) is created and registered as a persistent object in a database. In an actual implementation, we must make choice to use what kind of databases (for example, relational database or object-oriented database). The external view and the conceptual view of our system will be implemented by object-oriented language C++. It will be efficient for object-oriented language to access an object-oriented database. Actually, in an object-oriented database, the language and the database are usually designed as a whole system [2, 3]. But in our experimental environment, object-oriented database in each node is not available. Therefore, we decide to use a relational database called INGRES. To use a relational database, the main problem is focused on how to map the directory schema to the schema of the database. To represent the directory schema which is a tree structure in a normalized relational form will need a lot of relations (tables). To solve this problem, we use unnormalized relational form to represent the directory. In the database, each directory class is represented by one relation, and several relations are used to keep the relationship of the directory tree.

Many of today's multimedia systems stored, manipulated and presented media locally. Networking places additional requirements upon languages, tools, applications and operating systems. To cater for sharing and data management of multimedia objects we have introduced persistent facilities into our object oriented model. The new implementation will consists of a new root object which supports versioning and locking, and a database object for managing reference to versioned objects. Persistence is realised by a new instance method, supported by a new root object class. This method can be invoked as part of an object's initialisation, allowing an entire class to be persistent or individual member to become persistent during lifetime. This approach also allows the programmer control of networks of persistence, in that the method can be modified to make associate objects persistent. Caching and locking is provided for using various instance methods. As it is the case with object-oriented environment these methods can be redefined, allowing for fine level user control. Using these primitives, the various coordination mechanisms can be realised.

The challenging goal of research is a crucial requirement for the system being applicable in real settings is the capability of integrating heterogeneous information managed by pre-existing information management systems not only with DBMSs but also with non conventional systems. The approach we are investigating aims at:

* providing a global view of the semantic content of the heterogeneous information bases. This view is uniformly incorporated in the D-QUELLE knowledge base [3];
* hiding the discrepancies of the operational interfaces within the same category of information management systems, i.e. RDBMS, image handlers and so on;
* hiding the location and distribution of the information;
* providing the user with an advanced interface for navigating the heterogeneous and distributed information.

5 Integrated example

As a summary , we present an integrated travel agency's office-related example which exploits all of the mechanisms. The example is illustrated in Figure 3.

The object being duplicated is a multimedia document representing a proposed customised travel route. A frame of the original route proposal is created by an employee by using a sample. The employee than copies the document remotely to a manager and archives the initial version of it. From now on, the copy at the manager's site is operated upon. The manager adds an abstract describing the scope of the proposed customised trip and its budget requirements. Afterwards, he moves the document to a technical employee in order to operate on the technical parts of the proposed customised trip, e.g., means of transportations. In addition, he keeps a local cached copy which is invalidated after the document is updated further.

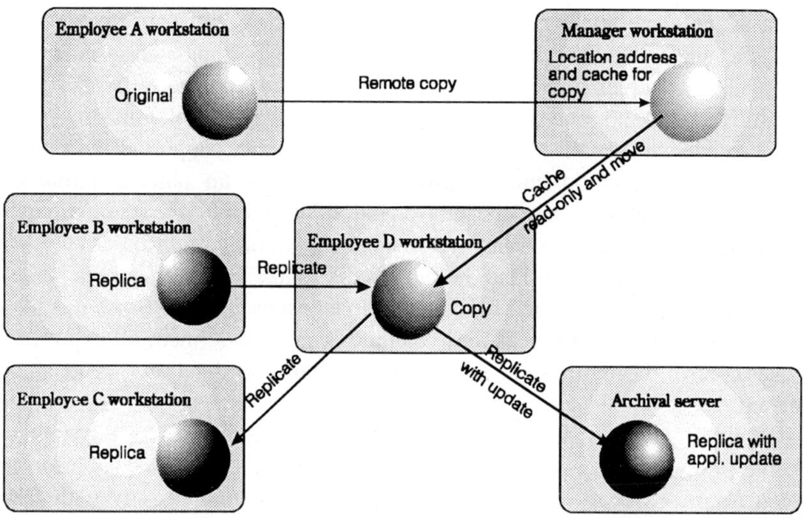

Fig. 3. Integrated example

This is to enable read access for reminding purposes if the technical expert should not act upon the document in a timely fashion. The senior employee delegates parts of the trip description to the appropriate staff and replicates the document for the purpose. Each staff member then performs updates of independent parts which are propagated to the other members. This way, each of them can directly refer to information within the other parts of the document. The first update propagation invalidates the cached copy of the manager who will then access the document remotely. In addition, replication with application-dependent update is used for checkpointing intermediate versions of the document to an archival server. A specific backup operation propagates updates from time to a backup copy at the server's site.

The example has shown that different mechanisms are important for the different access characteristics found within the given scenario. For example, migration with cached read-only copy was appropriate for the manager as he did not access the document while the staff was operating on it. Remote copying was used due to the need of keeping archival copies of the forwarded document. By integrating the mechanisms within a consistent framework, it has been possible to apply them in a uniform way without observing a variety of different, mutually inconsistent object access mechanisms.

6 Conclusion

The key point of the approach is the distinction between semantic and operational heterogeneity. At the semantic level heterogeneity arises when the various information sources are designed independently; that is the same entity may have been modelled in different ways in the various information bases.

A second level of integration called operational arises from heterogeneities due to the distinct software/hardware systems used to manage information. For example a picture can be a vectorial image and displayed by a CAD system or a raster image managed by some image editor and so on.The "operational" integration entails the abstraction of a common set of operations for accessing uniformly the physical supports, hiding the deeper heterogeneity of the access command language provided by the information management systems.

Our system focuses on how to abstract the meta-information from resources and how to manage these meta-information. The object-oriented approach provides us a modelling method. We can mention some characteristics of our system by comparing it to other systems. First, it provides an open-end resource management framework in a developing network environment. Second, the combining ability: existing resources can be combined to provide more services. Finally, easy construction: the existing operating systems and network facilities are utilized. We consider that these characteristics are important in practical distributed systems.

Intelligent presentation systems are important building blocks for the next generation of information systems, because they translate from the narrow output channels, provided by most of the current application systems, into high-bandwidth communications tailored to the individual user.

Our system is expected to be effective in the environment where new resources are extended frequently and the types of resources are various, for example, in office automation environment and travel industry. We think that the integration strategy cannot be unique for all the systems. Rather the way the coupling is performed depends on the nature of the application to be integrated. We can thus envisage different categories of systems for the different strategies. In our research the integration of non conventional applications managing images is approached using an operational mapping while for the connection with RDBMS a schems mapping approach is being investigated.

7 References

1. Black A.: Supporting Distributed Applications: Experiences with EDEN, Proc. 10th ACM Symposium on Operating System Principles (1985).

2. Wietrzyk, V., (1994), "QUELLE: A Knowledge - Based Approach to Systems Development". In Proc. of The Fourth International Conference on Information Systems Development - ISD'94; Methods & Tools - Theory & Practice. (1994).

3. Wietrzyk, V., (1994), "Development of Adaptable Information Systems in Tourism", In Proc. of International Conference on Information and Communication Technologies, Innsbruck, Austria. (1994).

From Structure to Process: A Vision of a process-based Organization

Kai A. Simon

Göteborg University
School of Economics and Commercial Law
Department of Informatics

Abstract. Organization design has for a long time been dominated by a functional perspective on organizations, considering them as hierarchies of authority and control. Current concepts, such as total quality (TQM, TQC) and reengineering (BPR) can be seen as an effort to overcome the traditional functional approach and to focus on the processes performed within the organization rather than on its structure. However, when looking at the results of total quality implementations and reengineering projects one can conclude, that the basic idea about organizations as being a structure rather than a set of processes is not actually replaced. Functional departments are replaced by teams, hierarchy levels are removed, but designing structures still appears to be the main emphasis of organization design.

This paper is not primarily intended to provide proven research findings, but to present a *vision* of a process-based organization concept, considering the organization as being a set of dialectic, hierarchical, integrated processes, and to receive feedback on the feasibility of the concept.

Introduction

There is a growing insight among company leaders, that the traditional concepts for organizing, labour division and management no longer are applicable in a world of global markets, changing customer requirements and rapid communication.

The recipes for change, known as reengineering (BPR, BPI), kaizen (Japanese for continuous improvement), and total quality (TQM, TQC) are based on the same primary assumption: Companies will have to refocus on their basic task, satisfying customer needs (Hammer & Champy 1993, Davenport 1993, Creech 1994).

Even though the means for achieving this differ between the approaches, they share one commonalty: A focus on processes instead of functions. Nevertheless, the organizational redesign often comes short of this ambition as the new organization still is a conglomerate of structural relations, rather than a network of processes. Removing hierarchy levels, establishing teams and empowering employees will not shift the focus from structure to processes per se.

This paper is will approach this problemacy by providing arguments for the usability of emphasizing on organizational processes, while disregarding the structural component of organizations. A way of considering organizations as a set of dialectic, hierarchical, integrated processes will be introduced and the consequences of this view for organization design will be discussed with regard to their impact on several aspects of the design process. However, it is important to point out, that this article is not presenting findings yet proven by the standards of the scientific community. It should be considered as the presentation of a visionary idea about how organizations can be designed upon a process-basis, and an attempt to receive theoretical and empirical feedback regarding the feasibility of the ideas presented.

"There is in the literature a great disparity between hypothesis and evidence. Much of what we know or believe about organizations is distilled from common sense and from the practical experience of executives. The great bulk of this wisdom and lore has never been subjected to the rigorous scrutiny of scientific method. The literature contains many assertions, but little evidence to determine - by the usual scientific standards of public testability and reproducibility - whether these assertions really hold up in the world of fact."

James March and Herbert Simon, 1958

Background

Ever since the application of Smith's labour division principles on administrative science, we have had the same logical assumptions about how companies should be organized, indifferent from branch and primary competitive focus. Similar, functional tasks have been aggregated, rather than logically related activities. This view has generated corps of specialists, each of them focusing on his own bounded task, with the result of increased time-to-market, transactions-costs, workflow delays and problems in quality assurance.

Change concepts such as BPR, try to overcome the pathologies occurring as a result of over-focusing on functional production, while disregarding the aspects of transactions, by designing organizations based on value adding (core) processes.

When looking upon manufacturing-industries, the consideration of process, designed upon the basis of workflows along an assembly line has been a quite common phenomenon ever since the days of Henry Ford. However, even manufacturing processes have mainly been conceived as interrelated sets of functional activities. In order to handle the aspects of transaction among the elements of the process, there has been a focus on independence, instituted by buffering and stocking, rather than integration. However, the turbulence and accelerating environmental dynamics of the 1990s will have major implications for how organizations operate and are managed. The rapid spread of the just-in-time (JIT) system, which has the effect of removing organizational buffers, is a partial example for the emerging awareness of the need for new organizational forms. Rockart and Short (1991) have proposed networked organizations as a possible solution to the problem. A similar view has been proposed by Bush and Frohman (1991). They criticized the traditional up-and-down communication model, as well as the sequential flow of functional activities, and instead proposed a model for a concurrent network organization.

Both proposals are, however, not concerned with the feasibility of certain organizational forms to implement the proposed networked organization. My intention is to integrate process- and network-approach, in order to propose an organizational form that is better capable of facing the challenges of the future.

Analyzing processes and designing structures

Most of the current change concepts claim to have a primary focus on organizational processes instead of structures, and this can agreed with to a certain amount. While organization analysis is concerned with identification of value-adding processes, one can often conclude a tendency towards structural design in the re-organization stage of the change process. Repeatedly occurring measures are the removal of hierarchy levels, the establishment of empowered teams, and expanded spans of responsibility for remaining managers. These measures are based upon the presumption, that process management requires stable structures.

According to my opinion, it provides significant advantages to disregard the structural component of organizations and to primarily focus on the processes to be performed. Even though this implies considerable changes in the way of conceiving organizations, the distribution of work, reward systems and control a.o., this view enables a stronger consideration of the organizational outcome and the means to achieve it, rather than of the organization itself.

Towards a process-based organization

In order to overcome the deficiencies of focusing on structural, instead of processes design, it is necessary to make a clear distinction between two sub-elements of organizations. The german economist Erich Kosiol (1962) used a distinction between "structure-" and "process-organization". Even though Kosiol considered this distinction as a "scientific trick", aimed to reduce the complexity of conceptualizing organizations, I found it useful for my further considerations.

In current change management literature and seminars, e.g. Davenport (1993), Gartner Group (1993), organizational processes are often depicted as in fig. 1. (B), i.e. as a set of straight, sequential activities, lying above the existing, functional structure. According to my opinion, this description model is insufficient for a conceptualization of organizational processes, since it provides an image of processes as being a sequential flow of co-ordinated functional activities with well-defined boundaries, and that the preservation of an underlying functional structures is an implication for organization design on a process basis.

I will go beyond this foundations and provide a model under the presumption, that organizations can be designed based upon organizational processes only.

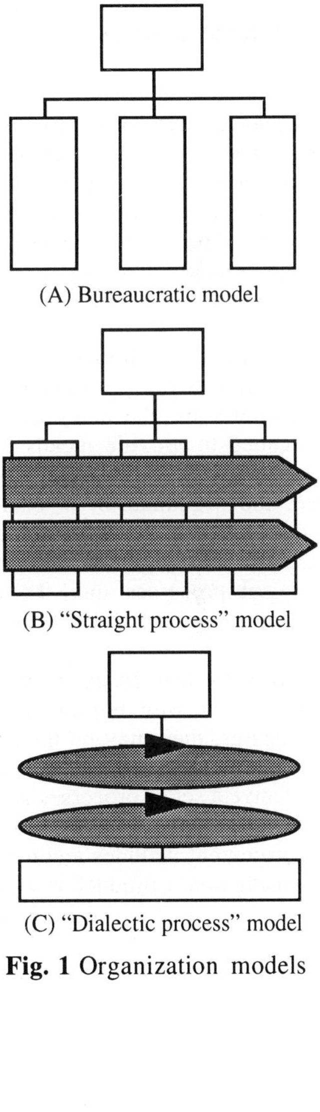

(A) Bureaucratic model

(B) "Straight process" model

(C) "Dialectic process" model

Fig. 1 Organization models

However, this includes abandoning many conventional implications concerning organizations, how they are managed, the role and behaviour of organizational members etc., which will then no longer be applicable. For my further considerations, I will first have to define some basic assumptions about organizations conceptually defined in process terms. The following assumptions will be used for the further discussion. A graphical depiction of an organization based on the assumptions given below is given in fig. 2.

Organizations are networks of processes

Instead of defining organizations in functional terms, dividing them into departments, business units, or teams, they can conceptually be defined as being networks of processes. This perspective enables a focus shift from the organization as an institutional phenomenon to its ends and the required activities and means to achieve them. The identification of activities and the integration of those into processes, their interrelation, and outcome, according to the organizations mission and process objectives then becomes the primary task for organization development, instead of providing a functional frame. As a result of this focus shift, an organizational structure occurs temporarily based upon the actual processes under performance.

Processes are dialectic[1]

By applying a dialectic perspective at organizational processes, we can overcome the limitation of a conception of processes as being sequential, i.e. as having a pre-defined starting- and end-point and incorporate enhanced organizational learning and process elevation in organization design at an early stage. This view includes a wide range of conceptual assumptions about organizational behaviour and individual and organizational learning.

Processes are hierarchical

As complexity is considered as being the major source of reduced manageability in organizations, the analytical school, mainly represented by Herbert Simon, is intended to provide means to reduce complexity and increase perspectiveness, independence and manageability. This is achieved by organizational fragmentation, i.e. the organization is broken down into a sub-set of tasks, each of them contributing to fulfil the objectives of their super-task. The same principle can be applied when organizations are considered as processes, which are then fragmented into sub-processes, until the desired level of complexity to remain is reached (as described by Emery (1969) for functional organizations).

Processes are integrated

In the same way as processes can be considered as being sets of interacting sub-processes, they may be integrated into one, or several, super-processes, given the presumption that they share common objectives. Process integration allows us to conceive a set of processes as a whole, instead of an assembly of parts. Thereby, co-ordination among the incorporated elements is improved, as the scope of process management includes a consideration of transactions as a critical factor, instead of focusing on the production of functional outcomes.

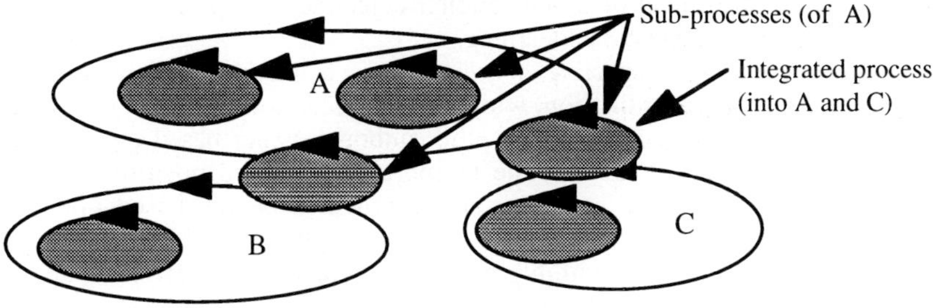

Fig. 2 The process network model

Discussion

Considering processes in above mentioned terms does not only impact the perspective at processes as being straight, sequential flows, crossing several functional boundaries. It will even challenge conventional wisdom regarding superiority and sub-ordination, reward systems, the concurrence of activities, a.o. I found that the following aspects, being discussed in the following, will have to gain increased attention:

- Superiority, sub-ordination
- Job assignment
- Reward systems
- Competence-pools
- Process evolution
- Goal congruence

Superirity and sub-ordination

Authority, superiority and sub-ordination are the current determining factors for depicting organizational structures. The hierarchical organizations resulting from this design principle are based upon a fragmentation of the organization into similar functional tasks, instead of value adding processes, often resulting in a departmental self-containment and a focus on the production of functional outcomes. The structure then tends to become a self-purpose, i.e. an institution, where the primary focus is to maintain the current state, power-bases and control structures. Within these organizations, the career of organizational members is determined by a person's formal position within the hierarchy, not the individuals contribution to added value, his skills, and commitment to the objectives to achieve. Additionally, promotion is single-directed, i.e. upwards. As described by the "Peter principle", this may result in promotion to incompetence, i.e. an individual is promoted until it reaches an hierarchical level, where task solvating is beyond its capacities.

Job assignment

For avoiding the institutionalizing of established structural relations within the organization, *temporary assignments* of individuals to processes appear to be an feasible approach, since this focus on process performance instead of functional positions keeps the organization in a *permanent state of change*, and the emerging "structure", i.e. a "snapshot" of the process network in a specific point of time, is continuously changing upon the basis of an *ongoing re-evaluation* of processes' contribution to the fulfilment of organizational objectives and process-elevation on the basis of enhanced organizational learning.

Even though a process perspective on organizations is intended to disregard formal structures, the need for co-ordination, within a process as well as among interacting processes, remains unchanged. However, this authority is not based on a formally determined span of control, but on the temporarily assigned position within an organizational process. These positions are assigned to people based upon their personal skill profile and their ability and will of committing to the objectives of the process. By assigning positions within processes to people temporarily, a continuous performance evaluation is enabled according to the required performance of the process. The individual may now qualify, or disqualify, itself for the assigned position. As these assignments are temporary, determined by processes' cycle-time, it is ensured that positions are not occupied by people with competence lacks for an unpredictable period of time ahead. It is a common phenomenon to "promote away" individuals who are not fulfilling the expectations focused on them. Through temporary assignments this proceeding becomes obsolete, since individuals not being able or willing to fulfil the requirements related to their position will not be allowed to be assigned to positions beyond their capabilities, due to the required match between their skill-profile and the process requirements.

Skill-profiles and reward-systems

In order to ensure the qualification and competence of individuals having process positions assigned to themselves, the individual's skill profile must be corresponding to the required competence for the position within the process. It may be desirable, however, to allow individuals with a potential capability to assign positions beyond their core competencies to themselves, since competence broadening and individual skill development is a necessary implication for incorporating organizational learning and the continuous improvement of process performance.

Due to the temporary nature of positions, the conventionally used reward systems occur to be inapplicable. Alternatively, there are two options to choose: Either can individuals be rewarded upon the duration of their organizational membership, or upon the temporary positions they currently possess. While the first alternative implies that experience and competence is a matter of age and will increase automatically, there are no incentives for gaining increased competence and knowledge, which is a demotivating factor and hinder for the continuous competence development that is required in dynamic environments. Since rewards have to be related to the responsibilities taken by the individual and its commitment to organizational objectives, it occurs natural to base the reward structure on the current assignments. This may result in a reward structure, where a basic reward is allowed to all employees, but all additional rewards are based upon the

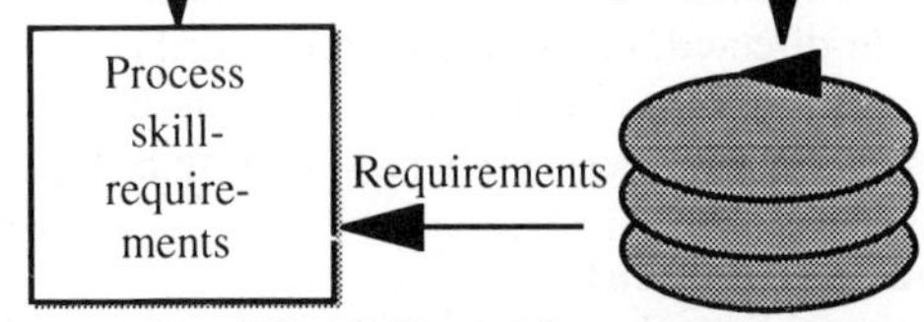

Fig. 3 Reward structure

position within the process. By continuous competence development, the individual may then be allowed to assignments on a higher co-ordinative level within the process network.

A methodology approach to employee ranking is described by Nadler and Gerstein (1992). Their concept consists of thirteen steps, starting with a job or job-cluster identification, and appears, even though being originally developed for executive staffing, to be a feasible approach to matching individual skills with job requirements.

Competence-pools

Since organizational members are not belonging to pre-defined organizational units, and the processes being performed within the organization are not stable as far as their existence is concerned, new forms have to be found to define organizational membership. It appears suitable, to use a competence-pool, basically containing all organizational members, and used for training and education, as the basic unit. This would include a concept of the organization as being intentionally peer-based, where superiority and sub-ordination is determined by the actual position within a process that the member is currently assigned to, as it was described above. Basically belonging to the pool, individuals are then temporarily assigned to process-positions, and returning to the pool after having finished their assignment. Since there are e.g. legal implications, a need for continuity in strategic decision-taking, policy definition etc., the concept is, however, not applicable on all organizational members. A small group of top executive staff members has to be excluded in order to ensure the requirements for continuity.

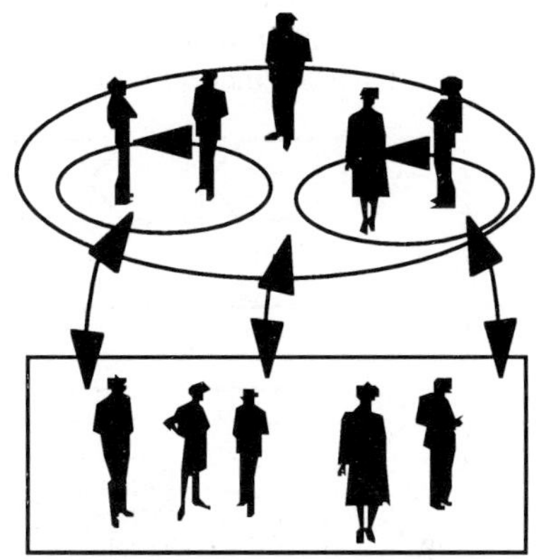

Fig. 4 The competence-pool

Process evolution

In their striving for reduced time-to-markets, many organizations being involved in product development are using concurrent engineering (CE) as a tool for reducing the waiting states of interdependent entities within the organization and to integrate the organization's activities across the firm's value adding chain. This integration, described by Lawrence and Lorsch (1967) provides opportunities for reducing the time required from product-design to -delivery, quality improvement regarding the conformance to customer requirements, and cost-reduction. Even though this concept was originally defined for functional integration, it occurs to be applicable on process-organizations as well. By taking needs, capabilities, and results of interacting processes into account and re-considering them dialectically, lengthy, iterative development processes can be eliminated.

This can be practically achieved by defining "transaction tokens", i.e. points of times when preliminary process outcomes are transferred to depending processes, thus providing them with a basis for their own activities at an early stage, and thereby reducing the need for achieving final results before transferring them to the next process. The output of one sub-process is then successively incorporated into the results of depending processes to become a part of the outcome of the super-process. Since these preliminary results are rapidly spread throughout the entire process-network, a "prototype" of the final outcome of the super-process can be achieved faster, allowing to match it against customer requirements and fine-tuning it during the further development process.

This concept can be considered as a "dialectic process evolution" and is comparable to the concept of incremental system development, being widely used in software engineering. There is one major difference, however: While incremental development is based upon modularity, i.e. entire clusters of the system are produced and delivered, the evolutionary approach uses preliminary results through the entire development process as a basis for incorporation and fine-tuning.

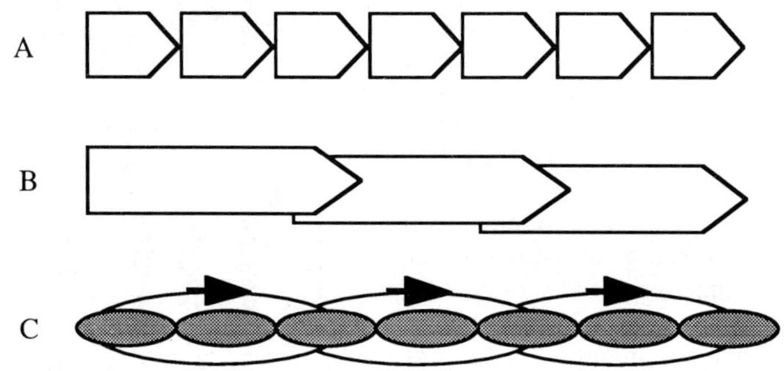

Fig. 5 Value-added chain (A), "collapsed" value-added chain (B) and "process evolution" (C)

Goal congruence

An aspect not yet discussed is the basis upon which processes are fragmented, respectively integrated. In hierarchical organizations, the similarity of tasks is the determining factor, but this principle appears not to be usable in a process organization, due to the diversity of the activities being performed within the processes. Using goal congruence as determinator appears to be a more feasible way for fragmenting and integrating in a process-organization, i.e. processes are put into relation to each other depending on their capability to contribute to achieve objectives. Depending on the characteristics of the processes under concern, these objectives may be of qualitative, as well as quantitative nature. This can be exemplified by looking at the qualitative objectives of a sales- , service-, and customer contact process:

- Sales objective: Presenting our products as the solution to customers problems. This can be achieved by establishing and maintaining close relationships with existing and prospective customers, since we thereby show our concern for customers problems.
- Service objective: Through close customer contacts we can provide a superior service, since we are aware of the specific situation of our customers and can thereby respond quickly to their service needs.
- Customer contact objective: Maintaining close relationships with our customers.

Apparently, both the sales- and the service-process are depending on good customer relationships. The customer contact process' objective, in turn, is a sub-set of the objectives of both other processes. When fragmenting the process-hierarchy, i.e. using a top-down approach, the customer contact process is therefore considered as a sub-process by both super-processes, while an analysis of process-integration would reveal customer contacts as being integrated into two super-processes.

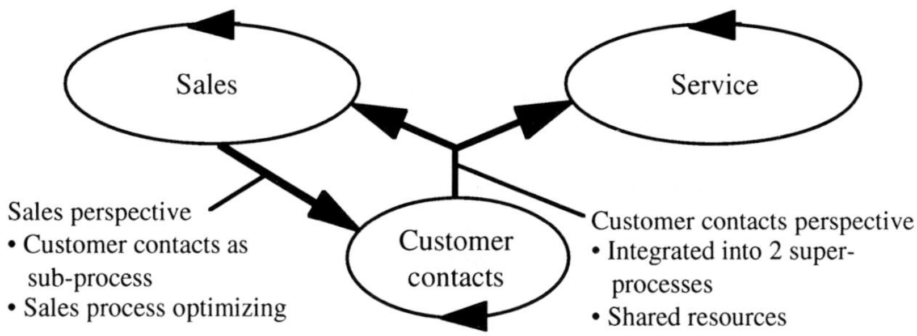

Fig. 6 Process perspectives

One could consider this as a zero-sum game, since fragmentation, as well as integration will result in the same number of relationships, however, taking a perspective from a singular process, the results will lead to different conclusions. Both super-processes are intended to maximize their own performance, i.e. to employ the resources of customer contacts in a way that maximizes their own goal achievement, while, on the other hand, customer contacts has to co-ordinate its activities with those of two super-processes, share its resources of its activities among them and contribute to the achievement of different goals. The difference between those two perspectives is depicted in figure 6. To increase the workability of both super-processes, there must be an agreement that satisfies the mutual expectations of the parts involved.

Conclusions

In this paper I have presented a vision of an organization being conceptually based on processes instead of hierarchical structures. Several aspects of such an organization and their impact on organization design have been discussed. However, several issues had to be disregarded due to the complexity of the topic and a lack of theory, as well as empirical research. My literature studies revealed, that a lot research remains to do, and a lot of experience to be gained, in order to overcome the deficiencies of current approaches and for being able to define a solid bedrock in this field. The issues to be investigated in the future may include:

- The distribution of responsibility.
- How to migrate from a bureaucratic to a process-based organization.
- The changing roles of organizational members.
- IT for supporting process-organizations.

Nevertheless it can be claimed, that the process-approach to organization analysis and design will have to gain an increased attention, since it provides mechanisms for a better adaptation of the organization to environmental dynamics, imposed by globalized markets, increasing competition and rapidly changing customer requirements.

Bibliography

Bush and Frohman (1991), John B. Bush Jr. and Alan L. Frohman, *Communications in a "Network" Organization*, In: Organizational Dynamics, Autumn 1991

Creech (1994), Bill Creech, *The five pillars of TQM: how to make total quality management working for you*, Truman Talley Books/Dutton, Penguin group

Davenport (1993), T.H. Davenport, *Process Innovation: Reengineering work through information technology*, Harvard Business School Press, Boston

Emery (1969), James C. Emery, *Organisation planning and control systems*, Macmillan, New York

Gartner Group (1993), Gartner Group handouts, BPR seminar Stockholm

Hammer & Champy (1993), M. Hammer & J. Champy, *Reengineering the Corporation*, Harper Business

Kosiol (1962), Erich Kosiol, *Organisation der Unternehmung*, Wiesbaden

Lawrence & Lorsch (1967), P.R. Lawrence and J.W: Lorsch, *Organization and Environment: Managing Differentiation and Integration*, Homewood

March & Simon (1958), J. March and H. Simon, Organizations, Wiley, New York

Nadler & Gerstein (1992), David A. Nadler and Marc S. Gerstein, *Strategic Selection: Staffing the Executive Team*, in: Organizational Architecture, David A. Nadler et.al., Jossey-Bass

Rockart & Short (1991), John F. Rockart and James E. Short, *The Networked Organization and the Management of Interdependence*, in: The Corporation of the 1990's, edited by Michael S. Scott-Morton, Oxford University Press

Schubert (1972), Schubert, U., *Der Management-Kreis. In: Management für alle Führungskräfte in Wirtschaft und Verwaltung*, Stuttgart

Taylor (1911), Frederick Taylor, *The principles of scientific management*, New York

White (1994); Tom White and Layna Fischer (eds.), *New Tools for New Times: The Workflow Paradigm*, Future Strategies Inc.

Other sources of information

Internet discussion lists

BPR@MAILBASE.AC.UK

BPR-L@IS.TWI.TUDELFT.NL

TQM%PUCC.BITNET

Footnotes

[1]A dialectic process is, in this concern, defined as "a process, where input is incorporated into existing knowledge, and where this new, enlarged body of knowledge is used as bedrock for further activities.

Evaluation of Hypermedia Tourism Applications

Franca Garzotto [(1)], Luca Mainetti [(1)], Paolo Paolini [(2,1)]

[(1)] Hypermedia Laboratory - Politecnico di Milano °
[(2)] University of Lecce

Abstract: This paper discusses the problem of evaluating hypermedia applications. We will show that a design model can be used to *analyse* the structural and dynamic features of a hypermedia, and we will propose some general *evaluation criteria*, that are independent from the specific application area, from the user profile(s) and from the user task(s). The method proposed in this paper is *design-oriented*, and is complementary to other evaluation techniques proposed in the literature. It will be exemplified by analysing and commenting a commercial application in the tourism field ("Italia", by Touring Club Italiano and Opera Multimedia).

1 Introduction

The problem of evaluating a hypermedia application can be regarded under different perspectives. One can look at the application from a pure *engineering* view point, and apply well known software engineering techniques to measure features such as software robustness, efficiency, performance, portability of the code, and similar. A different (complementary) approach to evaluation is to look at a hypermedia from a user-oriented perspective, and to analyse its *usability*. Paraphrasing Jacob Nielsen's definition ([8], p.25), hypermedia usability can be defined as the question of how well users can use the functionalities of a hypermedia application. Assessing the usability of an application, in general, requires an extensive testing with end users. Since sometime this is impossible (e.g., because of budget or time constraints), this paper suggests a different approach to hypermedia evaluation. The proposed method is *design-oriented*, being concerned mainly with the *internal strength* of the design, neglecting the relationships with the user profiles and tasks. By its very nature, our method does not involve end-users, and is therefore complementary to user-oriented evaluation techniques that are based on usability tests [8][9][11]. We believe however that in most cases the results of the design-oriented evaluation will be reflected also in the user-oriented evaluation. In addition, a preliminary design-oriented evaluation

° Authors' Address: Department of Electronics and Information, Piazza L. da Vinci 32, 20133 Milano, Italy. Phone: +39-2-23993520; Fax:+39-2-23993411; e-mail: garzotto@elet.polimi.it could be used to detect problems and weaknesses of a hypermedia application, and to better focus the usability tests.

The ability of systematically analyzing a hypermedia application is a prerequisite for an objective evaluation. Defining analysis methods is difficult, due to the lack of standardization of the basic components of a hypermedia application, and the lack of a precise terminology to describe them. Our first goal has been therefore to identify what should be analyzed, and to define the main "dimensions" under which a hypermedia application can be inspected and modeled. Then we have adopted a model to describe the analysis results, namely, the Hypermedia Design Model HDM. The final step has been to identify some *general criteria of good design* that are independent from the specific application area, from the user profile(s) and from the user task(s). They can be applied in order to identify possible problems and weaknesses that are independent from the specific goals of the application, and to provide some preliminary feedback's on usability before or without actually involving users.

Our approach will be exemplified by analyzing a hypermedia application in the tourism field, namely, the "Italia" CD-ROM, by Touring Club Italiano and Opera Multimedia [9].

2 Analysis Dimensions

The different "dimensions" under which one can inspect a hypermedia application are *structure*, *presentation*, and *dynamics*. They can be described at two levels, *in-the-large* (i.e., at the global level) and *in the-small* (i.e., in detail). Analysis dimensions are discussed using the Hypermedia Design Model - HDM. This model allows to standardize the description terminology, and to identify some standard constituents of a hypermedia application. The primitives of HDM are introduced very synthetically, and the interested reader is referred to the bibliography [1][2][3] [4] for a more complete description.

Structure

Analyzing the structure of an application means inspecting the *organization* of the pieces of information contained in the application.

To describe the *structure in-the-large* of a hypermedia application, we use the HDM concepts of *entity*, *entity type*, *collection, link*, and *link type*,

An *entity* groups together a number of information segments in a granule that corresponds to some real-world conceptual or physical "object" (e.g., the town "Venice" or the subject "Italian Landscape"). The constituents of an entity are called components, discussed below. The arrangement of the components, within an entity, can vary, according to the topology of the entity itself: they can be organized in a sequence, in a set, in a tree, etc. Entities that correspond to domain objects of the same class are grouped in the same *entity type* (e.g. "Town"), and all share the same topology.

A *collection*[1] groups together a set of objects, called *members* of the collection [2]. Members of a collection can be entities, constituents of entities (i.e., components or single nodes) or other collections (*nested collections*). Objects can be organized into collections in order to represent a taxonomy, according to some objective criteria, or they can be grouped together simply to improve application readability and help the user to better find his way around in the application. A collection also holds a distinguished node, associated to the collection itself and called *collection-node*. The purpose of the collection-node is of illustrating the content of the collection itself, and also to provide access paths to the members of the collection.
Links (also called *webs* in HDM) are connections among nodes, entities, or collections. HDM defines various categories of links: *structural links*, *applicative links, index links, and guided tour links. Structural links* tie together the different nodes belonging to the same entity; they are, in general, implicitly defined by the structural features of the entities (tree, sequence, etc.). *Applicative links* connect together two "objects" - a node, an entity, or a collection - according to some intended relationship. Links that have similar meaning and connect objects of the same category or type are grouped under the same *link type*. *Index links* connect the collection node to the members, and vice versa; *Guided tour links* interconnect the different members. Index and collection links are collectively called *collection links*

To describe the *structure* in-the-small of a hypermedia application, HDM introduces the concepts of *slot, frame, node, component.* A *slot* represents an atomic piece of information. It can be of a simple type, such as an integer, or of a complex type, such as, for example, a video synchronized with sound [5]. A *frame* is an aggregate of slots, put together in order to create a cohesive granule of information. Frames with similar slot structure are grouped in the same *frame type*. A *node* is a navigational unit. In HDM, a node is always associated to a frame that represents the node content. The type of a node is defined as the type of its frame. A node is, in general, interconnected to other nodes (while frames only aggregate slots, with no connections to other information granules).
A *component* is a group of nodes that constitute a logical unit within a given entity. Components grouping nodes of the same type belong to the same *component type*.

Dynamics
We use this term to indicate both two different aspects: *dynamics-in-the-large*, that refers to the way the user can move around across the different pieces of information, and *dynamics-in-the-small*, that refers to the interaction of the user with each piece of information.
In modern hypermedia applications, *dynamic in-the-large* amounts to a combination of Navigation (i.e., link traversing), Data Base Queries, and Content-based Search, with relative relevance depending upon the “style” and the intended use of the application. We will examine in this paper only the dynamic features concerning *navigation* aspects, which are the most specific of hypermedia applications. If passive

[1] Components, entities, and collections, are all examples of *composites*, in the sense defined by the Dexter Reference Model [6].

media only are considered, activating a link from its source leads to the activation of its destination and the de-activation of its source. This basic concept needs some extensions when active, time-dependent media are taken into account. If active slots were being played in the source node, for example, it must be defined the state in which the source itself is left (e.g., the original state, or the state reached at the moment of departure from the node) [7]. If, for example, a video and a sound were being played, it must specify whether those slots are to be *suspended*, or *reset* at the beginning, or whether one of them must *continue* playing [3]).

Different categories of links induce different *navigation patterns*. The natural way of exploring an entity is to follow the structural links for *Structural Navigation. Applicative Navigation* is the most traditional (in the hypertext sense) style of navigation, and corresponds to traverse applicative links. It allows the user to move across different entities or collections. As far as navigation within a collection is concerned, there are two styles, that can be intermixed: *index navigation* and *guided tour navigation*, collectively called *Collection Navigation.* In *index* navigation, the collection node is used to access a member via collection links, and from a member it is possible, in general, to navigate back to the collection node. In *guided tour* navigation, it is possible to move from one member directly to another member (again following collection links) without need to traverse each time the collection node. A typical combination of index and guided tour allows the random selection of a member, and from this the subsequent exploration of other members.

Dynamics in-the-small concern the interaction with slots and frames. Slot interaction is strictly related to the type of the slot itself. If the interaction with an integer or a string is virtually not existent, the interaction with a multimedia value can have complex features. Zooming on pictures, playing control over video, sound, or animation, etc., are all examples of hypermedia interaction at slot level. In most hypermedia applications, multimedia is confined at slot level, in the sense that the peculiar features of active media are used to build (complex, but conceptually atomic) objects [5]. The dynamics related to a frame consists in coordinating the presentation of its slots. If a single active slot is included in a frame (an audio track, for example), it may be played by default, or it might be played upon request, as an option to the reader. When several active media slots are involved (say multiple sound tracks, videos, animation, etc.), there are more complex issues concerning parallel presentations with proper synchronization, or well-sequenced presentations.

Presentation

Presentation refers to how the content, the structures, and the dynamic features of the application are "shown" to the reader. Presentation in-the-small concerns the lay-out of individual granules of information, i.e., the way slots and frames are arranged on the screen, and the way of visualizing to the reader the functionalities for interacting with these presentation elements. Presentation in-the-large concerns the way in-the-large structures are presented to the reader (e.g., showing a diagram of the entity structure) and the way dynamic in-the-large features such as navigation are visualized.

3 Criteria of Hypermedia Design Evaluation

Once an application has been analyzed and precisely described, there is a potential huge number of criteria, i.e., "heuristics" [8], that can be applied to evaluate its design [9][11]. In this paper, we will consider a very small subset of them - *richness, easiness, consistency, self-evidence*, and *predictability* - that are intended to be to each of the analysis dimensions, both in-the-large and in the-small. The relative weights of these criteria, their range of validity and their impact on the usability of a hypermedia application, actually depend on the intended uses of the application, and should be assessed each time a different application is being examined.

Richness

It denotes the search power of an application, and expresses the fact that the application provides abundant and articulated ways to reach the various pieces of information (either by search, by browsing, or by navigation). As such, it is mainly concerned with dynamics in the large.

Easiness

It describes how easy is to use the information and the operations made available by the application. It is dependent on the quality of the presentation (both in the large and in-the-small) and on the ability of the presentation design to convey the meaning of the various objects and features through expressive lay-out elements.

Consistency

It can be synthesized by saying that *conceptually similar elements should be treated in a similar fashion, while conceptually different elements should be treated differently*. Consistency is consider by several authors [8][9][11] as one of the crucial evaluation criteria, and probably the most important one. It applies to all the analysis dimensions discussed in the previous section, both in-the-large and in-the-small.

Self-evidence

It denotes the capability, for the reader, of guessing the meaning and the purpose of whatever is being presented to him for the first time (either content or structure or navigation or presentation element).

Predictability

It expresses the possibility, for the user, of "guessing" the outcome of an operation (by analogy of what he has already experienced). It relates to all the analysis aspects, can be regarded as an extension of the concept of self-evidence, and is strongly affected by consistency.

We will finally use the term *readability* to denote the simultaneous consideration of all the above factors.

It should be noticed that we have omitted from our discussion any consideration about the actual *content* which refers to the actual information provided by an application, and is a further dimension that should be considered in the analysis and evaluation of a hypermedia application. Content analysis may be considered as the most important aspect to be evaluated in order to assess the quality of a hypermedia, since, at the very end, all other factors become negligible for the usability of an application if it provides incorrect, or incomplete, or wrong information. Content analysis requires, however, a specialist of the application domain and a deep knowledge of the user's profiles and tasks; as such, it is outside the scope of our analysis and evaluation method.

4 Design Analysis of a Tourism Application

This section will analyse a commercial hypermedia application, the "Italia" CD-ROM by Touring Club Italiano and Opera Multimedia, and will elaborate some considerations on its design. “Italia” is a truly enjoyable application, that allows the user "to discover and learn about the natural, artistic, and historic wonders of Italy" [10]. Its content is relatively complex, since it concerns over 250 places and 600 masterpieces in Italy, described by over 800 photographs (mostly full screen), hundred of pages of text, several short video clips, music, and animations across which the user can interactively navigate.

We will show that a design model, such as HDM, can be used to describe an application that was designed with no knowledge of the model itself, and that the systematic description thus obtained can be helpful in detecting possible design problems within the application, with respect to the heuristic criteria discussed in section 3.

“Italia” is organized in two main sections, that address different goals and have different access styles and interaction facilities. One section is called “Guide to Italy” and is more “information search” oriented. The user who wants to learn about Italy, or to plan a tour, can “visit” one of Italy’s twenty regions, looking at regional features (wines, cuisine, art, nature). In addition, “Italia” offers, in the section "Discover Italy" a range of different tools and games containing video clips, slide shows, and animated sequences on topics of particular interest, that allow “discovery Italy” in a more playful (and simple) way. For lack of space, we will analyse only the "Guide to Italy" section of this application.

4.1 Structure in-the-large and in-the-small of “Italia”

The “Guide to Italy” section of “Italia” concerns artistic, historical, or natural places and regions of Italy[2]. We have modeled the organization of these contents by defining *two entity types* and a number of *nested collections* (i.e., collections of collections), closely interconnected each other, and accessible through a number of hierarchical indices. The only links available in “Italia” are structural links (to navigate within entities) and collection links (to navigate within and across collections).

Entity Types

Entities of “Italia” represent physical places located in Italy, that have some historical, artistic, or natural interest. The distinction between entities of the two types, called “*Minor Place*” and “*Major Place*”, depends from the amount of content associated to them and in the organization of such content, i.e., in the *structure* of the

[2]"Italia" is provided both in Italian and in English, within the same CD-ROM. The two versions are isomorphic and independent, and we will analyze the English one.

entity type. An entity of type "Minor Place" is defined by a linear sequence of homogenous components of type Place. A component of type Place consists of a single frame of type F-Place. An F-Place frame contains a number of slots, including a picture slot, a text slot with a short descriptive text commenting the picture, and some text slots storing the name of the place or the monument, its region, the subject of the picture, etc. An entity of type "Major Place" is structured as a tree of components. The root component has the purpose of allowing the user to select one of the three components History, Surroundings, or Tour of the Town. The History component contains one frame that consists of a sound slot (a voice explaining the town history), a title label with the town name, and an animation slot storing an animated sequence of images presenting monuments, places, or personages that are relevant for the town history. Surroundings has a sequence of frames, each one of type F-Place (described above). The component Tour of the Town has a frame type Map storing a picture slot with the map of a town, and a label slot with the town name. This component is connected to other components, each one with a frame of type Map showing a specific area of the town. Each of these components stores a sequence of frames of type Place.

Collections

Entities are organized in various collections, according to the combination of various three criteria: Region, Topic, and Subtopic. Topics are Art and Nature. Subtopics of Art are Art Periods: Prehistoric Times, Etruscans, Ancient Greeks, Ancient Romans, Middle Ages, Renaissance, Baroque, 18th-20th Centuries. Subtopics of Nature are Seaside Resorts, Mountain Resorts, Countryside, Parks, Lakes, and Spas. Collections have complex *nested structures*.

- *Lowest level* collections

  They are sequences of places organized by Region *and* Sub-topic (e.g., "Lake Places in Tuscany", or "Renaissance Places in Veneto"). The frame in the collection node is of type "F-region", and consists of a picture slot (a region map), and four text slots describing the region, its wines, and its local cuisine.
- *Second level* collections

  They have as members lowest level collections.

  There are two categories of second level collections, based on two different grouping criteria: *by "Subtopic",* or *by "Topic and Region".*

  Collections "by-subtopic" group lowest level collections that concern the *same subtopic*. Examples are the collections "*Renaissance Art* in Italy", grouping all collections of type "*Renaissance* Places in *R*", or "*Lakes* in Italy", grouping all collections of type "*Lake* Places in *R*" (R denotes a region). In collections of this kind, the frame in the collection node is of type "F-country", and consists of a picture slot (the map of Italy) and a text slot with a short presentation of Italy.

  A second level collection "by Topic and Region", groups all lowest level collections that share the same Region, and concern a Subtopic of the same Topic. An examples is the collection "*Art* in *Veneto*" (grouping all collections of type "AS in Veneto" where AS is a subtopic of Art). The frame in the collection node is of type "F-region" (defined above).

- *Third level* collections.
  They have as members second level collections.
  There are several third level collections. One is called "Art in Italy", grouping all second level collections of kind "AS in Italy", where AS is a subtopic of Art (e.g., Renaissance, Baroque, etc.). "Nature in Italy", is defined in a similar way (for subtopic of Nature). In both cases, the frame of the collection node is of type "F-country". Furthermore, for each region R there is a third level collection "R by-Art&Nature" that groups the two second levels collections concerning the region R, and Art or Nature. The frame in the collection node is of type "F-region".
- *Fourth level collection*
  There is one fourth level collection, called "Regions", whose members are the third level collections of type "R by Art&Nature".
- *Fifth level collection*
  The only fifth level collection - called "Master" - groups the two third level collections "Art in Italy" and "Nature in Italy", and the fourth level collections "Regions"[3].

Our consideration on the structure of "Italia" is that, while entity types are relatively simple and predictable, collections very sophisticated but less intuitive, due to the many levels of nesting and to the difficulty, for the normal user, to immediately grasp the many combinations of organization criteria. This has impact on dynamics in-the-large, discussed in the next section.

4.2 Dynamics in-the-large of "Italia"

Let us now proceed with discussing the navigation facilities of "Italia". As already mentioned, there are no application links in this application, and therefore the only navigation patterns to be considered concern structural navigation and collection navigation.

Structural Navigation

Structural navigation within an entity of type "Minor Place" is extremely simple, and consists in moving backward and forward, via Next and Previous commands, along the sequence of nodes corresponding to the only component of the entity. Structural navigation within entities of type "Minor Place" is induced by the tree-like structure of this entity type, and is slightly more complex. From the node of the root component, the user can select one of the children components - History, Surroundings, or Tour of the Town, and access its first node. Within nodes of the

---

[3]In addition to the above collections, there is simpler collection which is called "Index". It organizes all places (entities of type "Minor Place" and "Major Place"), relevant monuments (components of Places), and regions (third level collections of kind "Region R by Art&Nature"), in an alphabetic order.

Surroundings component, the user can navigate in a strictly linear fashion. From the node of component Tour of the Town (showing a town map), the user can select a child component concerning a specific area of the town, and access the sequence of nodes describing the selected area, in a linear fashion. In addition, the user can jump to the root node from any of the above visited nodes inside an entity.

Structural navigation in Italia is very usable. Structural links are consistent, and therefore predictable. Their presentation is intuitive and make self-evident their use. The lay-out of link placeholders (buttons) highlights the distinctions between links across different components and links within a single component. The richness of links provides quick ways of exploring the various entities. A minor burden is created by the purely linear way to scanning components of type Place: when a Place component stores a large amount of information and has many nodes, the lack of direct jumps to the last or the first member can be disappointing, and can reduce the efficiency of use. This choice has the advantage of keeping the presentation interface simple, but it has the disadvantage of an obvious weakness in the richness in the navigation features.

Collection Navigation

Collection navigation follows different patterns depending on the kind and level of nesting of a collection. The simplest collection is the Index, which allows the user to select any topic he is interested to, jump there, and return to the index at any time (and from any node of the application).

Navigation on all other collections is significantly more complex is , and complexity increases with the increasing nesting depth.

Within a lowest level collection (e.g., “Lake Places in Tuscany”), user can navigate both in index and in guided tour mode, according to three patterns: the user can directly access a member from the collection node, or can move from a member to the *next* and *previous* one, according to the order established by the collection, or can return from any member to the collection node. Direct access to all members is provided on the collection node, by showing the members (i.e., the places) on a map. Forward and backward scan in the collection is provided by the left and right arrowhead buttons on the members, which are located on the bottom of the screen. If the current member is the last one of a collection, the right arrowhead button is visible but it is inhibited. For example, the user who is located on a Place (say, “Venice”) within collection “Renaissance Places in Veneto”, can move from Venice to Verona by following a “next member” link, return to the collection node which shows all the Renaissance places in Veneto, and directly select a different place (e.g., Vicenza).

Overall, navigation in lowest level collections is consistent, self evident, and predictable. We have found only a minor mistake in “Countryside in Veneto”, where members are organized in a circular list, and going Next from the last member takes the user to the first member (instead of being prohibited, as it is in general).

The dynamics of navigation within second level collections is slightly different. Navigation within second level collections based on Subtopic, combines index and guided tour modes. From the collection node of “*Renaissance* Places in Italy”, for example, the user can select a specific Region, e.g., Veneto, and access the lowest level collection "*Renaissance* Places in Veneto". From here, he can access the adjacent members by navigating forward or backward, or return to the collection node of "*Renaissance* Places in Italy". Differently from lowest level collections, members of second level collections of this kind are arranged in a *circular list*: once he reader has reached the last member collection, he can continue forward and access the first member collection (arranged in alphabetic order, base on the Region name). For example, from "*Renaissance* Places in Veneto" (Veneto is alphabetically the last Italian Region) the link Next takes the user to "*Renaissance* Places in Abruzzo", since Abruzzo is the first Italian Region in the alphabetic order. This inconsistency with respect to lowest level collections is sometime disorienting, since it is not predictable nor self-evident at all.

Let us now consider navigation in second level collections based on "Region and Topic", such as "*Art* in *Veneto*". From the collection node, the user can select a member, i.e., a lowest level collection, and from any member he can directly access any other one. For example, once the user is on the collection node of "*Art* in *Veneto*", he can select any lowest level collection in the set "Prehistoric Times in *Veneto*", "Ancient Romans in *Veneto*", "Middle Ages in *Veneto*", "Renaissance in *Veneto*", etc. From "Renaissance in *Veneto*", for example , the user can directly switch to "Prehistoric Times in *Veneto*". Lack of linear scanning of members is inconsistent with respect to navigation in second level collections of the first category, and slightly disorienting when the user accesses a collection of this kind for the first time. This inconsistency is however compensated by a good presentation (which leaves the list of all lowest level collections always visible from the root and from all members, consistently in all collections of this kind).
The same navigation pattern is provided for all other collections at higher levels, with the exception of the Master collection. The collection node of the Master collection is only used to select a collection among "Regions", "Art in Italy", "Nature in Italy". There is no way to return to this node from its constituents collection (or from their members, whatever the level).

On the one hand, "Italia" collection navigation is extremely rich and powerful for expert users. On the other hand, learning how to use the many collection navigation patterns, and exploiting the richness of navigation features, may be significantly too complex for an average user. The main problems are related to the depth of the collection hierarchy (four levels), the different dynamics of collections, i.e., the different navigation patterns available at different levels, and the fact that the user can reach the leaves of the collection hierarchy (i.e., the actual content about Places) in several different ways. Collection navigation is complicated by the fact that the user is allowed to jump across non adjacent collections in the hierarchy, skipping some levels, and sometime in a context dependent way. For example, from the collection node of "Renaissance in Italy"(second level), the user is allowed to jump to the collection node of "Nature in Italy" (third level) as well as to the collection node of "Regions" (fourth level). If the user is on the collection node of "Baroque in

Veneto", and selects Venice (member of a lowest level collection), he can activate a "jump" and go to the collection node of "Baroque in Italy" (third level collection).

4 Conclusions

This paper has discussed the evaluation of a touristic hypermedia - "Italia" - from a design perspective, which is complementary to other approaches to hypermedia evaluation defined in the Software Engineering and Human Computer Interface fields. Using "Italia" we have shown that precise design primitives not only can help the hypermedia design and development process, but can also improve the possibility of analyzing hypermedia applications, and to perform a systematic design-oriented evaluation. The analysis of our test bed case has also highlighted that the complexity of sophisticated, i.e., structurally and navigationally rich, hypermedia applications can be mastered by end users only if consistency is strongly enforced. Finally, it has pointed out the problem of solving the trade-off between learnability for novice users and efficiency of use for expert users, that is inherent to hypermedia design.

References

1. Garzotto F., Paolini P., Schwabe D. "HDM - A Model for the Design of Hypertext Applications", *Proc. HT'91- ACM Conf. on Hypertext*, Dec. 1991
2. Garzotto F., Paolini P., Schwabe D. "HDM - A Model Based Approach to Hypermedia Application Design" In *ACM Trans. Off. Inf. Syst.*, 11 (1), Jan. 1993
3. Garzotto F., L. Mainetti, P. Paolini "Adding Multimedia Collections to the Dexter Model". In *Proc. ECHT'94 - ACM Conf. on Hypermedia Technology,* Edinburgh, UK, Sept. 1994
4. Garzotto F., Mainetti L., Paolini P., "Hypermedia Application Design: A Structured Approach". In *Designing User Interfaces for Hypermedia*, W. Schuler, J. Hannemann, N. Streitz (eds.), Springer Verlag, 1994 (in press).
5. Gibbs S., Breiteneder C., Tsichritzis D., "Data Modeling of Time-Based Media". In *Proc. ACM SIGMOD*, Minneapolis (USA), May 1994
6. Halatz F., Schwartz M. "The Dexter Hypertext Reference Model". In *Comm. ACM, 37 (2),* Feb. 1994
7. Hardman L., Bulterman D.C.A., Van Rossum G., "Adding Time and Content to the Dexter Model". In *Comm. ACM, 37 (2),* Feb. 1994
8. Nielsen J., "Usability Engineering", Academic Press, 1993
9. Preece J., "Human-Computer Interaction", Addison Wesley, 1994
10. Touring Club Italiano & Opera Multimedia, "The Italia CD-ROM, 1994
11. Shneiderman B., "Designing the User Interface", Addison Wesley, Mass. 1987

Tourism promotion needs multimedia information system

Ms. Jaro Berce, Andraž Oblak, Igor Tršan

SIP&A, ltd., Mlinska pot 20, 61231 Ljubljana, Slovenia

Abstract. Information technology (IT), as a fast growing field, is used in almost all spheres of everyday life. To follow modern concept requirements in tourism and to satisfy more and more demanding tourists, a project of using advanced IT with multimedia in the Republic of Slovenia has been recently introduced. Project has been designed to collect electronic tourism data, to connect different systems that are already in use in tourism through EU-ISDN, and to "bring" this data to users. Tools and principles used in the process of setting up the IT environment are user-friendly. The standardisation of paths, links, as well as data gathering and representing were our first steps. How to fulfill a missing tourism data formulation, how to build up links between the systems and how to unify and symbolize tourism data icons is certainly a challenging future task.

1 Introduction

Tourism information system is a complex environment covering different segments of life milieu. The tourism industry is more appropriate viewed as a market rather than an independent industry sector, as it is spread across a wide diversity of services and industries. We must know that the demands of world tourists have shifted considerably over the last decade. They are now more unconstrained and better informed, and they seek greater flexibility in their vacation arrangements, none-the-less a more appropriate quality and diversity of services. The tourism industry is a prevalent, very complex network of businesses contracted in the lodging, feeding, travel arrangements and mostly entertainment of tourists. Therefore a tourist seeks not for hotel accommodation but for the whole atmosphere of the place he or she visits.

To provide for such a requirement and to differ from concurrence one should build a system that can be flexible, updated with necessary data and events, and most of all easy to understand and easy to use. All these requirements are met by multimedia information technology and world area network -- WAN connection. All prior stated assumptions were the concepts and objectives of a project organization for Tourism Information System of Slovenia -- TISS.

Fig. 1. Tourism Information System of Slovenia elements

TISS should bear the variety of connected systems :

- **directly related** to tourism as: hotel booking, travel agency, ...;
- **partly related** to tourism as: cultural, sports etc. events, point-of-sale (stores), ...;
- **indirectly related** to tourism as: police, whether report, custom, ...;
- **support**: geographical information system (GIS), telephone (PTT, ISDN, GSM), medical care etc..

TISS also contributes some other specific functions which are not directly related to and/or included in linked systems:

- enables to support connection abroad;
- enables to input the data that are not gathered with computers;
- a "unique" way of retrieving or using data by users;
- provides outputs for tourism promotion of Slovenia;
- etc..

The heart of the TISS system is so called *general tourism system* (GTS) which adds accurate basic tourism information into the system. Different information (e.g. cultural, historic, sports events etc.) arise at the local level, whereupon it is gathered and input into the system. The credibility and genuineness of the data is assured. GTS resides at the *local*, *regional* and *state* level and contributes prior stated type of data. Through standardized tasks the preparation and gathering of data at *tourist information centers* (TIC) is performed.

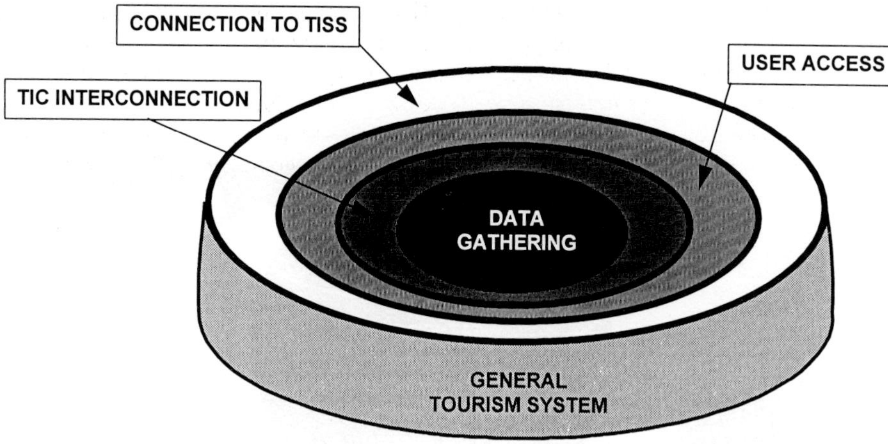

Fig. 2. Structure of GTS

2 Project goals

By using modern concepts at the information technology level the project goal is to support the promotion of tourism of a new born country - Slovenia.

At the initial stage of the project the search for necessity of IT, and technical basis for the new environment was performed. A questionnaire on the type of tourism data and systems in use, on the pressure of joining systems, on how tourism system should be build etc. was mailed. The research comprised two main groups

- *Tourist Association of Slovenia* with more than 350 members and
- respecting ministries, tourist agencies, communities, police etc. approx. 120 addresses,

and brought out very similar and encouraging results. Major answers (98%) of research reflected the need for "unified" computerised system for tourism. There were also some considerably alarming facts such as the level of computer knowledge of future users (TIC) and the lack of the computer equipment in TIC.

Therefore to gain time and resource during next years the project was split into several subprojects with partial but parallel goals:

1. a part of GTS for electronic data gathering performed by TIC, setting up an organization part of the system (named ***RAC.T.I.***), a general tourism data presentation to the users (e.g. state, regional and local level) is on this stage performed by tourist operators in TIC;

2. connection of TICs through ISDN network should be established for the purpose of exchanging interesting and representing tourism data between cities with computerised TIC. Other tourism industry users would also be attached to this system. This should become a backbone of the future TISS.
3. opening of the system to the outside world by setting the touch screen connections and disperse them throughout the country. Now it is the time to consider how to invite the system to our homes;
4. setting up the interconnection of new parts in the tourism industry which are required to bring different tourism data in the TISS. These new parts are already established and used as the islands of information systems in different fields (travel and agency booking; hotel reservation, police, other government "agencies" with general tourism data /visas, rules for "importing" animal(s), health care, local and day-light saving time .../ , etc.);
5. last not least part of this project is the connection of the TISS system to the "external tourism computer world" through ISDN.

There are also accompanying subprojects supporting the main stream in establishing the whole information system:

- organisation framework of the system;
- standardisation of data (EDIFACT standard);
- standardisation of representing non-traffic (tourism) signs;
- standardisation of computer icons for tourism information (still not existing in European Community),
- defining and distinguishing between "payable", "free" and protected data;
- use of ISO standards;
- communication standards;
- etc..

Final goals to be achieved with this project are:

- to connect different systems (banking, booking, police, ...);
- to bring tourism data to the locations where they are needed (touch screen, computer in agencies, home, ...);
- to support new technology by which the system can be friendly and easy to use (GIS, intelligent agents, virtual reality ...).

3 A practical example of building GTS in Slovenia

Since the tourism is a significant branch in the Slovenian economy, several efforts were attempted to build an efficient tourism information system during past years. None of them completely fulfilled the actual needs, either because of the unsatisfactory computer equipment, or the insufficient preparation and improper concept of information and organisation of a system. However, a few partial solutions have been developed e.g. agency database, automobile club information system, hotel booking etc.. Nevertheless none of those databases was suitable to cover the general tourism data.

Therefore we decided to develop the most vital part of TISS -- GTS. The project is carried out in several phases:

Phase 1

As mentioned before, the questionary on the available hardware and computer knowledge of the employees of TICs all over the country was carried out. This phase showed the insufficient equipment as well as the lack of the computer education of the people involved. Therefore the professional proposal as the most feasible solution was to design software on middle range PC computer (486) with MS Windows as operating system platform.

Phase 2

An interdisciplinary group of 13 people mostly from different tourist organizations as well as experts in computer science was brought together. The main task of the project group was to make the basic guidelines for the progress of GTS as the backbone in development of TISS. A general consent was reached that the software should facilitate as well as improve the daily work in TIC. The following requirements for software were agreed upon:

- to introduce a user friendly software with an efficient graphic user interface;
- to allow fast retrieval of records in the database, which is distributed between TICs;
- to automatically exclude out-of-date information, which means that the information has to be divided into three categories: *static* (borders, location of museum, roads etc.), *slowly changing* (rate of exchange, regulations, etc.) and *rapidly changing information* (weather, road traffic, etc.);
- records should incorporate multimedia objects wherever available (pictures, sound and video clips). Considering the nature of data and its diversity, records must be ordered in the B+ tree structure. Each branch defines the scope of information in the unique way shown at the figure 3.;
- every record has the approximate geographic position, as geographic maps are also included in the software;
- data pointers frequently and automatically transfer between already connected TICs to allow any user of the network the access to all the information in the system;

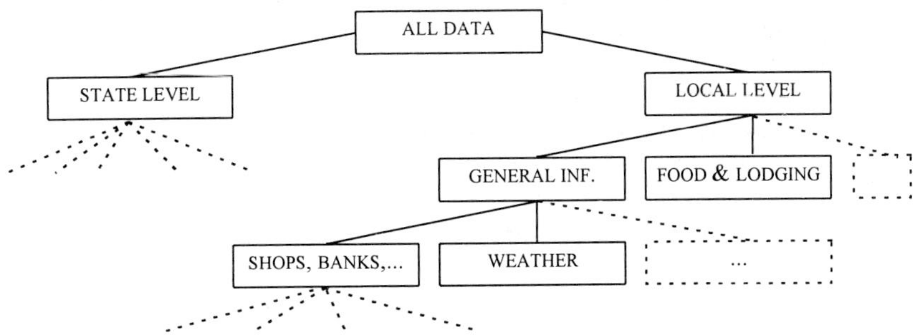

Fig. 3. Part of data organization structure

- software is proficient to handle *generally accessible*, *protected* and *chargeable data.*

Phase 3

The software was developed and tested on six preselected locations in such a way that different environments were applied -- from local to regional and state level TIC. As mentioned before, the only generally available communication in Slovenia is modem communication with speeds from 2400 to 9600 bits per second. Because of this the transmissions between TICs were delayed, especially when transferring large files such as pictures, videos etc.. The problem was partially solved with background communication which enables the user to proceed with other tasks while the transmission is in process. For several computers trying to communicate to each other simultaneously this solution is still too slow. Therefore it was necessary to use a powerful graphic compression tool. After testing several different options we used fractal compression, which, in combination with background communication, provided a sufficient solution of the problem. The software testing showed a necessity to divide the input information into the obligatory part, which enables the users to find what he/she is looking for, and the descriptive part, which serves as a more profound information of the subject.

Phase 4

The installation of software in all TICs wherever the predefined computer equipment was available.

Present situation

Currently we are bringing to an end Phase 4. At this point there are 21 active TICs. We expect this number to grow up to 30 by the end of the year 1994. This number should guarantee at least the rough coverage of general tourism data in Slovenia. The program at this stage allows collecting data at three levels: state, regional and local level.

At the same time we are further developing the program and the GTS in the application levels as follows:

- new communication module that will support Euro ISDN as soon as it is available in Slovenia;
- "view-only" application for hotels, agencies etc. that allows only look-up of data (as professional users of the system);
- touch screen application (for normal users -- random tourists or others).

At present we proceed with establishing connections to some other databases as for instance: weather service, GIS etc..

4 Conclusion

After more than ten years of efforts to build the computer support for tourism industry the first successful steps were achieved. The process of setting up GTS as a backbone of future TISS has begun. Users in more than twenty TICs fill in the distributed tourism database of Slovenia with multimedia data. New steps for connectivity and upgrading the GTS are now in the process. Different users from other fields show strong interest to link their tourism data into the system.

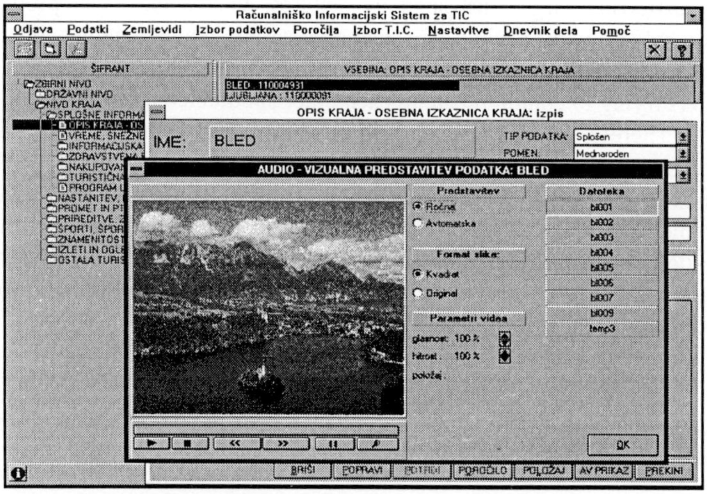

Fig. 4. Sample screen of the actual program

The presented concepts and solutions are the beginning of a new way of promotion of tourism in Slovenia. There will always be place for paper posters and people communication but tools to upgrade this work will be done by IT. There will also be more recent information for better advertising as well as higher service. Promising tourists will be able to observe "in real" the destination they intend to visit. This will result in less depressing search for correct information and misunderstanding of it.

Acknowledgments

We gratefully acknowledge support from Ministry of Science and Technology, Ministry of Economic Affairs and Tourist Association of Republic of Slovenia. We thank all members of users group past and present for their help in building and testing the application.

References

1. Berce, Jaro: Computer information is the backbone of modern tourism. DELO, (znanje za razvoj, p. 6, 15. June, 1994).
2. Berce, Jaro: Information in tourism - where is it?, Lipov List (vol. 7-8 y.35, p.185-186, 1993).
3. Commission of the European Communities: Panorama of EC INDUSTRY 93, ISBN 92-826-5428-1, ECSC-EEC-EAEC, Brussels, Luxembourg, 1993.

Multimedia Information Systems for Hotel Guests

Christian Weiser
Institute for Information Management, University of St. Gallen
Dufourstrasse 50, CH-9000 St.Gallen, Switzerland
E-Mail: 89612337s@sgcl1.unisg.ch

Abstract. We introduce the term Multimedia, and highlight some of the resultant problems. Then we select from the total number of hotel guests specific groups according to their demands. Subsequently, we show how these requirements are answered by information systems. We then give a description of existing systems with their advantages and disadvantages. We conclude with a look into how these systems could develop in the future.
The systems and developments described here are limited to Switzerland and reflect the situation as of the summer of 1994. This paper, while not strictly representative does aim to highlight trends expressed by hoteliers and multimedia producers.

1 Multimedia

Today many products carry the label 'multimedia' when in actual fact they have little to do with it. In the literature the following criteria are considered characteristic of multimedia:
Integrated use of various media: In multimedia, as the name implies, various methods of presentation (or media) are employed. The definition of media is not always described in the same way in the literature [1,2,3] but is usually made up of the following groupings: text - static image (raster-, vector graphics) - moving pictures (film, video and animation) - sounds (music, noises, speech). This list is not definitive since in the future other types of media may also be included, for example touch support was developed in an experimental *virtual reality* environment.
Use of static and dynamic media: On the one hand the message of a dynamic medium is dependent on temporal sequence, e.g. a film or a sequence of sounds. But there are static media where this factor is not relevant, e.g. in photography.
The perspective of an electronic document: Media components may be integrated into what is known as a common document. This document can be comprised of one or more physically separate files.
Open specification: No commitments should be made to any particular hardware or software components.
Computer Support: Without this particular criterion the term multimedia could also apply to just about anything, e.g. a passing car. By computers we do not just mean personal computers but also a wide variety of electronic equipment, e.g. CD-I players.

In summary multimedia could be said to have the quality of an electronic document, integrating several static and dynamic media whilst being computer-supported. Multimedia information systems are defined as "a system architecture based on the use of different media to carry the data and application programs" [4]. This description does not yet consider the element of interactivity. Users should be able to obtain adequate information according to their individual needs. Here a problem arises with television which has not yet found its place in the multimedia world, but will do so in the near future under the heading of *Interactive TV* (ITV).
After this brief introduction to multimedia we shall now focus on hotel guests and their information needs.

2 Different groups of hotel guests and their information needs

We are dealing here with guests who have already decided upon their location and who have already booked their hotel. That means we can exclude all reservation systems, especially those in the travel agents, from our study. The information need by the traveler has a great deal to do with the reason for his trip. These reasons can be looked upon as a motive, which themselves can be collected together in groups. Kaspar [5] categorizes five *motivation groups*:

- Physical (Recuperation, convalescence and sport tourism)
- Psychical (Adventure)
- Inter personal motivation (Relatives, Club, Adventure, Escapism)
- Cultural (Educational, Pilgrimage also alternative lifestyle tourism with the goal of understanding another culture.)
- Status und Prestige (Personal development, Skill development, trips which one can boast about.)

From this list we get the following *types of tourism:*
Relaxation, sport, cultural, social, business and politically motivated. Depending on which one of these being examined there are some further issues which come into play such as age, gender, liquidity (financial power), travel experience, social position, length of stay, etc.
In numerous discussions with key individuals in the hotel business, two types of hotel guest are well understood, namely: the holiday guest and the businessman. These two types have different needs. In the following section we characterize the extreme forms of these two types, whereby the distinction between them tends to be fluid.

2.1 Characteristics and Information needs of the Traveler

The *Tourist* is of course undertaking his journey voluntarily and is looking for entertainment, enjoyment and some rest. His emotional state is of primary importance, which leads him more and more to select small cozy, family type hotels [6]. Personal contact between the guest and the hotel employees is important and sought out by both sides.

The *Information needs of the tourist* are directed towards enjoyment, with entertainment taking an up-front position. Nevertheless, the tourist has to feel the benefit of using an information source. If portability is an important factor, then of course brochures make sense because they can be taken anywhere. If entertainment is one of his goals, then a multimedia based information system could be more appropriate. On arrival, the tourist needs to make an assessment of what is on offer in the way of entertainment. In discussions we noted that short tours through a location, with appropriate highlights is especially welcome for the tourist in gathering initial information.

The *Business traveler* on the other hand is to some extent a counterbalance to the tourist. He is on a trip for business reasons and probably wishes to keep his trip as short as possible. He uses his time in a much more rational way and the functionality of the activities he undertakes is key. The personal contact with the hotelier is less important. The *Information needs of the businessman* are focused on his business activities. He is clearly biased towards the usefulness of the information sources he has at his disposal. Both the accuracy and speed of access of information is important. Facts have the highest priority which is why multimedia presentation is not of such importance. A further important point is the sensitivity of information. Nobody should know about what interests him or not. Especially relevant here are business data.

From the perspective of the *Range of information presented*, the following categories are distinguished:
Destination information: Apart from information about the hotel, this includes material about the locality or region. The business guest is most interested in infrastructure data (such as timetable), the tourist may want to know about sightseeing locations, sport amenities and upcoming events.
Travel information: This might include travel information or the weather, state of the roads etc. This of course depends less on the type of guest and more on the mode of travel he has used.
Entertainment information: In this category we have concerts, theater, cinema, sporting or other events.
Reservation information: is largely dependent on the extent of entertainment information available. Next to hotel bookings this includes ticket reservation and payment information.

2.2 Point of Information

A differentiation can be made whereby information is made available. Of course there is a preference for delivery to be *in the hotel room*. This is because it is much more comfortable and private. Another possibility is in the hotel lobby or hall. This is not ideal due to the general commotion and the short time that people tend to stay in this location. Another alternative is to provide information in some public places. These so called *Information kiosks* can be situated in well frequented places like a railway station, museum, shopping centers or at motorway service points. They are of course targeted at a wide public, not just the hotel guest, which also includes local people. Information kiosks have been used very successfully. In the future we can expect to see tourist information available on a global basis such as over communication wires like the Internet, partly because information is thereby free from any locality and temporal constraints.

2.3 Hotel categories and their Information offering

The reason for a trip obviously influences both the information needs and the type of accommodation selected by the traveler. On this basis we can assume that the type of accommodation is in some way tied up with the information required and how it is presented. Again, the two types of hotel guest apply.

Tourists often prefer small hotels with a family atmosphere. At the moment interactive multimedia information systems are *not used in this type of hotel* for a number of reasons:
Size and a certain skepticism: Avoidable loss of the personal touch.
Reducing Investment: This argument is important in small hotels, especially in todays difficult business environment, amplified by short seasonal business.
Length of stay: In comparison to the duration of a business trip, this is longer for the tourist. Note also that interest in information is higher at the beginning of a stay followed by a swift drop off. Follow on use depends very much on how attractive the system is.
Another accommodation possibility is the quasi hotel market. In 1992 53.4 % of overnight stays in Switzerland were in this category [7], which includes private accommodation, camping, caravans, youth hostels, etc. Delivering information to guests in this type of accommodation is very difficult and costly. Information kiosks are an obvious delivery vehicle for this market.

Business Travel: Hotel selection is normally done on a strictly rational basis like location, transport connections, availability of rental cars, check in and out times. These things are important. The typical business guest nowadays also expects certain information to be available in his room, including perhaps international finance information in textual form (e.g. Reuters). Some room based information systems allow the guest to go through a complete check out procedure on his own.
Because entertainment is not a key issue for the businessman, multimedial presentation is less important. This generalization is of course not applicable in every instance since the businessman also sets aside some time to relax.

3 How current systems meet the needs of the hotel guests

Using the same characterization of the hotel guest and his information needs we introduced in the last section, we show how the two types of need can be met by hotel room information systems and kiosks.

3.1 Hotel room information systems

To present information in the room, we need some equipment. This can take on a number of forms. The following types have resulted from discussions with various experts:

Decentral Multimedia Device: In each room there is a complete multimedia installation:

- *CD-I - Device:* Each room is fitted out with a CD-I player attached to a normal TV. The guest can play any multimedia title when he wants, including interactivity. One of Zurich's five star hotels is planning to do this.
- *Multimedia PC:* Once again, each room is equipped with a complete system, including PC and CD-ROM player. This type of installation is very costly and takes up a lot of space which needs to be careful planned. We saw no indication of any hotel wanting to do this. However, with the widespread use of laptops, this approach could become attractive in the future.

Central CD Device: A remote control device in the room provides access, but such a configuration can't be used by more than one guest at a time due to technical restrictions. This can be got around by having a number of devices available for the exclusive use of individual guests interested in CD based material. If there are more guest interest than available devices a waiting queue is established. Devices used in this way can be either CD-I, CD-ROM or Photo-CD.

Autonomous Presentation Systems (Configured as Inhouse or Regional TV systems): A central player is the source for rolling, possibly multi-lingual, presentations which are fed into a TV cable. Encompasses all device types including video. An installation of this type already exists in Zürich.

Check out - Systems: Teletext and control signals are sent in addition to the usual TV channels. The end user device is a modified TV with additional, separately addressable Radio and control units. This system is interactive, but can handle only text or teletext type graphics. It is possible to connect this system to international finance network. This class of system allows the guest to make reservations, interface with Pay-TV (video) and order goods/services. Any number of these configurations have been installed in hotels, mainly in establishments focusing on the businessman.

Table 1 provides an overview of the key aspects of the different systems. Installation and operating expenses for each hardware configuration can be listed individually. The major expense is however associated with *gathering and preparing content,* specifically pictures and animated sequences. A study [8] revealed the following figures: (The goal was to build a pilot CD based system for hotels. Three categories of information were included and associated costs were calculated on the basis of US$ 60 per picture and US$ 65 per min. sound - for one language.)

Standard hotel information	with 12 pictures and	71 min. sound:	*US$ 5435*
Special hotel information	with 9 pictures and	35 min. sound:	*US$ 2865*
Locality information/events	with 29 pictures and	290 min. sound:	*US$ 21000*

What we see here are *very high costs,* whereby about 80% reoccur on a monthly basis. We do not see any way to significantly reduce these costs in the future. This component is the area on which to focus for a breakthrough in information systems. Note also that these costs are relevant for all types of system.

Table 1. Characteristics of different kind of information systems in hotel rooms

	CD-I + TV distributed system	PC distributed system	CD - Station centalized	Autonomous Presentation Systems	Check-out Systems
Hardware in each room	TV with CD-I - player	PC with CD-ROM	TV with controller	TV	TV with radio and control unit
General hardware	-	-	Network, CD-player	Network, CD- or Video player	Network, database with editor
Cost per room	about US$ 1200	about US$ 3200	different	TV-set	different
Control Equipe-ment	joystick	mouse, touchscreen	keyboard ?	-	remote con-trol of TV
Multime-dia	yes	yes	yes	yes	no
Interacti-vity	yes	yes	yes (only for activ user)	no	yes
realiza-tion	not known, planned in a Swiss hotel	unknown	in some hotels in USA	in some hotels in Switzerland	at many pla-ces, esp. bu-siness hotels

3.2 Information Kiosks

This second group of guest information systems is similar to the decentralized PC/CD-ROM solution shown above. Computer, monitor - sometimes using touch screen technology - loudspeakers, perhaps printer and telephone communications equipment are installed in as usually attractive housing with a computer (PC or Macintosh) and a CD-ROM device. Information is presented in a multimedia form using a interactive, intuitive interface. Factors for the success of such kiosks are similar to those of cash machines [9,10] as follows:

- Intuitive and easy to use, with recognizable elements and symbols
- Small number of easily learnt controls
- If possbile located in a quiet, safe atmosphere
- Usefulness - fast access to current, well presented information
- Mold into the environment at key locations
- Protection against Vandalism

Based on these theoretical considerations, we look at two examples of implementations in Switzerland.

"Multimedia Graubünden": The motivation for this prize winning system was to present information about the canton Graubünden to tourists. Apart from general information such as weather forecasts and road information, this system included information on sport meetings, specific localities, events and accomodation. The system was brought very much to life by "Conradin" an animated figure under the motto of "motivation through fun!" [11]. Beside being able to find information, the tourist call directly to his selected hotel by the press of a button. All this is done with a Macintosh computer.

"Info Z": This other, more recent system offers information about the canton of Freiburg. Information is available covering multiple areas: accommodation, restaurants, traffic information, public transport, leisure activities, culture, sport, attractions, shopping, services (e.g. banking, hairdressing), emergency health services and general subjects like local information, police, fire department, post and telephones. The individual service operator (e.g. a shopping center) can add additional information to this palette. Four languages are supported, French, German, Italian and English [12]. This system should be useful for the local population as well as the tourist. Info Z runs on a PC with DOS/Windows. Four kiosks have been installed by the end of November; from December on there will be installed ten new units every month.

4 Weakness and disadvantages of todays systems

Hotel room - information systems in Switzerland are currently limited to check out and stand alone presentation systems. This means either multimedia or interactive operation, but not both, something which will have to change if there is to be wider acceptance. Additionally, systems will have to provide users with the possiblity to print selected information, not just show it on a screen.

Information kiosks. The situation here is a little better since they have multimedia as well as interactivity and usually include a printer. However, there are some negative environmental effects such as noise levels and general hectic. Also the availability of kiosks can depend on the opening times of the location. By locating kiosks in areas which are well frequented reduces the level of privacy usual desirable, due in part to the construction of the housing which normally allows several people to look at the information being shown and the sounds being broadcast. This can put the user under psychological pressure from other waiting users. Some critics see kiosks as a purely interim solution [13], until such time as all hotel rooms and homes have direct access to information systems. But as the situation with the public telephone system shows, this argument might well be fallacious. Of course such a development would exclude the quasi hotel business altogether.

5. The systems of the future - their architecture and use

Generally it is prudent to look at what might be technically possible in the future by looking at the overall sense of the system and the real needs of users. Some of the possibilities to make usage easier for future travelers are:
Language recognition: The system should be usable through verbal commands. At the moment there are technical reasons why this is not possible. (Environmental noise, voice differences, accents and acoustic intermingling of words.)
Digital video sequences: These require significant computer power. At the current time there has been no use of such clips due to their low quality. (Small picture size, stutter, long load times.)
Handwriting recognition: Current system usage is limited to selecting information, whereby the method of selection can be tedious. With handwriting recognition things could be a lot simpler. At the moment this technology requires an extended learning phase.
Transaction processing: A change from todays simple information selection to full ordering capability including credit card or smart card support.
Integration of all elements: Moves towards a networked solution other information processing systems will lead to easier data management and more up-to-date information. This will make data supply to kiosks and installations in individual hotels much simpler, as well as providing input for regional TV stations, videotext, teletext, international tourist databases and the Internet.
This last connection provides 24 hour access to multimedia information worldwide. Further, support can be given this way with services to small hotels and quasi hotel operations. A precursor to this is demonstrated by the TIS (Tourism Information System) in Tirol [14].

6. Conclusion

Next to the information needs of the guest are the requirements of the hotelier and the local tourist association. The people interviewed did not express any quantitative or qualitative measurements regarding information supply. Information content depends on the type of guest. Even if in theory we destinguish between different classes of guest, this is not done in practice. *Two guest types are assumed;* tourists and businessmen. The latter wants up-to-date information quickly and puts little value on multimedia presentation. He avoids kiosks in open areas and ideally wants to use an information system in his room. The tourist on the other hand wants to have information presented in an entertaining way, for which multimedia is well suited (Infotainment). Small hotels put a lot of emphasis on personal contact. Overall attention has to be paid to the emotional side with tourists.

During implementation, the requirements of the guest have to be respected, even if the interface for each class of guest may be different. In the future presentation may be selectable dependent on guest type. A special inquiry session at the commencement of a session could be used to adapt to the situational behavior of the individual.

Systems currently running reflect these needs. Multimedia is rare in hotels, text in a tree structured form is the order of the day. The cost of multimedial systems, particularly in small hotels is prohibitive. Such systems are of course also technically complex and require a solid infrastructure in the hotel. Interactivity will increase these costs due to the need for more expensive hardware.

Kiosks are good for multimedia presentation, even if substantial work has to be put into a user friendly interface. The ideal position for such kiosks is in train stations, post offices, shopping centers, motorway rest areas, etc. Use of them in hotel needs further study, especially in respect of reducing their disturbance factors (selection of position away from access doors, disturbance through noise).

Multimedia presentation has to be useful to the guest and his host. In most cases the financial payback is difficult to establish, using such measurements as increase in turnover. In practice we see that guests are generally interested in the few systems which have been developed. As an example, the Graubünden kiosk has been used by 60,000 people in its first year [15]. In future the market for multimedia will continue to grow steadily because more and more people in charge recognize the positive impacts of these systems. Another trend is towards the user being able to make transactions/reservations with the system and not just gather information. This way the full potential of multimedia systems will be opened up for both the guest and the hotelier.

References

1. Lesch, A.: Integration von Telekommunikationsdiensten in einem Hypermedia-System. In: Häusser, E. (eds.): Online '92 - Kongressunterlagen zur 15. Europäischen Congressmesse für Technische Kommunikation, Velbert, 1992. Congressband V, V.27

2. Schmenk, A.; Waetjen, A.: Multimedia - Multimedia verstehen, planen, einsetzen. München: DTV, 1993

3. Ziegler, J.; Koller, F.: Die Komponenten von Multimedia. In: Förster, H.P.; Zwernemann, M. (eds.): Multimedia - Die Evolution der Sinne. Berlin: Luchterhand, 1993, p. 13

4. Longley, D.; Shain, M.: Van Nostrand Reinhold dicitionary of information technology. New York: Van Nostrand Reinhold, 1989

5. Kaspar, C.: Die Struktur der Tourismusnachfrage unter besonderer Berücksichtigung der Bundesrepublik Deutschland. In: Storbeck, D. (eds.): Moderner Tourismus: Tendenzen und Aussichten. Trier: Geographische Gesellschaft, 1988

6. Witt, D.; Wichert, J.: Anforderung an die Hotelqualität aus der Sicht der Gäste - Probleme der Hotelklassifizierung. In: Kaspar, C. (eds.): Jahrbuch der Schweizerischen Tourismuswirtschaft 1992/1993. St. Gallen, Institut für Fremdenverkehr und Verkehrswirtschaft, 1993, pp.173-196

7. Bundesamt für Statistik (eds.): Statistisches Jahrbuch der Schweiz 1994. Zürich: Neue Zürcher Zeitung, 1994, p. 236

8. Rees, B: Costs For A Hotel CD-ROM Project 1994. Zürich: Rees Innovation, 1994

9. Meyer, P.: Bürger-Information "live" - Elektronisches Besucher-Informationssystem "Info-Treff" in Leutkirch im Allgäu im Einsatz. In: Office Management, 6/1992, pp. 36-37

10. Stippel, P.: Das Multimedia-Szenario: So verändert die neue PC-Generation das Marketing. In: Absatzwirtschaft, Nr. 6/1992, pp. 38-45

11. Fietz, G.: Provokation der Informationspuritaner. In: Frankfurter Allgemeine Zeitung, Nr. 59/1992, March 10. 1992, p. B34.

12. ADK Informatique SA: Info Z, die interaktive Säule für die Vermittlung von Informationen. Fribourg, 1994

13. Ritz, D.: Elektronische Märkte verändern die Tourismusbranche. In: io Management Zeitschrift, Nr. 1/1992, pp. 77-81

14. Ebner, A.: TIS - Das Tirol Informations System. In: EM - Elektronische Märkte, Nr. 3/1992, p. 4

15. Anonymous: MultiMedia Graubünden: Tausendmal berührt. In: Saison, Nr. 34/1993, p. 5

OuR-TOWN: A Distributed, Multi-media System for Travel and Tourism

Stephen W. Clyde
Computer Science Department, Utah State University,
Logan, UT 84322-4205

Todd Landfried
Natural Resources and Rural Development
U.S. Department of Agriculture, Extension Service

Abstract. To help rural communities and small business, the USDA initiated a program called OuR-TOWN that would enable them gather and diseminate up-to-date travel and tourism information over the Internet in a cost-effective manner. Here, we present the architectural design of the OuR-TOWN information system and discuss how it mets the USDA's objectives. Several prototypes, our current development status, and future plans are also discussed.

1 Introduction

The OuR-TOWN information system is a distributed, multimedia software application for travel and tourism currently under development at Utah State University. It contains detailed, up-to-date information on items of interest, such as possible destinations, natural and manmade attractions, recreational areas, historical sites, accommodations, restaurants, and cultural events. OuR-TOWN was originally conceived in 1992 by the U.S. Department of Agriculture as a repository of information on travel and tourism opportunities in rural America. Since then, it has evolved into a global information and decision-support system for a wide range of users. However, the system is specifically designed so rural communities and small businesses can promote their unique resources cost-effectively.

We divide the users of the information system into two main categories: providers and consumers. The information providers include organizations, businesses, and government agencies that have information to give to travelers. Through user-friendly, data-entry programs that run on their own computers, providers will be able to access and update their own information directly whenever they want to. The data-entry programs will also help them organize the information into attractive on-line brochures. These brochures can look similar to printed brochure with multiple columns, pages, and sections. However, the on-line brochures can also contain multi-media presentations, such as slide shows, sound clips, and motion video. Furthermore, they can include interactive hyper-links between different presentations and brochures.

The primary information consumers include current and future travelers, travel agents, tour planners, meeting and conference planners, and travel writers. For simplicity, we to refer all of these groups collectively as the *travelers*. Their main use of the system will be for exploration and planning. With a graphical-user interface on a desktop computer, a traveler will be able to quickly locate items of interest and view multi-media presentations about those items. If they want, travelers can also download this information to their own systems for quick future reference. In addition, if they are not sure where they want to go, travelers can request assistance from an on-line trip planner.

Other information consumers include universities, government agencies, and marketing businesses. They will use OuR-TOWN primarily for demographic studies and research related to travel and tourism. For this reason, the system will keep statistics on accesses and downloadings on a per item basis. It will also allow a traveler to enter comments on any item in the system and then automatically pass these comments onto the appropriate information providers.

The idea of making travel and tourism information available electronically is certainly not new. Professional travel agents have had access to computerized airline, hotel and car rental information for many years through *computerized reservation systems* (CRSs). Services such as SABRE and APOLLO provide detailed information on availability, timetables, rates, and commissions. They also facilitate making reservations, printing tickets, authorizing credit card transactions, and providing reservation confirmation numbers. Most of these text-based networks are hosted on mainframes and can only be accessed through dial-in or dedicated leased lines. Monthly access fees typically range from $750 to $1,500 per terminal. Also, CRS information services are complicated systems that require hours of training in how to use them effectively. Because the major airlines, hotel chains and automobile rental companies own these services, they are the primary information providers. Although CRSs do include information on other attractions, businesses pay thousands of dollars each year to be listed. These high fees and the need for specialized hardware makes it difficult if not impossible for small businesses to take advantage of CSRs.

Consumer-oriented services, such as EASY-SABRE, Worldspace, OAG Electronic Edition, and TravelFile, tend to be less complicated than professional-oriented services. In addition, many of them are accessible through commercial online services such as CompuServe, Prodigy, and America Online. However, the information is usually limited to flight availability and fares, hotel addresses and facilities, location information (distance from downtown), various kinds of telephone numbers, business services, and accepted credit cards. Like the CSR's, consumer-oriented services are text-based. Also, they tend to focus on those attractions that are part of corporate chains or have paid large fees to be listed. Thus, the types and quality of information in rural areas is fairly low.

With the introduction of the World-Wide Web (WWW) and Mosaic as a means of making the Internet easier to use and more visually pleasing, a growing number of travel information sources have began to appear. The ease at which WWW documents can be prepared has enabled information providers to deliver photographs in addition to the textual information that already exists in other online sources. Like professional- and consumer-oriented services, these information sources tend to focus on well-know destinations or compilations of existing published materials. One of the more popular WWW services is the Global Network Navigator (GNN) Traveler's Center. GNN is also the home to Fodor's Worldview System which focuses on events occurring in major cities around the World. Some travel agencies have also begun to do business over the Internet by allow users to make airline, hotel and car reservations online.

The main differences between OuR-TOWN these other systems lie in its architecture and in the underlying objectives that motivated the architecture. Section 2 describe the high-level architecture for the OuR-TOWN information system. In Section 3, we recast our objective in terms five major features and show how the architecture provides those features. We briefly discuss several prototypes and their results in Section 4. Section 5 describes our current status and future plans. Finally, we summarize in Section 6.

2 Architecture

The OuR-TOWN system consists of five logical components: the information subsystem, distribution and network support layer, application server layer, traveler interface, and provider interface. Figure 1 shows the relationships between these components.

2.1 Information Subsystem

The information layer consists of thousands of inter-related software objects. Figure 2 contains an *Object-Relationship Model* [3] that describes some of the different kinds of objects in the information subsystem and their relationships with each other. The boxes in Figure 2 are *object classes* which represent sets of objects, e.g. the box labeled *Tourism Object* represents the set of items that are of interest to travelers. The lines are *relationship sets* which define how objects in the connected object classes can relate to each. For example, the line between *Tourism Object* and *Tourism-Object Type* allows tourism-object types to classify tourism objects. The min:max pairs near the ends of the relationship sets are called *participation constraints*. A participation constraint restricts how many times objects in the connected class can participate in the relationship sets. For example, the *1:** near the *Tourism Object* object class says that each tourism object has to be classified by one or more tourism-object types.

The relationship set with both sides connected to *Tourism-Object Type* organizes the tourism-object types into a super-type/sub-type lattice. It links a general type, such as "restaurants", with specializations of the types, like "Chinese restaurants" and "Italian restaurants". This lattice not only helps organize the data, but it provides a basis for creating hierarchical legends and selection controls in the traveler interface.

Another important component in the information system is the *On-line Brochure* object

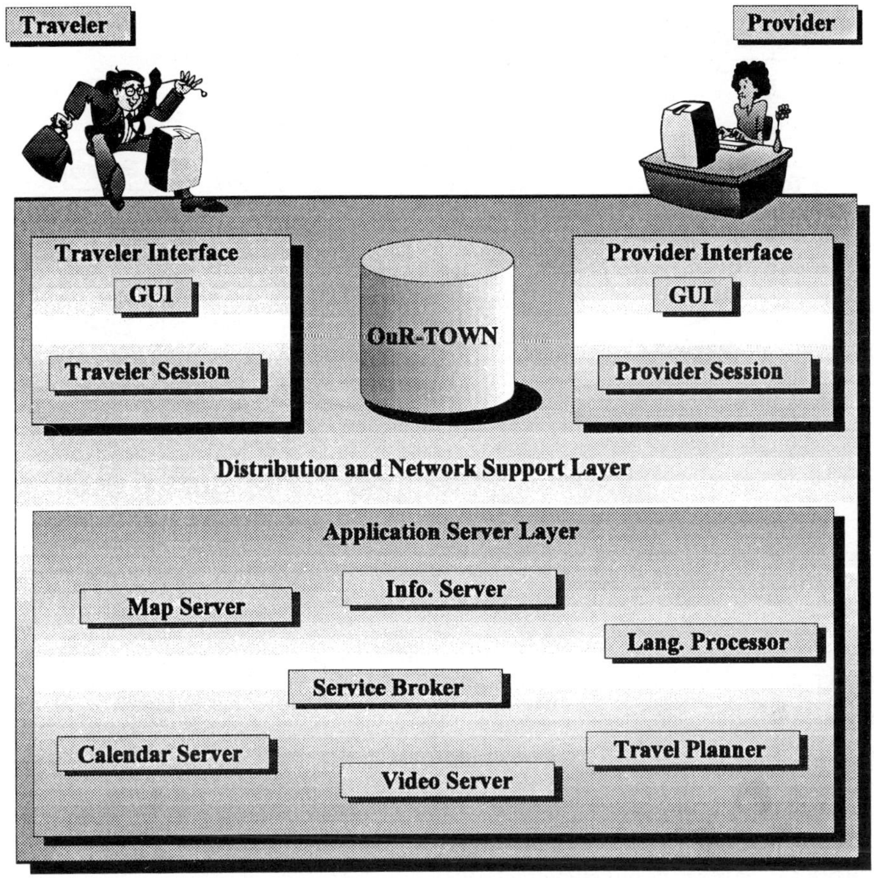

Figure 1 Overview of OuR-TOWN Architecture

class. On-line brochures contain the same kinds of information found in printed brochures. In fact, they are even displayed to appears like printed brochures. Each on-line brochure includes one or more pages, which in turn contain presentations. A presentation, as indicated by the generalization/specialization symbol (the open triangle) in Figure 2, can be either a text block, image, slide show, sound clip, or video. Also, some pages start new sections, which can be used to organize brochures in topic areas. Finally, unlike printed brochure, on-line brochures can be interactive. This is accomplished by allowing pages to have hot spots that trig various actions, like starting a video, moving to another page, or opening another brochure.

2.2 Distribution and Network Support Layer

The distribution and network support layer handles all low-level communications with complete access and location transparency [2]. For example, consider a traveler in

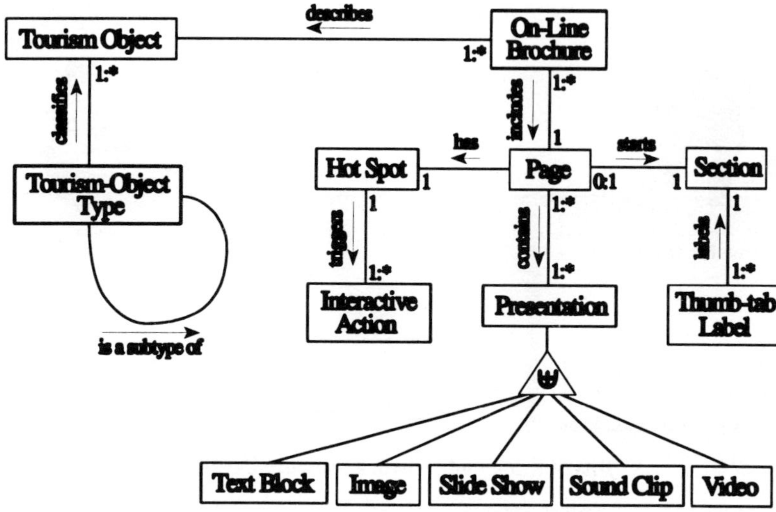

Figure 2 Partial ORM of OuR-TOWN Information System

Europe who requests a historical brochure on Moab, Utah and that brochure is physical located on a computer somewhere in the United States. The support layer will find the requested brochure and transmits it to the traveler's computer without the traveler every having to worry about where it was located or who else was accessing it at the same time.

To help balance the load on the network and provide better throughput, the support layer can migrate and/or replicate objects and parts of objects (object fragments) across the network [3]. It bases its migration/replication decisions on recent access patterns, object size, and network performance. The replication activities also have the added advantage of helping to protest against down time due to network or node failure. All object migrations and replications are complete invisible to other subsystems.

2.3 Server Layer

The server layer in Figure 2 is a collection of various network programs that provide specialized, high-level services to the traveler and provider interfaces and to other servers. For example, the information servers provide secure, high-level access to objects in the information subsystem. Any user interface or server that needs to access an information object can do so through this server.

The map and calendar servers generate custom maps and calendars occurring to parameters specified by the user. For example, Figure 3 shows a window that allows travelers to request custom maps by selecting specific types of tourism objects from the hierarchical legend on the left and then drawing a marque box around the desired region on the right. The type selections and region specifications are packaged into a request and sent to the nearest map server. Using a local road database and objects from the information subsystem, the map server generates the request map and sends it back to the traveler interface.

The route servers calculate possible routes according to user-specified optimization criteria. For example, a traveler can request a route between Salt Lake City and Jackson Hole that minimum distance, has the most scenic vistas, or is the most economical. Like the map servers, a route server accesses its own local road database and the objects in the information subsystem to complete its task. However, the route server also uses a local knowledge base of routing rules.

The trip planners in Figure 2 are an intelligent agents that can make suggestions about where to go, what to see, when to go, where to stay, etc. As a traveler interacts with the system through a traveler interfaces, a travel session (part of the traveler interface) develops a profile of the traveler's general tastes and a profile of the trip currently being planned. The travel session gathers the information for these profiles from the calendars and maps currently open in the user's workspace, various fill-in blank forms, and free-form dialog. Then, when the traveler asks for a suggestion, the travel session generates a request to a trip planner by sending it the traveler and trip profiles. The trip planner tries to match these profiles to travel cases in an extensible knowledge base. Some of the travel cases are very specific and therefore will only match detailed profiles. Other travel cases represent general rules or heuristics, similar to those used by travel agents.

The natural language processors (NPLs) are used to translate free-form text into sets of fuzzy data structures that try to capture the meaning of the text. The trip planner will eventually use these data structures to help match profiles to travel cases. Each fuzzy data structure consists of an ordered list of triples (P,C,F), where P is a word phase, C is an index into a concept dictionary, and F is a fuzzy value. A NPL generates triples by first extracting phrases from a block of text using a grammatical analyzer. Then, for each phrase P, it tries to match significant words in P to keywords in a concept dictionary. Each entry in the dictionary associates a single travel/tourism concept with a set of keywords that are often used to express that concept. The keywords are weighted to indicate their relative importance with respect to the concept. When it finds a good match, the NPL sets C to the concept's index and calculates a fuzzy value F to represent its level of confidence in the match.

Other servers include the video servers and the help servers. The video servers format and compress on-line video clips according to user-specified quality parameters and transmit these clips over the network. The help servers provide context-sensitive help on how to use the traveler and provider interfaces.

Servers can join and leave the environment dynamically. When a server comes on-line, it registers itself with a service broker, which is itself a special kind of server. The service brokers are a key innovation that will enable OuR-TOWN to become self-sustaining because they facilitate the evolution of an open market by allowing clients to shop for services and servers to compete for clients. For example, a service broker can help a client shop for the best deal that on trip planning services. Once a server is engaged to perform a desired service, the service broker establishes a connection between the client and server so they can communicate directly. However, it still keeps track of usage information so it can do the proper accounting. To facilitate network-aware shopping for services, the brokers can also estimate costs, negotiate prices, and evaluate network traffic.

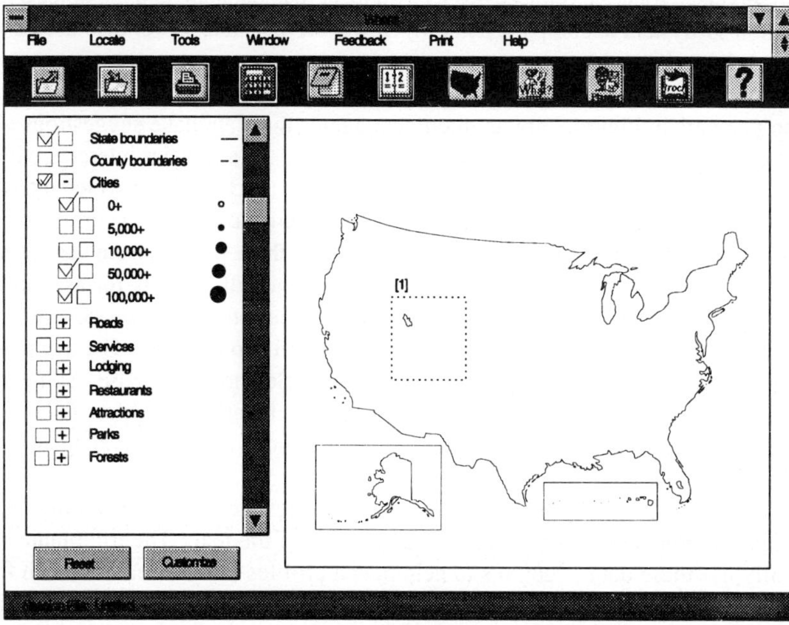

Figure 3 Sample screen from traveler interface for customer map requests

2.4 Traveler Interface

As mention earlier, a traveler interface is the means by which a traveler access the information system. Traveler interfaces will run on personal computers and communicate with the network either through direct connections or dial-in lines. Eventually, we will have traveler interfaces for a variety of platforms. However, our initial plans only include Windows- and WWW-based interfaces. Both will allow travelers to interact with maps, calendars, and hierarchical legends to search for interesting objects. Once some interesting objects are located, the interfaces will also allow the travelers to browse, download, and print on-line brochures. In addition, they will allow travelers to request suggestions from a trip planner. The Windows-base interface will have some additional features including multi-window displays, persistent traveler and trip profiles, itineraries, and personal annotations.

2.5 Provider Interface

Like the traveler interfaces, the provider interfaces run on personal computers connected to the Internet directly or indirectly through dial-in line. They consists of various data-entry and maintenance screens that will allow information providers to access and update their data easily. However, when a provider makes an update, it does not go into the information system immediately. Instead, it goes to an automated quality-control processor (QCP) that first performs some basic checks, like looking for multiple listings of the same tourism object. The QCP sends the results of its tests back to the provider, who can then confirm or cancel the request.

Not only does the QCP help maintain the database's integrity, but it also provides some basic security. Information providers are only allowed to update their own objects. However, if someone tries make bypass the access controls and update someone else's object, the owner will able to reject the update request, because the verfications are always sent to the object's owner, not the requester.

3. Objectives

The purpose of OuR-TOWN can be characterized by five fundamental objectives. These objectives have greatly influenced the architectural design of system and therefore correspond directly to specific features.

The first objective is to provide travelers with detailed and up-to-date information on a wide range of items. The information subsystem is the primary key to providing this feature. It contains a robust and efficient set of data structures capable of capturing information about virtually any kind of tourism object.

The timeliness aspect of the information, on the other hand, is supported by the provider interfaces. Some of tourism objects correspond to relative static entities in the real world, such as states, cities, tourism regions, parks, forests, etc. Most of the information about these objects changes relatively infrequently and so they are not a big problem. However, many of the objects represent dynamic entities in the real-world, such as culture events, recreational activities, seasonal information, visitation patterns, etc. The data for these types of objects must be kept current on a regular basis; otherwise, travelers will loose confidence in the system and eventual stop using it. With OuR-TOWN, we have adopted a decentralized approach for data collection, i.e. there is no central data acquisition organization. The data-entry interfaces described above allow the information providers to maintain their own data. The WWW is an excellent example of global information system build on a decentralized philosophy.

A second objective is to provide an inexpensive and effective way for small organizations to market their services and attractions. This means that OuR-TOWN has to support quality presentations that are equivalent to or better than other forms of advertisement.

Simple directory listings and short textual descriptions are inadequate. The on-line brochures in OuR-TOWN can be multi-page, multimedia presentations that rival even the best printed materials. Thus, they can help small organizations to present themselves is a very professional and cost-effective way.

A third objective is to provide a cost-effective way for organizations to disseminate information that is short-lived or likely to change frequently, such as current weather conditions, community events, occupancy, visitation patterns, etc. The information subsystem and provider interfaces are against the keys to achieving this objective. The information subsystem provides structures that can hold this kind of data and the data-entry interfaces allow it to be maintained by the providers.

Offering alternative marketing and information-distribution channels gives rise to a fourth objective, namely global accessibility. Travelers from around the world must be able to access the OuR-TOWN information system through existing communication networks. The distribution and network support layer and traveler interfaces enable this kind of access without creating unnecessary bottlenecks.

A fifth objective is for OuR-TOWN to become economically self-sustaining. The service brokers in the service layer help meet this objective by creating an open economy for the sale of electronic services. Electronic service providers can establish their own rates and advertise their services with the brokers. Clients (i.e. user interface programs and other servers) can shop for the best deals on the services they need.

4. Prototypes

As part of our analysis and our subsequent design activities, we developed several prototypes to test various approaches and implementation techniques. One prototype consisted of screen mock-ups for a traveler interface. Another focused on the structures in the information subsystem. A third dealt with the functional aspects of the traveler interface. Finally, a fourth explored some of the implementation concerns associated with the service and support layers. We evaluate the results of each prototype within the development team and used several of them to help validate the objectives and features of the system with potential users.

The information we gathered from the prototypes helped us refine the requirements and create more friendly user interfaces. They also gave us considerable insight into possible design and implementation techniques. In addition, since some of the prototypes were relatively complex, they helped us refine the development process for the production version. The most important result of the prototypes, however, was the basic ideas were feasible with current state-of-the-art technology and that the system met several critical needs for the rural communities in the United States.

5. Current Development Status

At this point, we have complete a full analysis and architectural design of the entire system. The architectural design gave us a natural break down of the development effort by subsystem. Currently, we are implementing the first production version of a Windows-based provider interface, traveler interface, quality-control processor, information subsystem, map server, and calendar server. Allow these initial products will communicate over the network, they will not rely on the full service and support layers. Instead, they will communicate with each other directly through an intermediate protocol.

After we complete this initial development effort, we will shift our attention to the server and support layers. When they are operating satisfactorily, we will then update the communication logic in the others products to go through their services.

6. Summary

The OuR-TOWN information system will use state-of-the-art technology to give users immediate access to travel and tourism information and expert trip-planning assistance. OuR-TOWN will also provide travel and tourism related organizations with a cost-effective way to market themselves. Although the production version of OuR-TOWN is still under development, its architectural design is sound and meets all the original objectives. Also, through several prototypes we have concluded that its implementation is not only doable, but very worthwhile.

References

1. Clyde, S., Embley, D., Woodfield, S., "Dynamic Distribution of Object Fragments", Technical Report, *Brigham Young University*, September, 1994

2. Coulouris, G., Dollimore, J., Kindberg, T., *Distributed Systems*, Second Ed., Addison-Welsey Publishers Ltd., 1994

3. Embley, D., Kurtz, B., Woodfield, S., *Object-oriented Systems Analysis: A Model-Driven Approach*, Prentice-Hall, Inc., 1992

Business travellers' expert advisor

Faria Y.Y. Ng
Department of Management Studies, University of Surrey
Guildford, Surrey, GU2 5XH, UK

Abstract. This paper describes the construction of an 'expert system' prototype — *Business Travel Counsellor (BTC)* for business travel counselling. It is aimed to provide assistance to travel agent staff to match the available products with the needs of inquiring customers. Knowledge acquisition was done in consultation with experienced travel consultants to build the rule base. The complexity of human decision making is reflected by the *'scoring scheme'* in which rules are formulated to handle complex users' requirements and different weighting/importance levels. The structure of the SABRE system was analysed for the design of the database. Special emphasis was put on the feasibility of the *integration of expert systems and Central Reservation Systems (CRSs)*. BTC serves to prove the concept of valuable applications of expert systems in travelling counselling. The aim is to provide efficient and reliable information to ensure a better *customer-product match*.

1 Introduction

Travel choices are relatively high-involvement decisions, and customers tend to engage in active information gathering (Moutinho, 1987). As the industry enters the mature market phase, competition for available tourists will increase. This mature market for the tourism industry will almost certainly usher in an era where price will no longer be sufficient to assure success. Rather, a strong reliance on *'expertise'* to deliver individual services will become necessary for survival.

Expert Systems are computer programs that embody the knowledge of one or more human experts in a narrow problem domain and can solve problems in that domain matching the expert's level of performance (El-Najdawi and Stylianou, 1993). Capturing expertise in the form of an expert system gives permanence to the expertise and allows it to become ubiquitous, which is termed as 'attaining corporate immortality' by McMullen (McMullen, 1987). Since an expert system can easily be duplicated, it is possible for inexperienced travel consultants to gain specialised assistance without having to deal with the time and location limitations that restrict human experts (Hruschka and Mazanec, 1990). In other words, there will always be an expert around to help. The implementation of an expert system that makes sophisticated travel counselling possible for everybody and everywhere, therefore, represents an important opportunity for the travel agent industry (Crouch, 1991).

2 Problem identification

A field research was conducted in one of the travel management centres (TMCs) of Thomas Cook. The consultants are assisted by the SABRE Central Reservation System. They will look up the customer profile in SABRE once receive a call. Based on the information from the profile and the present requests of the customer, the consultants will send commands to SABRE to check the availability of the products that the customer wants. SABRE will then generate a list of alternatives. The consultants will advise on the option that is supposed to meet the requirements of the client most appropriately.

2.1 The performance gap

A *questionnaire* analysis on the characteristics of travel consultants showed that the level of experience of consultants varies significantly. Though a large proportion (70%) has two to five years' experience, the rest of them show a dimension ranging from less than one to more than 16 years. Therefore, the same customer with the same requirements may be recommended different products by different consultants. Moreover, human decisions are inconsistent by nature. The same inputs do not always produce the same decisions. This may be due to external distractions, forgetting to get key pieces of information and even changes in an individual's mood. Therefore, even the same consultant may have varied performance at different times. In other words, there is no guarantee that the customer really gets the most suitable product.

Based on a *performance review* carried out in the same TMC, the consultants were evaluated in terms of their efficiency and productivity.

Table 1 Details of the calls received by the observed team in the TMC

	No. of Calls	ABD*	ABD%	TSF%+
Monday	63	9	14.2	87
Tuesday	64	2	3.1	83
Wednesday	73	6	8.2	89
Thursday	57	2	3.5	83

* ABD is the number of calls abandoned.

+ TSF% is the amount of calls answered in 15 seconds after being put through.

The consultants in this team were *interviewed*. It was found out that the team performed below average on Tuesday (83%) and Thursday (83%). The criterion for assessing performance is by the standard set by Thomas Cook, which is 85% of calls to be answered in 15 seconds for a day.

2.2 How expert systems fit in?

With the use of a *criteria checklist* (Liebowitz, 1989), it was found out that travel counselling meets all the major criteria as an appropriate narrow problem domain since the task requires strategic use of heuristics. As an expert system can encode the *pooled expertise* of the experts into a computer, it will not only *smooth individual variances*, but also help to *diminish the variances across decision-makers*. Moreover, an expert system can offer speedy 'customer-product' matching because it thinks like a human expert, applying rules in a non-procedural manner, jumping to quick hypotheses and offering speedy conclusions. By this, consultants will become more efficient and productive. The *ABD% can be reduced and TSF% increased* as clients' waiting time is minimised with the improvement in the speed in decision making.

3 The functional architecture of BTC

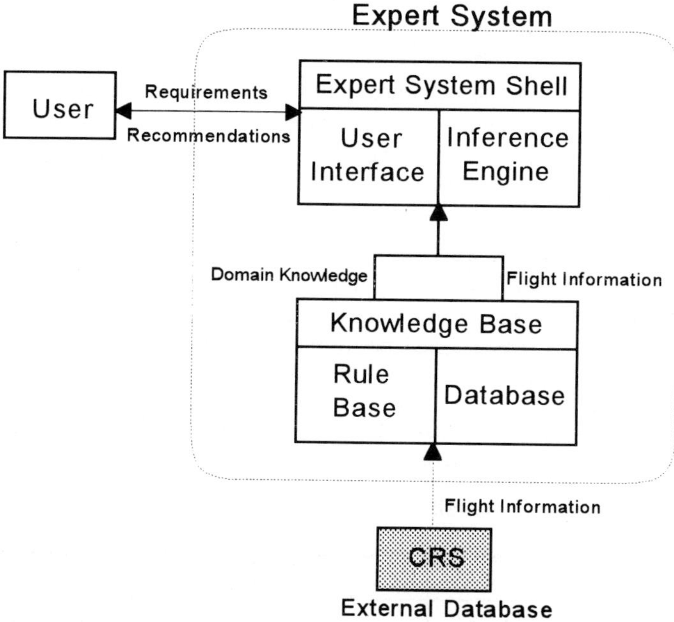

Figure 1 The functional architecture of BTC

BTC was constructed using a simple commercial expert system shell. The shell provides the inference engine and tools for building graphical user interfaces. The inference engine derives conclusions from the knowledge base that includes both a rule base and a database. The rule base contains heuristic knowledge collected from the field research concerning how travel consultants make decisions. The database contains information received from a CRS, in response to actions triggered by the inference engine. The user interface collects users' requirements such as date, time, class of travel, etc., and displays details of the recommended flights together with other information useful to the trip. The custom components of BTC will be explained in the following sections.

4 The database design

The BTC database structure is designed with the practical idea of interfacing to an external CRS. After accepting the user's requirements, BTC will start processing them and then sent commands to the CRS system to extract relevant information, typically a list of relevant flights. The information extracted is assumed to be rearranged in a *machine-readable format* that can be further analysed, i.e., a database. This, in fact, will take place internally without the user noticing at all. Though the real time connection was not tested, the structure was accurately simulated. Such kind of integration has been recognised as an important functional element in future global distribution systems (Goeldner, 1994; Martin and Oxman, 1988; Sheldon, 1992).

4.1 The analysis on SABRE

By entering the date, the destination pair and the preference for the departure time (if any), a list of flights available will be shown.

Table 2 SABRE — flight availability

```
1. NW 49 F4 C4 Y4 B4 M4 H4 Q0 V0    LGWBOS 1215 1435 747 DS 0
2. AA109 F7 C7 Y7 B7 M7 V7 X7 Q7 H7 LHRBOS 1130 1400 767 LS 0
3. VS 11 J4 W4 Y7 B7 L7 A7 S7       LGWBOS 1500 1710 747 LS 0
4. BA213 F7 J7 M7 S7 B7 K7 Q0 V0    LHRBOS 0955 1230 767 D  0
5. BA215 F7 J7 M7 S7 B7 K7 Q0 V0    LHRBOS 1645 1900 747 D  0
```

It shows information such as airline and flight no., e.g., NW49, the classes of seat available, e.g., F4 means four in first class, the departure and arrival airports, e.g., LGWBOS (London Gatwick and Boston), the departure and arrival (local) time, e.g., 1215, 1435, the type of flight, e.g., 747, meal services, e.g., DS (dinner and snack) and the number of stops, e.g., 0 means no stop.

Specific flight details such as the length and the total miles of the flight can be obtained. To deal with seat preferences, a seating plan showing the availability and particulars of seats can be displayed. Seats are shown relative to the position of toilets and the screen for movies. Information on fare bases can be requested to see if the customer is eligible for a particular fare base, e.g., youth and standard adult tickets. Each type of fare will impose different restrictions on the traveller.

4.2 The BTC database structure

The BTC database is *relational* and consists of four linked files, namely SCHEDULE, CLASS, FARE, and SEAT. The database structure is designed to handle full flight information supplied by SABRE, though not all possible details are included in this prototype. The problems are not trivial, e.g., the representation of the complex fare structure of individual seats, which depends on the date of travel, length of stay, ticket restrictions, etc. Another problem is to represent the seat plan such that not only aisle and window seats can be selected, but adjacent seats can also be determined.

General flight details are stored in SCHEDULE to which all three files are linked. Both FARE and SEAT are linked to CLASS. Their relationships are explained in Figure 2.

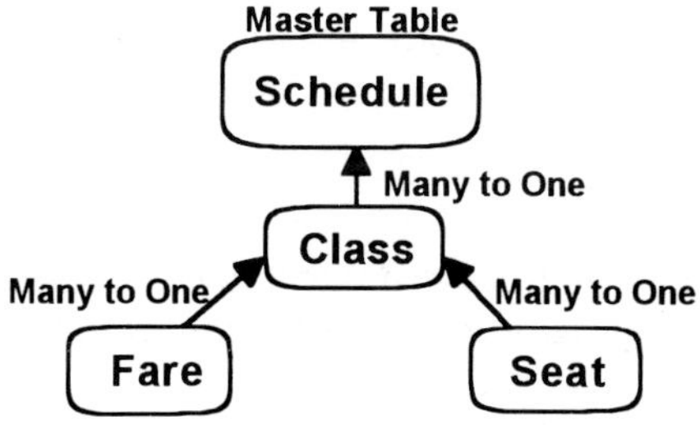

Figure 2 Structure of the relational database

SCHEDULE shows flight availability. Basic flight information, such as *Board and Off-Points*, *Airline and Flight No.*, *Times of Departure and Arrival*, *No. of Stops* and *Equipment* are stored. *CLASS* gives information on the types of class available for the flights. The field *Availability* gives information on the number of seats available for a particular class. *FARE* stores information on fare base. The fields *Before Day* and *After Day* denote the period within which a particular fare base may apply, i.e. season. *SEAT* shows the variety of seats *(Seat Type)*, such as window, aisle, front and back seats. The field *Vacant* tells if a particular seat is available. The particulars of each seat are represented by specifying what lies on its right side *(Seat No. on the Right)*. For example, if there is an aisle/a window on the right, it is an aisle/a window seat; if both sides are vacant seats, then the user may know that adjacent seats are available, and so on. *Smoke* distinguishes between smoking and non-smoking seats.

5 The rule base

5.1 Knowledge acquisition

As no single method will suffice for complex knowledge acquisition, a 'mix and match' method (Hart, 1991) , *protocol analysis* plus *interviews,* was employed.

Protocol analysis. Protocol analysis involves a knowledge engineer observing how a domain expert solves problems. The knowledge engineer may directly query the expert. Alternatively, the knowledge engineer may passively observe the expert 'speaking out loud' while working through a problem (Chadha et al., 1991; Kim and Courtney, 1988, Sussmann and Ng, 1994). In the case of BTC, multiple counselling sessions of a team of expert travel counsellors were recorded. From the actual dialogue between the clients and the consultants, it was possible to extract not only the knowledge needed for the expert system, but also a benchmark against which to compare the prototype once developed. The observations were supplemented by an analysis of transcripts produced from recorded notes of the 'speaking out loud' problem sessions. Interference with the expert consultants' decision-making process, which might be caused when asking questions, was minimised.

Interviews. Follow-up interviews were conducted to complement the results from the protocol analysis. The experts were asked why they make 'such and such' decisions. Sometimes, they have formed a close relationship with their clients that they simply apply what they know from the customers' profiles, e.g., a customer is a member of the frequent flyer program and prefers to fly with a particular airline every time, or a company will put price in the first place when they book flights for their staff. The consultants were asked to verbalise their immediate thoughts behind their decisions.

5.2 The 'scoring scheme'

The knowledge elicited are then translated into a 'scoring scheme'. The principle of the 'scoring scheme' is to assign an overall score for each unique option based on two aspects: *'matchability'* and *'weighting'*.

By 'matchability', it assesses how much the option can fit into the user's requirements, e.g., if the customer want to be at the destination before 1500, a flight arriving at 1400 will certainly has a *lower mark* for the 'arrival time' (field in database) than a flight reaching the airport at 1700.

RULE	**arrive_before_b**
IF	arrival_time_requirement = before and preferred_arrival_time > scheduled_arrival_time
THEN	time_score = ((preferred_arrival_time - scheduled_arrival_time) x cost scale)

The scores are worked out by calculating the discrepancies between the preferred arrival time and the scheduled arrival time plus an adjustment according to a *'cost scale'* with £100 as the base fare. These costs are then adjusted in proportion to the actual fare. For the flight arriving at 1400, the scale is *£2 per hour* as the traveller can still manage to reach the destination before the preferred time, though a bit earlier than the exact hour he wants. For the flight arriving at 1700, the scale will be *£5 per minute*, as late arrival would cause much more inconvenience to the traveller.

In terms of 'weighting', the importance that a particular traveller associates with a field is also considered as travellers will have individual preferences. The relative importance of the fields also depends on circumstances. For example, the arrival and departure times are less important in long-haul flights as absolute punctuality is not easy and the traveller will probably allow for some reasonable delay in such cases.

The total score for each candidate flight is the sum of the products of individual field marks and their weights. Though human experts do not work with numerical scores, they do consider 'matchability' and 'weighting' (Kattan, 1994). BTC attempts to emulate human experts except that the final assessment is quantitative. The advantages of using a structured scoring scheme are consistency, ease of averaging expert opinions and simplicity of software maintenance.

6 The user interface

The design principle for the user interface is: *(1) to exploit the advantages of using an expert system to arrive at a user friendly interface; and (2) to design a user interface that exhibits expert behaviour in data collection.*

6.1 The intelligent form

BTC is designed to interact with users via an *intelligent form*, as shown in Figure 3. The use of a form allows information to be gathered in arbitrary sequences that do not hinder natural conversation with customers whilst operating BTC.

The form is divided into *windows*, each contains a number of *fields* in which the operator will enter the data. Key information such as date and time of travel, travel class, etc., are entered in the main window. These are the most likely details that customers will tell their consultant. The number of *key fields* is kept to a minimum as a consultant will not ask a lot of unnecessary questions. On the other hand, a large number of *optional fields* are provided to satisfy individual customer preferences that are occasionally specified, e.g., seat, smoking and airline preferences. These optional fields are placed in a number of *auxiliary windows* that are only displayed when their selection buttons are activated on the main window.

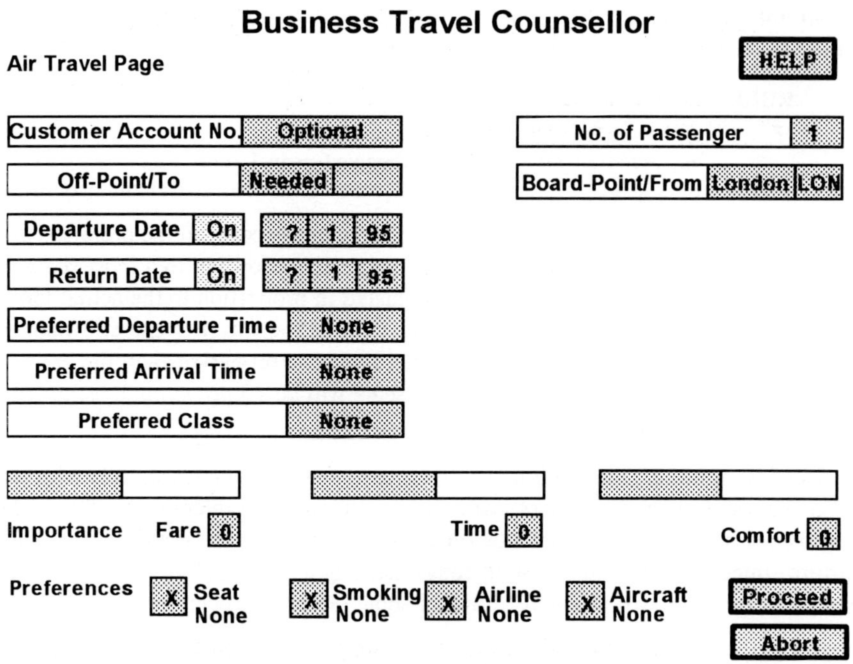

Figure 3 The BTC consultation screen

Context sensitive fields. *Context sensitive fields* are implemented to speed up form entry, which is illustrated as shown for the preferred departure time in Figure 4.

If the customer wants to depart around a specific time, the BTC operator then point and click at *None* to display the options. A *pull-down menu* appears which provide options such as *Morning, Afternoon, Evening, Around, Before, After* and *Between*. The time field is dynamic, i.e., if *Morning* is selected, the field will disappear immediately, whilst an additional question mark will appear for *Around* and two additional question marks for *Between*. This design avoids large number of unnecessary fields and labels obscuring the screen.

Defaults. *Default values* suggesting highly likely answers are supplied if possible and they may change dynamically. For example, the current month and year are the defaults for all dates, and the default month/year of the return trip are those of the outward trip.

Range and relationship checks. Whenever a field changes value, special rules associated with the field are triggered. These rules are used to check likely mistakes in the data and, more importantly, the likely conflicts amongst fields. Rules on individual fields are mostly range checks to guard against mistakes such as trips to the past. More complex rules examine the interrelations amongst fields, e.g., if both preferred arrival and departure times are entered, the initial entry will be cleared since the fixed flight (travelling) time will not allow both fields to be specified arbitrarily.

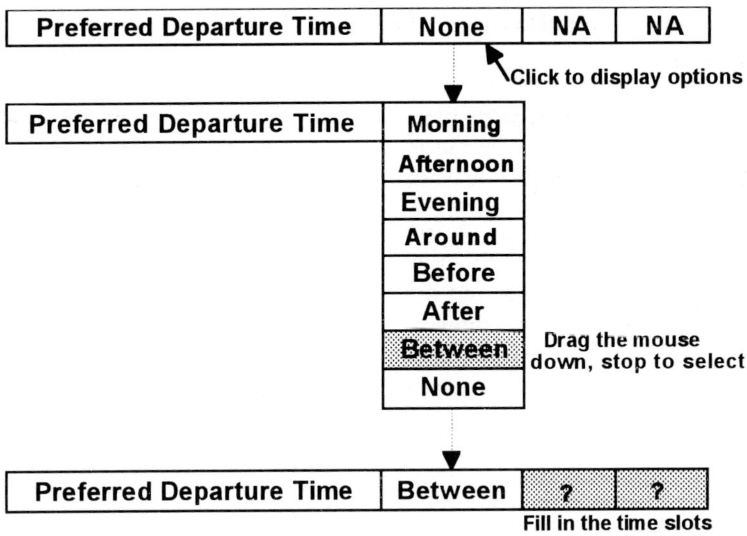

Figure 4 Context sensitive fields

Horizontal gauge. The relative importance, or weights, of the fields are determined by rules as explained in section 5.2. Customers are unaware of individual weights, but three importance levels, *Fare, Time* and *Comfort* are provided to allow customisation. The default values of these importance levels are one, i.e., the three criteria are equally important to the customer. The importance levels can be changed by direct data entry, or by sliding horizontal gauges. Individual field weights are then derived from the importance levels by a set of rules. For example, if Time is greater than one, the schedule of the flight that matches the customer's requirement is given higher priority.

Auxiliary windows. The options for seat, smoking and airline preferences are provided in auxiliary windows, popping up on the blank space to the right hand side of the screen only if one of the buttons has been activated. An example on seat is shown in Figure 5.

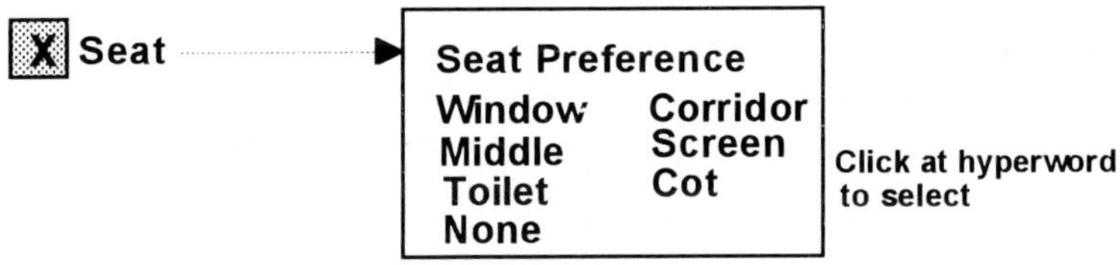

Figure 5 Auxiliary windows

Context sensitive HELP. *Context sensitive help* information is provided at all times implemented by *hypertext* tools of the expert system shell. Help menus relevant to the current user action are located in pop-up menus, error message boxes and all windows.

6.2 The consultation screen

If there are no reported errors and all mandatory fields are completed, the user can leave the intelligent form and enter the consultation screen. The operator is presented with a split screen, on which the customers' requirements are shown alongside the recommended flights so that it is easy to check if the requirements are handled satisfactorily. An example is shown in Figure 6.

In this case, the customer wants to go to Innsbruck from a London airport on 17/1/95 and return on 21/1/95. The preferred departure time is morning and economy class is needed. The only personal preference is a window seat. The OS234 flight is recommended, which departs from London Gatwick to Innsbruck at 1005 and reaches the airport at 1350. A non-smoking window seat is allocated.

If the customer is satisfied, the operator then starts the computerised booking procedures, otherwise, BTC can be aborted or the intelligent form can be restarted and modified. Extra information is displayed in boxes highlighting ticket restrictions, destination information, visa requirements, etc.

Figure 6 The consultation screen

7 Future work

Recent market analyses show a common and coherent trend — decrease in the importance of standardised travel packages and inclusive tour (Bennett, 1993; Hitchins, 1991). With travel information more and more readily available, there will be a trending towards *independent travelling*, i.e., the customers will mix and match travel products for their self-planned holidays instead of going to the tour operators for a pre-arranged package. Coupled with this trend is the changing role of the travel agents, which evolves from providing convenient booking to help *giving customised advice* as valued added services (Bruce, 1994). Therefore, research is currently continuing into the development of a more comprehensive expert system, using Prolog, to cater for both the business and independent travellers (Ng and Sussmann, 1994).

The future of expert systems depends on the cracking of the so-called knowledge acquisition bottleneck. The knowledge acquisition bottleneck limits the scalability of expert systems. While it is relatively straightforward to populate a small-scale knowledge base, it becomes more difficult to maintain consistency and validity as the knowledge base grows. Thus, it is important to automate the knowledge acquisition process (Rubin, 1993). An expert system in no way mimics human intelligence — unless it is adaptive — unless it learns. Learning is perceived as an integral part of expert systems in the future (by Kick in Rubin, 1993). Intelligence must be viewed as an evolutionary adaptation (by Fogel in Rubin, 1993). Therefore, the next version of BTC will address the 'learning' issues of knowledge elicitation.

The use of *multi-media* has also showed its importance as a competitive tool (Sheldon, 1994). We are sure to expect an increasing number of multi-media booking and information systems emerging in the market, such as SABRE*vision* which can show coloured photos of hotel exteriors and interiors, deck and cabin of cruise ships (SABRE, 1993), the Thomas Cook Travel Kiosk at their Marble Arch branch that shows still images of destinations (CD ROM User, 1994), etc. Though BTC was designed to assist the travel agent staff, it has the capacity of involving the customers as direct end-users. With the audio-visual output of product information, the system is able to appeal to the psychological needs of the customers, making the products more tangible by allowing customers to actually 'feel' the products on the screen. An expert system with direct customer involvement through multi-media is going to be as important as the knowledge it encapsulates.

8 References

Bennett, M. M., (1993), Information Technology and Travel Agency: A Customer Service Perspective, *Tourism Management*, August, pp. 259-266.

Bruce, M., (1994), Technological Change and Competitive Marketing Strategies, in Witt and Moutinho (eds.) *Tourism Marketing and Management Handbook,* Prentice Hall, Hemel Hempstead, pp. 430-433.

CD ROM User, (1994), The Information Highway: Virtual Holidays, July 1994.

Chadha, S. R., Mazlack, L. J. and Pick, R. A., (1991), Using Existing Knowledge Sources (cases) to Build an Expert System, *Expert Systems*, November, 8(4), pp. 3-12.

Crouch, G. I., (1991), Expert Computer Systems in Tourism: Emerging Possibilities, *Journal of Travel Research,* 29(3), pp. 3-10.

El-Najdawi, M. K. and Stylianou, A. C., (1993), Expert Support Systems: Integrating AI Technologies, *Communications of the ACM*, 36(12), December, pp. 55-65.

Goeldner, C. R., (1994), Tourism Information Systems, in Witt and Moutinho (eds.) *Tourism Marketing and Management Handbook,* Prentice Hall, Hemel Hempstead, pp. 178-182.

Hart, A., (1991), Report of Workshop on the Use of Knowledge Acquisition Techniques with Structured Systems Methods, Held at BP, London, 5 December 1990, *Expert Systems*, November, 8(4), pp. 38-40.

Hitchins, F., (1991), The influence of technology on UK Travel Agents, *Travel & Tourism Analyst*, No. 3, pp. 88-105.

Hruschka, H. and Mazanec, J., (1990), Computer-Assisted Travel Counselling, *Annals of Tourism Research,* Volume 17, pp. 208-227.

Kattan, M., (1994), Inductive Expert System vs. Human Experts, *AI Expert*, April, pp. 32-38.

Kim, J. and Courtney, J. M., (1988), A Survey of Knowledge Acquisition Techniques and their Relevance to Managerial Problem Domains, *Decision Support Systems,* 4, pp. 269-284.

Liebowitz, J., (1989), Problem Selection for Expert Systems, in Liebowitz, J. and De Salvo, D. A. (eds.), *Structuring Expert Systems, Domain, Design, and Development,* Yourdon Press Computing Series, Prentice Hall, Englewood Cliff, NJ, pp. 3-23.

Martin, J. and Oxman, S., (1988), *Building Expert Systems — A Tutorial,* London, Prentice-Hall International (U.K.) Limited.

McMullen, M., (1987), Artificial Intelligence in the Airline Industry, *IATA Review,* April/June, 1987, pp. 16-18.

Moutinho, L., (1987), Consumer Behaviour in Tourism, *European Journal of Marketing,* 21(10), pp. 1-44.

Ng, F. and Sussmann, S., (1994), The Expert Business Travel Counsellor, *Tourism: The State of the Art,* University of Strathclyde, Glasgow, Scotland, 11-14 July, 1994.

Rubin, S. H., (1993), Machine Learning and Expert Systems, *AI Expert*, June, pp. 32-37.

SABRE Travel Information Network, (1993), SABRE*vision*, 7 February 1993.

Sheldon. P. J., (1992), Researching Consumer Information: Destination Information Systems: Examples of Electronic Market Places, *Proceedings of the 23rd Annual Conference,* Travel and Tourism Research Association, Minneapolis, MN, June 14-17, pp. 37-49.

Sheldon, P. J., (1994), Information Technology and Computer Reservation Systems, in Witt and Moutinho (eds.) *Tourism Marketing and Management Handbook,* Prentice Hall, Hemel Hempstead, pp. 126-130.

Sussmann, S. and Ng, F., (1994), A Prototype Expert System for Business Travel Counselling, *Annuals of Tourism Research* (forthcoming).

A Decision Support System for Tourism Destination Choice

R. Mulye and J. Rickard
Faculty of Business and Economics, Monash University, Australia.

E-Mail: Raju.Mulye@BusEco.monash.edu.au

Abstract. A decision support system based on the analytic hierarchy process (AHP) is proposed as a tool in tourism destination counselling. The AHP constitutes a useful paradigm for integrating existing expert systems to provide a more accurate representation of tourist preferences for destinations. The system is designed on the basis of consumer choice set theory and propositions on size of the evoked set and decision rules used by tourist. The conjunctive rule is used in the first stage of the evaluation process to narrow down the alternative destinations to six and then the AHP procedure is applied to systematically evaluate the alternatives and choose the best destination.

1. Introduction

The development of computers and their widespread application in the last decade or two, have made it possible for travel organisations to deal efficiently with increasing volumes of business. The primary impetus for diffusion of information technology (IT) in tourism has come from the airline industry, which adopted computer reservation systems to streamline their ticketing operations. Subsequent development was led by tour operators aiming to achieve greater cost efficiencies in their operation through the introduction of interactive on-line computer networks bringing together various elements of their product mix, through a reservation system encompassing airlines, coaches, hotels and car rentals [11]. However, the nature of IT development in tourism seems to be primarily driven by product orientation rather than consumer orientation. Much of the industry and academic research in this area has focused on the development of IT systems with the emphasis on a managerial paradigm. Considerably less attention has been given to technologies related to travel counselling and understanding the behaviour of the final consumer - the tourist when in fact the majority of tourism related inquiry stems form tourists seeking travel agents' advice on some aspect of their vacation destination. Recent surveys of tour operators in the US, Europe and Australia suggest that travel agents simply act as "information brokers," providing little assistance to travellers in their travel choice, and many lack expertise in travel counselling [3,7]. This has raised important quality of service issues in the industry. A decision support system using state of the art developments in artificial intelligence seems to be a promising approach in circumventing at least some problems arising from variation in the skills, knowledge, experience and intuition of the travel counsellors. Hruschka and Mazanec [7] note that an expert system designed for the travel agent to assist in travel counselling has not yet been introduced. This may be due to the inherent complexity in modelling preference for an intangible product and the array of influences on the decision process. A starting point in developing such an expert system is study of the consumers' decision making process and factors that influence this process. A considerable amount of literature in consumer behaviour exists on this topic; however, very few of these studies have investigated this issues in the context of tourism, though efforts to examine various aspects of the tourist destination choice [eg. 4,5,8,9,11,14,15] are noteworthy and highlight the relationship between consumer behaviour and marketing strategy.

The aim of this paper is to introduce a decision support technique to help the final consumer select an appropriate holiday destination. Specifically, the paper introduces the use of the analytic hierarchy process (AHP) in combination with choice set theories and motivation factors as a tool in complementing existing tourist counselling systems. First, the existing expert systems relevant to some aspect of tourism counselling are discussed, followed by literature on choice set theory relevant to modelling the consumers' decision process in choosing vacation destination. The AHP modelling process is then described along with its application in tourism counselling in the context of selecting alternative vacation packages.

2. Expert systems

An expert system (ES) is an information system that uses expert knowledge to attain high levels of performance in a well-defined area [1]. We were able to locate only four studies given below on the topic of computer assisted travel counselling.

Bose and Padala [2] introduced Globetrotter - a personal flight scheduler for developing an optimal travel itinerary. Optimisation is achieved through satisfying certain constraints such as cost, flying time, stopovers etc. and a set of assumptions about the traveller. The assumptions are based on an expert's interpretation of information provided by the tourist. For example, if the traveller identifies himself as a business traveller then the program automatically prioretises travel time, number of connections, date of travel and exact destination, and puts less emphasis on cost. The program reasons with incomplete knowledge by constructing a model of the traveller and searches for a set of optimal flights based on user-provided constraints.

Bodi and Zeleznikow [1] have criticised the model because it "makes unwarranted assumptions about the traveller," instead of asking the traveller for his specific requirements. They have addressed this limitation by proposing an expert system based on a deductive database called CATA - computer aided travel assistant. CATA is an extension of the airtravel expert database developed by Freitag and Biernath [6]. Both expert systems operate by using several heuristics, subject to user provided constraints. Some heuristics used in the two systems are: a) search for the shortest route; b) restrict search to international airports; c) consider the best connecting flights with respect to an overall flight time estimate; and d) provide an optimal solution by modifying some of the user specified rules.

Hruschka and Mazanec [7], have proposed a prototype for computer assisted travel counselling using an expert system and retrieval approach. Two programming approaches are proposed - use of an expert system shell and an AI programming language PROLOG. The system operates on the "diagnosis/prescription" paradigm of matching the traveller's concept of an ideal tour from one sector with the tours available in the market on another sector. In the prototype database 127 tours described on more than 100 characteristics were included to provide a match for the tourist specified requirements.

These are important tools that could help the travel agent in structuring their consultation and provide a complete range of travel alternatives that match customer requirements [1,7]. When used in conjunction with existing computer reservation system, they can provide a definite competitive advantage. However, there is considerable scope to improve these expert systems by incorporating state of the art research on consumer choice modelling. For example, all the above systems have relied solely on the conjunctive rule to select the final destination, whereas many studies related to tourism destination choice have recognised that consumers use the compensatory rule at some stage of their decision process [4,5,8,9,11,14]. Le Blanc [8] based on an empirical study concluded that decision models based on the assumption of only one rule in selecting a final destination are likely to have low predictive validity. Thus, a good understanding of the tourist decision making process is crucial in developing an expert system that will adequately represent a travellers preference.

3. Tourist decision making process

Selecting a tourism destination involves complex trade-offs and risks due to the intangible nature of the product and the wide range of available alternatives. Furthermore, cognitive psychologists have confirmed through numerous experiments that there is a finite limit to the capacity of the human brain to process information relating to a large number of alternatives [4,12,13]. A widely accepted theory on how consumers resolve this complexity and arrive at a purchase decision is the notion of choice sets [4,5]. According to this theory, a vacation destination choice can be viewed as emerging from a funnelling process consisting of three phases: i) development of an initial set of destinations called the awareness set, ii) elimination of some destinations from this set to arrive at a smaller acceptable number of destinations, called evoked set, and iii) a final destination selected from those in the late consideration set.

Applying the choice set framework to the consumer decision making process for vacation destinations results in six stages, namely, problem recognition; passive internal search; formation of an initial consideration set; active external search to evaluate destinations in the initial consideration set leading to the formation of the late consideration set; active external search to evaluate destinations in the late consideration set leading to selection of a destination; and postpurchase evaluation [14,15]. "The core of this six-stage model consists of the three central stages that, it is agreed in the tourism literature, constitutes the core process used by potential tourist [5]." However, these three stages of shortlisting alternatives do not illustrate the dynamics of the evaluation process, i.e. the decision rules which are adopted at each stage of the process. Crompton [5] notes that there is no study done on this topic in tourism and suggest three propositions on this issue: a) consumers use different strategy for selecting alternatives for the late consideration set as compared to selecting the final destination from the late consideration set; b) the decision strategy used in evaluating alternatives from the early consideration set will primarily focus on the relative merits of the destination attributes, while the decision strategy used to evaluate alternatives in the late consideration set will focus on the constraints associated with each of the alternative destinations; and c) the number of evaluative criteria used for selecting alternatives at both stages is inversely related to the number of destinations at each stage.

3.1 Decision strategy. Consumers are known to use various decision rules or heuristics to simplify their task of alternative evaluation to arrive at a decision. The rules can be used in combination (mixed strategy) and may vary with the stages of the decision process. The rules are commonly classified as *compensatory* or *noncompensatory* rules [4,9,10,11,12]. In noncompensatory rule trade-offs between attributes do not occur. For example the tourist may evaluate the alternative destinations on two or three key criteria and eliminate destinations that fall short on these key criteria. There are three types of noncompensatory rules: the conjunctive, disjunctive and the lexicographic rule. In a *conjunctive* rule, a destination is selected if it meets the minimum standard on all the criteria. In a *disjunctive rule* a destination is selected if it is perceived to be excellent on one or more key criteria. The *lexicographic* rule uses all criteria but in a stepwise manner. Destinations are evaluated on the most important criterion first. If there is a tie, then the choice is based on the next most important criterion, and so on.

Compensatory rule, on the other hand, assumes a complex cognitive structure and demands the greatest effort on the part of the decision maker of all the decision rules. It requires a systematic and balanced evaluation of all the alternatives on all the criteria and then summing up of the evaluations to derive an overall preference score for each destination. Thus, the weakness of a destination on one criterion can be compensated for by strength on another. The *weighted linear compensatory rule* is similar, with the exception that the criteria ratings are weighted by their importance before they are summed [4,9,10,11]. A reflection of this approach is the analytic hierarchy process described in the next section.

4. The Analytic hierarchy process (AHP)

In this section we provide a brief description of the AHP. Readers unfamiliar with the method can refer to any of the several textbooks written on the subject. A technical text on this topic is listed in the reference section [13]. The Analytic Hierarchy Process proposed by Saaty [13] is a technique used to solve different types of multicriteria problems. The unique aspect of AHP is its flexibility in dealing with qualitative factors, multiple objectives and multiple decision makers. It combines both qualitative and quantitative factors into an integrative framework based on ratio scales from simple pairwise comparisons of objects. It is available on several commercial software packages. The technique can be succinctly described in three steps: structuring the hierarchy; pairwise comparisons to yield priorities; and synthesis of the priorities into composite measures of the decision alternatives or options.

4.1 Structuring the Hierarchy. The first step is to decompose the problem into a hierarchy of interrelated elements such that the overall objective to be achieved is placed at the top level, followed by levels for criteria, subcriteria, and lastly the alternatives or options under consideration. The hierarchy can have more than three levels but for simplicity we will only consider three levels in our illustration. For example, to select the best possible package tour (top level), one has to examine the extent to which the evaluative criteria or benefits (second level) are offered by the alternative package tours (bottom level).

4.2 Pairwise comparison to derive priorities. The next step is to ask a respondent to compare the elements of a level in a pairwise fashion as to their relative importance with respect to an element in the next higher level. This comparison process requires the respondent to answer two questions for each pair of alternatives - 1) with respect to cost which vacation package is more desirable

A or B?, and 2) by how much or how many times? At the level of criteria the questions are 1) with respect to choosing the best package tour which criteria is more important, cost or activities? and 2) by how much or how many times? A semantic differential 9 point ratio scale is used for making the comparison. The paired comparisons are placed in a positive reciprocal matrix ($a_{ij}=1/a_{ji}$) and is the input to the AHP problem of deriving a ratio scale of relative weights of elements at any level of the hierarchy. The matrix contains a certain level of inconsistency ($a_{ij}xa_{jk}=a_{ik}$) due to subjectivity in the respondents' judgement. Under these circumstances the eigen vector method is shown to yield the correct priorities for the elements of the matrix. These priorities are in ratio form and are normalised to sum to one.

The comparison process generates an *inconsistency ratio* which provides feedback to the tourist on how consistent their judgements are and even points out inconsistent comparisons that need to be altered.

4.3 Synthesis of priorities into composite weights. Once the weights are established for each element of the hierarchy, the final step of aggregation can begin. This involves multiplying the weights through the hierarchy and summing up to obtain a composite score for each alternative. The composite score captures the effect of all higher level elements and can be used to rank order the destinations or select the best destination.

5. Application of the AHP in destination choice

The major deficiency of the existing destination counselling systems is the extensive reliance on the conjunctive rule to represent a consumers decision process. In contrast, much of the research on this topic has recognised that consumers' use "mixed strategies"- combination of rules in a sequence to arrive at the final choice [4,5,8,9,11,14]. We propose that in selecting a tourist destination, a non-compensatory conjunctive rule is used first to eliminate alternative destinations quickly and arrive at a manageable number, all of which posses a set level of the evaluative criteria and then a compensatory rule is applied for a more thorough evaluation of the alternatives before making the final purchase decision.

An expert counselling system similar to the one proposed by Hruschka and Mazanec [7] for selection of vacation packages can be used in the first stage to arrive at a manageable number of alternatives via the conjunctive rule. Then the compensatory rule of the AHP procedure is applied to refine the final choice from the evoked set of alternatives. This is done through the systematic evaluation of alternative vacation packages on the evaluative criteria to select the most preferred vacation package. The outcome of the AHP procedure can be input to an expert database such as Globetrotter [2] or CATA [1] to develop an optimal travel itinerary through satisfying constraint provided by the user during the consultation process.

A good expert system for tourism counselling must go beyond the technical details of the tour and incorporate other predictor variables related to destination choice such as travel motives, benefits sought, destination images, and perceived risk [7]. However, there is no set method of designing an expert counselling system and factors such as characteristics of the knowledge representation, rules of reasoning, specification of constraints and so on, dictates its development. Given the developmental nature of the proposed methodology, commercially available expert system shells can be used to design the first stage of the consultation to develop an evoked set of alternative destinations. The knowledge database can be created by itemising the components of the tour and setting a value for each item corresponding to a tour. Several qualitative research techniques such as brainstorming sessions by experts, indepth and focus group interviews of the sample travellers from the target market, repository grid technique and secondary data on destination choice research are available at this stage of developing the items. The matching and retrieval technique of the expert system will provide a set of destinations by eliminating destinations that are totally unacceptable. The conjunctive rule can be used to rapidly reduce the vast number of alternatives in the consumers awareness set. We propose that the elimination process should stop once the number of alternative destinations is reduced to six. This is based on consumer research findings on the upper limit on the number of alternatives from the evoked set a consumer is willing and able to use in their purchase decision [4,13,15]. Next, the tourist may be asked to identify evaluative criteria from a set of possible criteria, which can be used to compare the alternatives through the AHP procedure to select the best destination.

The question of whether the proposed counselling method performs better than the existing methods need to be resolved empirically. The authors are conducting an experiment to test the predictive and convergent validity of the proposed method in the context of evaluation of package holidays.

6. Discussion:

Decision support systems (DSS) in Tourism have mainly focused on tourism planners and practitioners to the complete exclusion of the final consumer - the tourist. Selecting a tourism destination involves complex trade-offs due to the intangible nature of the product, wide range of possible alternatives and the inherent risk of making a wrong decision. The reliance on travel agents intuition does not guaranty the selection of best possible destination. The existing expert systems are also unlikely to result in optimal decisions since they fail to recognise the use of mixed decision strategies used by tourist in high involvement decisions such as destination choice. A decision support system based on the AHP seems to be a very practical and intuitive approach in overcoming this shortcoming of existing expert systems. The AHP can be easily incorporated into the expert system modules to provide a comprehensive framework for a destination counselling system.

A major advantage of using the AHP method in tourism destination choice that is not obvious is its potential role in reducing consumers' post purchase dissonance. It is conjectured that clients who go through the AHP evaluation procedure of selecting a holiday package may experience more satisfaction in their post purchase phase than clients who relied mainly on the travel agent. A client who is involved in every aspect of the decision is more likely to feel responsible for that decision and would not only seek out positive information to support that decision, but also recommend the destination/travel agent to other members in his/her social group to reduce his dissonance.

7. References

1. Bodi A., Zeleznikow J.: CATA: A computer aided travel assistant, In: Faulkner B., Fagence M. (eds): Frontiers in australian tourism: The search for new perspective in policy development and research, 425-432 (1988).

2. Bose P.K, Padala A.M.: Reasoning with incomplete knowledge in an interactive personal flight planning assistant, In Proceedings of the Seventh Avignon Conference on Expert Systems, Avignon, France, 1077-1092 (1987).

3. Choice, Travel agents on trial, Choice, 29, 33-37 (March 1988).

4. Crompton J.L, Ankomah P.K.: Choice set propositions in destination decisions, Annals of Tourism Research, 20, 461-475 (1993).

5. Crompton J.L.: Structure of vacation destination choice sets, Annals of Tourism Research, 19, 420-434 (1992)

6. Freitag B., Biernath O.: An airtravel expert database, In Proceedings of the 3rd International Conference on Data and Knowledge Bases, Jerusalem (1988)

7. Hruschka H., Mazanec J.: Computer-assisted travel counselling, Annals of Tourism Research, 17, 208-227 (1990).

8. LeBlanc R.P.: An exploratory investigation into the relationship between evoked set decisions and final purchase choice, Developments in Marketing Science, 7, 7-11 (1989).

9. Mansfeid Y.: From motivation to actual travel, Annals of Tourism Research, 19, 399-419, (1992).

10. Middleton T.C.: Marketing in travel and tourism, Oxford:Heinemann 1988.

11. Moutinho L.: Consumer behaviour in tourism, European Journal of Marketing, 21(10), 1-44 (1987).

12. Mulye R,: Modelling consumer choice: a comparison of methods, In: Southern Marketing Theory and Applications, Proceedings of the Refereed Section of the 1994 Australian Marketing Conference, Adelaide, 457-474, (1994).

13. Saaty T.L.: The analytic hierarchy process, New York: Mc-Graw Hill 1980.

14. Um S., Crompton J.L: Attitude determinants in tourism destination choice, Annals of Tourism Research, 17, 432-448 (1990).

15. Woodside A.G., Lysonski S.: A general model of traveller destination choice, Journal of Travel Research, 27(4), 8-14 (1989)

International marketing via broadband networks - Building the local network in a Norwegian region

Kari Aanonsen*, Yngve Lindsjørn*, Georg Kamfjord**

*NR, Norwegian Computing Center, P.O. Box 114, Blindern, 0314 Oslo, Norway
phone: + 47 22 85 25 00, fax +47 22 69 76 60
Kari.Aanonsen@nr.no, Yngve.Lindsjorn@nr.no

**BI, Norwegian School of Management, P.O. Box 4636 Sofienberg, 0506 Oslo, Norway, phone: +47 67 57 05 00, fax: 67 57 05 70
Olympia Utvikling - Troll Park, Elvegata 19, 2600 Lillehammer, Norway
phone: +47 612 89 900, fax: +47 612 63 665

Abstract. To introduce the Tourism Information and Marketing system TIM in a geographical region, a number of steps have to be taken at the organizational and the technological level. Some strategic considerations and decisions are also necessary. This paper discusses these steps and decisions, based on our experiences from introducing TIM in the Norwegian region Troll Park, and on the strategic analyses we carry out nationally for further introduction of TIM in Norway.

1. Introduction - Information technology in tourism distribution

International network systems for marketing and selling tourism products are emerging in Europe, gradually introducing new parts of the tourism industry to the benefits of information technology. Up until now the area has been dominated by the large CRSs (Computerbased Reservation Systems) like Amadeus, SABRE and Gallileo (J.Olaisen, 1993, P.J.Sheldon 1993). The CRS service is a distribution tool mainly aiming at the business markets to which the large international companies sell standard products with high volume and high value. Information technology has so fare not been available in form of affordable, effective marketing and sales tools for the part of the industry consisting of medium and small service suppliers scattered around in rural areas, serving the rapidly growing leisure market. A leisure market which growth seems to be based on more specific needs and wants, and thus a demand for more differentiated products on every thinkable resource, activity and experience.

The TIM system (presented elsewhere) represents a further step in the development of advanced telecommunication services to the benefit of numerous small and differentiated service providers throughout the whole tourism industry in Europe (and the world). Local providers of tourism products can use TIM to distribute multimedia information about their products to sales organizations throughout a European wide network. The products can be booked and sold directly via gateways to local and central reservation systems. A Norwegian regional tourism company, Olympia Utvikling - Troll Park, has participated in the TIM project since it started in 1992. Troll Park is now building the organizational and technical network for using TIM to market and sell the various products of the region. The paper is based on experiences from this process. It is also based on analyses performed by the NR, Norwegian Computing Center, as part of our work for the Norwegian Research Council in defining a strategy for using information technology within the tourism business in Norway. NR is also a technical partner in the TIM project.

2. Short description of Troll Park

The Troll Park region covers a large area of mountains and valleys (approx. 155.000 sq. kmts) with Lillehammer as a natural tourism center. There are about 12.000 commercial beds in the area producing some 2.2 million guestnights a year The Troll Park area provides activities such as cross country and alpine skiing in winter and hiking, rafting, tracking, canoeing, cycling, fishing and sightseeing in summer. There also a couple of attraction in the Lillehammer-area and facilities to host meetings and conferences mostly at the national level.

Today these offers are being *promoted* both individually by the single producers by means of traditional media, and through brochures created and published by the local and regional tourist boards. The *selling* is mainly taken care of by the service providers themselves on the national markets, and by traditional tour operators on the international markets. The local or regional tourist boards are not into actual selling of the products. Olympia Utvikling - Troll Park LTD is a company established by the tourism industry and the public interests in the region with the traditional functions of a regional tourist board, but partly due to the increased service to the industry that opens up through the TIM system, the company have decided to serve as a commercial intermediary for the industry in the region.

3. Technical and organizational requirements for a regional TIM network

The TIM system is a distributed multimedia database using ISDN network to transfer information throughout a European wide network. The overall requirement on the TIM architecture is: Multimedia marketing material produced locally, at PoO (Point of Offer) sites should be distributed at user determined times across Europe to user determined locations (PoS/PoI - Point of Sale/Point of Information sites). The multimedia information is stored locally at database servers at all PoO and PoS sites. A *global supervising node* organizes database updates and system use; it does not store the multimedia data. Booking is partly being provided by a *Gateway Server* in Rome. TIM has implemented gateways to some of the big CRSs in Europe (Galileo and Amadeus) for booking of those products that are part of the inventory in these systems, and to one region booking system (Integra) which is also based as a wide area network. As most of the products in question are not on any CRS, booking of these products will take place through a booking facility in the TIM system directly to each PoO. All database servers are running Microsoft NT advanced Server with Microsoft SQL_Server database management system (DBMS). The terminals are running Microsoft Windows for Workgroups on top of MS DOS. Multimedia data as video and sound is central to TIM. The video standard under Microsoft Windows, with AVI video and standard software, is used both in the digitizing, editing and compression process.

The TIM system requires extensive cooperation between partners at the different organizational levels. First of all the regional PoO, representing the product range of the region must establish a close and trustful relationship to the producers that want to be on the system with their product. The structure with one regional PoO will be needed for three main reasons. Firstly because most of the providers will be too small to invest in the technical equipment and human resources necessary to function as a separate PoO or a full TIM node. Secondly it will raise a number of commercial and legal problems if one and each of the service providers should establish his own business relationship to every possible PoS. Thirdly it will represent a crucial possibility for quality control of the products being offered by a specific region to have them presented by a regional company that is also responsible for handling market information, knowing international standards, meeting financial requirements, legal issues etc. These are all advantages for the region with respect to long term image and credibility building, as it is to represent a wide range of the regions diversified and specialized product to a number of target groups on the international markets. This paper focuses on the relationships on the regional level, but it must be noticed that it is left to the regional PoO, according to this structure, to establish business relations to European PoS that might be interested to sell tourism products from the region. This latest issue depends among other things on how the TIM system eventually will be set up internationally.

4. Steps to be taken at the organizational level

To create the network or infrastructure required for TIM, a number of steps have to be taken at the organizational level. We will here describe them as five different steps, but they are closely connected and should not be performed in a strictly sequential order. It will also be fruitful to go through some of them again as the network itself changes and improves.

Different models for the organizational network can be chosen depending on the size of the region, the kind of organizations and businesses involved, their ambitions in regard to international marketing and their access to information technology. (Kamfjord,93). Normally a organizational network for TIM will consist of one or more TIM-representatives which will act as a full TIM-node within the TIM-system representing a number of providers in the region. The central elements forming the economical ties between the participants, will be provisions for booking and advertising costs.

Step 1 - Establish contact with a set of participants

The first step in creating a TIM network is to chose the participants. As a system for marketing leisure products for individual travelers, TIM will contain products from small providers. Involving them in the organizational network is therefore crucial. The role of the tourist boards is central, both in regard to this and because TIM will include general information and marketing material from a region. Since TIM will consist of products that can be booked on-line, an important question for defining their role in the TIM network is whether they can be involved in actual booking activities.

As the regional tourism company in the Troll Park area Olympia Utvikling - Troll Park LTD was the natural unit to take responsibility as the regional PoO. Due to the whole concept of TIM, the company must grow out of the role as a traditional tourist board and prepare for the role as a commercial intermediary in selling the regions tourist products through this new channel of distribution. The bookings will be carried out through an allotment system, but with close relationships to the suppliers involved. Some products like accommodation with capacity limits and individual wishes will obviously need closer follow up than standard products like lift tickets, bicycle rental and other products.

Step 2 - Establish marketing strategy

Regional tourism marketing has for many good reasons, conceptually, historically and financially, not been seen as a very sophisticated contributor to the art of marketing. The introduction of a multimedia distribution system will force the industry to develop knowledge and experience at a new and higher level. The new set of tools are in many senses much stronger, the message needs to be much more concentrated and targeted to build images and brands that are compatible in a marketplace with continuously stronger competition.

The market strategy that needs to be developed must consist of substrategies first of all for products and promotion (image). The product strategy must sort out the overall most profitable product categories, according to demand and product availability and quality, and it must be decided to which extent the products should be presented in the electronic folders as single products, product groups or prepacked products. The promotion strategy must deal with crucial question from the very top dealing with which generic profile if one, the region should tie all its products into, and down to more creative questions related to the communication that takes place in all its new forms. The more one relies on the single suppliers or local tourist boards to participate in the development of inserts (video-clips, pictures, sound, texts and other images) to the electronic folders, the more one will need specific guidelines as help and quality control in the preparations.

Step 3 - Establish routines for cooperation and collaboration

The next step is to specify routines for collecting and producing the multimedia marketing material. The material is built from elements created with standard PC tools. It is therefore a number of ways for the providers and the representative to cooperate in creating the folders for TIM.

Participants without any computer support will have to produce their material the traditional way by filling in forms produced by the TIM representative. Images have to be sent to the representative as negatives or on paper. Videotapes can also be sent as part of their contribution. The TIM representative will then have to type inn the text, scan the images and digitize parts of the video tapes to create the inserts. Finally the representative will have to create the folders with its front cover, and include the inserts. Distribution of the folders to other TIM nodes in Europe will also be done by the representative in this setting.

Participants with standard PCs and basic administrative tools such as a text editor will be able to create the text insert themselves and send these on a disk to the TIM representative. Images and video will be handled the traditional way. The next level of technical support is when the providers have standard equipment for handling multimedia material, i.e. scanner for digitizing images, tools for modifying them and cards for digitizing video and creating AVI-files. With these tools a participant can create most of the material, i.e. all the inserts for a TIM folder. In this setting the representative will only have to create the folder and include the inserts. Text and images can be sent to the representative on disks, but video clips are normally too big. A network connection between them is therefore the next step.

Cooperation can be made much more effective if there are some sort of network connection between providers and representatives. Forms for specific information, text files, images and video clips can then easily be exchanged. Network connection opens for the use of tools such as sending fax directly from the PC, transferring files and using electronic mail. Video telephony can be introduced if the sites have ISDN connections.

The technically most sophisticated way of cooperating, can take place when the participant has a full TIM point-of-offer application with all the tools for handling multimedia and full ISDN network connections. The participant can then create the whole folder and use the TIM system to distribute this to any other TIM node.

Step 4 - Introduce suitable tools and technology for each participant

As described in step 3 the TIM environment is well suited for introducing a wide range of tools and technologies depending on the ambitions and economic abilities of each participant. The tools used for creating marketing material and communication in TIM can also be used for other purposes, such as managing archives for digital images and performing ad hoc communication. The utilization of information technology varies greatly within the tourism business. Part of the business are using advanced systems and networks while many of the actors are using very simple or no technology at all. This is partly due to economical premises and partly due to lack of knowledge about available technology and how to chose the right systems.

As part of introducing TIM in a region, a program for introducing standard tools and technology, including basic network, should therefore be established. This would increase the effect of their marketing efforts within the TIM network and within the business in general. Such a program should include analyses of each participants requirements and specify a step-by-step investment and development plan. The plan should start with basic general tools and technology which can be used for a number of purposes in addition to TIM.

Step 5 - Organize training and support functions

Since many of the participants in the TIM network will be small providers with little experience from this kind of technology, training will be a critical factor for success when establishing the local network. Training will be needed both for using standard PC-tools and for using TIM specific tools. Designing and creating multimedia presentations require specific training where experts in graphical layout should be involved. Communication via networks also requires certain training. Finally establishing new routines for cooperation will require training or special attention for a period of time.

The establishment of support functions will be another critical factor. Small providers will seldom have computer experts within their company and will therefore depend on external arrangements. This can for instance be local vendors. For some of the participants it might be possible to establish support in cooperation with local public administrations centers.

5. Steps to be taken at the technical level

The following description is based on the technical solution in a commercial system, and not in the research phase in which the project is at the moment. The figure on the next page gives an overall idea of the architecture of the system.

Troll Park will typically be a PoO representative in their region in Norway. The PoO representative will normally have 486 DOS/Windows terminals connected to Windows NT server as their basic configuration. The terminal/server solution can alternatively be either 1) server and terminal in one machine or 2) running NT also on the TIM terminals in a LAN network. This solution will give better performance and solve the problems of integration between the DOS operating system and all the other software and hardware. All DOS/Windows software can be run from NT. The Global Supervising Node will be distributed to National level as well as the Gateway Server.

Since small providers seldom have their own booking systems, each PoO representative can have a local booking system which is represented in the National Node as a gateway. The National Node also has a gateway to the big CRSs. The National Nodes play the "Routing" and the "National Booking Gateway" function, and only one machine is needed. Only the PoS nodes and PoO nodes will store multimedia information. The National Node keeps track of all "National folders"; from which PoO representative they "belong" and to which PoS/PoI nodes they are distributed. All the distribution of folders is going through the National Nodes. The PoS/PoI nodes store the folders together with the "Booking Information". When a folder is booked at a PoS a request is sent to the "National Node Booking Gateway" to which the folder belongs. A folder belongs to the PoO representative in the country where it is created.

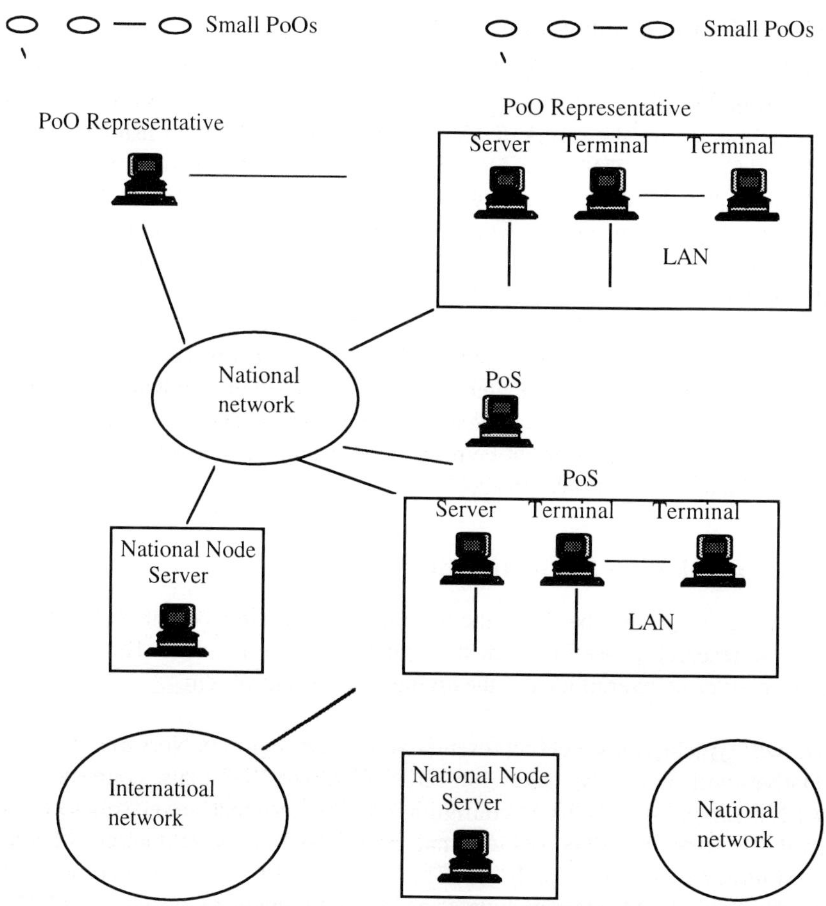

To become a PoO representative, the whole TIM configuration is needed. One or more PCs with at least 1 GB disc, an ISDN line connection (commercial available in most European countries), an ISDN router, NT advanced Server Software, Microsoft SQL-Server DBMS and of course the TIM database and application is minimum. In addition, external hardware and software is needed to make the folder inserts. A scanner is needed to digitize paper based pictures, and a video card is needed to digitize video. TIM uses the *Captivator digitising card.* To play the video and sound, TIM uses the *928 Movie card*. Video for Windows, which has become a standard on PCs today, is used to edit the video. Editing text and pictures for TIM can be done with standard PC software tools such as Microsoft WORD, Word Perfect, Paintbrush, Corel Draw etc.

As described in chapter 2, the small PoOs can be connected to TIM in many ways. One way is not to be "technically" connected at all (not even have a stand alone machine) and let the PoO representative do all the work.

One possible technical solution is to use a stand-alone PC, and make some of the folder-inserts. The first step is to create text based information and simple images. The minimum technical requirement is then standard software for text and image processing. To be able to create multimedia information, the video card and the sound card must be added to the configuration. The economic investment is not more than 1000 ECU. But often, a more powerful processor and larger disc (especially when working with video) is needed. If the PoO wants to have good quality images from paper, a scanner is needed.

One step further is to have an ISDN communication line. Using ISDN, it will take 5-10 minutes to transfer a holiday-product (a *folder* in TIM- terminology) from one site to another, depending on the folder size. The price for the ISDN connection will vary from country to country, but in most cases it is comparable with the cost of the telephone (both connection and use). In addition, an ISDN router or an ISDN adapter card is needed, and will cost approximately 2000 ECU. With this communication line the PoO is able to send inserts to the PoO representative. Other basic network services such as e-mail, file transfer and access to general common information will also be available.

The last step is to invest in the full TIM configuration (as described above), and become a "professional folder maker". To become a PoO representative is now a short step technologically.

6. Strategic challenges

Most of the questions that one will face by entering in to the age of information technology in overall tourism marketing has been pointed at in the paper. A couple of key issues should though be focused on in the end. They are all dealing with economy. First of all one will need a close follow up with business case studies and

Macrodata-integration support for electronic tourism marketing

Karl Anton Froeschl

Institut für Statistik, Operations Research und Computerverfahren
Universität Wien, A-1010 Wien, Austria

Abstract. As tourism information systems come to be also the organizational backbone of tourism management and decision making, the *online* availability of up-to-date and comprehensive market information gains increasing importance. Utilizing the technology of digital network communication tourism information systems already rely upon, an approach to *integrate*, actually *combine*, and *feed back* electronically tourism data aggregates obtained from tourism information systems participating in the network is proposed. The paper discusses a metadata-based model of *semantic* macrodata integration after clarifying the role and difficulties of macrodata integration. The example of bednight statistics is used to illustrate the data model.
Keywords. Tourism information systems, macrodata, data integration.

1 Introduction

Electronic telecommunication media, based on technologies such as ISDN, MAN, or ATM, have already begun to change irreversibly the marketing strategies also in the field of tourism [20]. What is taking place in front of us is a gradual but definite shift away from traditional selling of tourism products by travel agencies towards direct marketing methods exploiting the technological capabilities of electronic (digital) end consumer networks - tourism information becomes delivered directly to the consumers' living rooms. Tourism information systems (TIS, for short) outclass printed advertising matter for several obvious reasons: advertising becomes more effective (market coverage, targeting of market sectors, multimedia presentation), information becomes easier to access and up-to-date. Likewise, TIS equipped with direct-booking facilities will, to a considerable degree, circumvent traditional commercial product distribution channels. Hence, simply speaking, TIS are regarded as important strategic marketing tools in the - electronic - tourism marketplace [10].
In addition to the emphasized orientation of TIS towards end consumers, however, TIS may become indispensable tools for economic disposition [3] and strategic management [19] as well. Stimulated by electronic telecommunication media, tourism markets grow both more transparent and diversified economically, a situation calling for decisions - on the suppliers' side - at tremendously decreasing reaction times based on recent and detailed market information. Apparently it will no longer be sufficient to offer services electronically; economic success (or even bare

survival) will depend on knowing *how* to really sell what is offered in a rapidly changing market. In a broader perspective, it will be even more important to figure out in time *what* one must offer to stay competitive at all. In this respect, complementary to the role of end consumer information systems, TIS possess a not yet fully recognized potential as *strategic* decision support systems. Particularly, as soon as TIS are extended from "simple" one-way tourism information broadcasting media to bidirectional, interactive booking and reservation systems, they constitute a prime source of market information hardly available otherwise (especially non-profit tourist organisations would benefit from the profoundly increasing market information rendered back from the TIS they are running). In fact, TIS are capable to provide efficiently, in a timely fashion, records of market information previously either out of scope or obtainable by expensive market research only. In particular, aggregate data - termed *macrodata* in statistics - summarizing low-level case data (such as travel or hotel bookings) represent valuable assets of "back end" information about trends in customer and market behaviour limited in extent and granularity of data being kept for analysis by cost considerations only.

Typically, a TIS operates at destination level - that is, it comprises a geographic region's touristic offer - since, for reasons of scale, regions (cities) are the basic economic market participators in the context of global competition. As an immediate consequence of this, information about competing destinations is required for devising touristic marketing strategies at the management, destination, or governmental level. This, in turn, raises the problem of making tourism macrodata from different TIS technically and - more important - semantically compatible with each other before consolidated, "global" market information can be *fed back* electronically to local TIS at the strategic management level. At present, however, ready-made solutions for *online* macrodata integration, fully utilizing - at little additional cost - the technological framework and infrastructure TIS already operate in, are still missing. Having that objective in mind, this paper sets out to bridge the apparent gap in tourism data processing by proposing a macrodata integration approach originating from the official statistics domain.

After discussing the functions and effects of macrodata in future tourism marketing, section 3 presents a logical data model designed to integrate macrodata of comparable semantic content but coming from different *heterogeneous* (that is, differing in structure as well as terminology) data sources based on the concept of *metadata* (which, coarsely speaking, is data *about* data [11]). For the sake of illustration, an example is sketched in section 4. The closing section summarizes some - preliminary - conclusions.

2 Tourism information systems and macrodata

In a TIS including booking facilities the basic information transmitted refers to individual accommodation and travel bookings. In general, this basic information is supplemented with information specific to both, individual suppliers of tourism services and the respective destination as a whole. Provided that different types of transactions (such as bookings, information requests, etc.) can be captured in standardized data formats ("records", *microdata* in statistical terminology [13]), it is fairly easy - and cheap - to collect the transaction instances for further processing (as a pertinent example of data capturing by point-of-sale monitoring cf. [14]). Formally, a transaction record ("case") comprises a predetermined set of case characteristics ("observed variates") describing a case's features of interest. For instance, a hotel booking transaction record may consist of data about hotel category, type of room booked, tourists' nation of residence, duration of stay, etc. Applying statistical data aggregation functions to such instance collections yields macrodata at the TIS level (to be precise, *log-time* macrodata and *transaction-time* macrodata have to be distinguished, the latter concerning the actual state of a TIS - such as the number of hotel rooms currently vacant - and not being considered further). Essentially, TIS log-time - that is: time-tagged - macrodata can be viewed as multi-dimensional tables (of counts) broken down by various taxonomic criteria (such as hotel category, source country of traveller, accommodation type, etc.). These - series of - tables are open to further data analytic investigation to figure out market as well as end consumer behaviour either at enterprise or destination level and can be passed on directly to computerized data analysis systems (such as TourMIS, cf. [22]).

Viewed strategically, given that TIS indeed provide market information in terms of macrodata, the *integration* of macrodata becomes practically relevant in order to combine data at yet higher (national and international) levels or - for developing effective marketing policies - to compare competing destinations by, for instance, generating market portfolios, etc. Traditionally, at a national level tourism data has, by law, to be reported periodically conforming to legal standards typically using paper as primary data carrier. Despite the advantage of national uniformity of collected tourism (macro-)data, this procedure is hopelessly out of date because (i), apparently, it tends to be slow and tedious and (ii), what is more severe, much of the collected information is lost on its way due to intermediary aggregation steps cutting down the volume of reported data. This is particularly unfortunate since already incurred data production costs are wasted unduly. From an open systems view, neither should available data be destroyed voluntarily nor should data be lost simply because of differing technical or semantic standards. It is, however, a fact that different data sources (most evidently at the international level) obey different formats just as individual TIS (will) use different technical standards, logical data models and terminologies ("data languages"). As a natural consequence, the integration of heterogeneous distributed data - constrained by attainable compulsory standards and technically manageable flexibility - becomes a valuable research target.

Amongst the obstacles to data integration to be overcome, *semantic integration*, or data harmonizing, is the most intricate one. Doubtlessly, technical integration is an indispensable prerequisite to any kind of data harmonizing but those tasks (setting up data interchange formats, for instance) have turned out to be solvable easier than subject-matter issues which are entangled intimately with questions of local data source autonomy: as soon as a data integration approach is about to threaten this autonomy, it is almost certainly doomed to fail (and only partly so due to cost concerns regarding local system adaptation). Besides, semantic data integration does not only involve the spatial dimension; every now and then data semantics change even within local data sources (for instance, by redefinition of classifications forced by changes in legal regulations, etc.). Any data integration approach incapable to cope with discontinuities in either of the dimensions, space and time, were a disastrous misconception since it would fall short of maintaining and providing a comprehensive body of market information to the economic decision maker.

Consequently, any viable data integration design necessarily builds a new semantic layer "above" existing and evolving sub-systems (relying on, of course, and drawing advantages of preceding technical sub-system integration). A starting point for semantic integration layer definition is provided by current national subject-matter standards (for instance, quality classifications) which have, in future at least, to be supported by all involved - local - TIS anyway. Expectedly, some local systems will surpass minimal data reporting requirements (for internal information services, at least) by orders of magnitude; thus, in principle, these systems could deliver considerably more information than required legally (however, surplus information might not be accessible free of charge).

In the present context, a semantic data integration approach is advocated which intentionally preserves local data source standards (such as legal constraints, data production schemata, nomenclatures, data quality, etc.) most extensively except that a couple of weak, though mandatory *interface* conventions have to be met. Essentially, by introducing a metadata framework (that is, predefined *second-order* data structures describing first-order data formally) these requirements are confined to (i) a canonical self-description of interface data structures in terms of metadata to be conveyed in conjunction with macrodata such as to enable subsequent automated data processing and (ii) a unified data export format of local macrodata (and, of course, of metadata as well) which - some aspects of data privacy possibly excepted for the time being - are brought about rather easily (e.g., cf. [1]'s macrodata generator proposal). Now, on top of these plain conventions data sources (that is to say: TIS) are joined in an *aggregate tourism information network* (ATIN, for short) representing a heterogeneous distributed database operating in client/server mode (with respect to a similar approach cf. [17]) where

- local data sources (TIS) act as *servers* (points-of-offer), data request sites - TIS again, for instance - act as *clients* (points-of-demand);
- only *global* meta-information necessary for navigating through the ATIN and indispensable for resolving data requests (normally) reside at client sites whereas local metadata as well as the bulk of macrodata is stored distributed at local data producing sites (thus avoiding artificial mega-databases and focussing on "lean", demand-driven data traffic over the network);
- data aggregation from source macrodata up to high-level aggregates ready for user display and investigation is deferred until as late as possible (that is: until demanded actually), thus accounting for the cardinal design principle of enabling definite derivation of *all* statistical aggregates logically possible within the ATIN;
- the traditional data reporting paths are replaced by electronic media, thereby obtaining both required transmission speed and data volume transmission rates.

At the very core of the ATIN approach there is a *global semantic (meta-)data model* actually integrating the local sites encompassed in the network. In other words, there is a comprehensive formal-theoretic domain language capable to re-express the semantics of the local sites' data languages. The only preparatory measures to actually integrate a TIS into the ATIN with respect to agreed-upon interface conventions comprise (i) the compilation of (low-level) data aggregates - from data of the TIS's transaction component - delivered to the ATIN and (ii) the generation of local metadata describing those aggregates formally. It should be noted that, compared to attempts of full-fledged multimedia integration of TIS (such as [2]), this task is considerably simpler due to "innate" data type homogeneity. Moreover, with respect to macrodata the situation is completely analogous to the task of integrating official statistics (macro-)data - for instance, merging national aggregates at the European community level - for which reason a transfer of technical approaches and experiences to the field of tourism seems advisable.

3 A macrodata integration approach based on metadata

During the last decade research in statistical databases - as contrasted with more conventional, traditionally commercially oriented (relational) databases - has established its own field [15]. In spite of superficial similarities, both data semantics and database operations differ considerably between both domains [21], a circumstance which, unsurprisingly, gave rise to the development of specific statistical data models and operators tightly geared to them. With respect to database querying, however, in both domains - in favour of easy usage of databases - a strict separation of query *statement* and the subsequent query-answering *process* is aimed at: ideally, a database query states a particular *view* on data non-procedurally (that is, in terms of a logical assertion, or theorem) whereas the actual derivation of responses is brought about deductively, mainly by using a database's self-descriptive information (such as data dictionaries). This *problem solving* view of database querying has been accentuated particularly with statistical databases since, evidently, the derivation of (higher-level) data aggregates requires, in general, a little more than simple retrieval of stored data. As a rule, query answering now also involves a statistical-methodological transformation (summing, weighting, estimation, etc.) of either case or pre-aggregated data. This, in turn, touches on the endeavours in statistical analysis strategy formation undertaken in the development of so-called *statistical expert systems* [5] which strongly emphasized the role of statistical metadata [12]. Hence, viewing statistical databases as specific query-answering, or problem solving, systems the mechanics of query processing coincide with a formal proof procedure in a metadata calculus generating, as "side effect", database responses at the (macro-)data level [8]. One particular approach to develop such a metadata calculus [7] stresses the semantic macrodata integration aspect in the field of official statistics databases and is presented in its outlines subsequently since it is precisely targeted at the integration of distributed, (semantically) heterogeneous databases, that is, it fits perfectly the ATIN structure as defined above. Throughout, it should be kept in mind strictly that a formal *data model*, not an implementation scheme, is discussed.

Conceptually, the starting point of the proposed data model is a distinction of well-defined *populations*, viz. collections of "homogeneous" instances (sampling frames, statistically) each of which is described in terms of a *property space* (PS, for short). More precisely, the PS of a population is generated by a couple of descriptive dimensions (variables) to each of which a set of values is assigned (for the sake of uniformity and model simplicity, all value sets are assumed finite-discrete and ordered); thus, formally, a PS can be identified with the Cartesian product (cross-classification) of the descriptive dimensions' value sets. Together, descriptive dimensions and value sets, termed (population) *frames*, provide a set-algebraic intensional *data language*. In general, there is a lot of semantic structure in such a data language (like relationships between descriptive dimensions as well as within value sets) to be represented formally in a metadata-based DBMS which, however, will not be considered here for the sake of brevity.

Given that PS induce well-defined classifications of their respective populations, any instance of a population matches one (and only one) value combination ("tuple") of the attached Cartesian product. Apparently, this condition assures the *additivity* property of frames mandatory for statistical data aggregation and tuples can be used properly as count registers holding the number of occurrences (statistically) of value combinations (viz. instances) or as instance identifier containers. Note that, for all frame dimensions, an instance's values represent the PS "coordinates" determining its logical storing, or counting, register. In general, a domain of discourse consists of several such population frames the instances of which may be linked by (binary) relationships associating instance identifiers. Furthermore, the data model assumes that - after some preprocessing, possibly - each macrodatum refers to exactly one of the discerned frames.

Now, in view of a *distributed* domain of discourse producing macrodata - in different places at different times - pertaining to (some of) the population frames defined in the domain we may state that

- macrodata can be represented generally in PS format (this means, in particular, homogeneity of representation of aggregate, or sum, information) basically by reversing the view of instance (or: micro-) data as a one-element key (identifier) accompanied by n attribute fields to an n-attribute key with an identifier label attached;
- *local* PS usually differ with respect to frames, that is, descriptive dimensions and - particularly - value sets (this means heterogeneity of classifications).

Provided that the discerned populations can be agreed upon in a given subject-matter domain (which should not turn out as controversial issue) the cardinal task of data integration consists of arranging a *translating relation* between the source macrodata's PS (in fact, there are considerably less data sources than macrodata objects conforming to - quite constant - local terminological standards since, in general, each data source produces (time-) series of macrodata; thus, by and large, local PS become associated with data sources rather than individual macrodata). In contrast to arranging a symmetric translating relation between all involved local PS, which might imply prohibitive efforts, it seems favourable to devise a - fictitious - global PS (for each frame) with a data language fine-grained enough to allow the formal re-expression of local data languages in terms of PS-*mappings*. Technically, this amounts to defining a function, for each local PS, associating each local frame tuple with the semantically corresponding *set* of global frame tuples (details cf.

[7,8,9]). In plain words, local PS are re-defined as (not necessarily exhaustive) typologies at the global data language level. These mappings, or *embeddings* (represented formally as *semantic metadata* [6]), of data sources into the global frames provide the backbone of semantic macrodata integration to be held at the client sites of a distributed database like the ATIN.
Addiction to the global PS approach beneficially yields a neutral (with respect to local idioms) data language that can be utilized as uniform *query language* as well. Access to source (that is: local) macrodata is facilitated internally, at the semantic level, by means of embedding metadata and, thus, may proceed entirely hidden from the system's users. This way only the data aggregates of interest need to be stated assertively, leaving questions of data language translation to local frames and request routing to the DBMS.
In formal terms, database requests are yet another sort of macrodata differing from source macrodata mainly with respect to a drastically reduced set of cross-classifying dimensions (in a sense, output macrodata correspond to rather *coarse* typologies of populations). Hence, in addition to a *selection* of source macrodata (which, basically, implies a selection of servers within the distributed database framework), request processing involves internally also a *data aggregation* step comprising, in general, the table management operations of *restricting* (selecting values of descriptive dimensions), *(re-)grouping* (combining values into groups or clusters), and *projecting* (dropping descriptive dimensions entirely) [8]. Although individual requests may become fairly complex, they can be broken down to a sequence of elementary table management operations throughout, possibly augmented with interspersed statistical (table) operations such as weighting or estimating (scaling up). Nested tables as well as tables of other summary type (such as *rate*) are dealt with easily by appropriate alignment or arithmetic processing of elementary tables ("flat" tables of summary type *count*). Furthermore, frequently repeated requests can be "frozen" to *standard database views* such that intermediate or high level data aggregates are provided directly rather than generated anew each time they are requested.

4 The case of bednight statistics

As an example illustrating the proposed macrodata integration approach, bednight statistics will be considered since it has been of predominant interest in tourism statistics. The model does not, of course, preclude any extensions in scope.
Typically, in tourism statistics periodically recorded data comprise both sales-oriented and supply-oriented data. The latter refer to tourism enterprises (service providers) described in terms of enterprise characteristics (hotel category etc.), (lodging) capacity as well as various accommodation features (additional services offered such as indoor swimming pools etc.). Enterprises physically belong to tourism destinations (more specifically: political administration units); thus, they implicitly get classified spatially as well. Sales-oriented data, on the other hand, record information about tourist arrivals and bednights. Since generated by enterprises these data records are - or remain - closely linked to supply-oriented data. In traditional data tapping schemes, no information describing destinations as a

whole is captured - this, however, is likely to change with spreading usage of TIS since destination data build a fundamental part of TIS services.
Among the data aggregates of prime interest are absolute figures of enterprises, beds, tourist arrivals, and bednights, as well as derived figures such as averages like firm size (beds/enterprise), stay in days (approx. bednights/arrivals), or bed utilization (bednights/beds). Usually, aggregates are broken down with respect to one or more classifications such as accommodation type/category, source country of travellers, region/municipality, time/season, travelling motive, etc. (as an example cf. [16]). Quite in contrast, no information about price levels etc. is provided for various reasons.
In view of the data model introduced in section 3, there are different ways of frame definition conceivable. A rather parsimonious domain model, taking its traditional bearings, could consist of a single frame encompassing *all* of the descriptive dimensions involved. Apparently, individual enterprises would have to be the frame's instances and making provision for a lossless representation of instance data on, say, a daily basis of reporting would have to include a separate frame dimension for each independently recorded enterprise feature. Using the codes *E*, *B* and *N* for scale types *enumerative*, *binary* (that is, an *E* scale with two values - yes and no - only), and *(finite) cardinal*, respectively, stating clusters of related frame dimensions upper case, and letting denote composed (that is, to be factored out) dimensions by the ⊗ sign, the resulting global PS would consist of descriptive dimensions as follows:

- *accommodation type* (hotel, pension, hostel, camping site, ...): *E*;
- *category* (*, **, ***, ****, *****, ...): *E*;
- *n*-BED-ROOM (*1-bed, 2-beds, ...*) ⊗ ROOM-FACILITES (*hot water, shower, bath; central heating; room telephone; TV-set; ...*): *N*;
- GENERAL-FACILITIES (*indoor swimming pool, tennis court, sauna, ...*): *B*;
- SOURCE (e.g., nations of residence) ⊗ FREQUENCIES: *N*;
- *space* (e.g., community districts): *E*;
- *time* (e.g., days): *E*.

Dimension clusters may be as simple as FREQUENCIES comprising only two items, viz. *arrivals* and *bednights* (resulting in frame dimensions like *France.arrivals*: *N* and *France.bednights*: *N*), or as complicated as ROOM-FACILITIES which itself, in Austria at least, is a collection of lower-level dimension clusters (thus producing frame dimensions looking like *1-bed.bath.central_heating.phone.TV.minibar*: *N* or *2-bed.shower.central_heating.no_phone.no_TV.no_minibar*: *N*). Given that *n*-BED-ROOM comprises *b*, ROOM-FACILITIES *r*, GENERAL-FACILITIES *a*, and SOURCE *s* dimensions, this *enterprise* frame bears a sum total of $4+a+b*r+2s$ dimensions for each of which an individual instance may carry a value (although, for a particular enterprise, most of the time only the values of $2s$ dimensions will change daily). Practically, due to differences in local data source PS only part of these dimensions might be covered; moreover, source dimensions as well as values may be in *1:n* relation to global PS dimensions and/or values thereof. With respect to this "missing" information instance counts pertain to *collections* of frame tuples as defined in PS mappings [7]. Since, in general, TIS cover a certain geographical area, data sources (local PS) become aligned along the *space* dimension. The temporal

axis is added as yet another dimension formally, gathering the temporal reference points of cross-sectional source macrodata.
In this simple data model, the derivation of aggregates requires merely summing up (with respect to *E* scales) or weighted summing (with respect to *N* scales) operations. For instance, obtaining the sum total of *bednights*, for some point or period of time, amounts to (i) aggregating over all dimensions except *bednights*, thus obtaining - somewhat unusual - an *enterprise* count c_j for each possible bednight value (j=0,1,2,...,J), and (ii) computing $\sum_{j=1}^{J} jc_j$. Should this, say, be broken down with respect to source countries of travellers, the very same procedure had to be repeated separately for each SOURCE-country (such as *France.bednights*, *UK.bednights*, ...).
Because of its conceptual simplicity, the one-frame domain model is rather terse. For instance, the SOURCE ⊗ FREQUENCIES portion could be modeled as a separate frame of population *sold-night*, possibly augmented with further traveller feature dimensions (as obtainable, say, from registration forms at check-in time, etc.) and linked to the *enterprise* frame by a *n:1* instance relation. Adding destination data suggests a further extension of the model to comprise a *destination* frame, linked to the *enterprise* frame by a *1:n* instance relation.

5 Conclusions

At present, it is rather difficult to assess the impact of TIS on the overall structure of the tourism market. Even more difficult is predicting seriously how marketing policies will respond. Less doubtful, however, is the role of aggregate market information in future tourism marketing: any marketing policy will make use of tourism macrodata and even better so, if information is readily available *within* TIS. The proposed data integration model tries to anticipate an answer to this emerging demand by advocating an open systems, client/server approach easily adaptable to changing technical as well as terminological standards. Although being open to *any* data source of tourism macrodata which can be integrated in terms of PS mappings, the outlined approach, admittedly, indicates a possible information-technological solution only; it leaves open intricate economic, social and legal questions. Just to mention one facet, the then still present market imperfections may call for specific legal regulations as to who will be admitted access to which type of available market information in what time and at which prices - apparently, the ubiquitous presence of global market information will definitely change market dynamics and offer hitherto unknown opportunities to those having means and know-how to exploit the new information resources. Thus, the development of technical solutions must be accompanied with serious economic as well as ethical considerations, if technology - once again - should not introduce problems involuntarily it is bound to resolve.

References

1. Appel, G.: A Metadata Driven Statistical Information System. In: [4] (pp. 291-309).

2. Austin, W., et al.: Processing Travel Queries in a Multimedia Information System. In: [18] (pp. 64-71).
3. Ernst, M., Walpuski, D.: Information Technologies and Tourism Markets. In: [18] (pp. 228-235).
4. EUROSTAT: Statistical Meta Information Systems. Luxembourg: Office for Official Publications of the EC 1993.
5. Froeschl, K.A.: Mechanisierte Statistik: Numerische Algorithmen und formale Strategien. Doctoral thesis, Univ. Wien 1989.
6. Froeschl, K.A.: Semantic Metadata: Query Processing and Data Aggregation. In: Dodge, Y., Whittaker J. (eds.): Proc. in Computational Statistics - COMPSTAT '92. Heidelberg: Physica 1992 (pp. 357-362).
7. Froeschl, K.A.: Towards an Operative View of Semantic Metadata. Stat. J. UN/ECE 10 (2), 181-194, 1993.
8. Froeschl, K.A.: A Metadata Approach to Statistical Query Processing. To appear in Statistics and Computing.
9. Froeschl, K.A.: Metadata-Based Processing of Statistical Data Aggregates. Habilitation thesis, Univ. Wien, forthcoming.
10. Froeschl, K.A., Werthner, H.: Die Konzeption von Tourismus-Informationssystemen. In: Schertler, W. (ed): Strategische Bedeutung neuer Informations- und Kommunikationstechnologien im Tourismus. (In print).
11. Hand, D.J.: Data, Metadata and Information. Stat. J. UN/ECE 10(2), 143-151, 1993.
12. Hand, D.J.: Statistical Expert Systems. Chance 7(1), 28-34, 1994.
13. Lenz, H.-J.: A Rigorous Treatment of Microdata, Macrodata, and Metadata. In: Dutter, R., Grossmann, W. (eds.): Proc. in Computational Statistics - COMPSTAT '94. Heidelberg: Physica 1994 (pp. 357-362).
14. Maartmann-Moe, E., Byerley, P., Guinanco, R.: The TIM Project: Tourism Information and Marketing. In: [18] (pp. 164-170).
15. Michalewicz, Z. (ed): Statistical and Scientific Databases. New York et al.: Ellis Horwood 1991.
16. ÖSTAT: Der Fremdenverkehr in Österreich im Jahre 1993 - Beiträge zur österr. Statistik, Heft 1.132. Wien: Österr. Staatsdruckerei 1994.
17. Sadreddini, M.H., Bell, D.A., McClean, S.: Metadata for Integrating Distributed and Heterogeneuos Statistical Databases. In: [4] (pp. 207-219).
18. Schertler, W., et al. (eds.): Information and Communications Technologies in Tourism. Wien-New York: Springer 1994.
19. Schertler, W.: Tourism 2000 - an Information Business. In: [18] (pp. 20-26).
20. Schmid, B.: Electronic Markets in Tourism. In: [18] (pp. 1-8).
21. Shoshani, A.: Statistical Databases: Characteristics, Problems and Some Solutions. In: Gentle, J.E. (ed): Proc. Computer Science and Statistics: The Interface. Amsterdam, New York: North Holland 1983 (pp. 9-23).
22. Wöber, K.: Strategic Planning Tools Inside the Marketing-Information-System in Use by the Austrian National Tourist Office. In: [18] (pp. 201-208).

Acknowledgement. *Hannes Werthner* encouraged me to write this paper; he also made valuable comments on earlier drafts of it.

The system architecture of CitySoft/GermanSoft

Dr. Raymond Fleck

Ploenzke Informatik, Business Unit Travel/Transport/Tourism,
Wilhelmstraße 48, 65183 Wiesbaden, Germany

Abstract. The ideas and the components of CitySoft/GermanSoft (CGS), a reservation system for the regional tourist market in Germany, are described.

1 The aim of CitySoft/GermanSoft (CGS)

CGS is a reservation system (under development) for the regional tourist offices in Germany. It should provide a system for the tourist market in the whole country.

Every service provider in CGS will be able to sell his products to other CGS-participants, to travel agencies and later on direct, to the customer. The way to the travel agencies is explained in more detail in the following section.

An important factor in the success of CGS is the large amount of products, which can be booked over the system. The basis for a broad range of providers within the system is in place. These include existing contracts with important service providers, the possible connection from so-called umbrella systems, and another possibility for existing software solutions to connect their system to CGS.

At a later time it is planned to merge the CGS-System with the system TicketSoft, which is already installed at several service providers, to one system. TicketSoft is a system, developed from START Ticket, to sell tickets, e.g. for theatres. If the necessary broad basis for CGS is reached, it can become an important reservation system for the regional tourist market in Germany.

But there are also international aspects involved, like multi-lingual abilities and the consideration of different tax systems, which already have focussed the interest of several other european countries in CGS.

2 Selling the products through the travel agencies

The distribution channel of the products from CGS through the travel agencies is made possible with a connection between CGS and the most important user-interface for tourist reservations in Germany, the TOMA-procedure. Through TOMA the travel agencies are used to book flights, hotels and other touristic services.

TicketSoft connects to KART, a similar user-interface for the selling of tickets by travel agencies.

TOMA and KART were developed by START Informatik GmbH, the leading distribution provider of a computer reservation system in Germany.

The connection to TOMA is made possible through an interface between the central computer of CGS and START.

3 The central computing unit of CGS

The central computing unit of CGS serves both the direct management of single providers and the control of the connection to all CGS-systems, especially for using the TOMA-procedure. The information about the products from all connected systems is stored in this central unit and lessens the burden of communication within the CGS-net.

With this mechanism it is possible to wait for sending a message to a CGS-system as long as possible within the booking process.

But the load in this central unit is enormous, the need for storage memory can get a problem in the future, depending on the success of CGS. Therefore the software has to be constructed in a transparent way, as far as "getting the information" is concerned. So one has the possibility to *distribute* the storage if necessary.

4 A CGS-system

A CGS-System consists of the different modules, which are needed and seperately bought by the purchaser of a system.

For this reason CGS is modular, you can first buy a limited version and easily extend your system afterwards.

Within one CGS-system you can manage many service providers with their quotas or you can connect to so-called individual solutions.

5 Connection to individual solutions

In this context with individual solution we denote software programs, e.g. for smaller regional tourist offices, which originally were not developed for use within CGS. The developers of such systems can get the description for an interface to CGS and therefore expand their systems by a connection to CGS. Therefore it is possible to book the products of the individual solution within CGS and through a travel agency.

It is already planned to perform such connections to CGS.

Through this interface it will be possible to reach a broad spectrum of cities and regions.

6 Service providers

Hotels and tour operators can hold their quotas at a CGS-system or the central CGS-computer. To buy a CGS-system makes sense for larger companies or whole regions.

7 Multimedia-Info-Towers

Later it is planned to create information towers with multimedia components. First they are used as a POI (point of information), but later on they will be expanded to POS-stations (point of sale).

In the project TicketSoft, some work has already been done in the area of POS.

8 Direct access for customers

Also there are plans for a possible direct connection to the customers. Then they can use their PC at home for the booking of the next holiday. At least one can get information this way, perhaps using the 'Datex-J'-net of the German Telecom, and then book the products through one of the travel agencies, which are included in the system.

9 The 'Touristische Informationsnorm' (TIN)

The Tourist Information Norm TIN is a proposed standard for reservation systems, which in many cases is influenced by TOMA. A great part of it deals with the selection of products. One of the aims of CGS is to use this standard for their system, making TIN popular to the rest of the reservation community.

10 Object-oriented development

Another interesting feature in the development of CGS is, that the whole project is based on an object-oriented method. After an OOA and OOD the language for implementing CGS will be C++.

The OOA was based on a study, in which the requirements for a reservation system were discussed with users and experts of existing software. So it was possible to consider the essential aspects together with the necessary improvements.

As method we used OOA/OOD by Coad/Yourdon. To manage the dynamical aspects of the problem domain we established scenarios.

References

1. Touristische Informationsnorm (TIN), Marketing-Beratung Dr. Helmut Fried & Partner

2. TOMA-Verfahren, Trainingshefte, START AMADEUS Vertrieb

3. Untersuchung der Einsatzmöglichkeiten von Standardsoftware für CitySoft für die START Holding GmbH, Ploenzke Informatik, GS Verkehr/Transport/Touristik

4. Voranalyse zum Projekt CitySoft für die START Holding GmbH, Ploenzke Informatik, GS Verkehr/Transport/Touristik

5. Voranalyse zum Projekt GermanSoft für die START Holding GmbH, Ploenzke Informatik, GS Verkehr/Transport/Touristik

6. Projektdefinition City-/GermanSoft für die START Informatik GmbH, Ploenzke Informatik, GS Verkehr/Transport/Touristik

7. Unterlagen aus der Analysephase

Tourism and Technology

Peter Kruger

Abstract The nature of tourism today and, if present trends continue, the form it is likely to take at the end of the decade, has the potential to cause widespread disruption in many parts of the world. There are two sides to tourism in the age of mass travel; for the western traveller the private beach in the Bahamas represents peace, seclusion and relaxation in idyllic and luxurious surroundings, it is, however, seen in a different light by the native population to them it as part of their homeland from which they are excluded and within which they are regarded as a second class citizen. The question we must ask is can technolo gy be used to solve the problems tourism causes or will it make matters worst for the tourist industry, the tourist and the host countries?

Tourism on Trial

Whether it is poverty pushed into the back streets out of sight of tourists, or the false and degrading interpretation of local customs re-enacted to reinforce the preconceived notions of visitors. Whether its the Oberammergau reduced to the status of Disney World or fishing villages in Spain destroyed and rebuilt as British and German fun factories. Often the scale of damage to indigenous culture is on a par with that caused by a small war. In some respects mass tourism has become a cultural battle between the materialism of the West, and the way of life enjoyed by the rest of the world. The armies who set off on twentieth century crusades do so with the aim of forcing the countries they invade to either modify their culture or in some cases abandon it altogether. There are limits to the continuance of this behaviour, even if the terrific waste of resources which it represents can be supported by the troubled economies of the developed world resistance in areas which already suffer from cultural will ensure further growth is limited.

The Role Of Automation

Technology has the potential to accelerate the growth of tourism. Computerised booking, point of sale terminals is making travel more efficient, more accessible and in some cases almost impulsive - for example last minute holidays at airports. This is, however, serving to expand the least desirable and potentially most troublesome area of the tourist industry. Appreciation of local customs and a desire to absorb alternative cultures is hardly uppermost in the mind of someone who only decided on their destination an hour before getting on the aeroplane.

Possibilities for Virtual Reality

The applications, other than those used to enhance administration, for technology in the tourist industry. Holidays could become virtual, we would only view other cultures via television or experience other environments using data gloves and headsets. Even if computer and communication technology advanced to the point where this was not a sub-standard experience, we would merely be exchanging a sociological for a psychological problem and in the long run if all mans experiences become virtual how do we justify his physical presence anywhere. Virtual reality has a part to play in a balanced application of technology. We are seeing a growth in the number of enclosed holiday centres where the climate - one of the prime concerns for the holidaymaker - is controlled and the weather is guaranteed. In these holiday centres there are many and varied applications for virtual reality and related technology for example as infotainment for children.

The Need For Appropriate Technology

There is now potential using ISDN and ATM for simulated face to face contact and the downloading of multimedia information. So far the only real application in the tourist industry has been the selling of package holidays or previewing destinations as part of a multimedia holiday brochure. The same technology can be used to address individual needs of the tourist to some extent taking the “mass” out of “mass tourism” and changing the motivation for travel. This is more likely to affect the younger generation as access to modern communication technology will appear first in education and not have a significant impact for another decade . Enhanced communication systems can be used to develop inter-personal contacts with people in other countries and also to view and gain an understanding of cultures different from their own. There is no longer a need to pre-package tourist information. The ‘Tele-presence’ provided by video conferencing means there is no need to invade the space either of the society or the individual to gain a better appreciation of the region they intend to visit. The motivation to travel can change from a mere sightseeing trip to a social visit and the psychological barrier which prevents tourists visiting other countries as a family unit or as an individual can, to some extent, be overcome.

Work has already been carried out in Europe and America to assess the impact of enhanced inter-personal communications between groups from different and varied cultural backgrounds. Some of this work has been carried out by Digithurst and trials have been undertaken to assess the impact of inter-personal communications on the attitudes of young people as a preliminary process prior to an actual physical visit or holiday.

Conclusion

It would be wrong to believe that, in the future, there will be no demand for package holidays, this will always exist due to the economies of scale There must, however, be a change in attitude towards tourism and the scope for providing a richer and more rewarding experience for the traveller - which in the long term will benefit the industry as a whole. Although these changes seem radical and idealistic it is likely that they will arise from necessity rather than a desire to improve the image of the tourist or tourism. Nevertheless the role of technology within this process of change cannot be ignored.

OOSEM - a complete oo-development process for developing touristic framework

Dr. Josef Withalm

SIEMENS AG AUSTRIA (Europe)

Abstract. There are so many different methods in use for oo-software development, but almost none of them covers the complete development process (analysis, design, realization, application, project-management, quality-assurance, configuration-management). There are also only few strategies for testing.
The tutorial gives a survey of OOSEM (Object-Oriented System-Engineering Method), a method comprising a set of guidelines covering the whole lifecycle of oo-software development. This lifecycle is divided into several phases (start,analysis, class-design, subsystem-design, class-specification, class implementation, integration, systemtest, product-acceptance and application), each phase is described by its requirements, activities and results. The project-management has to decide in what order which phases to use and which technical activities to perform. the quality-assurance has to decide which activities to plan and/or to perform to make sure that all quality requirements are supported. You will be informed how to perform project-control. A small case study is used to explain the methodological steps.

Following this OOSEM we are developing a touristic-framework in two steps:

1. by implementing concrete projects both in the incoming and outgoing sector for well-known tour-operators
2. by installing three developing teams making
    - analysis
    - application development
    - framework development

1 Introduction

As already mentioned in the abstract none of the different methods for developing oo-software covered the complete development process. So we tried to develop a new method which meets the following requirements:

- usable for developing object-oriented software
- method without any new and specific notations
- tries to use the opportunities of structured analysis and design
- is not a rival to the functional approach.

In 1989 we decided to adapt the existing method for software development of PSE (SEM) for object-oriented technology. 1990 we started a cooperation project with the Technical University of Vienna. The aim was an object-oriented methodology (MOOD). In 1992 „MOOD" was completed. The result was OOSEM.

2 OOSEM Method

OOSEM is a method for development of object-oriented software at Siemens Austria PSE.

2.1 Generel

The basic structure of OOSEM is adopted from SEM (System-Engineering-Method). It is divided into

- ooEM (Engineering Manual) - WHAT is to do ? and
- ooDPM (Development Procedures Manual) - HOW to do the task.

OOSEM describes a possible and well organized way to execute projects for software-development. All important aspects as:

- technical software engineering
- quality ensurance
- project management and controlling

are handled.
Furthermore it makes appointments for

- project organization
- planning and organizing projectphases
- project management
- configuration management
- quality ensurance
- reusing and reusability of components

By using OOSEM for handling an object-oriented software engineering project you have got several advantages:

- a list of all possible phases and principle activities exists
- a suggestion for the sequence of phases is given
- all possible and useful preconditions, results and postconditions for each phase are described
- there is an „unit construction system" for building individual forms of organizing phases
- the use of international known forms of notation for the technical activities and documentation as

OMT (Dr. James Rumbaugh)
OOA/D (COAD/yourdon)
OOD (Booch)
SOM (Sinz/Ferstl)
RDD (Wirfs-Brock)
...

is allowed.

- standardizations for handling topics - not mentioned or only touched by many other methods - (e.g. user interface, sharp line between the phases, iteration of phases) are defined.

2.2 Lifecycle-model

2.2.1 Phases-overview

Using OOSEM the development process is split up into the following phases:

- analysis (initiation, study)
- design (subsystem-design, class-design)
- implementation (class-specification, class-implemetation, integration, system test, product-acceptance)
- application

A detailed description of these phases is given in chapter 2.4.

2.2.2 Organizing the phases

Phases are organized by selecting a set of features listed in the ooEM, i.e. you have to select the:

- phases needed in your lifecycle
- sequence of the chosen phases
- preconditions for the chosen phases
- activities to be performed for all chosen phases

and to define the results for each chosen phase.
If you leave out obligatory topics you must add your reasoning to your project documetation.

2.3 Handling a project

Handling a project with OOSEM means regarding the following items:

2.3.1 Project-organization

You have to define answers to these questions:
- What kind of tasks has the project management to do?
- Who is responsible for what?
- Which structure of phases do we need?
- What results do we expect for the overall project?
- What results are expected by the client?
- What about support?

2.3.2 Project-management

Project management means:
- Planing:
  - decision about paradigm (object-oriented, functional)
  - method (ooSEM, OOA/OOD, OMT)
  - product structure (object structure)
  - project structure (phases, activities)
  - project organization
  - the process (supplies, milestones, dependence of the chosen activities on each other)
  - human effort, working materials, training, traveling and the costs
  - risk management (trouble shooting and avoiding)
- controlling:
  - the adherence to the given plans
  - the actual costs and efforts
  - dates
  - development results
  - can be done the whole project, for each phase seperately or for single activities.
- coordination, administration, organization:
  - communication between client and contractor
  - organization and holding of meetings
  - definition of the contract
  - coordination of developers and their training programs
  - organization of resources
  - initiation of (planned) activities in critical situations
  - reporting

2.3.3 Configuration management

A configuration management system can be object-oriented itself. The administered units (classes, subsystems, design models) can be elements of an inheritance structure and the aggregation can be used to handle different versions.

Administered units can be (especially for object-oriented development):
- object-oriented models of analysis and/or design,
- class specifications,

- complete implementation of classes,
- prototypes,
- software-tools together with their documentation,
- compiled (and probably linked) components (e.g. subsystems)

2.3.4 Quality ensurance

Quality ensurance must be done by every team member in his own area. Planned activities have to be performed for avoiding, detecting and removing errors. Further topics are: testing, reviews and reporting.

2.3.5 Reuse - reuseability

Developing reusable software needs some extra effort for building reusable components and for the search of the solution. It also needs a reuse-structure for the whole company and acceptance by all employees, but it saves much effort by not „inventing the wheel a second time".

The description of a reusable component consists of

- the kind of the component (class specification, pure data, prelinked subsystem)
- description and definition of all possible applications
- description of the interface(s)
- listing of all planned modifications
- a list of contents
- developed by which method

There are some rules for creating reusable components, you should create

- classes with very general responsibilities
- algorithmic classes
- „complete" classes
- classes with a very small interface

2.3.6 Documentation

Some important aspects for documentation are

- homogeneous documentation over all phases of the development process
- for object-oriented development there should be as much graphical documentation as possible
- to all graphical documentation textual descriptions must be added.

2.3.7 Testing

Most important is the state of an object (and related objects) and not the relation input/output data. Further testing topics are

- the checking of preconditions, postconditions and the execution of the designed methods
- testing methods the usual way
- specifying a list of cases to be tested for each object (object-identification, list of defined states for this object, list of methods to be executed for each case, list of events to be generated for each case, list of external conditions for each case, scenarios, state-transition diagrams)

2.4 Phases in OOSEM

2.4.1 Initiation

To define the requirements out of the declarations made by the client you have to

- establish objectives (development of a new product, improvement of the control of a given product, rationalization, consideration of future influences)
- make iterative definitions of the requirement (together with the client in interviews and internal with brainstorming)
- represent the requirements - may be object-oriented but it is not a must („speak the language of the client")

Then you have got to prepare a product proposal (requirement definition) which on the one hand defines the checked requirements of the client for the contractor (view of the client) and on the other hand is a base for the product specification (task definition) in the phase „study". This product proposal must be checked whether all

- requirements are included
- all requirements are documented correctly
- all definitons are clear, unisonous and of only one meaning

Now you can do the fine planning for the next phase (study).
The results of initiation are

- product proposal
- market analysis
- brief project plan

2.4.2 Study

Aim of this phase is the preparation of a binding (for the client and the contractor) definition of tasks and project-efforts. These definitions are represented by systems of objects and classes, documentation of associations between them and their dynamical behaviour and descriptions of the different tasks to be performed by these objects.

You have to decide what has to be developed, whether it is possible to do so and choose one of the several different ways to solve concrete (technical) problems and you also have to prepare the user interface (prototype).
Structure of the product specification

- aims
- tasks (+)
- external interfaces (userinterface and systeminterface) (+)
- technical requirements
- quality requirements
- conditions for realization (*)
- documentation requirements (*)
- acceptance requirements
- special requirements
- preconditions
- appendix (literature references, definition of special phrases)

(+...object-oriented models, *...strong influence by the object-oriented approach)

The results are:

- product specification
- solution studies
- provisional plan for quality ensurance
- provisional project plan
- quality report
- list of components that may be reused
- phase acceptance report
- installed configuration management system

2.4.3 Subsystem design

Refering to the conditions of realization the system architecture is defined. A building of system components is made by paying attention to topics as user-interface and simplifying the structure of connections inside the whole system. Therefore one of several concepts (layers and components by Coad/Yourdon or modules-OMT) is used. In addition an integration plan is prepared.
There are some rules for defining subsystems:

- a subsystem is a set of classes and objects connected by logical structures (interdependences, responsibilities)
- a subsystem may consist of further subsystems, but the leafs of the tree have to be classes and objects
- a subsystem communicates with other components of the whole sytem only by a clear defined interface which should be less complex than the sum of all internal interfaces.

Results of subsystem-design are:

- system specification
- integration plans

- datastructures for test-cases
- test plans
- extended quality ensurance plan
- quality report
- extended project plan.

2.4.4 Class design

Class design means a binding definition of the class-hierarchies and of the public interfaces of classes and subsystems. Therefor you need

- an implementation-dependent representation
- elimination of multiple inheritance if necessary
- definition of the conversion of the design-notation to structures of the implementation-language
- optimization of the class-hierarchies
- optimization of access-paths
- inclusion of class-libraries.

You also have to do the following items:

- extension and modification of the existing models
- definition of the dependences of each class to the whole system
- definition of algorithms and data-structures
- extension of the integration plans
- extension of the test plans (adding test-cases and data-structures)
- decision which elements to be subject of a code-review.

Results of this phase are:

- extended sytem specification
- extended integration plans
- test plans and data-structures
- product proposals for subcontractors
- final quality ensurance plan
- quality reports
- extended project.

2.4.5 Class specification

Parts of this phase are:

- the specification of the interface of each class using structures of the implementation language (offered services, needed interfaces)
- providing a provisional user-documentation
- creation or procurement of test-tools
- execution of code-reviews.

Results:

- final system specification
- provisional user-documentation
- extended integration plans
- provisional technical SW-documentation
- class specifications
- quality reports
- extended test plans
- extended project plan
- confirmations of ordered supply.

2.4.6 Class implementation

Now all classes and their methods are implemented. A precise conversion of all models of analysis and design with adherence to conventions, inline documentation, class tests and definition of the final integration plans are made. After finishing this phase you have got:

- extended user-documentation
- final integration plans
- extended technical SW-documentation
- tested classes
- quality reports
- test reports
- extended project plan

2.4.7 Integration

A usable application is created by the integration adhere to the integration plans and by the creation of tools.

2.4.8 System test

By testing the whole system using the view of the client (therefore mostly functional oriented) application should achieve maturity.

2.4.9 Product acceptance

In this phase the mature product is delivered to the customer, who accepts that the product meets the defined requirements.

2.4.10 Application

When the customer uses the delivered product he needs training, service and maintenance.

3 Case study - Designing a wrist watch

The customer has got some hardware-parts he can assemble to a wrist watch. These parts are:

- a digital display
- 4 buttons (waterproofed)
- 2 impulse units (timer)
- a „motherboard“ for cpu, memory and electric switches
- a buzzer (waterproofed)
- a light unit (additional to the display)
- a body (waterproofed)
- a power supply unit (battery)

We (the designers) have to develop the appropriate software to make that watch usable.
The client has got these wishes:

- this watch shall display the normal (local) time AND the time in several cities all around the world
- it must be possible to use this watch as an alarm-clock
- with this watch he wants to determine how fast his kids can run.

Then he makes concrete definitions:

- for the cities he wants New York, London and Hongkong
- he wants to take time of a race with the hundreth part of a second as the degree of accurancy

So we work out this product proposal:

1. AIMS
The controlling software (firmware) of a wrist-watch shall be developed. The services of the watch shall be divided into several sequential changeable modes. The basic hardware is known and available to the contractor. This watch will be the result of an individual production.

2. TASKS
2.1 LOCAL TIME DISPLAY
Standard display. Displays the actual time - hours, minutes, seconds. Displays the actual mode - local time. The displayed time must be adjustable. It must be possible to enable and disable the alarm-clock function. The state of the alarm has to be displayed.
2.2. WORLD TIME DISPLAY
Displays the time of a selected city - New York, London, Hongkong. The displayed time must be adjustable. The actual city must be changeable to one of the other specified cities. The actual city has to be displayed.

4 oo-Development - Tourism

Each object has got

- a memory
  - own status
  - events
  - object-neighbours
- services
  - behaviour
  - information
- local control
  - „self-managing"
  - comprehensible

In oo-applications you use objects for describing things of the real world. Therefor in touristic-oo-applications you have got objects with the typ

- hotel
- country
- region
- room
- .....

When you are working e.g. on an information terminal (or internet or BTX or ..) you can get information of the objects via the infosystem ORB (=object request broker).

5 Summary

So we can say that OOSEM has got several advantages:

- OOSEM covers the complete development process for object-oriented software
- it has got no own notation - it makes use of existing ones
- gives instructions and hints for newcomers
- changes to the recommended system should only be done by experienced professionals and must be included in the technical SW-documentation, the process plan and the phase plan
- it is an alternative to the existing method SEM (based on the functional approach)

W. Schertler, B. Schmid, A M. Tjoa, H. Werthner (eds.)

Information and Communications Technologies in Tourism

Proceedings of the International Conference in Innsbruck, Austria, 1994

1994. 116 figures. XII, 286 pages.
Soft cover DM 98,–, öS 686,–
ISBN 3-211-82543-6

Prices are subject to change without notice

The proceedings of the conference ENTER - International Conference on Information and Communications Technologies in Tourism provide an international forum for the discussion of the role of telecommunication and information systems in tourism, inform potential users and people concerned with the importance of such technologies and to explain their functioning, and finally intensify the contact and the communication between researchers, system developers and users. Tourism and leisure industry experiences a fast technological development, however, the different participants in this market are very differently prepared to meet this challange (e. g. big airlines with their reservation systems versus a rather small structured supplier on the other side). This is the background to the discussion presented in this volume, dealing with questions like how an equal and fruitful cooperation for all participants can take place, when one should participate in this development and enter the electronic market, what are the dangers of entering too early or too late, whether the environment is prepared for such a development, and what can be learned from other sectors. The results of this discussion are of interest for scientists, researchers and practitioners in tourism as well as in the computer industry.

Springer-Verlag Wien New York

Sachsenplatz 4–6, P.O.Box 89, A-1201 Wien · 175 Fifth Avenue, New York, NY 10010, USA
Heidelberger Platz 3, D-14197 Berlin · 3-13, Hongo 3-chome, Bunkyo-ku, Tokyo 113, Japan

Wolfgang Herzner, Frank Kappe (eds.)

Multimedia/Hypermedia in Open Distributed Environments

Proceedings of the Eurographics Symposium in Graz, Austria, June 6-9, 1994

1994. 105 figures. VIII, 330 pages.
Soft cover DM 118,–, öS 826,–
ISBN 3-211-82587-8

(Eurographics)

Prices are subject to change without notice

While multimedia applications are rapidly becoming an integral part of stand-alone, single-user systems, the problems encountered when moving into distributed environments are only beginning to be identified. This book represents the results from the Eurographics symposium on "Multimedia/Hypermedia in Open Distributed Environments", held at June 6-9, 1994, in Graz, Austria. About 20 contributions cover a broad range of problems related to this topic. Organized in the six sessions "Standards and Standards Exploitation", "Demonstrations", "Tools", "Hypermedia and Authoring", "Architectures", and "CSCW and Information Services", the book gives a comprehensive overview about the state of the art in research, development, and standardisation in the areas of hypermedia (hm) encoding and presentation, distributed multimedia (mm) tele- and information services, mm/hm development and authoring tools, cooperative development environments, and new architectural concepts. In addition, the future mm/hm encoding and presentation standards MHEG and PREMO are presented. As a result, the reader will profit from this book in getting up-to-date information about the current trends in (the development of) mm/hm services and applications in open, distributed environments.

Springer-Verlag Wien New York

Sachsenplatz 4–6, P.O.Box 89, A-1201 Wien · 175 Fifth Avenue, New York, NY 10010, USA
Heidelberger Platz 3, D-14197 Berlin · 3-13, Hongo 3-chome, Bunkyo-ku, Tokyo 113, Japan

Martin Göbel, Heinrich Müller, Bodo Urban (eds.)

Visualization in Scientific Computing

1995. 150 figures. VIII, 238 pages.
Soft cover DM 118,–, öS 826,–
ISBN3-211-82633-5

(Eurographics)

Prices are subject to change without notice

Visualization is the most important approach to extract relevant information from the huge amount of data produced in today's computational and experimental sciences. Selected contributions from the fifth in a well established series of workshops on "Visualization in Scientific Computing", organized by the EUROGRAPHICS Association, held at May 30 to June 1, 1994, in Rostock, Germany, treat topics of particular interest in current research: visualization of multidimensional data, flow visualization, data modeling, time control, interaction, and volume visualization. Examples of applications for instance come from flow simulation, chemistry, medical imaging, and geography. Readers will profit in getting insight in state-of-the-art techniques which might help them to solve their visualization problems.

Springer-Verlag Wien New York

Sachsenplatz 4–6, P.O.Box 89, A-1201 Wien · 175 Fifth Avenue, New York, NY 10010, USA
Heidelberger Platz 3, D-14197 Berlin · 3-13, Hongo 3-chome, Bunkyo-ku, Tokyo 113, Japan

Springer-Verlag
and the Environment

WE AT SPRINGER-VERLAG FIRMLY BELIEVE THAT AN international science publisher has a special obligation to the environment, and our corporate policies consistently reflect this conviction.

WE ALSO EXPECT OUR BUSINESS PARTNERS – PRINTERS, paper mills, packaging manufacturers, etc. – to commit themselves to using environmentally friendly materials and production processes.

THE PAPER IN THIS BOOK IS MADE FROM NO-CHLORINE pulp and is acid free, in conformance with international standards for paper permanency.